Econometric Analysis of Regional Economy

Sachiyo Asahi

Econometric Analysis of Regional Economy

Springer

Sachiyo Asahi
Faculty of Humanities
Law and Economics, Graduate School
of Humanities and Social Sciences
Mie University
Tsu, Mie, Japan

ISBN 978-981-99-8706-1 ISBN 978-981-99-8707-8 (eBook)
https://doi.org/10.1007/978-981-99-8707-8

This Springer imprint is published by the registered company Springer Nature Singapore Pte Ltd.
The registered company address is: 152 Beach Road, #21-01/04 Gateway East, Singapore 189721, Singapore

Paper in this product is recyclable.

Preface

The Japanese economy is the third largest in the world, as indicated by its nominal GDP of 4.94 trillion US dollars in 2021,[1] and has abundant social capital and economic vitality. On the other hand, since the early 1990s, the Japanese economy has been in a 30-year period of low growth. This is the result of a combination of factors, including a decline in demand since the collapse of the bubble economy, a drop in supply capacity due to sluggish productivity growth, a decline in the working-age population, and some redesign of the economic structure itself, including in response to the rise of international globalization.

In recent years, global warming has also had a deep impact on climate, ecosystems, and even ways of life, and the international community has begun to take concerted action, with no exceptions made for economic activities. This has also affected energy issues, which have become even more serious, leading to international conflicts. In addition, Japan has faced natural disasters including the Great Hanshin Earthquake and the Great East Japan Earthquake.

These natural disasters and the economy have had a major impact not only on Japan as a whole but also on its regional economies. Low birthrates and population aging have resulted in a rapid population decline almost everywhere, and extreme depopulation is on the rise locally. The social capital of a region needs to provide a resilient infrastructure that is able to respond to disasters and at the same time needs to have a low environmental impact and increase the economic vitality of the regional economy. In addition, in response to the hollowing out of regional economies through the relocation of Japanese companies overseas, efforts have been made to attract and foster regional industries, preferably of types that are less damaging to the environment and able to use energy in a more efficient manner. Tourism as an active use of regional resources also deserves promotion as a way of working toward the economic revitalization in a region through the strengthening of an industry that has a broad scope for sending out ripple effects to other industries.

---

[1] This is the GDP given in the United Nations Statistics Division. Retrieved September 9, 2023, from https://unstats.un.org/unsd/snaama/Downloads.

To address issues of productivity and population, resilience and revitalization, this book offers an analysis of problems confronting Japanese regional economies in this period of rapid change. Most significantly, it presents thoughts about policy proposals capable of setting better perspectives for an economic future. It aims to ensure this by using economic data and econometric methods to identify the mechanisms most actively at work in particular regional economies.

This book is a collection of studies in four chapter areas for which quantitative analysis can profitably shed light on key issues facing Japan's regional economies: the areas of tourism, population, the balance of energy and environment, and social capital.

This book comprises six chapters:

Chapter 1—Introduction:Significance and Role of Regional Economic Analysis in Japan
Chapter 2—Study of Total Fertility Rate of Women in Employment, by Industrial Sector: Estimation of Japanese National and Prefectural Data Using the Own-Children Method
Chapter 3—Analysis of the Impact of Overtourism in Japan: The Effects of Congestion Phenomena
Chapter 4—Analysis of Environmental and Economic Effectiveness of Wind Power Generation in Japan
Chapter 5—Economic Ripple Effects of Choice Factors and Disaster-related Investments at Nagoya Port
Chapter 6—Summary and Future Tasks

Chapter 1 describes the relationship between regional economics and regional economic analysis in Japan and outlines some relevant case studies based on regional statistical data and econometric analysis methods. This is also where my ideas and research positions in this book are initially presented.

Chapter 2 analyzes the total fertility rate, one of the causes of Japan's population problems. A special feature of this study is that it examines the fertility rate from an employer-side perspective. Accordingly, total fertility rates (TFRs) are calculated by the industrial sector. First, it summarizes trends of childbirth and employment in Annual Population and Social Security surveys. Next, previous research is summarized concerning the Own-Children method and fertility rates. It gives an outline of the data to which the method is to be applied in this paper and explains in more detail the procedures to be used for estimating characteristics of TFRs by the industrial sector for Japan and the 47 prefectures. Finally, there is a summary of results, including also the relationships between the TFR of industrial sectors and regionality. This concludes with an examination of how consistent these results are with preceding research and surveys and in relation to agglomeration indicators.

The background reasoning behind estimating TFRs by the industrial sector in this way is as follows. When a worker enters into employment in Japan, there is a bewildering diversity of contract conditions, and there are cases where even the work category is not clear or fixed. Furthermore, the type of work may change in the course of employment depending on the worker's aptitude, the management circumstances of the company itself, or evolution in the working environment. However, the industrial sector of employment will not change unless the worker changes jobs. Within sectors, there are sometimes craft or industry unions that transcend the boundaries of individual enterprises. Although labor unions in Japan are generally company unions, many of them are also organized into industry-wide alliances. For reasons like these, the issue of declining birthrate cannot very well be discussed outside of the issues of employment choices and work environments within industrial sectors.

Chapter 3 is a study on tourism as a means of regional revitalization, and an estimation of the tourism demand function of international visitors to Japan. The purpose of this is to analyze the impact of congestion, one of the phenomena of "overtourism" involving international visitors and to discover which economic variables affect the numbers. In recent years, the trend toward local overcrowding has developed into an international issue and in Japan, too, this is attracting attention. Cities such as Kyoto and Kamakura have encountered overtourism problems already.

This chapter will begin by summarizing trends in the number of international visitors to Japan in recent years. This will be followed by an overview of the research on congestion phenomena related with tourism. Next, the model to be used in this study will be introduced. The purpose of the model is to estimate the demand function of international visitors to Japan, taking into account of variables that indicate congestion phenomena. An analysis will then be performed to estimate the effect that these variables are likely to have on the numbers of international tourists visiting Japan in the future. Finally, based on these results, estimates for future variations in congestion phenomena will be displayed and summarized. Broadly, the empirical results of this study show that governments, local governments, and tourism operators in popular destinations need to devise measures to reduce the congestion phenomenon.

Chapter 4 examines recent advances in wind power generation in the different regions of Japan and finds a positive cost-benefit balance in favor of the expansion of generation capability. The aim of the chapter is to analyze the effective use of the natural environment for wind power generation and to compare regional initiatives in this activity area, using existing survey results of wind power generation facilities in Japan and established research methods. First, an overview is offered of the current state of wind power generation and of the purposes and challenges of moving into this new area. This is followed by an analysis of the amount of wind power currently generated, the CO_2 reduction effect, and the economic efficiency. In addition, the ripple effect of the construction of wind power generation plants on regional economies is analyzed, including the employment aspect.

Chapter 5 analyzes the impact of disasters on local economies, using the Port of Nagoya as a case study to clarify the effects of investment for social capital, including disaster prevention. In one of the greatest natural disasters of recent times, the Great East Japan Earthquake of March 2011, vessels in many ports were washed ashore by tsunami, causing extensive damage to the whole port area. At the same time, congestion in supply chains reduced the production capacity of companies. The overall impact of disasters on local economies varies in the extent and absolute severity of the damage sustained depending on the scale of the disaster, the level of production activity, and the local industrial structure.

Imagining such a blow striking a major port such as Nagoya, I first attempt to identify factors that lead companies to use the port in the first place, and then review circumstances that might force them into changes of plan, including choices of ports in other areas. I will focus particularly on factors relating to natural disasters and countermeasures, first summarizing the investments that are required to ensure a major port's safety and resilience against risks of disasters and then analyzing the further impact these investments have on the whole Nagoya region, especially Aichi Prefecture.

The final Chap. 6 will provide an overall summary and a list of remaining issues, to indicate the direction of future research tasks.

Research for the chapters in this book was reported at the Nagoya Workshop on Econometric Studies. I am indebted for the useful advice I received from the now late Dr. Soshichi Kinoshita (Professor Emeritus, Nagoya University), who first organized this study group, Dr. Mitsuo Yamada (Professor Emeritus, Chukyo University), and Dr. Taiyo Ozaki (Professor Emeritus, Kyoto University of Advanced Science). I also thank the other researchers who participated. Dr. Yamada, in particular, gave me many previous years of guidance, without which I could never have written the papers, and provided further advice at each stage of devising the book's structure. Further years of guidance came from Dr. Akira Yakita (Professor Emeritus, Nagoya City University), the now late Professor, Tsunetada Kawate (Professor Emeritus, Yokkaichi University), Dr. Yoshitaka Nitta (Professor Emeritus, Yokkaichi University), Dr. Yukimasa Takemoto (Professor Emeritus, Yokkaichi University). Dr. Yasuyuki Nishigaki (Professor, Ryukoku University), and Professor Daijiro Fujii (Professor Emeritus, Yamaguchi University) gave me valuable opportunities to pursue my research. In arranging the parts, David Dykes (Emeritus Professor, Yokkaichi University) provided continuous constructive guidance. His contribution was crucial to getting the book together. Finally, Mr. Yutaka Hirachi, my editor from Springer Tokyo, always provided unfailing support. I would like to thank all of these people once again.

This book is essentially a compilation of the following five papers. Chapter 1, however, is offered for the first time, as an opening for this book. The work was supported by JSPS KAKENHI Grant-in-Aid for Scientific Research (B) Number 19H04380.

Chapter 2 was based on my previous paper, published in April 2016, Study on Total Fertility Rate of Female Employed Persons in Employment, by Industry: Estimation of National and Prefectural Data by the Own-Children Method—(Chukyo University, Institute of Economics, Discussion Paper Series, 1602) (in Japanese), into which some amendments, additional data and reanalysis results were incorporated. The earlier Asahi (2016) paper was supported by JSPS KAKENHI Grant-in-Aid for Scientific Research (B) Number. 25285091 "Research on Macroeconomy and Economic Policy under Demographic Change" (Principal Investigator: Dr. Akira Yakita), the Ministry of Education, Culture, Sports, Science and Technology (MEXT), Japan, for the fiscal years 2013–2015. I am grateful to Associate Professor Hajime Ihara (Associate Professor, Institute of Economic Research, Hitotsubashi University) for providing much useful information. Dr. Yoko Konishi (Senior

Research Fellow, The Research Institute of Economy, Trade and Industry (RIETI)) kindly allowed me to use her data on agglomeration indices.

Chapter 3 began from earlier work that I published in March 2020, Chap. 6, Analysis of the Impact of Congestion due to Tourism in Japan, in M. Yamada., J, Masuda. (Eds.), The Globalization and Econometric Modeling of Regional Economy (Chukyo University, Institute of Economics Economic Research Series 27). Tokyo: Keiso Shobo (in Japanese), with amendments, additional data and some reanalysis results. I express my gratitude to the publisher, Keiso Shobo for giving me the opportunity to publish this material. The work was originally supported by JSPS KAKENHI Grant-in-Aid for Scientific Research (B) Number 19H04380. It was also a fruit of the 2012–2019 research project of the Chukyo University Research Institute, "Research on Econometric Modeling of the Global Economy" (Principal Investigator: Dr. Mitsuo Yamada).

The beginnings of Chap. 4 were in my work published in March 2005, Chap. 8, The Environmental and Economic Effectiveness of Introducing Wind Power Generation, H. Terada. (Ed.), Theory and Policy of Environmental Problems. Kyoto: Koyo Shobo (in Japanese), incorporating amendments, additional data and reanalysis to reflect environmental changes of the past 20 years. My gratitude to the publisher Koyo Shobo for permission to republish this chapter. The earlier paper, Asahi (2005), was a product of work achieved in the Yokkaichi University Energy Education Research Group at a time when the university was acting as a "regional hub for energy education" under an initiative run by the Socio-Economic Productivity Center. This Center itself is a branch of the Energy Agency, attached to the Ministry of Economy, Trade and Industry. Project funding was thus from government organizations. I thank Dr. Yoshitaka Nitta (Professor Emeritus Yokkaichi University) for giving me the opportunity to conduct this research.

Chapter 5, lastly, was based on my research published in June 2013, Economic Ripple Effects of Choice Factors and Disaster-related Investments at Nagoya Port—(The Japan Port Economics Association, Chubu Division, Port Studies, Volume 34) (in Japanese), again incorporating amendments and additional data and subject to partial reanalysis. I would like to express my gratitude to the President of the Chubu Division of the Japan Port Economics Association, Dr. Toshikazu Oshima (Professor Emeritus, Chubu University) for approving the republication of this part of the book.

Finally, I would like to express my heartfelt gratitude to my late father Haruo and my sister Yoko, who have supported me throughout my research life.

Tsu, Japan
October 2023

Sachiyo Asahi

Contents

1 Introduction: Significance and Role of Regional Economic Analysis in Japan 1
1.1 Introduction 1
1.2 Regional Economic Modeling and Regional Economic Analysis 3
1.2.1 Input-Output Analysis Research 3
1.2.2 Econometric Modeling Research 10
1.2.3 Panel Data Analysis 14
1.3 Setting the Objectives of Regional Economic Research and My Previous Research as a Whole 19
1.3.1 How to Go About the Process of Econometric Research in a Regional Economy 19
1.3.2 The Place of My Previous Studies in My Regional Economic Research Career 21
1.3.3 Plan and Chapter Structure of this Book 22
Appendix A 27
References 30

2 Study of Total Fertility Rate of Women in Employment, by Industrial Sector: Estimation of Japanese National and Prefectural Data Using the Own-Children Method 33
2.1 Introduction 33
2.2 Childbirth and Employment Trends in Annual Population and Social Security Surveys 35
2.3 Previous Research on the Own-Children Method and the Fertility Rate 39
2.3.1 Research Using the Own-Children Method 40
2.3.2 Research on TFRs in Specific Industries 41
2.3.3 Research on the Relationship Between Region and Fertility Rate 42

2.3.4 Research in Japan that Has Dealt with the Own-Children Method 43
2.3.5 Research on the Relationship Between Japanese TFR and Other Economic Variables 46
2.4 Statistical Data on Fertility Rates 46
2.4.1 Data 46
2.4.2 Industrial Classification 47
2.4.3 Use of the Own-Children Method 48
2.5 Data Used and the Estimate Method 50
2.6 Results of Total Fertility Rate Estimates by Industrial Sector in Japan and the 47 Prefectures 56
2.6.1 Evaluation of TFR Estimate Results for a National Census Year 56
2.6.2 Evaluation of TFR Estimate Results for Japan and Its 47 Prefectures, 2000–2015 67
2.7 Analysis Results: Total Fertility Rate and Its Relationship with Regions 69
2.7.1 Background of Analysis 69
2.7.2 Indicators of an Agglomeration Economy 73
2.7.3 Analysis Results Obtained with TFR and Agglomeration Economy Indexes 86
2.8 Conclusions 96
References 102

3 Analysis of the Impact of Overtourism in Japan: The Effects of Congestion Phenomena 107
3.1 Introduction 107
3.2 Trends in the Number of International Visitors to Japan in Recent Years 109
3.3 Research by Means of a Tourism Demand Model Including Congestion Phenomena 114
3.3.1 Definition of Overtourism 114
3.3.2 Life Cycle (TALC) Analysis of Tourist Destinations 115
3.3.3 Research on Congestion Phenomena in Tourism 116
3.3.4 Research Using a Tourism Demand Model 117
3.3.5 Variables of Congestion in Tourism Research 119
3.4 Analysis Method and Data Used 119
3.4.1 Tourism Demand Function Including Congestion Variables 119
3.4.2 Variables Indicating Tourism Demand 122
3.4.3 Variables Indicating Tourism Congestion 123
3.4.4 Other Variables Relating to Tourism Demand and Formulas Used for Analysis 124
3.4.5 Variables Indicating the Strength of Tourism Supply 125

3.5 Results of Analysis ... 125
3.5.1 Tourism Demand Among International Visitors to Japan, by Prefectures of Stay ... 125
3.5.2 Tourism Demand Among International Visitors to Japan, in Six Prefectures ... 131
3.6 Conclusion ... 133
References ... 134

4 Analysis of Environmental and Economic Effectiveness of Wind Power Generation in Japan ... 137
4.1 Introduction ... 137
4.2 The Present State of Wind Power Generation in Outline ... 139
4.2.1 Background to the Introduction of Renewable Energy ... 139
4.2.2 Efforts to Introduce Wind Power Generation ... 141
4.3 Factual Situation of Wind Power Generation ... 145
4.3.1 Current Status of Wind Power Generation in Japan ... 145
4.3.2 Issues in Introducing Wind Power Generation in Japan ... 146
4.4 Research on CO_2 Reduction Effect in Wind Power Generation ... 148
4.5 The CO_2 Reduction Effect of the Introduction of Wind Power Generation ... 149
4.5.1 Measurement of the Amount of Energy Supplied by Wind Power Generation ... 149
4.5.2 The Effect of Wind Power Generation in Reducing CO_2 Emissions ... 151
4.5.3 Measuring the Costs of Wind Power Generation ... 155
4.6 Regional Economic Effects of Wind Power Generator Plant Constructions ... 161
4.6.1 Measurement of Economic Ripple Effects Using Data from Interregional Industrial Input–Output Tables ... 161
4.6.2 Analysis of the Ripple Effects from Construction Investment ... 167
4.6.3 Results of Analysis ... 169
4.7 Conclusion ... 176
References ... 179

5 Economic Ripple Effects of Choice Factors and Disaster-Related Investments at Nagoya Port ... 185
5.1 Introduction ... 185
5.2 The Impact of the Great East Japan Earthquake on Port Logistics ... 187
5.2.1 The Impact of the Great East Japan Earthquake on Japanese Port Economies ... 187
5.2.2 Freight Logistics at the Port of Nagoya ... 188
5.3 Analysis of Factors Favoring the Choice of the Port of Nagoya ... 191
5.3.1 Previous Papers Regarding Port Choices ... 192

5.3.2 Factors for Port Selection with Regard to the Port of Nagoya ... 194
5.3.3 Analysis of Selection Factors for the Port of Nagoya ... 197
5.3.4 Selection of Ports Other Than Nagoya During an Earthquake Situation ... 200
5.4 Economic Ripple Effects of Port and Harbor Disaster Mitigation Projects on Local and Other Regional Economies ... 206
5.4.1 Data and Analysis Methods ... 208
5.4.2 Analysis of the Economic Ripple Effects of Public Investments in Nagoya Port ... 216
5.5 Conclusions ... 227
References ... 229

6 Summary and Future Tasks ... 231
6.1 Background, Aim and Structure of the Book ... 231
6.2 Summary and Future Tasks in Each Chapter and Overall ... 232
6.2.1 Significance and Role of Regional Economic Analysis in Japan ... 232
6.2.2 Study of Total Fertility Rate of Women in Employment, by Industrial Sector ... 232
6.2.3 Analysis of the Impact of Overtourism in Japan ... 235
6.2.4 Analysis of Environmental and Economic Effectiveness of Wind Power Generation in Japan ... 236
6.2.5 Economic Ripple Effects of Choice Factors and Disaster-Related Investments at Nagoya Port ... 238
6.2.6 Future Tasks for This Study ... 240
References ... 240

Chapter 1
Introduction: Significance and Role of Regional Economic Analysis in Japan

1.1 Introduction

Many activities in cities or urbanizing regions become extremely diversified and, even while remaining intricately connected, build up into a wide range of economic systems, or even life cultures, relating to people's modes of life. Regional economics is a way of understanding the various phenomena occurring in a regional space of this sort. Nijkamp and Mills (1987) show how a regional economic analysis—meaning one that makes use of regional economics—manages to clarify the spatial dispersion of economic activities while respecting their coherence. They also show some of the attempts that have been made in this way to deal lucidly with spatial issues.[1]

An important point here is how to visualize a region. It can be given a wide range of definitions, which may also allow for integrated regions made up of distinct countries as units, areas grouped together as units of a region within one country, and smaller replications of this group-of-units pattern on ever more local scales. Okada et al. (2007) describe the concept as a multilayered structure with several layers, ranging from the town or village up to the global level.[2] Within the bounds of one country, this implies "a (self-sustaining) economic zone that is geographically divided off inside a national economy."[3]

Although problems of regionally integrated unit areas within countries, or of trading relations among groups of unit countries, have always been treated where necessary, the emergence of "spatial"—in most cases "regional"—economics as a concept with its own logic has recently led to more rigorous treatments of interregional trade, also extending to pluri-national regions. Regional economics can now be seen as a study field not only of regions within a country, but also having a more general and inclusive scope.

---

[1] Nijkamp and Mills (1987), pp. 1–2.

[2] Okada et al. (2007), pp. v–vi.

[3] Kuroda et al. (2008), p. 1.

S. Asahi, *Econometric Analysis of Regional Economy*,
https://doi.org/10.1007/978-981-99-8707-8_1

McCann (2013) uses geographical space as a basis for identifying cities and regions. Once a region has been located in this way in relation to a greater international region, it can next be taken more specifically as a region within a country, which may correspond individually to one town or village, city, prefecture/province, or so forth. Or alternatively, at this level, it may be brought into a larger grouping of regions on this scale dimension so as to constitute an area. Or again, a region can be considered as a multilayered space in itself. Regions may thus be considered as combinations of various kinds of geographical units, depending on the type of economic event being handled.

Regional economics tends to be related to urban and transportation issues, environmental issues, and in many cases, regional resource issues. This means that it is necessary to consider appropriate approaches to each of these problem areas separately. In the view of Nijkamp and Mills (1987), the three analytical methods most likely to contribute to the economic theorization of regional economics are locational analysis, use of regional economic models and methods, and consideration of regional economic development and policy.

In early stages, locational analysis was developed theoretically and empirically in the work of von Thünen, Weber, Lösch and Christaller, and more recently these basics have been revisited in the New Economic Geography of Paul Krugman.[4] As for regional economic models and methods, these have had a growing influence on regional economic analysis thanks to the availability of a variety of data, including those originating from regional and urban economies, and thanks to the development of new statistical methods for use alongside the traditional econometric and statistical tools. In practice, these methods can be used to monitor the state of the regional economy in real time and to evaluate regional economic policies. Regional economic development and policies, finally, are being consulted as a means for raising people's living standards and social well-being by attending to the intersects between economic efficiency and socioeconomic equity. This kind of scrutiny has always had an especially important place in regional policy analysis, not to mention the key role it plays at a global level between countries, but also between regional communities, where common shared mishaps can be spotted and solved through a more accurate and realistic recognition of a situation or a better clarification of problems. Advances of this kind in regional economics have brought deeper insights into regional economies and shared well-being across regional communities.

The studies that I pursue as a researcher of regional economy are grounded in the theoretical and mathematical analysis of economic phenomena. In this chapter, I will be presenting a regional economic model and an accompanying methodology as one of my own contributions to the economic theorization of regional economics, along with some practical examples of policy analysis performed with the support of these tools.

The plan of the chapter is as follows. I will first give an outline of the regional economic model and analysis illustrated with statistical data from actual past research

[4] This has been shown in Barnes (2003), Johnston and Sidaway (2015), Hubbard and Kitchin (Eds.) (2010).

that I have worked on. Proceeding from there, I will then explain the essentials of problem setting for regional economic research and offer an overview of my previous studies and of my thoughts regarding this book.

1.2 Regional Economic Modeling and Regional Economic Analysis

In order to reach a more accurate understanding of a given economic event, we need to consider economic activities in a consistent way by integrating our economic theory and data. This is the same when treating regional economies. For example, in order to decide which policy choices are important, policy makers need to base their decisions on a more exact grasp of the event they are targeting.

Econometrics is the study of the current state of economic events and problems and the way it approaches them is through an integration of economic theory with real data, which can then be analyzed using statistical methods. At the same time, econometrics can also be used to consider regional economic issues in regional economies. In this way, regional economic research can lead to a surer grasp and fuller examination of regional economic issues in terms of econometrics. A basic prerequisite for a quantitative analysis of a region, urban area, or city is the availability of data for the analyst. In addition, the analyst must have the capability of processing these data and handling them appropriately.

Many modeling and analysis methods have been developed for understanding regional economies. In fact, one good way of constructing a model is by comparing and examining the various earlier ones that have served as bases for previous analyses.

In this section, using examples from my own research, I will first explain the basics of panel analysis, a statistical analysis approach that has grown out of classic multivariate input-output analysis, econometric modeling, and multiple regression analysis.

1.2.1 Input-Output Analysis Research

1.2.1.1 National-Level Input-Output Tables and Regional Input-Output Tables

Input-Output (I-O) analysis was developed by Leontief, Isard, and other researchers, and continues to this day. The interconnected structure linking production sectors at the country level, their production activities, and their relationship to the final demand and value-added can be analyzed by means of an input-output table, an important statistical processing frame that reveals the basic structures of that country. This analysis is one of several methods that analyze economic effects such as induced domestic production and induced employment by industrial sector, and is used to measure direct and indirect effects of public investments while estimating sectoral spillover, or ripple effects. It is also used to verify a nation's economic structure, prepare the ground for various economic policies, and analyze the economic ripple effects from government measures. One consequence of this analysis table approach is that economic analysis is required not only at the country level, but also at levels such as a metropolitan area or a region. This means that modifications are needed before input-output analysis can be used at a regional, or other sub-national level. The input-output model has to be altered, or even set up afresh, to reflect the specificity of regional (or sub-national) issues.

Miller and Blair (2009) have the following to say about the ways in which particular characteristics of regional economies affect the practices of input-output analysis viewed more generally.[5]

> First, although the data in the national input-output coefficients table are obviously some kind of averages of data from individual producers located in specific regions, the structure of production in a particular region may be identical to or it may differ markedly from that recorded in the national input-output table.
>
> Secondly, it is generally true that the smaller the economic area, the more dependent that area's economy is on trade with "outside" areas – transactions that cross the region's borders – both for sales of regional outputs and purchases of inputs needed for production.

In view of these characteristics of regional economies, the structure of production in a particular region may differ so far from that recorded in the national input-output table, that a separate regional table is necessary. Moreover, the smaller the economic area, the greater the importance of inter-regional trade. From this point of view, too, an inter-regional input-output table is needed. For a regional economic analysis to be viable, then, there is a need for a regional table that is tailored to the objectives of the analysis and to the characteristics of the region being analyzed.

In Japan, the Regional Bureau of Economy, Trade and Industry within the Ministry of Economy, Trade and Industry produces an inter-regional input-output table, and each of the 47 prefectural governments also produces its own regional table. In some cases, I-O tables are also drawn up at city level, chiefly for the ordinance-designated major cities. The extent to which these lower-level input-output tables have been provided for the needs of regions, prefectures and major municipalities, including the provision of inter-regional tables, can be verified on the website of the Pan Pacific Association of Input-Output Studies (Papaios).[6]

In practice, the boundaries of an area covered in a regional economic analysis do not always correspond to those of an administrative district, so the analyst may need an input-output table that divides the prefectural table into smaller sub-areas. In addition, for many cities and towns regional input-output tables are not available,

---

[5] Miller and Blair (2009), p. 69.

[6] See input-output tables for Japan and its 47 prefectures, http://www.gakkai.ne.jp/papaios/iotable-m.html.

For input-output tables of cities, http://www.gakkai.ne.jp/papaios/iotable-m.html.

For other input-output tables, http://www.gakkai.ne.jp/papaios/iotable-d.html.

which means that the analyst may need to produce one of her own in a form suited to the region under study. And finally, regional economies are recently coming to depend on collaborations between more than one prefectural economy. Large-scale projects may involve a number of regional economies working together. Analyses to assess the effects of such an undertaking will require an input-output table linking the economic activities of this area-level group of regions. This is also the case for regions at city and town level.

1.2.1.2 Creation of a Regional Input-Output Table

This section will begin by presenting Asahi (2003) as a case study of a city-level I-O table. At the same time, information on earlier papers will also be supplied as required. Asahi's study concerned Nagoya in Aichi Prefecture, a major city that has since produced its own I-O table (for 2015), but prior to that had not produced one for many years. For comparison purposes, in her 2003 paper, Asahi needed data for Nagoya City from 1995. But the only way to obtain that was by modifying data from the 1995 Aichi Prefectural table. Accordingly, that is what Asahi did, while leaving a record of how she was able to create this "Nagoya 1995 I-O Table" *ex post facto.*

Producing regional input-output tables requires many types of statistical data. As a designated major city, Nagoya has relatively more statistical data than other cities, making it possible even for researchers with limited access to administrative records to produce an input-output table of a reasonable standard.

To prepare a city input-output table of this kind, the first step is to estimate the total value of production in the city (CT: control total). The next is to estimate intermediate inputs by multiplying this total production value by the input coefficients from the Aichi Prefecture input-output table. The final demand can then be estimated.

The most important and intricate work in producing a regional input-output table is the estimation of the transfers of exports and imports. As Ishikawa (2016) explains, when we estimate the induced production effect of final demand, the equilibrium output model includes a part where the self-sufficiency rate is calculated. The value of induced domestic products varies with the level of this self-sufficiency rate. As self-sufficiency is determined by the trade coefficient, it is necessary to estimate the inflow and imports data in the regional input-output table with a high degree of accuracy.[7]

Generally, estimates for transfers and exports are made using information from special surveys, such as ordinance-based commodity distribution surveys or surveys of outflows and exports, supplemented by interviews with major companies. However, when working on city input-output tables, researchers and analysts often do not have access to sources like these, or in many cases such surveys have not been conducted. The same situation hampered my first attempts to produce a regional input-output table for Nagoya. As there was no basic stock of information for trade between Nagoya and other regions, trade data had to be estimated using

---

[7] Ishikawa (2016), pp. 10–11.

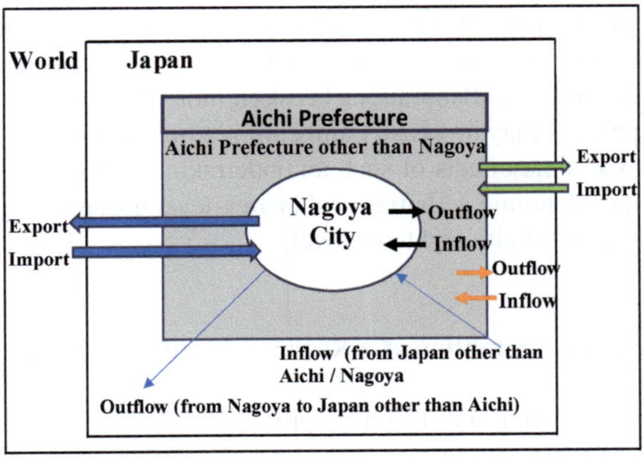

Fig. 1.1 Relations between Nagoya City and other regions in terms of outflows, inflows, exports and imports. *Source* Partly modified and schematized from Asahi (2003), p.19, Fig. 1

simple location quotients. This is one of the non-survey methods relied on in the location quotient method.

This method uses the specification quotients assigned to every production sector. Where the data for these quotients are above the standard value 1, the sectors concerned are outflow sectors to other regions, whereas sectors with quotients below the standard value are inflow sectors from other regions. The input coefficients can be adjusted accordingly. The advantage of this method is that the inter-regional trade value for each sector can be estimated purely from the data in the intra-regional input-output table and adapted theoretically to the overall state of the regional input-output table.

A number of studies have been undertaken on non-survey methods, including uses of Flegg's location quotient or a cross-industry location quotient rather than the simple location quotient. Studies including a scrutiny of these methods and their accuracy are Ishikawa (2004, 2005), Miller and Blair (2009), Nomura et al. (2013), Uchida et al. (2020) and many others (Fig. 1.1).

Research into more complex interregional input-output analysis is also being pursued in Japan using a variety of other statistical methods and data, either dividing regions into smaller subregions or though uses of multiregional input-output analysis.

For example, in another project in which I participated as one of the researchers, Nomura et al. (2011) constructed a four-region interregional input-output table for analyzing regional tourism policies in Yamaguchi Prefecture. The four regions in this instance were Yamaguchi City, Hagi City, the rest of Yamaguchi Prefecture excluding these two hubs, and everywhere outside of the prefecture boundaries. The particular focus of this study was to estimate the economic impact of tourists who stayed in Yamaguchi and Hagi Cities. For studies of regional tourism policies, it is not sufficient to evaluate policies only on the basis of prefectural tables because that overlooks the policy effects of more dispersed interactions occurring in the region. For capturing these, it is better to create inter-regional in this case, mainly sub-regional input-output tables.

It is very common for tourists to visit more than one place. The economic effects of round-trip tourism in a region also need to be measured in terms of their sub-regional impacts. The results of this study showed that the effects of policies at this sub-regional level, for example in towns and cities, included a good deal of demand leakage, especially when the policies were directed to visitors from other parts of the prefecture or from outside the prefecture altogether. It has to be admitted that demand leakage is not an inevitable effect of top-down tourism policy. In some cases, there also seemed to be rebound effects here and there. At any rate, it is important for regional input-output analysis at the sub-regional level, such as in cities or towns, to take into account the leakage from appeals addressed outside the region and counteract the effect through interactions between sub-regions.

For estimates of inter-regional trade coefficients at the sub-regional level, Nomura et al. (2013) compare and discuss differences between survey-supplemented "hybrid" approaches and various non-survey methods. The results of this analysis confirm the importance of developing a hybrid approach that can effectively combine the best of both worlds.

The problems with a logistics survey are the high cost of conducting the survey and the difficulty in obtaining responses about sub-regional trade dealings. The problem with not performing a survey, on the other hand, is that it becomes impossible to capture the interactivity of inter-regional trade. Also, in the absence of a survey method, estimates for inter-regional input-output tables that are actually combined out of several separate sub-regions will not lead to consistent estimation results, as distortions are concentrated in smaller-scale regions. To resolve these problems, it is important to utilize information obtained through surveys, but also to verify the results through complementary checking based on non-survey methods.

Another thing we need to consider when compiling a regional input-output table is the number of sectors. In the regional I-O table for Nagoya City drawn up by Asahi (2003), the number of sectors for value of production (CT) was 185, with 93 sectors for inputs and value added estimates. The reason for using such a dense array of sectors to estimate the value of production in the city is in order to reproduce the sector characteristics as far as possible. To put this another way, in a large sector for which we have grouped together transaction details, we assume that an estimate based on such a sample will lead to effectively the same result as when the whole sector is observed as a lump sum. In reality, however, the sectors in each sub-category perform transactions differently. It is important to guard against this problem as far as possible within our data constraints.

Nomura et al. (2011) have also produced a sector classification in conformity with the Tourism Satellite Accounts in the UNWTO Manual. Not only will this help researchers to find the sectors necessary for their analysis purpose, but if the classes and numbers of sectors commonly used in regional input-output tables can be distinguished as clearly as possible, they can be used in a more standard way across a variety of analyses.

1.2.1.3 Construction of an Employment Table for Use in a Regional Input-Output Table

In regional input-output analysis, the effect on production also has an influence on employment, which is indicative in its turn of the specific situation of regional production activities. This is particularly important in view of the fact that promotion of the regional economy and security of employment are important issues for local administrations. The use of employment tables alongside regional input-output tables greatly facilitates the analysis of ripple effects on the local employment base.

In an earlier paper, Yamada and Asahi (2000) began by reporting the state of data estimates for prefectural input-output and employment tables for the years 1990 and 1995. Using this as a base, they then produced their own updated employment estimates for Mie Prefecture from which, with the further aid of the regional input-output tables for Mie and other regions, they went on to analyze the impact of overseas expansion of the Mie manufacturing industry on production and labor in Mie itself. One finding from this was that 24 prefectures out of 47 had issued tables of persons engaged in productive employment for 1990 and that a further 8 were due to do so in 1995. A subsequent look at a more recent situation showed that all 46 prefectures that issued prefectural input-output tables in 2015 had also published employment tables. Similarly, of the 16 ordinance-designated major cities that had issued an input-output table, 11 had also issued an employment table. While there had been a steady increase in employment tables in prefectures and major cities over the past 30 years, however, cities in the next rank down had not yet made a start in this direction.

To issue tabulations of work data or the like, cities or other regional authorities need to keep stocks of data which can be retrieved and combined in a complementary way for display. Furthermore, when data from different survey years have to be collated together, it may be necessary to estimate what the more exact figures would have been for the year required. In addition, statistics from different work locations may need to be recombined into a single activity-based table. As already mentioned, the preparation of a table like this will require knowledge of the contents of various statistical surveys.

At the close of their paper, Yamada and Asahi (2000) evaluated the validity of their employment estimates by placing their Mie Prefecture results alongside those obtained using official employment tables in the adjacent prefectures of Aichi and Gifu, which belong to the same "Tokai" manufacturing area. They then verified for accuracy by comparing deviations between the employment coefficients in these three Tokai prefectures, and also with other parts of Japan. The result was that the Mie results fitted aptly enough with the adjacent and national patterns to justify a conclusion that they could be used for regional analysis. Finally, specific results were analyzed regarding the impact of Mie manufacturers' expansion overseas on production and labor in Mie.

1.2.1.4 Environmental Evaluation

As the input-output table also shows supply and demand relations of raw materials for products, input-output analysis can further be used to estimate energy consumption and emissions of environmental pollutants in manufacturing processes.[8] This is thanks to the quantitative evidence that can be presented when considering the spillover effects of industrial, energy and environmental policies. As environmental and energy problems are closely linked, a number of analyses have been carried out on the impact of renewable energy sources such as domestically supplied solar and wind power on the economy and on employment in Japan.

In Japan, the National Institute for Environmental Studies (NIES)[9] has developed a database called Embodied Energy and Emission Intensity Data for Japan Using Input-Output Tables (3EID). The input-output tables have approximately 400 sectors classified by the type of production activity, and show the environmental load for each type in terms of the energy consumption and greenhouse gas emissions per unit of production activity (this unit is equivalent to 1 million yen of production value). The latest version of this database is from 2015 and covers the emission substances CO_2, CH_4, N_2O, HFCs, PFCs, SF_6 and NF_3. The fuel inputs in each sector, consumed in forms of coal, oil, petrol and natural gas etc., are estimated from statistics.

The database also estimates greenhouse gas emissions from the energy consumption of households and firms. The actual function of the database is to assess environmental impacts, for example by calculating the amount of CO_2 emitted during the manufacture of a product or over the period of a life cycle assessment (LCA). The results of this LCA calculation then show the carbon footprint of the product or service (CFP), meaning the CO_2 emissions load over the entire period of its production and use.

Examples of regional analysis studies using this database are Long et al. (2017, 2021). These have provided CFP estimates for household consumption activities in Japanese cities and drawn up inventories of urban household emissions.

Asahi (2005a, 2005b) analyzed the spillover ripple effects of wind farm constructions on regional economies, including employment and environmental aspects, using a 9-region inter-regional input-output table issued in 1995 by the then Ministry of International Trade and Industry (MITI) along with unit data for CO_2 emissions from the 3EID.

Asahi (2013) analyzes the Yokkaichi pollution problem that affected a localized area in Mie Prefecture during the period of rapid postwar economic growth. While production activities led most directly to sulfur oxide (SO_x) emissions in Yokkaichi City itself, local products affected by SO_x emissions were also input into other goods produced in areas away from Yokkaichi. In addition, increases in demand from areas

---

[8] See Leontief (1986).

[9] The 3EID database is summarized in Nansai (2009) and data are presented on the website below. Nansai and Moriguchi (2006) analyze two methods for estimating an environmental load unit.
https://www.cger.nies.go.jp/publications/report/d031/jpn/datafile/index.htm.

outside may have stimulated production in Yokkaichi, placing a still greater environmental burden on the location. This study analyzes these linked economic impacts. To do this, it uses a two-region inter-industry input-output table that makes dual reference to the 1975 Mie Prefecture input-output table and to the national table for the same year. More specifically, the study uses survey data of the same period from companies in the Yokkaichi petrochemical complex and data on SO_x emissions and coefficients from the Input-Output Table for Analysis of the 1973 Industrial Pollution[10] issued by the Research and Statistics Department of the Minister's Secretariat (Ministry of International Trade and Industry, 1976). From these materials, and using the same 30 sectors as in the Ministry document, I created a two-region inter-regional input-output table with Mie prefecture as one region and locations outside of Mie as the other. The results obtained were as follows. For the year 1975, 75% of the total production value of products in Yokkaichi's chemical and petroleum industry was absorbed in Mie Prefecture, leaving a 25% overspill to locations outside the prefecture. The cost of SO_x emissions due to this petrochemical production divided into 79% borne by Mie as against 21% outside. Hence, the environmental impact due to the SO_x pollution, even if considered alongside benefits obtained from the industry, fell disproportionately heavily inside the prefecture rather than outside. To put it simply, regions outside Mie had to produce more to obtain transfers of Mie petrochemical products for use in other productions. This increased external demand then had a knock-on impact on Mie, and on Yokkaichi in particular, resulting later in still higher levels of SO_x emissions in the surrounding urban region.

Various studies in waste input-output analysis (WIOA) have also been conducted to determine the amounts of waste generated and disposed of in landfills in Japan and its cities and regions. One such study, by Nakamura and Kondo (2002), uses a waste input-output table (WIOT), developed by the authors and divided into sectors for a detailed classification of waste types and treatments to allow an analysis of waste flows. In another study, Tsukui et al. (2015) extended an existing input-output table for the Tokyo Metropolis to take in city-level data from the 46 other prefectures and the rest of the world. They used this table to estimate and compare waste amounts and treatments and performed an evaluative analysis. In ways like these studies, new methods of waste flow analysis have been developed by applying existing input-output methods.

1.2.2 Econometric Modeling Research

1.2.2.1 Econometric Models

Many kinds of econometric models have been developed. The basic ideas of structural macro-econometric modeling were laid out in America by the Cowles Commission, at first based on real business cycles but then modified in the direction of "dynamic

[10] See Research and Statistics Department, Minister's Secretariat, MITI (1976).

stochastic general equilibrium" (DSGE) models. Numerous econometric models, of DSGE and other types, have since been developed. Their transitions and characteristics are described in Fukač and Pagan (2010a, 2010b) and Murphy (2017). Two Japanese treatments are Taguchi and Vu (2018) and Takahashi and Yagihashi (2019), both of which offer examples of the use of macroeconomic models in institutions outside Japan.

In the management of economic policy, econometric models of this kind are used to assess economic prospects and various policy effects by national governments, central banks and international organizations. Central banks have rapidly progressed in their use of DSGE models, which are based on the dynamic optimization behavior of economic agents. The Bank of Japan, following a "suite of models" approach that favors diverging types of model for different uses, has created a DSGE-type Japanese Economic Model (JEM)[11] for some purposes, and for others a hybrid-type Quarterly-Japanese Economic Model (Q-JEM)[12] that relaxes theoretical rules to some extent to focus on data fitting. In addition, it has published a Financial Macroeconomic Model (FMM).[13] From within the Cabinet Office, the Economic and Social Research Institute has developed and published economic and fiscal models of its own[14] while the Office for Econometric Analysis (2018) has brought out a Short-term Japanese Economic Macroeconomic Econometric Model.[15] For its part, the Research Institute of Economy, Trade and Industry (RIETI) has developed a hybrid-type MEAD-RIETI Model (MRM)[16] which works on quarterly economic data.

1.2.2.2 Construction of a Regional Econometric Model

Various regional econometric models have been developed to cope with different regional issues. The Asia Pacific Institute of Research has developed a macroeconomic model for short-term economic forecasting in Kansai (the area around Osaka), a region with relatively up-to-date data by national standards.[17] There is also an extended version that incorporates the main economic variables of all seven Kansai prefectures. This extended model can be used for empirical investigations and simulations of the Kansai region on dynamic stochastic general equilibrium (DSGE) principles.[18]

In municipalities below the rank of ordinance-designated cities, regional econometric modeling analysis runs into the problem of insufficient data, as smaller cities and towns keep considerably smaller amounts of continuous long-term economic

[11] See Fujiwara et al. (2005), Teranishi et al. (2004).

[12] See Hirakata et al. (2019).

[13] See Abe et al. (2023).

[14] See Matsumae and Hasumi (2016).

[15] See Maruyama et al. (2018), Sakamaki et al. (2022).

[16] See Fukuyama et al. (2010).

[17] See Inada and Irie (2013), Irie (2014, 2019).

[18] See Okano et al. (2015).

data in the first place, and the kinds that they do keep are limited to narrower ranges of categories. Therefore, for regional econometric modeling analyses on this level of small cities or below, intensive preparations are required in the form of collecting or estimating the data needed for new projects and evaluations or for regional policies. What is more, once the first run of the analysis is completed, follow-ups with new data are rarely undertaken, let alone ongoing revisions of the kind that demand changes to the model structure and equations or to the estimation work.

Around the year 2000, I worked with several researchers on the project of creating a regional econometric model with an environmental and economic policy focus for Yokkaichi City. This was an example of a one-off model limited to a definite period as its purpose was to verify past policies. It was a six-year project carried out in cooperation with Mie Prefecture, Yokkaichi City and a local International Center for Environmental Technology Transfer (ICETT). Since then, the model has not been revised to allow further policy analysis. But as one case example of a regional econometric analysis of this sort, I will now explain about the economic development and later changes in environmental regulations that led to a pollution problem in the Yokkaichi area becoming the occasion of a regional econometric model for environmental and economic policy.

Yokkaichi air pollution was a problem that affected a localized area during the period of rapid economic growth from the end of the 1950s to the early 1970s. Four regional outbreaks of pollution-induced disease are widely remembered from this period in Japan: Minamata disease, Niigata Minamata disease, itai-itai disease in Toyama Prefecture and Yokkaichi asthma, and the pollution that caused the Yokkaichi asthma became known as the "Yokkaichi pollution." Its main cause was sulfur oxide (SO_x) emissions from the plants of several companies grouped in the city's petrochemical complex.

The study used several analytical tools. Of these, the regional econometric model was purpose-built for this environmental policy evaluation. For more details, see Kito et al. (1998), Asahi et al. (1998), and Nishigaki et al. (1998). The estimation period for the model was 1965–1994, which included the period of high SO_x emissions and the subsequent period during which these emissions declined due to stricter regulations. A previously existing econometric model for environmental policy that was referred to in the analysis was the Kanagawa Prefecture Regional Environmental Economic Model of 1994.[19] However, there seem to have been no prior instances of regional econometric modeling analysis at ordinary city level for the assessment of past cases of air pollution.

Macroeconomic econometric modeling analysis at the ordinary city level had been studied previously by Hashimoto (1992) for Amagasaki and by Inagaki (1992) for Yokkaichi. We used these as references for the construction of the Yokkaichi Region Econometric Model for Environmental and Economic Policy.

In Inagaki (1992)'s framework, in which the purpose was to analyze environmental policy, public finance functions were simplified into a single "supply block" for the city's "industrial block." To this first core, it was then necessary to add further blocks

---

[19] See Research Institute, Mitsui Knowledge Industry (1994).

for the petrochemical complex/environmental sector, and for distribution, prices and demand. In a similar way, the model for environmental and economic policy had a central core made up of three blocks for the industrial complex, the environmental effects and various economic and environmental indicators, and then other blocks for demand, supply, distribution, public finances, prices and other economies in Mie Prefecture. In addition, it was necessary to bring in macroeconomic blocks for exogenous effects.

Figure 1.2 shows a flowchart of the Yokkaichi Regional Environmental and Economic Policy Model. The model is relatively small-scale, with 33 stochastic (or behavioral) equations and 32 identity equations, for a total of 65 (Fig. 1.3).

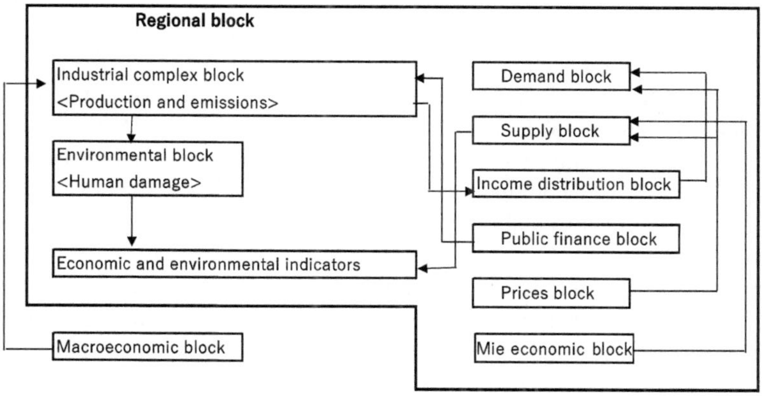

Fig. 1.2 Flowchart of the Yokkaichi Regional Environmental and Economic Policy Model. *Source* Asahi et al. (1998), 108, Fig. 1, rewritten in English

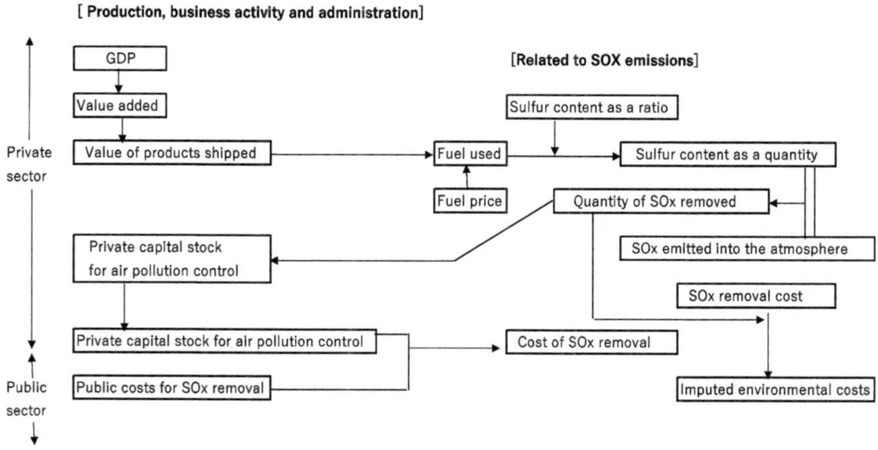

Fig. 1.3 Flowchart of "Industrial complex block". *Source* Asahi et al. (1998), 108, Fig. 2, rewritten in English

The industrial complex block includes variables relating to production activities of the companies grouped in the complex and the pollution-related variables generated by them. The environmental block includes variables for SO_X concentration levels and for the numbers of patients identified under the Act on Compensation for Pollution-related Health Damage as being due for relief. This needs to be entered because of the serious impact that the SO_x emissions from the industrial complex had on the health of the local population. On these grounds, the environmental block was introduced as a system of equations explaining these relationships.

The relationships were obtained through estimates, as follows. First, a simulation of SO_x diffusion was undertaken based on the amounts of SO_X emitted by the companies and the SO_X concentrations around the complex, using a mesh with 500 m intervals, and relying on smoke source data from 1975. Estimates of the numbers of new patients were based on the results of these diffusion estimates and on the local population distribution each year for each cell of the mesh.

The two indicators included in the economic development indicator block are the net national welfare (NNW) indicator and the Green GDP. The NNW indicator was calculated by subtracting total human damage costs and SO_x removal costs from the net national (citizen) product of Yokkaichi City. Similarly, the Green GDP was found by subtracting attributable environmental costs from the net national (citizen) product.

The supply block includes the value added of the city's manufacturing industry excluding that of the petrochemical complex. This value added is determined by macroeconomic trends and by the operating status of companies' tangible fixed assets. The simulations for the project were then also used to analyze the effects of the new environmental policies implemented at the petrochemical complex to bring local SO_x concentrations down to the levels determined by the new and more stringent standards. The impacts of three new limits were analyzed: SO_x concentration limits, K-value limits (controlling the concentrations reaching the ground) and limits for total emission amounts.

1.2.3 Panel Data Analysis

1.2.3.1 Panel Data Analysis: An Overview

Statistical data can be presented in three basic ways. The first way is in a time series showing changes over time, the second is by using cross-sectional data to describe the characteristics or status of some country, prefecture, household, or enterprise at a single point in time, and the third way is by tracking individual household or enterprise data over a longer span of years.

In this next section, I describe an analysis that uses panel data, sets of cross-sectional data collected within one country or prefecture and presented across a number of time points. Panel data thus combine properties from cross-sectional data (multiple instances at one point in time), and from time series (across multiple time points).[20]

Econometrics has had to develop a number of ways to avoid bias arising from omitted variables. Multiple regression and instrumental variable methods are representative examples. One advantage of using panel data is that this offers a way of avoiding variable bias omission without any actual need of observing additional variables.[21]

Methods of panel data analysis can be divided into two types: static and dynamic. The static methods divide into fixed effect and random effect estimation. Dynamic methods divide into those using instrumental variables and those depending on the generalized method of moments (GMM). The essential difference between static and dynamic panel data analysis lies in the use or non-use of lagged explanatory variables. In static panel analysis, the explanatory variables in the estimating equation do not include values carried over from the past (i.e., with a time lag), but in dynamic panel data analysis, they do.

I will begin first from the fixed-effects estimation method in the static approach.[22] Here, the individual effect is considered specific to the one case, and thus constant over time. An effect of this kind cannot be used as an explanatory variable in a regression analysis because it is not observable in the data. The individual effect is therefore included in the error term. No correct estimate is possible if the error term occurs correlated with the explanatory variables. Thanks to the panel data, however, it is possible to control for this. There are four typical ways of doing it: the Least Square Dummy Variable (LSDV) method, difference estimation, "within estimates," and "between estimates." Using one or other of these methods, it becomes possible to remove individual effects.

In cases where individual effects and explanatory variables are correlated, they can be regarded as fixed and can be estimated using a fixed effects model. Random effects are also individual and do not change through time. However, unlike fixed effects, they do not correlate with explanatory variables. Thus, individual effects not correlated with explanatory variables can be taken as random. The way to distinguish individual effects is to use a Hausman test to see whether or not they change through time (i.e., whether they are random). Briefly, this allows testing whether there is a correlation between individual effects and explanatory variables.

This exploits the fact that regression analyses give differing estimate results from fixed effect and random effect models. If differences between estimates are large, the unchanging ones that stay fixed are the ones that are correlated with the explanatory variables. In general, in cases where fixed effects can be estimated, this fixed effect can be considered the effect of an unobservable element staying constant through time.

---

[20] For a more detailed treatment, see Higuchi et al. (2006). Chaps. 1 and 2.

[21] Baltagi (2008), 4–9, points out seven advantages backed up with references to Hsiao (2003) and Klevmarken (1989).

[22] See Okubo (2021).

At any rate, analysts need to be aware of the difference between fixed and random effects. Especially, in situations where only random effects are usable, there is a need to consider carefully what assumptions can be made about the randomness of the data when conducting an empirical analysis. In such circumstances, an F Test can be used to verify whether one is warranted in assuming that there are no fixed effects in the panel data that would rule out the option of a pooling estimate using the ordinary least square method. The Lagrange multiplier is another test that can be used to determine whether a randomness assumption is justified before a pooled estimate is attempted. In addition, time-fixed effects should also be tested for, to ensure that there is no omitted variable bias arising from variables changing over time cycles.

Panel data can be useful for understanding the causes of serial correlation in economic variables. In particular, when thinking about the implications for a model, it makes a considerable difference whether variations are due to unobserved heterogeneity in the phenomenon being analyzed or in state-dependent effects. Unobserved heterogeneity can be dealt with on static assumptions, using fixed or random effect models. However, state-dependent effects cannot be addressed in this way. Dynamic effects need to be considered. Arellano and Bond (1991) used dynamic panel models in their attempts to analyze state-dependent effects. This enabled them to find consistent estimators for estimate parameters, although only for use in static panel analysis. In dynamic analysis, these estimators may lose their consistency. In particular, the dynamic panel data model can be used together with the static GMM method to obtain a consistent estimator.[23]

1.2.3.2 Case Studies of Regional Economic Research Using Panel Analysis

Panel analysis is used for empirical testing of various matters in regional economic research. This section presents examples of panel data analysis in Asahi (2000, 2001b). These studies analyze the impact of social capital on the local economy.

In the view of the Japanese government, one important effect of social capital is to increase the working aptitude of the population through the productive capacity and amenity effect of improved living conditions, as industrial and living infrastructures are developed in accordance with the objectives of government projects.

Another additional role of public investment and social capital is to work toward the correction of income inequality in local economies because it also functions to redistribute income.[24] Based on this, Asahi (2000) analyzed how actual social capital relates to the production and characteristics of each region. The period of analysis covered 21 years from 1976 to 1996. Asahi (2000) analyzed the stock of

---

[23] Vector autoregression (VAR) models for dynamic panel data analysis are described in Holtz-Eakin et al. (1987, 1988).

[24] Alternatively: Director General for Economic and Fiscal Management, Cabinet Office (2001), Part 1, Chap. 1, Sect. 1.
https://www5.cao.go.jp/j-j/cr/cr01/chiikireport01_01-01-01.html.

social capital in terms of investment in educational facilities in particular, and in total. Asahi (2001b) analyzed the stock of social capital and the social discount rate.

First, the effects of social capital on productivity were estimated with Cobb-Douglas Production functions, using data from all 47 prefectures. Second, a panel analysis was carried out to take regional characteristics into account. This added dummies to the production functions at the prefecture level, allowing purely regional characteristics to be extracted. An analysis was then run on the fixed effect model using panel data for production factor variables and income for all 47 prefectures. Using this fixed effect model, the estimate results for the 1976–1985 and 1986–1996 data sets both turned out good. The social capital parameter was found to be significantly positive when region-specific characteristics were taken into account. This indicates that the social capital supplied in the prefectures was having a productive effect. When the analysis for the production functions was subjected to a constraint of constant returns to scale, a lower parameter of social capital was apparent only in the private sector. The Hausman test results, too, showed an evident correlation between the regional characteristic variables and the other variables.

Based on this, the fixed effect model was selected, leaving open the possibility that it might include problems of simultaneity[25] with the social capital. The two-way fixed effects model was then used to obtain estimates for the data from 1966 to 1984. The results allowed reasonable parameter estimates, while the estimate results for the data from 1976 to 1996 showed that the parameters of the social capital stock were not significant. Using the fixed effect model case which provided better measurement results, the analyzed results were then used to compare how regional (prefecture) characteristics related to production and social capital stock in these two time periods (Table 1.1).

Changes in regional characteristics were obtained by subtracting the standardized data values for 1976–1996 from the later ones for 1986–1995.The greatest differences between the two sets were from the rural prefectures Shimane, Iwate, Miyazaki, and Kochi, while the smallest differences came from the urban prefectures Tokyo, Osaka, Kanagawa, Aichi, and Saitama. More generally, too, regional characteristics showed a wider range of variation between different time periods the farther removed the regions were from the large urban areas.

Figure 1.4 shows a scatterplot of the regional characteristic variables and the output per unit of labor in 1996. The correlation coefficient between these data is extremely high at 0.905. This result implies that differences in output between regions are accountable not only to numbers of production components, but also to regional characteristics. Regional characteristics are therefore positively correlated with income levels. Figure 1.5 shows another scatterplot of regional characteristics and the social capital stock per unit of labor in 1996. The correlation coefficient between these data is $-$ 0.806. But the correlation coefficient for the same variables in 1976 was $-$ 0.393, indicating that social capital has some impact on reducing the disparities. The correlation coefficient between the social capital stock of educational facilities and regional characteristics in 1996 is $-$ 0.40. This indicates that in the

[25] Hayashi (2003) is an account of simultaneity and endogeneity for social capital.

Table 1.1 Results of panel analysis subjected to constant returns to scale (case analysis from a fixed effect model)

Paper	Social capital coefficient			Private capital coefficient	Statistics	
	Total	Social capital stock of educational facilities	Social capital stock other than educational facilities	Private capital stock	Adj R^2 Std. error	Hausman
Asahi (2000)		0.14** (0.02) *6.5*	0.22** (0.02) *8.0*	0.88** (0.01) *0.8*	0.92 0.05	85.63**
Asahi (2001b)	0.33** (0.01) *26.2*			0.11** (0.12) *9.2*	0.92 0.05	60.96**

Source Based on estimates in Asahi (2000) and Asahi (2001b)
Note Absolute values of estimated t-statistics in italics. Coefficient estimates marked **are above critical 1% level. Standard errors in parentheses under coefficient estimates. Adj R^2: adjusted R-square, std. error: standard error of regression. Hausman stats. marked **significant at 1% level. Estimates obtained using TSP4.5

educational world, too, the stock of social capital in each region has an influence on the reduction of regional disparities.

As the prefectural estimates do not take into account spillovers from other prefectures, the statistics were also analyzed in another way by reassigning the prefectural data to the 11 larger regions into which the 47 prefectures are often grouped. The results did not differ significantly from the prefectural ones. The larger-mesh regional characteristic values were still clearly higher in large conurbation areas such as South Kanto, Tokai and Kinki, and lower in Hokkaido, Chugoku and South Kyushu.

In other results calculated for the marginal productivities of social and private capital, the study showed that subregions with social capital deficiencies below prefecture level are concentrated in urban areas while the earlier shortages of social capital on the prefectural scale are decreasing. As for the contributions of social and private capital to production in the manufacturing sector, the findings were complex.

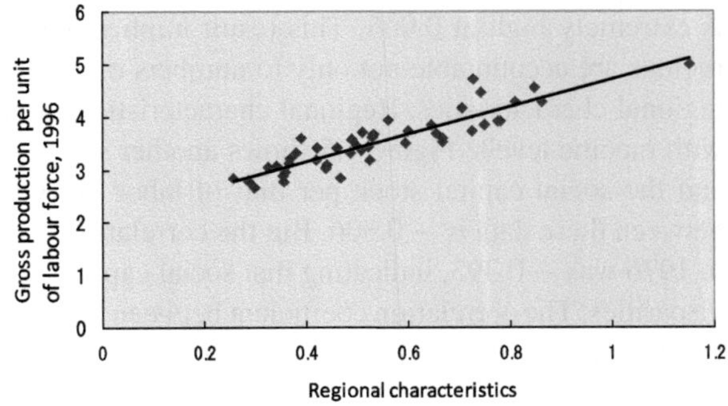

Fig. 1.4 Scatterplot of regional characteristics and gross production. *Source* Asahi (2001b), 138, Fig. 2-1, rewritten in English

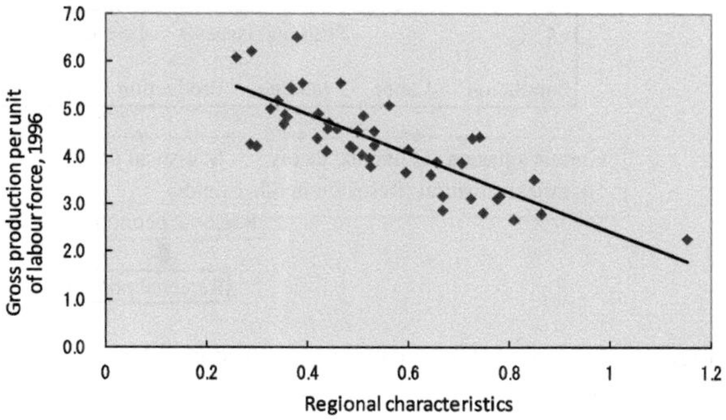

Fig. 1.5 Scatter diagram of regional characteristics and social capital stock. *Source* Asahi (2001b), 138, Fig. 2-2, rewritten in English

Generally, the estimated parameters were much better for private than for social capital. However, the measured results for marginal productivity of social capital showed that prospects were a good deal higher in certain specific regions. This indicates that investing in regions with high marginal productivity for social capital is also appropriate from an efficiency perspective.

1.3 Setting the Objectives of Regional Economic Research and My Previous Research as a Whole

1.3.1 How to Go About the Process of Econometric Research in a Regional Economy

In this book, I attempt a regional economic analysis of a number of issues currently confronting Japan in a rapidly changing environment. My aim in this is to clarify the evolving situation and introduce the policy options from which solutions are to be sought at the regional level, using economic data and econometric methods to identify the mechanisms concerned.

A processual overview of how to undertake an econometric study of a regional economy is offered in Fig. 1.6. Regional problems nowadays include population, labor, income, production, energy, environment and many others. The solution for any of these problems involves taking stock of the current situation and drawing on economic theory or on other research and information. Statistical data then need to be collected and supplemented by estimates to fill gaps in the analysis. The results of the research are obtained using these and various additional analytical methods.

To understand regional economic phenomena, it may not be enough to rely solely on this or that set of published statistical data. To ascertain more, it may be necessary to undertake a broader analysis using econometric methods applicable to regional economic problems, or estimates that take into account the deeper links between regional statistics of various kinds and their ultimate knowledge base in economic theory. In this kind of way, regional econometric problems are analyzed and results

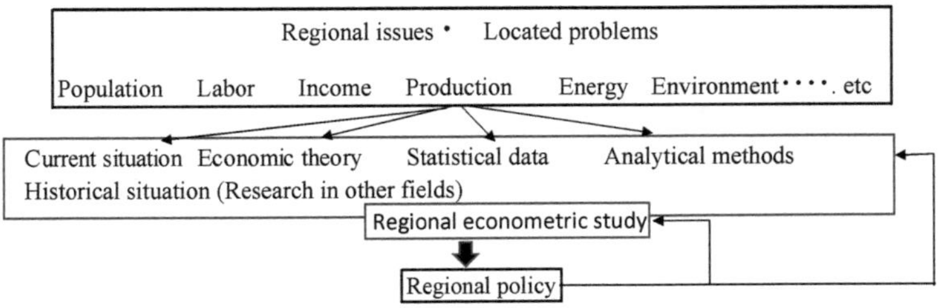

Fig. 1.6 Overview of how to undertake an econometric study of a regional economy. *Source* Created by the author

are won. It is then up to regional policymakers to use the results and decide on the policies to make. Alternatively, in some cases, regional econometric studies are needed to build up the stock of analytical information needed for the policymaking process and there are also cases where regional economic research papers of broader scope have to be written. Sometimes, along the way, the researched content of regional econometric studies may also be modified in various ways to fit more exactly into the formulation of a policy.[26] Ultimately, regional studies will be validated by what can be done with them.

The best commentary I can offer for this is a simple reflection on my own experience. We get all kinds of information every day, from online media, books and magazines, from friends and family, or colleagues at our institutions or workplaces. We are also informed about ourselves and the people around us, at local, regional or country level, and all of this gives us an insight into current situations and problems. I have sat on various regional administration committees over the past 25 years, where I have had my fair share of chances to attend meetings about my region (Tokai region or Mie) and all the challenges and issues it faces.

Regional econometric research begins with an understanding of the issues and problems in the region and questions about what is first needed to solve these problems. It goes without saying that it is important to know the current situation of the region you are researching. For this to be possible, statistical data need to be collected and entered into a database, and data describing the regional economic structures need to be compiled and made available. Regional input-output tables are one example of this.

To begin a particular study, you first have to look back over previous studies, and then update what you know of the analytical methods and the context and current state of the statistical data. Another thing to consider at this early stage is whether there are any analytical issues unique to the region, for example, regional specificities in the data. The analysis should be pursued in such a way that these statistical issues are also addressed. Further, and still thinking of analytical methods, regional econometric studies can also be included if there are statistical data to be found at the national level. In practice, however, data are often not available because few elaborate surveys

[26] Smith and Morrison (2012) refer to policy and input-output analysis.

have been carried out at regional levels. In fact, for any analysis at this level, there is likely to be a necessity to make up for gaps in the regional data. The methodology of how regional econometric analysis can supply this missing data is thus a vital part of the research.

In regional economy studies, then, regional issues and problems have a significant part to add to global and national issues. And this part can change significantly over time. Sometimes, when the problems faced by the national economy are gradually resolved, this also brings relief to the region. On the other hand, there are also times when the country as a whole may appear to have solved its problems, but particular regions have not yet managed to recover in the same way and remain as they were. Furthermore, each region has its own unique challenges and problems.

1.3.2 The Place of My Previous Studies in My Regional Economic Research Career

This section reviews my previous research into regional econometric studies. It shows the periods spent in these earlier studies along with the contents and analytical methods.

Figure 1.7, first, shows schematically the periods when I was occupied in my past research in regional econometric analysis. This includes a period wholly engaged in this one field, a single-year period occupied with a regional input-output table, a period of work on panel analysis, and then a period in which I estimated and presented my own economic data. The papers summarizing the results of my research are entered as items [1–28] on the right-hand side, with time bars or points corresponding to the respective years. These numbers all refer to papers I have worked on. Content indications can be found in Table 1.2 and for fuller details, there is a list of my publications just before the main References for this chapter.

Table 1.2 shows the subject matters, analytical methods, and data source accessibility for each paper, along with the analysis area (region) that was studied. From the perspective of the present book, 10 of these studies focus onon my own experience. the environment, 4 on tourism, 6 on social capital, and 7 on the economy in general, including population and labor matters. The number of papers on tourism research is small, but this reflects the developments in the statistical data following the establishment of the Tourism Agency in 2008, which recently led to an increase in time series of tourism data. In the future, tourism research should have a richer environment for econometric analysis. A further blow came very recently with the novel coronavirus (Covid-19) pandemic which had a significantly negative impact on the tourism industry. These fluctuations in the data will be a challenge for tourism research based on time series analysis, which requires long-term data. Research on social capital was also affected by the Great East Japan Earthquake in 2011, and environmentally-friendly social capital, including disaster prevention, is one of the current issues.

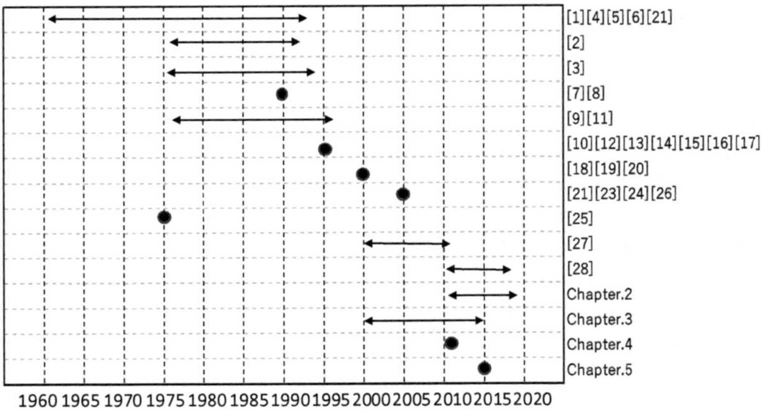

Fig. 1.7 Period of research devoted to the subject matters treated in previous papers. *Source* Created by the author

As for analysis methods, 4 of the studies use regional econometric models, 16, industry linkage analyses, 4, panel analyses and 5, other types. Note that when several analysis methods are used in a single paper, each method is entered separately.

The data source column in the table includes some cases of data released by national or regional administrative agencies and used directly, others where new data had to be estimated on the basis of agency data, others where surveys were conducted to be used as a source for complementary estimates, and cases where data were obtained through surveys. Regarding analysis areas, 11 studies concerned cities or localized areas around cities or towns, 5 concerned prefectures, and 12 were studies taking in all 47 prefectures.

The details of each study can be found in the respective papers. Note, however, that many were written in Japanese either because they are regional economic analyses of a limited area or because they were published in a book in Japanese. I regret the accessibility barrier that this represents for non-readers of the language.

1.3.3 Plan and Chapter Structure of this Book

Having set up a context for the kind of regional problems that can be tackled through an econometric approach to regional economies, and having also shown how the chapter contents of this book relate to my own previous research career, the time has come to explain the plan and chapter structure in order.

Figure 1.8 displays the interrelationships between the book's chapter topics. From a method viewpoint, this chapter has already supplied the required contextual overview of regional economic research and its analysis methods, illustrated with econometric examples. The content chapters that follow will try to apply this approach to four key issues of the regional economy: the decline in the total fertility

Table 1.2 List of research subjects, analysis methods, data sources and analysis areas

	Subject	Content and keyword	Year	Analysis method	Data source	Analysis area (region)
[1]	Environment, economy, business	Corporate activities and pollution issues	1960–1992	Path analysis	Public, research	Yokkaichi City and surrounding areas, Japan
[2]	Social capital	Efficiency of social capital	1976–1992	Econometric model analysis	Public, research	Yokkaichi City, Japan
[3]	Social capital	Efficiency of social capital	1975–1994	Panel data analysis	Public, research	47 Prefectures, Japan
[4]	Environment, economy, business	Pollution and the economy	1960–1992	Econometric model analysis	Public, research	Yokkaichi City, Japan
[5]	Environment, economy, business	Pollution and the economy	1960–1992	Econometric model analysis	Public, research	Yokkaichi City, Japan
[6]	Environment, economy, business	Pollution and the economy	1960–1992	Econometric model analysis	Public, research	Yokkaichi City, Japan
[7]	Economy	Hollowing out problem	1990	Input-output analysis	Public, research	Mie Prefecture, Japan
[8]	Labor statistics and economy	Hollowing out problem	1990	Input-output analysis	Public, research	Mie Prefecture, Japan
[9]	Social capital (education)	Efficiency of social capital	1976–1996	Panel data analysis	Public	47 Prefectures, Japan,
[10]	Environment and economy	Environmental preservation and economic efficiency	1995	Input-output analysis	Public	Tianjin, China
[11]	Social capital	Efficiency of social capital	1976–1996	Panel data analysis	Public	47 Prefectures, Japan
[12]	Environment and economy	Environmental preservation and economic efficiency	1995	Input-output analysis	Public	Tianjin, China
[13]	Regional statistics	Evaluation of regional I-O table	1995	Input-output analysis	Public	47 Prefectures, Region, Japan

(continued)

Table 1.2 (continued)

	Subject	Content and keyword	Year	Analysis method	Data source	Analysis area (region)
[14]	Regional statistics	Creation of I-O table for the city	1995	Input-output analysis	Public	Nagoya, Japan
[15]	Social capital (port)	Social capital productivity and effectiveness	1995	Panel data analysis, input-output analysis	Public	Nagoya, Aichi Prefecture, Japan
[16]	Energy, environment, and economy	Wind power generation, environmental economy	1995	Input-output analysis	Public, research	47 Prefectures, Region, Japan
[17]	Energy, environment, and economy	Wind power generation, environmental economy	1995	Input-output analysis	Public, research	47 Prefectures, Region, Japan
[18]	Regional statistics	Evaluation of regional I-O table	2000	Input-output analysis	Public	47 Prefectures, Region, Japan
[19]	Tourism statistics and analysis	Tourism statistics and ripple effects	2000	Input-output analysis	Public	47 Prefectures, Japan
[20]	Tourism statistics and analysis	Tourism statistics and ripple effects	2000	Input-output analysis	Public	Orange County, Florida, USA
[21]	Tourism statistics and analysis	Tourism statistics and ripple effects	2005	Input-output analysis	Public, research	Yamaguchi, Hagi, Yamaguchi Prefecture, Japan
[22]	Environment and economy	Economic growth and environmental impact	1960–1992	Statistical analysis	Public, research	Yokkaichi City, Japan
[23]	Earthquake impact and social capital	Earthquake disaster ports selection and port capital	2005	Factor analysis, input-output analysis	Public, research	Nagoya, Aichi Prefecture, Japan
[24]	Regional statistics	I-O analysis	2005	Input-output analysis	Public, research	Yamaguchi City, Yamaguchi Prefecture, Yamaguchi Area, Japan

(continued)

Table 1.2 (continued)

	Subject	Content and keyword	Year	Analysis method	Data source	Analysis area (region)
[25]	Environment and economy	Pollution and the economy	1975	Input-output analysis	Public, research	Yokkaichi, Mie, Japan
[26]	Energy, environment and economy	NIMBYs and wind power	2005	Logit analysis	Public, research	47 Prefectures, Japan
[27]	Population issues and analysis	Total fertility rate and regions	2000–2010	Statistical analysis	Public	47 Prefectures, Japan
[28]	Tourism statistics and analysis	Tourism demand and congestion phenomenon	2010–2018	Panel data analysis	Public	47 Prefectures, Japan

Source Created by the author

rate (Chap. 2), which is connected via demographics to the fabric of social structure, tourism as an industry that interacts with population (Chap. 3), and the sustaining resources of energy (Chap. 4) and social capital (Chap. 5). If the issues in Chaps. 3 and 4 come together in a concern for a sustainable environment, the resources in Chaps. 4 and 5 also meet in their common role as public goods. I will close by briefly previewing these four topics.

A serious problem in Japan today is population decline due to a falling birthrate and aging. The national and regional governments are working on policies to support child raising, but there has been no significant improvement in the situation. Population is a basic statistical indicator of social stability, and the current imbalance is having a significant impact on demographic trends. For this reason, regional population

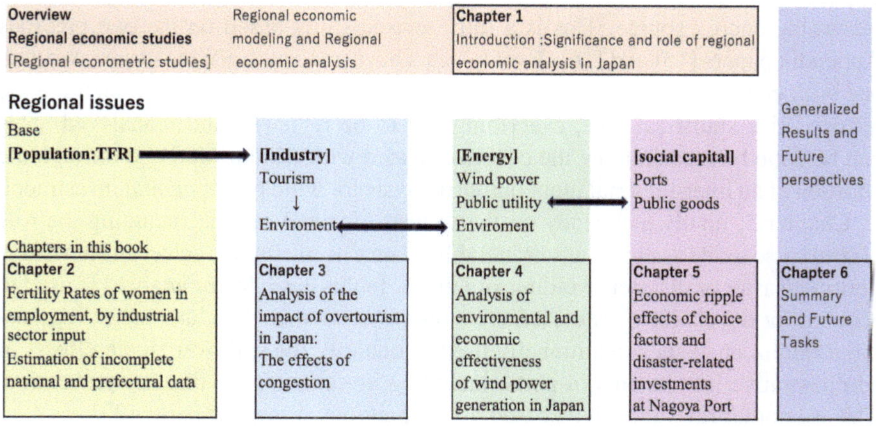

Fig. 1.8 Interrelationships between chapter topics. *Source* Created by the author

estimates, that is, estimated variations in total fertility rates (TFRs) and the economic variables that affect them in each region, were selected as an appropriate topic for Chap. 2. Another important objective was to demonstrate a method of data display for regional economic statistics that is capable of handling large numbers of data and measurement methods. The case study chosen as an example is one that revises an earlier paper (item [27] in the Appendix list below) by adding an additional five years to the period covered. As data for the issue of declining fertility, it calculates industry-specific TFR estimates for all 47 prefectures in the hope that this will encourage the various industry sectors to address the issue each from their own position. The study also examines relationships between these data and the respective regional characteristics.

Low regional birthrates lead to regional depopulation, and to decline in the regional economy. The national government is therefore promoting tourism as one of its policies to revitalize regional economies. International tourism, in particular, favors transfers of income from tourists' home countries to the destination countries they travel to. Chap. 3, accordingly, is arranged as a study of tourism using dynamic panel analysis. To be sustainable, however, tourism needs to benefit all economic agents—residents, tourists, tourism operators and governments. Regional tourism should also not place a burden on the regional environment itself. The conclusion of the analysis, therefore, is that tourism policy needs to recognize and avoid the negative effects of creating tourist congestion in certain areas. This case study is an extended revision of item [28] in the Appendix list with one additional year of data analysis. It was not possible to extend the data farther in this instance, as the years from 2020 on showed a significant impact from the novel coronavirus (Covid-19) pandemic.

A society with a low environmental impact is a requirement not only for tourism, but also for various economic activities. The power industry is also under social pressure not to seek energy from petrochemical resources due to global warming issues. At the same time, a stable energy supply is essential for Japan and its regions. Electric power is a private good, but can also be understood as a public utility and permanent necessity for all people. Chapter 4, then, is a study of wind power as a renewable energy source. This is a fully revised study based on the two previous Appendix papers [15] and [16]. Twenty years have gone by since those were written, and with changes in Japanese and global environmental policies, not to mention the retrospective statistical data, everything has to be reviewed and reanalyzed. This can be done by recalculating the costs associated with wind power, and through the addition of an inter-regional input output analysis for wind power capital investment.

Chapter 5, finally, is a study on the subject of social capital, including the role played by seaports as public assets, notably when a need arises to select an alternative port in disaster or disaster-avoiding situations. In this case, factor analysis is used to account for the choice of one alternative port over another. At a later stage, regional input-output analysis is additionally used to quantify the spillover ripple effects of administrative investments in ports, including investments for disaster prevention. This is another revisited study, based on the previous Appendix paper [23].

As mentioned above, key regional economic topics that I have previously worked on are revisited and revised in Chaps. 2–5. At the same time, they are also restructured with added uses of other analytical methods and applications of selection analysis in problematic or challenging circumstances akin to some recently faced in the Japanese regions. The final Chap. 6 adds a summary and a list of future tasks.

Appendix A

List of papers corresponding to the numbers in the Fig. 1.7 **and** Table 1.2

(Asahi, S's first-authored and co-authored papers are not included in the references of P. 30, but are all included in this Appendix A)

[1] Iijima, M., Takemoto, Y., Oka, Y., Kito, H., Nishigaki, Y., Kataoka, K., & Asahi, S. (1996). Economic aspects of environmental investment in plant facilities. *Computers & Industrial Engineering, 31*(3–4), 713–717. https://doi.org/10.1016/S0360-8352(96)00244-6

[2] Asahi, S., & Nishigaki, Y. (1996). Econometric analysis of the effects of social overhead capital: A case study with the Yokkaichi regional econometric model. *Ryukoku Journal of Economic Studies 36*(1), 79–113. (in Japanese).

[3] Yakita, A., & Asahi, S. (1998). Regional allocation of public investment and regional disparities, Japan. Postal Savings Funding Study Group Association, Postal Savings Fund Research—Research Grants, Vol. 5, pp. 229–257. (in Japanese).

[4] Kito, H., Oka, Y., Asahi, S., Takemoto, Y., Nishigaki, & Iijima, M. (1998). *Effectiveness of development policies that are environmentally friendly, econometric analysis of the Yokkaichi pollution.* Godo-shuppan. (in Japanese).

[5] Asahi, S., Oka, Y., Kito, H., Nishigaki, Y., Kataoka, Y. (1998). Econometric analysis on regional development and environmental evaluation: A simulation analysis on development and environmental policies for the Yokkaichi industrial complex (in: Japanese), Yokkaichi University, *Journal of Environmental and Information Sciences, 1*(1–2), 103–121.

[6] Nishigaki, Y., Kito, H., Oka, Y., Asahi, S., & Takemoto, Y. (1998). Economic evaluation for sustainable regional development—A case study on Yokkaichi petrochemical industrial complex. In G. Lu, V. Rudolph, & P. Greenfield (Eds.), *Sustainable energy and environmental technologies challenges and opportunities. Proceedings of the 2nd Asia Pacific Conference* (pp. 629–634), Brisbane, Australia.

[7] Yamada, M., & Asahi, S. (1999). Industrial hollowing and regional economy—A case of Mie prefecture. *Sangyo Renkan (Input-Output Analysis), 8*(4), 38–44. (in Japanese). https://doi.org/10.11107/papaios.8.4_38

[8] Yamada, M., & Asahi, S. (2000). Estimation of employment by sector within the regional I-O framework: A case of Mie prefecture (in Japanese). *Sangyo Renkan (Input-Output Analysis), 9*(3), 44–51. https://doi.org/10.11107/papaios.9.44

[9] Asahi, S. (2000). The regional characteristics factors and the effect of productivity for the social capital by an education on the regional economy. *Yokkaichi University, Journal of Environmental and Information Sciences, 4*(1), 87–103. (in Japanese).

[10] Asahi, S. (2001a). The effects of the soil improvement by the desulfurization gypsum on the agricultural production and the Tianjin economy: The case study of China's Tianjin city. In X. Hu & L. Yue (Eds.), *Sustainable energy and environmental technologies. Proceedings of the 3rd Asia Pacific Conference* (pp. 124–129), Hong Kong, China, December 2000, World Scientific. https://doi.org/10.1142/9789812791924_0021

[11] Asahi, S. (2001b). Productivity effect of social capital on the local economy. In M. Shirai, N. Kamata, & A. Yakita (Eds.), *Public economics research* (III, Chap. 7, pp. 133–154). Chukyo University Institute of Economics. (in Japanese).

[12] Asahi, S. (2002). (4) Estimation of the economic effects of introducing desulfurization equipment into Tianjin-Case study of effective use of by-product of desulfurization, Society for the Promotion of Science (JSPS), Research for the Future Program. Multidisciplinary: Interdisciplinary research on environmental protection and interdependence of the economy and the environment in Asia, Tokyo, Japan. Economic development and environmental conservation in Asia, Keio University Press, Tokyo, pp. 123–143. (in Japanese).

[13] Yamada, M., & Asahi, S. (2002). Comparison and evaluation of 1995 prefectural input-output. *Sangyo Renkan (Input-Output Analysis), 13*(3), 47–64. (in Japanese). https://doi.org/10.11107/papaios.10.47

[14] Asahi, S. (2004a). 1995 Input-output table of Nagoya city. *Sangyo Renkan (Input-Output Analysis), 12*(1), 16–24. (in Japanese). https://doi.org/10.11107/papaios.12.16

[15] Asahi, S. (2004b). Ripple effects on the local economy from public investments at Nagoya Port. *The Japan Port Economics Association Chubu Division, Port Studies, 25*, 54–79. (in Japanese).

[16] Asahi, S. (2005a). The effectiveness of introducing wind power generation on environment and economy. In H. Terada (Ed.), *Theory and policy on environmental issues* (Chap. 8, pp. 149–180), Koyoshobo. (in Japanese).

[17] Asahi, S. (2005b). Evaluation of the potential for wind power generation in Japan, Wellington. In S. Pratt & C. Davies (Eds.), *The Fifth Asia Pacific Conference on Sustainable Energy and Environmental Technologies* (pp. 150–156), Wellington, New Zealand, Massey University. https://natlib.govt.nz/records/21990244?search%5Bpath%5D=items&search%5Btext%5D=Small%252C+Clive. Accessed September 25, 2023.

[18] Yamada, M., & Asahi, S. (2008). Comparison and evaluation of 2000 regional I-O tables in Japan. *Sangyo Renkan (Input-Output Analysis), 16*(1), 3–16. (in Japanese). https://doi.org/10.11107/papaios.16.3

[19] Shioya, H., & Asahi, S. (2009). Overview and application of tourism statistics analysis using statistical survey on overnight travels. *Sangyo Renkan (Input-Output Analysis), 17*(1–2), 16–29. (in Japanese). https://doi.org/10.11107/papaios.17.1-2_16

[20] Hara, T., & Asahi, S. (2009). Comparative income distribution effects of tourism as an industry of host community. *Sangyo Renkan (Input-Output Analysis), 16*(1), 57–65. (in Japanese). https://doi.org/10.11107/papaios.17.1-2_57 (OK, no big problem).

[21] Nomura, J., Kinoshita, M., Saito, H., & Asahi, S. (2011). Economic impacts of trans-regional tourists' expenditures utilizing multiregional I-O table of Yamaguchi prefecture. *Sangyo Renkan (Input-Output Analysis), 19*(3), 72–93. (in Japanese). https://doi.org/10.11107/papaios.19.72

[22] Yakita, A., & Asahi, S. (2012). SO_X emissions reduction policy and economic development: A case of Yokkaichi. *Modern Economy, 3*(1), 23–31. https://doi.org/10.4236/me.2012.31004

[23] Asahi, S. (2013). Economic ripple effects of choice factors and disaster-related investments at Nagoya Port, Nagoya, Japan. *The Japan Port Economics Association Chubu Division, Port Studies, 34*, 1–28. (in Japanese).

[24] Nomura, J., Kinoshita, M., Saito, H., & Asahi, S. (2013). Estimation of inter-regional trade coefficients at a small region level: A hybrid approach based on the comparison between the survey method and the nonsurvey method. *Yamaguchi Journal of Economics, 61*(6), 85–112 (589–616). (in Japanese). https://petit.lib.yamaguchi-u.ac.jp/22405/files/155058. Accessed September 25, 2023.

[25] Asahi, S. (2013). An analysis of the effects of production activities on pollutions in Yokkaichi. *The Journal of International and Regional Economics, 14*, 27–42. Institute of Economic Research Nagoya City University. (in Japanese).

[26] Asahi, S. (2014). Wind power and NIMBY problems: Survey evaluation of an attempt to reduce environmental load in a region with the aid of wind power generation. *Wind Energy, 38*(1), 14–18. (in Japanese). https://www.jstage.jst.go.jp/article/jwea/38/1/38_14/_article/-char/en. Accessed September 25, 2023.

[27] Asahi, S. (2016). Study of total fertility rate of females in employment, by industry: Estimation of national and prefectural data using the own-children method. Nagoya, Japan, Chukyo University Institute of Economics, Discussion Paper Series, 1602, pp. 1–46. (in Japanese).

[28] Asahi, S. (2020). The impact of congestion on tourism in Japan. In M. Yamada & J. Masuda (Eds.), *The globalization and econometric model of the regional economy* (Chap. 6, pp. 175–206), Chukyo University Institute of Economics. Keiso shobo. (in Japanese).

References

Abe, N., Chikamatsu, K., Kanai, K., Kawasumi, Y., Munakata, K., Nakayama, K., Okuda, T., & Takano, Y. (2023). The financial macro-econometric model (FMM, 2022 version) (No. 23-03-30). Bank of Japan. https://www.boj.or.jp/en/research/brp/ron_2023/data/ron230330a.pdf. Accessed September 25, 2023.

Arellano, M., & Bond, S. (1991). Some tests of specification for panel data: Monte Carlo evidence and an application to employment equations. *Review of Economic Studies, 58*, 277–297.

Baltagi, H. (2008). *Econometric analysis of panel data* (Vol. 4). Wiley. https://library.wbi.ac.id/repository/27.pdf. Accessed September 4. 2023.

Barnes, T. J. (2003). The place of locational analysis: A selective and interpretive history. *Progress in Human Geography, 27*(1), 69–95.

Director General for Economic and Fiscal Management, Cabinet Office. (2001). *Breaking away from dependence on public investment and creating jobs.* Regional Economic Report 2001, National Printing Bureau, Tokyo.

Fujiwara, I., Hara, N., Hirose, Y., & Teranishi, Y. (2005). The Japanese economic model (JEM). *Monetary and Economic Studies, 23*(2), 61–142. Retrieved September 3, 2023 from https://www.researchgate.net/profile/Yuki-Teranishi/publication/5119977_The_Japanese_Economic_Model/links/02e7e5344b1402d2ea000000/The-Japanese-Economic-Model.pdf. Accessed September 23, 2023.

Fukač, M., & Pagan, A. (2010b). Structural macro-econometric modelling in a policy environment. In D. Giles & A. Ullah (Eds.), *Handbook of empirical economics and finance*. Routledge.

Fukač, M., & Pagan, A. (2010a). Structural macro-econometric modelling in a policy environment (No. RWP 10-08). Federal Reserve Bank of Kansas City. https://core.ac.uk/download/pdf/6576723.pdf. Accessed September 25, 2023.

Fukuyama, M., Oikawa, K., Yoshihara. M., & Nakazono, Y. (2010). Macro-econometric models and the outline of the MEAD-RIETI Model, RIETI. Discussion Papers, July 2010 10-J-045, Research Institute of Economy, Trade and Industry. (in Japanese). https://www.rieti.go.jp/jp/publications/dp/10j045.pdf. Accessed September 25, 2023.

Hashimoto, T. (1992). *Econometric analysis of the finances and economy of Amagasaki city.* Amagasaki Future Association Foundation. (in Japanese).

Hayashi, M. (2003). Simultaneity problems in the estimation of effect of public capital: A review of the Japanese studies. *Economic Analysis, 169*, 88–104. (in Japanese). https://warp.da.ndl.go.jp/info:ndljp/pid/11513838/www.esri.go.jp/jp/archive/bun/bun169/bun169e.pdf. Accessed September 25, 2023.

Higuchi, Y., Ota, K., & Shimpo, K. (2006). *Introduction to economic analysis using panel data.* Nippon Hyoronsha. (in Japanese).

Hirakata, N., Kan, K., Kanafuji, A., Kido, Y., Kishaba, Y., Murakoshi, T., & Shinohara, T. (2019). The quarterly Japanese economic model (Q-JEM: 2019 version) (No.19-E-7), June 2019. https://www.boj.or.jp/en/research/wps_rev/wps_2019/data/wp19e07.pdf. Accessed September 25, 2023.

Holtz-Eakin, D., Newey, W. K., & Rosen, H. S. (1987). The revenues-expenditures nexus: Evidence from local government data. Working paper 2180, March 1987, National Bureau of Economic Research. https://doi.org/10.3386/w2180

Holtz-Eakin, D., Newey, W., & Rosen, S. (1988). Estimating vector autoregressions with panel data. *Econometrica: Journal of the Econometric Society*, 1371–1395.

Hsiao, C. (2003). *Analysis of panel data.* Cambridge University Press.

Hubbard, P., & Kitchin, R. (Eds.). (2010). *Key thinkers on space and place.* Sage.

Inada, Y., & Irie, H. (2013). The revised econometric model for the Kansai economy considering energy constraint (in Japanese). APIR Discussion Paper, Series No. 30, Asia Pacific Institute of Research. https://www.apir.or.jp/wp/wp-content/uploads/310-1.pdf. Accessed September 25, 2023.

Inagaki, H. (1992). The regional fiscal model simulation on Yokkaichi area. *The Journal of Yokkaichi University, 5*(1), 61–90. (in Japanese).

Irie, H. (2014). The revised econometric model for the Kansai economy. *The Bulletin of the Junior College of Kinki University, 47*(1), 1–11. (in Japanese).

Irie, H. (2019). Kansai econometric forecasting model for 2008 SNA. *The Bulletin of the Junior College of Kinki University, 52*(1), 11–22. (in Japanese).

Ishikawa, Y. (2004). A three-region interregional input-output model using nonsurvey technique. Doboku Gakkai Ronbunshu No. 758/IV-63, pp. 45–55. (in Japanese). https://doi.org/10.2208/jscej.2004.758_45

Ishikawa, Y. (2005). Evaluation of nonsurvey method for interregional trade estimation in regional input-output analysis. *The Nanzan Journal of Economic Studies, 19*(3), 369–382. in Japanese.

Ishikawa, Y. (2016). Current status and issues of the regional input-output tables in Japan. *Sangyo Renkan (Input-Output Analysis), 23*(1–2), 3–17. (in Japanese). https://doi.org/10.11107/papaios.23.1-2_3

Johnston, R., & Sidaway, J. D. (2015). *Geography and geographers: Anglo-American human geography since 1945*. Routledge.

Klevmarken, N. A. (1989). Panel studies: What can we learn from them? *Introduction, European Economic Review, 33*, 523–529.

Kuroda, T., Tabuchi, T., & Nakamura, R. (2008). *Urban and regional economics*. Yuhikaku. (in Japanese).

Leontief, W. (1986). *Input output economics* (2nd ed.). Oxford University Press.

Long, Y., Jiang, Y., Chen, P., Yoshida, Y., Sharifi, A., Gasparatos, A., Wu, Y., Kanemoto, K., Shigetomi, Y., & Guan, D. (2021). Monthly direct and indirect greenhouse gases emissions from household consumption in the major Japanese cities. *Scientific Data, 8*(1), 301.

Long, Y., Yoshida, Y., & Dong, L. (2017). Exploring the indirect household carbon emissions by source: Analysis on 49 Japanese cities. *Journal of Cleaner Production, 167*, 571–581. https://doi.org/10.1016/j.jclepro.2017.08.159

Maruyama, M., Suzuki S., Kawamoto, T., Maeda, T., Hori, N., Yamazaki, T., Hori, M., & Iwamoto, K. (2018). The ESRI short-run macroeconometric model of the Japanese economy (2018 version): Basic structure, multipliers, and economic policy analyses. ESRI Research Note No. 41, Economic and Social Research Institute, Cabinet Office, Japan, Tokyo. (in Japanese). https://www.esri.cao.go.jp/jp/esri/archive/e_rnote/e_rnote050/e_rnote041.pdf. Accessed September 25, 2023.

Matsumae, T., & Hasumi, R. (2016). Impacts of government spending on unemployment: evidence from a medium-scale DSGE model. ESRI Discussion Paper Series No.329. Economic and Social Research Institute (ESRI). Retrieved September 4, 2023 from https://warp.da.ndl.go.jp/info:ndljp/pid/12298599/www.esri.cao.go.jp/jp/esri/archive/e_dis/e_dis329/e_dis329.pdf. Accessed September 25, 2023.

McCann, P. (2013). *Modern urban and regional economics*. Oxford University Press.

Miller, R. E., & Blair, P. D. (2009). *Input-output analysis: Foundations and extensions*. Cambridge University Press.

Ministry of International Trade and Industry (MITI). (1976). Report on the analysis results of the input-output table for analysis of pollution in 1973. In Minister's Secretariat, MITI (Ed.), *Ministry of International Trade and Industry*. (in Japanese).

Murphy, C. (2017). *Review of economic modelling at the treasury*. Report of the Australian Department of the Treasury. Independent Economics, 2017, https://research.treasury.gov.au/sites/research.treasury.gov.au/files/2019-08/Review-of-Economic-Modelling-at-Treasury.pdf. Accessed September 25, 2023.

Nakamura, S., & Kondo, Y. (2002). Input-output analysis of waste management. *Journal of Industrial Ecology, 6*(1), 39–63.

Nansai, K. (2009). *Environmental input-output database building in Japan* (1st ed., pp. 653–688). Springer. https://doi.org/10.1007/978-1-4020-5737-3

Nansai, K., & Moriguchi, Y. (2006). Practical determination of sectoral environmental burdens applied to input-output analysis. *Journal of Life Cycle Assessment, 2*(1), 22–41. (in Japanese). https://doi.org/10.3370/lca.2.22

Nijkamp, P., & Mills, E. S. (1987). Advances in regional economics. In P. Nijkamp (Ed.), *Handbook of regional and urban economics* (Vol. 1, pp. 1–17). Elsevier.

Office for Econometric Analysis, Cabinet Office, Japan. (2018). Economic and financial models. Resources (in Japanese). https://www5.cao.go.jp/keizai3/econome/ef2rrrr-all.pdf. Accessed September 25, 2023.

Okada, T., Kawase, M., Suzuki, M., & Togashi, K. (2007). Regional economics in the period of internationalization (3rd ed.). Yuhikaku. (in Japanese).

Okano, M., Ida, D., Kitano, S., & Matsubayashi, Y. (2015). Development of a regional DSGE model in Japan: Empirical evidence of economic stagnation in the Kansai economy (No. 1004265). https://www.apir.or.jp/wp/wp-content/uploads/DP38_Kansai_DSGE.pdf. Accessed September 25, 2023.

Okubo, S. (2021). How to use fixed effects models with panel data. *The Journal of Social Science, 72*(2), 55–68. (in Japanese). https://doi.org/10.34607/jssiss.72.2_55

Research Institute, Mitsui Knowledge Industry. (1994). Environmental policy and market economy research report: Development of a Kanagawa prefecture regional environmental and economic model. Study commissioned by The Institute for Public Policy, Kanagawa Prefecture. (in Japanese).

Sakamaki, T., Suzuki, S., Nakao, T., Kitagawa, R., Fukawa, K., Nakajima, T., & Hori, M. (2022). The ESRI short-run macroeconometric model of the Japanese economy (2022 version): Basic structure, multipliers, and economic policy analyses. ESRI Research Note No. 72, Economic and Social Research Institute, Cabinet Office, Japan. (in Japanese). https://www.esri.cao.go.jp/jp/esri/archive/e_rnote/e_rnote080/e_rnote072.pdf. Accessed September 25, 2023.

Smith, P., & Morrison, I. (2012). *Simulating the urban economy: Experiments with input-output techniques*. Routledge.

Taguchi, H., & Vu, T. (2018). Genealogy of practical economic models and the position taken in this project. Foundations and practice of macroeconomic models: Focus on East Asia. In J. Uemura (Ed.), IDE-JETRO 47 (Chap. 1, pp. 1–17). Institute of Developing Economies, Japan External Trade Organization. (in Japanese).

Takahashi, S., & Yagihashi, T. (2019). The Japanese Economy (90) frontiers of macroeconomic modeling: A study based on examples from overseas applications. Ministry of Finance (Ed.), Ministry of Finance Public Relations Report, Vol. 55(3), pp. 46–51. (in Japanese).

Teranishi, Y., Fujiwara, I., & Hara, N. (2004). The Japanese economic model: JEM. In Econometric Society 2004 Far Eastern Meetings (No. 723), p. 115. https://www.boj.or.jp/en/research/wps_rev/wps_2004/data/wp04e03.pdf. Accessed September 25, 2023.

Tsukui, M., Kagawa, S., & Kondo, Y. (2015). Measuring the waste footprint of cities in Japan: An interregional waste input–output analysis. *Journal of Economic Structures, 4*(18), 1–24.

Uchida, M., Sugimono, T., & Takamori, S. (2020). Estimation flow using the LQ method suitable for estimating regional input-output tables for Japan (in Japanese). The 66th Infrastructure Planning and Management Presentation and Collection of Lectures, Committee of Infrastructure Planning and Management, pp. 1–8.

Chapter 2
Study of Total Fertility Rate of Women in Employment, by Industrial Sector: Estimation of Japanese National and Prefectural Data Using the Own-Children Method

2.1 Introduction

Japan's population was 127.09 million at the time of the 2020 census. This is a decrease of 868,000 (− 0.68%) compared to the figure for 2015. Moreover, it was the first population decline recorded since the national census began in 1920. This decline in population has a serious impact not only on economic circumstances such as the shrinkage of the economy due to falls in domestic demand, the shortage of labor, and the imbalance between payments and benefits in the social security system, but also on the social infrastructure.

In order to push back against this population decline, the Japanese government has set an attainment target of 1.8 for the TFR, and is aiming to create a society more supportive of its child-rearing generation through marriage assistance, fertility treatment assistance, and a system of fixed-sum birth allowances.

One important issue for measures aiming to arrest the decline in the birthrate is how to support the balance between work and child-rearing. According to Annual Population and Social Security Surveys (The National Fertility Survey) reported by the Ministry of Health, Labor and Welfare in 2010 (14th survey) and 2015 (15th survey), 70% of married women continued to work after marriage in the period 2010–2014 (15th survey). Comparing changes in employment status up to and following the birth of a first child, the data for 2010–2014 showed a rise in the proportion of married women working up to their pregnancy compared with 2005–2009 (14th survey). The proportion leaving employment following their first childbirth, after increasing in both of the two previous survey periods, decreased this time by about 9%. With or without parenting leave, 38.3% of these first-time mothers chose to stay in their jobs.

There are many factors that now make it more feasible for women to continue working after the birth of a child. For example, important factors include changes in rules for childbirth and childcare support in companies where new mothers are employed, parallel changes in work-life rules for mothers and fathers, and support

S. Asahi, *Econometric Analysis of Regional Economy*,
https://doi.org/10.1007/978-981-99-8707-8_2

from other sources including local governments. This study examines work and birthrate from an employer-side perspective. Accordingly, total fertility rates (TFRs) are calculated by industrial sector.

The background reasoning behind estimating TFRs by industrial sector in this way is as follows. When a worker enters into employment in Japan, there is a bewildering diversity of contract conditions, and there are cases where even the work category is not clear or fixed. Furthermore, the type of work may change in the course of employment depending on the worker's aptitude, the management circumstances of the company itself, or evolution in the working environment. However, the industrial sector of employment will not change unless the worker changes jobs. Within sectors, there are sometimes craft or industry unions that transcend the boundaries of individual enterprises. Labor unions are company unions, although many of them are also organized into industry-wide alliances. For reasons like these, the issue of declining birthrate cannot very well be discussed outside of the issues of employment choices and work environments within industrial sectors.

The national TFR in Japan is further affected by interregional influences. The combined population of the nine most populated prefectures including Tokyo was 69.16 million in 2020, which accounts for more than half of the national total. This indicates that there are regional disparities in population. "Regionality," also, is not only a question of where people live, but has a mobility aspect of where they move to and interact. Therefore, along with the focus on industrial sectors in this study, there is also a regional breakdown of results among the 47 prefectures. The regional discussion of TFR, furthermore, proceeds in the light of what is found from the estimates in the industrial sectors. The study uses the "Own-Children Method" to estimate TFRs by industrial sectors, nationwide and in all 47 prefectures. TFRs of women in different occupational categories are published by the Ministry of Health, Labor and Welfare on the basis of surveys of population dynamics. However, no statistics of this kind are published for industrial sectors. This study therefore uses the Own-Children Method as a way of arriving at estimates for each industrial sector. It is a method used in demographics. In the Own-Children Method, TFRs are estimated by collating ages of mothers and of their own children living with them into "own children tables" which can be used retroactively with life tables to estimate the number of births a woman will typically have had by a particular age. This method is used especially to estimate the birthrate from the results of a population census.

In what follows, Sect. 2.2 summarizes trends of childbirth and employment in Annual Population and Social Security Surveys. Section 2.3 summarizes previous research concerning the Own-Children Method and fertility rates. Section 2.4 gives an outline of the data to which the method is applied in this paper, and Sect. 2.5 explains in more detail the procedures to be used for estimating characteristics of TFRs by industrial sector. Finally, Sect. 2.6 is a summary of results, including also the relationships between industrial sectors, and regionality. This concludes with an examination of how consistent these results are with preceding research and surveys.

2.2 Childbirth and Employment Trends in Annual Population and Social Security Surveys

The National Fertility Survey is one of a group of Annual Population and Social Security Surveys conducted through field research by the National Institute of Population and Social Security Research. It has existed as a government-approved source of statistics since 1940. As a survey, it is based on a national sample conducted every five years (since the second survey in 1952) to take in a five-year period. The formal name was changed at the time of the 10th survey (1992) from "The Fertility Survey" to: "Annual Population and Social Security Surveys (The Fertility Survey)." As explained in the 15th survey report, the Fertility Survey provides a regular account of the current realities of marriage and of the fertility of married couples along with a relevant background. The survey also collects other kinds of data that cannot be grasped from other official statistics such as vital statistics and national censuses. A further purpose is to supply basic data for the grasping of population trends for various related measures and future population estimates. In particular, these include simultaneous surveys of married couples and single people, which aim to investigate the current situation and issues concerning marriage, childbirth and child-rearing in Japan. I will now summarize the situation of married women with regard to employment and childbirth in Japan, based on the 15th (2015) and (14th (2010) National Fertility Surveys (Married Couples Surveys).

Figure 2.1 shows that the proportion of women who were working and did not stop upon marrying was increasing. The percentage continuing to work rose to 73.0% in 2010–2014. In Fig. 2.2, showing trends in the numbers of married women working beyond the birth of a first child, one tendency that appears is an increase in the proportion working up to their first pregnancy. In the most recent period shown, 2010–2014, there has also been a 10% decrease in the proportion leaving employment at the time of their first childbirth. Owing to this, the proportion of married women who were working and did not stop upon the birth of a first child was increasing. The percentage of married women in this situation has increased from 28.9% in 2005–2009 to 38.3% (with or without childcare leave) in 2010–2014. The number of employed women using systems of childcare leave is increasing. The percentage who used childcare leave to stay in their jobs rose from 19.4% in 2005–2009 to 28.3% in 2010–2014. Clearly, this system of leave is well established in Japan now and the number of users is increasing.

Figure 2.3 shows the proportions of married women continuing in employment beyond the birth of a first, second, or third child, respectively. The percentage who remained in work after the birth of a third child using a childcare leave system in 2010–2014 was 23.6%, or 11.2% higher than in 2005–2009. The percentage who remained without using such a leave system was 17.9%, which is 2.4% lower than in 2005–2009. This confirms the difficulty of continuing in work without using childcare leave.

Figure 2.4 is limited in its coverage to the percentages of women, employed be-fore marriage, who continued in work after marriage. Here, the proportion who

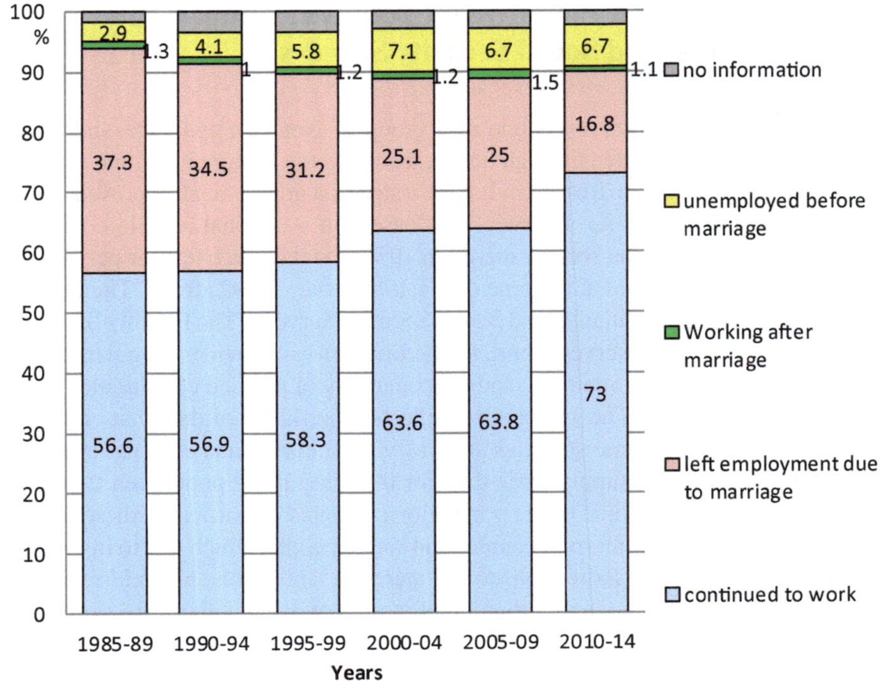

Fig. 2.1 Change and continuity in employment status of married women before and after marriage ("Years" = span in which the marriage occurred). *Source* National Institute of Population and Social Security Research (2017). "Marriage and Childbirth in Japan Today: The Fifteenth Japanese National Fertility Survey, 2015 (Results of Married Couples and Single Women Surveys)," p. 52, Chart II-4-5. *Note* Figure 2.1 created by the author based on p. 52, Chart II-4-5 of this source

went on working beyond marriage increased from 62.3% in 1990–1994 to 81.3% in 2010–2014, a rise of 19% over 20 years. Turning to Fig. 2.5, however, which shows the percentages of those remaining in work beyond the birth of a first, second, or third child, this percentage was 53.1% for the first child, 78.2% for the second, and 79.1% for the third. For the first child, the proportion remaining in work increased nearly 13% between 2005–2009 and 2010–2014, but the figures for the second and third child are not so different. The use of childcare leave systems for this purpose increased significantly between these two periods, irrespective of whether a first, second, or third child was concerned.

However, in the case of children other than the one born first, the proportion of employed women using systems of childcare leave is higher. The percentages in 2010–2014 were 51.3% for the second child and 45% for the third. As for regular/non-regular employment (as defined in Japan), 69.1% of the women surveyed were regularly employed before their first pregnancy in the period 2010–2014, an increase of 24.6% compared to the situation in 1990–1994 (44.5%). The proportion who were employed part-time or as dispatch staff in 2010–2014 was 25.2%. As for married

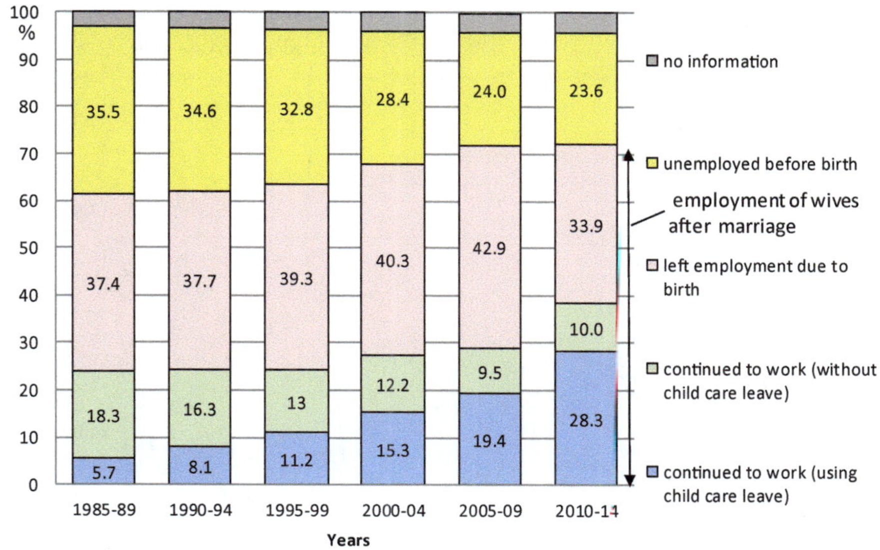

Fig. 2.2 Change and continuity in employment status of married women before and after the birth of their first child. *Source* The same as in Fig. 2.1. *Note* Figure 2.2 created by the author based on p. 52, Chart II-4-6 of this source

women with at least one child and planning to have at least one more in the 2010–2014 survey, 29.4% were regular employees and 19.9% were in part-time or dispatch work. Including also the self-employed, 52.7% were in employment. The employment rate of married women is increasing at all life stages.

In cases where regular employment continues after childbirth, 98.1% of women with children use a child-rearing support system/facility. In particular, 90.7% use prenatal/postnatal leave and 83.6% use childcare leave. The utilization rate of systems and facilities varies depending on the size of the employer etc. In large companies or government offices, the rate can be as high as 100%.

The percentage of working couples receiving help from a mother (the child's grandmother) in the first three years of the eldest child's life was 50% in the five years 2000–2004, 53.4% in 2005–2009 and 52.9% in 2010–2014.

To sum up, then, just as the number of working women continuing in work beyond marriage has been increasing over the years (as already shown above), so too, the proportion of married women who go on working after having children is increasing. Recently, various systems have been put in place to provide an environment in which women can continue to work, and many women now have access to them. At the same time, however, even among the regularly employed, there are still many women who leave their jobs to have a child, and in part-time or dispatch employment, the proportion is a good deal higher. It is necessary to create an environment where women like these who have left their jobs to have children can re-enter employment. As for later children, the high utilization rate of childcare and child leave systems

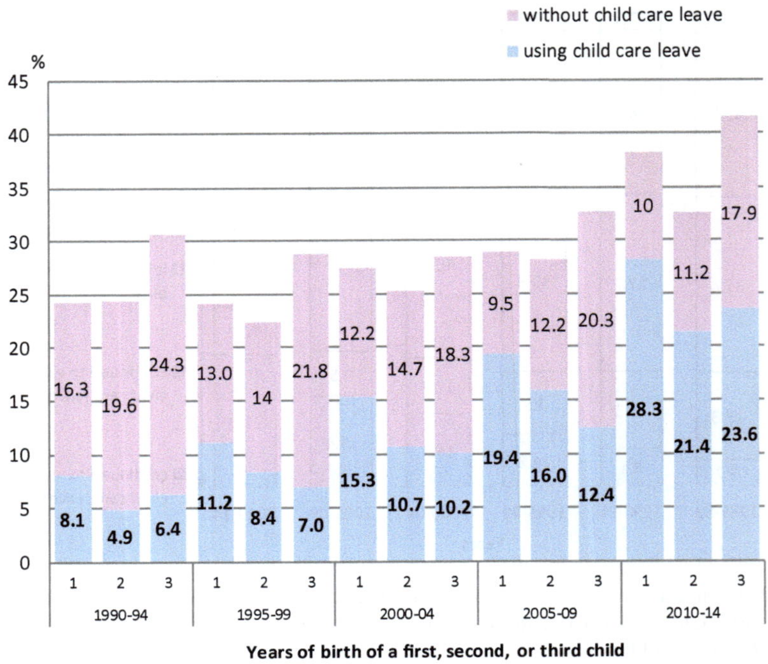

Fig. 2.3 Proportions of married women continuing in employment beyond the birth of a first, second, or third child. *Source* The same as in Fig. 2.1. *Note* Figure 2.3 created by the author based on p. 53, Chart II-4-7 of this source

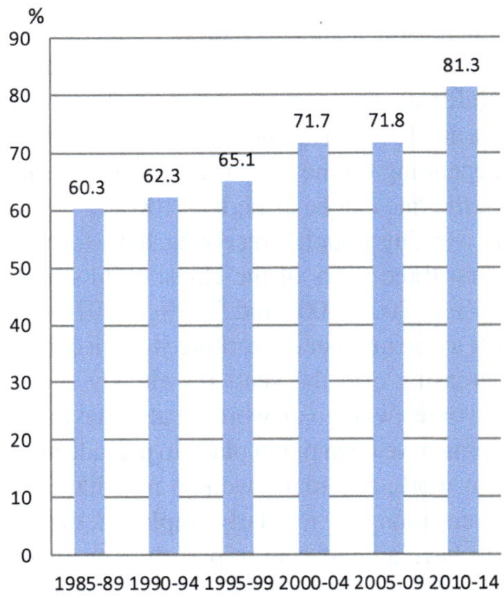

Fig. 2.4 Percentages of women, employed before marriage, who continued in work after marrying. *Source* The same as in Fig. 2.1

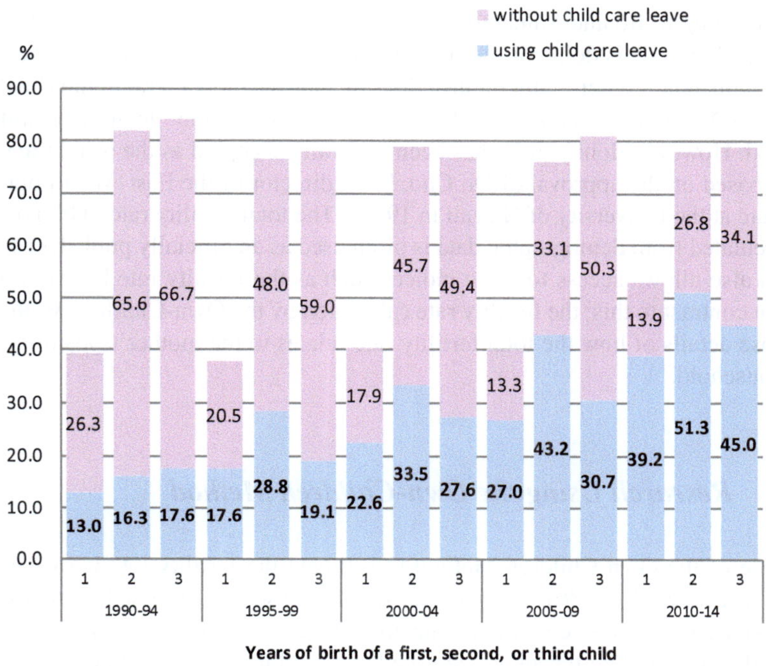

Fig. 2.5 Percentages of working married women continuing in employment beyond the birth of a first, second, or third child. *Source* The same as in Fig. 2.1. *Note* Figure 2.5 created by the author based on p. 54, Chart II-4-8 of this source

means in effect that a mother having a second child will also have the opportunity of continuing to work, and this remains the case when a third child is born, as well. What is most crucial, therefore, is to improve the working environment in a way that will assure the mother of a chance of maintaining employment continuity at the time of having her first child.

2.3 Previous Research on the Own-Children Method and the Fertility Rate

The Own-Children Method is used in demography. In this method, the fertility rate is estimated by retroactively estimating the number of births from the mother's age, using a life table based on the "Own Children Table", which is an aggregate tabulation of the ages of mothers and of the children living with them. The "Own Children Table" is generally used when estimating the fertility rate based on a population census.

According to Ito and Yamamoto (1977),[1] the Japanese translation for the "Own Children Method" is dohkyoji-ho, literally meaning the method based on "children living with their mother." Other translations include the more literal jibunji-ho ("Own Children Method," as above), and chakuji-ho, literally: the "legitimate children" method. However, dohkyoji-ho has been generally accepted as the usual translation term, based on the approval of Dr. Cho, L.-J., director of the East–West Population Institute at the University of Hawaii in 1976.[2] The total fertility rate (TFR) of Japan as calculated from demographic data is often used as an officially published statistic which also allows access to basic indices such as the fertility rate by the mother's age. In contrast to this, the fertility rate calculated by the Own-Children Method can disclose details of how the total fertility rate relates to the mother's position within the household.

2.3.1 Research Using the Own-Children Method

The use of the Own-Children Method to estimate the fertility rate is explained in detail in Cho et al. (1986). Many of the studies subsequently based on this kind of method used comparable ways of collecting, comparing and analyzing data.

Studies undertaken recently using the Own-Children Method include many that analyze the fertility rates of ethnic groups and immigrants because, as said above, this method makes it possible to estimate the fertility rate on the basis of the mother's position in the household. Bertoud (2001), for example, used this method to estimate the fertility rates of ethnic minority women in the UK from data in a Labour Force Survey with a particular focus on the teenagers. Similarly, Coleman and Smith (2005) used it to predict the future populations of immigrants and ethnic minorities in the UK; they calculated age-specific fertility rates and TFRs and revealed the differences between ethnicities. For their fertility rate research in Germany, Krapf and Kreyenfeld (2015) used German micro-census statistics and examined groups showing a specific mobility. They used the Own-Children Method to analyze the fertility rates of immigrants and non-immigrants.[3]

---

[1] See Ito and Yamamoto (1977), p. 16.

[2] See Cho (2021) and The United Nations (1986).

[3] Other studies include Zuberi and Sibanda (1999) applied the own-child law to the African census. There is also Wills (1973) for a static economic theory of lifetime marital fertility in US, Waller et al. (2014) for an analysis of fertility in the UK, Tamura et al. (2012) for a study of fertility differences in race.

2.3.2 Research on TFRs in Specific Industries

Albæk and Larsen (2014) used longitudinal data from the period 1997–2010 in Denmark to estimate the difference between female employees' fertility rates in the private and public sectors and to analyze the factors contributing to this difference. The average fertility rate was 2.23 in the public sector, and 1.91 in the private one, a difference of 0.32. Half of the difference was accounted for by the age group 25–29. 70% of the women in the data used worked in the same industrial sector. Approximately half of the difference in the fertility rate can be explained by the women's occupational choice. The women employed continuously in the private sector had a lower fertility rate than those in the public sector. The fertility rate of women who changed their employment between the two sectors lay somewhere between. From the results, it appeared that the women's work choices in their childbearing years were subject to conflicting influences from their preferences for motherhood on the one hand and from the immediate requirements of work conditions on the other. Albæk and Larsen consider preferences for motherhood as a factor in women's choice of an employment sector.

There are also studies that investigate the fertility rate in connection with other factors such as employment status. For example, Bratti et al. (2005) analyzed the labor market status of women after having children and traced the effects this has had on job characteristics in Italy. They paid special attention to women's work histories before their marriage and to factors affecting their degree of job participation after having their first child. Adsera (2005) examined data from the European Community Household Panel Survey in the period 1994–2000 and used the Cox proportional-hazard model to analyze fertility rates in 13 countries to see how differences in male/female unemployment rates, both overall and long-term, play out on the time intervals up to the births of a woman's first to third children. Based on these differences in male/female unemployment rates, Adsera (2005) further calculated estimates for the mother's age at the time of the birth of each child and for the transition times up to the births of the second and third children. Adsera (2011) also analyzes differences between the public and private sectors, showing that women working in the public sector have a second or third child earlier than women working in the private sector.

Conti and Sette (2013) analyzed the influence of employer types and employment contracts on women's fertility rates in Italy. Categories of employer type included public/private sector and small-/large-size business. The data used were from a representative sample of Italian women over a 30-year period. The results showed that women working in the public sector had a higher probability of having children than those in the private sector. Likewise, women working for large-size businesses, which provided better employment protection, had a higher chance of having children than those working for small-size businesses.

Begall and Mills (2013) compared the length of the transition to first and to subsequent births in relation to the mother's field of study and the gender-specific character of her occupation. Taking data from a repeated cross-section survey reflecting the Dutch population from 1940 to 1985, they estimated a series of discrete-time complementary log–log models to estimate variations in the transition time preceding each birth. For the first birth, the mother's educational field was significant. Women studying technology, economics or cultural studies had a longer transition than women in educational studies, for example. Another finding was that women whose occupations were related to business with a high level of specialty tended to postpone having their first child, but might have additional children faster.

Based on data for Jewish people in Israel, Okun et al. (2007) used a multinominal logit model panel to analyze the fertility rate of full-time and part-time female workers in the public and private sectors as well as non-working women. The results indicated a significant relationship between the sectors where the women were employed and their post-birth behavior; the women in the public sector were more likely to continue their jobs. This suggests the importance of encouraging women to be engaged in paid work after having a child.

Nakamura and Ueda (1999) analyzed decision-making of married women in Japan regarding job continuation at the time of having a first child. They used survey data from approximately 8000 married women and found that mothers' educational background and parenting behavior were important factors. Some features of the working environment also seem to have an influence, such as the type of industry and the size of the organization. In the public sector, for example, there was a greater tendency for women to stay with their jobs.[4]

De la Rica and Iza (2005) analyzed the relationship between fixed-term contracts and the delay in marriage and maternity in Spain. For men, the decision to marry was strongly and negatively influenced by unstable work contracts or not working. For women, in contrast, the question of having only a fixed-term contract was not a deterrent for the decision to marry. For all childless women, however, with or without a partner, holding only a fixed-term contract delays the decision to have a first child.

Other studies include Avery et al. (2013), which compares the low-cost Own-Children Method with the Full Birth History (FBH) method, utilizing information about children from surveys and censuses as a background. This is because an accurate civil registration, which is required for estimating a fertility rate, is lacking in many developing countries. The TFR estimate is found to be consistently higher than when the FBH method is used.

2.3.3 Research on the Relationship Between Region and Fertility Rate

Research on the relationship between region and fertility rate includes the following. Schultz (1985) analyzes various economic variables including demand for labor and

[4] Other studies of Japan's fertility rate are Atoh et al. (1986) Ogawa et al. (1986), Ohbuchi (1982), Takayama et al. (2000), Imai (1996), Shigeno (1996), Yamagami (1999), Abe et al. (1999), Shigeno et al. (2001), Ohkusa (2001), Kato (2001), Iwasawa (2002), Morita (2004), Abe (2005), Moriizumi (2005), Yamaguchi (2005), Yamashige et al. (2013).

women's wage rates as factors in determining fertility. In particular, this paper showed that rising wage rates for men led to higher fertility rates in 25 regions of Sweden, while rising wage rates for women contributed to lower rates. It showed further how concentrations of population due to the economy of agglomeration affected wages and might also affect the birth rate.

Sato and Yamamoto (2005), and also Zhang (2002) offer a theoretical explanation of the difference between overall and regional fertility rates. Sato (2007) extends this to take in relationships between birth and regional migration, using a two-period overlapping generations model of endogenous fertility to show that birth-rate differences between regions relate negatively to those regions' population densities and that external diseconomies from congestion have a negative effect on total fertility rate.

The agglomeration economy has both a positive and a negative effect on the birth rate. Positively, it raises wages, which has the effect of increasing disposable income. Increasing income encourages an increase in the birth rate. Negatively, however, a rise in the number of births has opportunity costs. Raising more children consumes more time, and to find this time, parents need to sacrifice hours in which they could otherwise be working. Thus, as people move from areas of low-density to areas of high-density population, this also leads to differences in net regional population change.

Morita and Yamamoto (2014) analyzed the disparity in fertility rates between regions resulting from the agglomeration of companies using an interregional trade model that included endogenous fertility rates. One finding was that the agglomeration of manufacturing companies in areas with a large population (a large working population, in their model) led to a lower birth rate than was the case in areas with a smaller population. Other conclusions from their study were that fertility rates in a region will decline if the price of goods is low relative to the cost of having children, and that they also decrease together with transportation costs, regardless of the local population size. Similar studies in which different countries are considered as if they were regions include Beine et al. (2009) and Goto and Minamimura (2015).

2.3.4 Research in Japan that Has Dealt with the Own-Children Method

Research in Japan that has dealt with the Own-Children Method includes the following.

Ito and Bando (1985) provides a summary of the calculation method of Cho, Retherford, and Choe. Ito and Yamamoto (1977) examined the accuracy of the Own-Children Method by comparing estimates of the fertility rate obtained this way from data in the Basic Survey of Welfare Administration (now: Comprehensive Survey of Living Conditions) with results obtained for fertility rate by mother's age from demographic statistics, i.e., mid-year population estimates and (registered) birth rates

Hardly any significant differences were observed in the results for fertility rate by age. However, in terms of the TFR, comparisons between the estimates and the official values showed a maximum error of up to about 5% during a one-year period, or about 1.8% for a 15-month average. The study also dealt with TFR estimates by regions, levels of household cash expenditures, and household occupation categories as well as offering an overview of TFR trends.

Oobayashi (1979) was another very early introduction of the Own-Children Method in Japan, based on an account in Cho and Feeney (1978) and offered fertility estimates by regions and various socio-economic categories. It was also the first study to propose the application of the Own-Children Method to data from the Japanese national census for which it pointed out a number of issues. For example, fertility estimates with a focus on regional differences cannot overlook region-specific aspects of population migration between prefectures. Also, rates of (registered) marriage may vary considerably from one prefecture to another. Matsumura (1980) used the Own-Children Method to calculate the Japanese fertility rate for the period 1961–1975 based on the 1975 national census and compared this with the fertility rate as obtained from the demographic statistics. This was not without problems. While demographic statistics use the annual number of births from January to December, the national census figures used here as input for the Own-Children Method estimates were for numbers of births from October 1975 to September of the following year. As a result, there were some differences between the two sets of data. Nonetheless, Matsumura calculated that the effect of this on the final results remained less than 3%, which is by no means far out. Matsumura also gives specific fertility rates for various employment sectors and for non-employed women.

Ito (1980) similarly used the Own-Children Method together with data from the national census to estimate the Japanese fertility rate and found a level of accuracy comparable with the results obtained through the demographic statistics. He also noted that the judicious choice of an input source (the 1975 Basic Survey of Welfare Administration in this case) favored greater completeness and reliability in the input data. For one thing, the data are recorded more precisely and with fewer gaps, especially with regard to age and the number of years of marriage. For another, the mother–child relationship can be confirmed more exactly. Further, the proportion of maternal-side stepchildren, that is, those living with a mother other than the one who bore them, is small. Finally, the mortality rate, that is, the ratio of children who will have died before the date of the survey, is low.

Kawasaki (1985) was another study that used the Own-Children Method and evaluated the results. Again, data came from an Own-Children Table, this time using the 1980 national census. On this basis, Kawasaki also calculated category-specific TFR values for the mother's educational background, employment status, occupational/industrial sector, and household economic, socio-economic, and home ownership categories.

Ito (1985) used the Own-Children Method again to demonstrate a way of estimating fertility rate specifically in relation to durability of marriage and to ascertain its accuracy. In a very different connection, Ito and Bando (1985) used the Own-Children Method in a similar way to calculate birthyear/prefecture-specific TFRs for the period 1964–1968, and examined whether the superstitious influence of the ill-omened "Hinoe-uma Year"[5] (Year of the Fire Horse) displayed any regional differences. Reactions to the Hinoe-uma alarm did indeed differ. The higher the initial fertility rate in a prefecture had been, the smaller the decline, and vice versa. In addition, the study also looked at the rates of recovery.

Retherford et al. (2004) used the Own-Children Table from the national censuses of 1980, 1990, and 2000 to calculate fertility rates specific to the mother's educational background, taking junior high, senior high, junior college or university as categories for the highest level of education completed. They demonstrated that the educational background is one of the factors that affect the changes in the fertility rate.

In recent years, Ihara, H. has been prominently engaged in research using the Own-Children Method. Ihara (2008) used data from the national censuses between 1980 and 2000 to estimate the fertility rates specific to particular industries and found notable differences between workers in agriculture and fisheries on the one hand, and those in other industries, on the other. Based on this, he cited the decline in agriculture as one factor in the decline of the Japanese fertility rate. Ihara (2011) used the Own-Children Method to estimate specific fertility rates of women in relation to current socio-economic categories for each year during the period 1961–2005, drawing data from the Own-Children Tables of the national censuses between 1975 and 2005. In particular, he compared the fertility rates specific to household economic categories, where an increase in the number of household members in employment contributed to a decline in the fertility rate. He took into consideration the feedback effects that the estimates for each year exerted on the mother's category status and showed how to connect together such retroactive results. Ihara (2012) followed the same method but estimated the fertility rates specific to the mother's occupational and employment status. Ihara (2013) used the Own-Children table of the national censuses of the same period, 1975 to 2010, to estimate and analyze fertility rates of working women raising children over the extended period 1961–2005. A comparison of the fertility rates in relation to age indicated two factors for the increase in the TFR from 2005 to 2010: first, a notable increase in the 30–45 age-group, and second a halt in the decline for women in their 20s. Ihara also analyzed the influence of the increase in women working while raising children on female employment trends more generally.[6]

[5] Hinoe-uma is the 43rd year of a traditional 60-year calendar cycle, renowned for disasters and the birth of women destined to kill their husbands" (definition from Iwanami Japanese Dictionay (Second Edition) (1975), Eds. Nishio et al., Iwanami Shoten Publishers).

[6] A similar study is Matsumura (2011) analyzed Parity-based population estimates based on the Own-Children Table in the National Census.

2.3.5 Research on the Relationship Between Japanese TFR and Other Economic Variables

There has been some recent fertility rate research in Japan which makes use of demographic statistics without focusing on the aspect of women living with their "own children." Yamauchi (2014) used population data in Japanese prefectures for the period 1980–2010 in order to examine the effect of a choice among four different birthrate indexes on estimates of future regional populations.

Toda (2007) used fertility rates from demographic statistics to analyze prefectural fertility rates for the period 1985–2004. He concluded that improvements in the employment environment might be conducive to an increase in the fertility rate but that the effect would be small.[7]

2.4 Statistical Data on Fertility Rates

2.4.1 Data

Statistics used to calculate fertility rates fall into two types: those deriving from surveys conducted by national or regional bureaus of statistics and those based on micro data collected independently for the purpose of analysis. In Japan's case, the fertility rate is first calculated from the demographic data collected by the Ministry of Health and Labor, after which the realities behind the trends in the rate are extracted and used for governmental policy making. The same data are also used for many other analyses.

Demographic statistics cover the total numbers of births, deaths, marriages, divorces and stillbirths reported under the Family Registry Law and the Regulations Relating to the Reporting of Stillbirths. These data are tabulated by month and year. Administratively, the data are arranged and made public at municipality level, and then within the 47 prefectures, and then again at the national level. But when fertility rates need to be analyzed under more special aspects, account has to be taken of various other factors, in many cases relating to the life situations of mothers or fathers. For that kind of purpose, it is also necessary to consider relations between the fertility rate and other demographic variables such as occupations and industrial sectors. The general framework for the publication of fertility data by occupations and industries is shown in Table 2.1.

[7] Tsutani and Higuchi (2009) showed the relationship between population decline and the economy. In addition, Wada (2015) provides a detailed explanation of population statistics.

Table 2.1 Demography by occupations and industries: mothers' main occupation categories

No.	Special count: not living with own children
1	Total
2	Employed
3	A. Agriculture and forestry
4	Agriculture
5	B. Fisheries
6	C. Mining and quarrying of stone and gravel
7	D. Construction
8	E. Manufacturing
9	F. Electricity, gas, heat supply and water
10	G. Information and communications
11	H. Transport and postal services
12	I. Wholesale and retail trade
13	J. Finance and insurance
14	K. Real estate and goods rental and leasing
15	L. Scientific research, professional and technical services
16	M. Accommodations, eating and drinking services
17	N. Living-related and personal services and amusement services
18	O. Education, learning support
19	P. Medical, health care and welfare
20	Q. Compound services
21	R. Services, other
22	S. Government, except elsewhere classified
23	T. Industries unable to classify
24	Non employed
25	Labor force status not reported
26	(Recount) Absent from work
27	(Recount) Unemployed

Source Statistics of Japan (2023, March 3). Demographic statistics. Retrieved September 22, 2023, from https://www.e-stat.go.jp/en/stat-search/files?page=1&toukei=00450011&tstat=000001028897&tclass1=000001053122

2.4.2 Industrial Classification

In the special study that follows, we will examine fertility data by industrial sectors in order to arrive at a set of estimates for planning in each sector. One problem here is that if the statistical standards behind the Japan Standard Industrial Classification (JSIC)[8] are revised, the classification of industries in the census will also change.

Normally, the data from different years should be based on the same standard. Where this is not the case, it is necessary to allow for rearrangements, using figures based on medium and smaller-scale data divisions. As far as concerns this survey, however, the industrial sector census data for mothers living with their own children go only as far as the general categories. In other words, the study will not be sensitive enough to take in finer industry-specific data. Finally, the data for 2005, 2010, and 2015 will need to be adjusted to match the classification of 2000, the census in which the number of categories was smallest. When calculating industry-specific TFRs, figures are available only for these census years 2000, 2005, 2010, and 2015, as these are the years for which detailed information was released. The matching adjustments between 2000, the year serving as a framework base for this study, and the other three census years 2005, 2010, and 2015 are shown in Table 2.2.

2.4.3 Use of the Own-Children Method

The national census includes detailed data for mothers living with their own-children. The numbers of own-children living with mothers are given, along with details of the mothers' employment status and industrial sector. These data are also available for the 47 prefectures. However, the national census is administered only once every five years.

The analysis in this study uses data about mothers, especially employment-related data by industrial sector and age. For this, it makes use of the Own-Children Method to estimate fertility rates based on the national census data.

The Own-Children Method allows fertility rates to be estimated by retroactively calculating past numbers of births based on the ages of mothers and of any own-children living with them. To do this, it utilizes a life table derived from the "Own-Children Table" previously developed in demographic studies to summarize ages of mothers and "own children."

This method is also used in other countries to estimate fertility rates based on data from population censuses. However, while this makes it possible to obtain estimates of fertility rates corresponding to differences in mothers' life circumstances, the estimates can diverge from reality if the circumstances themselves happen to change. For example, Ihara (2012) uncovers some divergences that occur in estimates of fertility rates by occupation. In the present study, also, the estimated fertility rates by occupation for employed women with children do not relate directly to numbers of children (in each occupation sector) expected to be born to employed women with children, but to estimates obtained by retroactively transferring the present life

[8] Japan Standard Industrial Classification (Rev. 14, 2023) (EFFECTIVE on April 1, 2024) Retrieved September 22, 2023, from https://www.soumu.go.jp/english/dgpp_ss/seido/sangyo/san14-3.htm.

Table 2.2 Main industrial sector categories in National Census

2000	2005	2010/2015 (no change)
01 Total	01Total	01 Total
02 Employed	02 Employed	02 Employed
03 A. Agriculture and forestry	03 A. Agriculture and forestry	A. Agriculture and forestry
04 Agriculture	04 Agriculture	Agriculture
05 B. Fisheries	05 B. Fisheries	B. Fisheries
06 C. Mining and quarrying of stone and gravel	06 C. Mining and quarrying of stone and gravel	C. Mining and quarrying of stone and gravel
07 D. Construction	07 D. Construction	D. Construction
08 E. Manufacturing	08 E. Manufacturing	E. Manufacturing
09 F. Electricity, gas, heat supply and water	09 F. Electricity, gas, heat supply and water	F. Electricity, gas, heat supply and water
11 H. Transportation and communications	10 G. Information and communications	G. Information and communications
	11 H. Transport and postal activities	H. Transport and postal activities
12 I. Wholesale, retail trade, restaurants	12 I. Wholesale and retail trade	I. Wholesale and retail trade
13 J. Finance and insurance	13 J. Finance and insurance	J. Finance and insurance
14 K. Real estate and goods rental and leasing	14 K. Real estate and goods rental and leasing	K. Real estate and goods rental and leasing
21 R. Services, other	15 L. Scientific research, professional and technical services	L. Scientific research, professional and technical services
	16 M. Accommodations, eating and drinking services	M. Accommodations, eating and drinking services
	17 N. Living-related and personal services and amusement services	N. Living-related and personal services and amusement services
	18 O. Education, learning support	O. Education, learning support
	19 P. Medical, health care and welfare	P. Medical, health care and welfare
	20 Q. Compound services	Q. Compound services
	21 R. Services, other	R. Services, other
22 S. Government, except elsewhere classified	22 S. Government, except elsewhere classified	S. Government, except elsewhere classified
–	23 T. Industries, unclassifiable	T. Industries, unclassifiable

(continued)

Table 2.2 (continued)

2000	2005	2010/2015 (no change)
Non employed	Non employed	Non employed
Absent from work	Absent from work	Absent from work
Unemployed	Unemployed	Unemployed

Sources Japan Census 2000, 2005, 2010, 2015.This Table was put together by the author based on these official sources

circumstances of employed women with children back onto the past years when those children were born.

According to Ihara (2012), the resulting estimate:

> indicates the fertility rate by occupations for mothers with babies aged zero; zero-year-old children are already born at the time of the national census but even if the mothers were employed until immediately before the birth, they are counted as having been born to a non-employed mother. Moreover, in order to examine the causes for the decline in the fertility rate, there is a need to analyze which occupations make it easier for women to have children. However, the Own-Children Table used for the estimate shows the mother's employment status after having the child, not before.[9]

The false assumption pointed out by Ihara is that the estimate here should be based on the interpretation that these women first have children and then enter employment. However, it is unlikely that women who have left their jobs to have children would then seek employment again immediately afterward; instead, cases like these are better read as referring to women who have continued in their respective employment categories.

2.5 Data Used and the Estimate Method

The estimate method used in this study is based on Ihara (2011, 2012, 2013) and provides fertility rates by occupation. The data used are taken from the Japanese National Census, in particular the Own-Children Table, the Female Population of Japan, the Complete Life Table, the Abridged Life Table, and the fertility rate by months for the four censuses of 2000, 2005, 2010 and 2015. Based on these, estimates of fertility rates by occupation are provided for the period 2000–2015 (counting each time from October 1), using the Own-Children Method. In the case of the life tables, the Abridged Life Table for each year is rectified using data from the Complete Life Table, which is compiled every 5 years. An adjustment also has to be made for the Own-Children Table. The table in the national census gives the numbers for male and female children combined; therefore, separate male and female totals need to be supplied based on the separate male and female figures from the life tables.

[9] Ihara (2012), p. 87.

- For the national data, a recreation of the population from 5 years before is obtained retroactively from the Complete and Abridged Life Tables, calculating back from the population of the year when the national census was conducted. Differences from the actual figures are then used to calculate correction coefficients for the past populations, based on the Abridged Life Tables, in order to rectify these abridged figures.
- As the prefectural data do not include the abridged data, the national Abridged Life Table is used instead.

1. As the population from the national census is counted for October 1 as a base, the fertility rate is calculated as the number of births for each month from October of one year to September of the following one, based on the data from the Demographic Survey. The number of births for each year, B (year), counting from October 1, is as follows.

   Number of births for each year, B (year), counted as of October 1.

$$\mathrm{B(year)} = \sum_{\mathrm{month}=1}^{9} \mathrm{B(year, month)} + \sum_{\mathrm{month}=10}^{12} \mathrm{B(year - 1, month)}$$

   B(year, month): The number of births for each month of that year

2. Fertility rates are calculated by the mother's age.

   Fertility rates are calculated according to the mother's age each year. For this, an estimate is calculated retroactively using the Life Table based on the national census and the proportion of each age-group among mothers with zero-year-old children as obtained from the Own-Children Table. The calculation of the retroactive estimate is as follows.

$\mathrm{c}(\mathrm{year}, \alpha_{\mathrm{age}})$: Retroactive estimate of number of births for mothers' age (β_{age}) for the calendar year (year)

$\mathrm{SR}(\mathrm{year}, \beta_{\mathrm{age}})$: Survival rate by age (β_{age}) of own children based on combined Life Table for males and females for the calendar year (year)

$\mathrm{C}(\mathrm{year5n}, \alpha_{\mathrm{age}}, \beta_{\mathrm{age}})$: Number of ownchildren by mother's age (α_{age}) and own-child's age (β_{age}) based on year of the national census (year5n).

Number of births in the previous year

$$\mathrm{c}(\mathrm{year5n} - 1, \alpha_{\mathrm{age}} - 1) = \mathrm{C}(\mathrm{year5n}, \alpha_{\mathrm{age}}, \beta_1)/\mathrm{SR}(\mathrm{year5n} - 1, \beta_0)$$

Number of births 2 years before

$$c(\text{year5n} - 2, \alpha_{\text{age}} - 2) = C(\text{year5n}, \alpha_{\text{age}}, \beta_2)/SR(\text{year5n} - 1, \beta_1)/SR(\text{year5n} - 2, \beta_0)$$

Number of births β years before

$$c(\text{year5n} - \beta, \alpha_{\text{age}} - \beta) = C(\text{year5n}, \alpha_{\text{age}}, \beta_{\text{age}})/SR(\text{year5n} - 1, \beta_{\text{age}} - 1) \\ /SR(\text{year5n} - 2, \beta_{\text{age}} - 2)/\cdots/SR(\text{year5n} - \beta, \beta_0)$$

Number of births for mothers' current age

$f(\text{year}, \alpha_{\text{age}})$: Estimate of number of births for mother's age(α_{age}) for the calendar year (year)

b(year): Combined number of male and female births based retroactively on the population of Japan in the calendar year (year) (counting from October 1)

$$f(\text{year}, \text{age } \alpha) = c(\text{year}, \alpha_{\text{age}}) * \frac{b(\text{year})}{\sum_{\text{age } \alpha}(\text{year}, \alpha_{\text{age}})}$$

3. The census indicates the number of own-children living with their mothers, by the mother's age and employment sector. Here, the data for 0-year-old children are particularly useful. Since births for children not living with their own mother cannot be directly linked to a "mother's employment" sector, they have to be allocated retroactively by matching the overall composition ratios for the total number of own-children for the mother's age.
4. The number of births in the yearly table of own-children is calculated as follows. First, the number of births for each 5-year period is interpolated directly, set out by the ages and employment sectors of the mothers, and then data for particular years are calculated in line with the proportion for each of the five years.
5. In this study, employment sectors are allocated to the following industrial categories: agriculture, forestry and fisheries; mining and quarrying; construction; manufacturing; electricity, gas, heat, and water; information and communications; transport and postal activities; wholesale and retail trade; finance and insurance; real estate and goods rental and leasing; scientific research, professional and technical services; accommodation, eating and drinking services; living-related and personal services; amusement services; education, learning support; medical, health care and welfare; combined services; other services; government, except elsewhere classified; non-classifiable industries; not employed, self-employed; unemployed.
6. The number of births by the mother's ages each year is calculated retroactively from the Own-Children Table by matching between the ages of the children in the five-year Own-Children Table and the proportion for each of the five years, as explained above. Following Ihara (2013), this is done through multiplying

by the proportions between the various industrial sectors while retroactively determining the numbers of births for each year in the Own-Children Table from the overall age totals (through dividing).

$$\mathrm{B_w(year5n,\ age)}\text{: Number of own-children by mother's age } (\alpha_{\mathrm{age}}) \text{ and employment (industrial sector) } (w) \text{ calculation based on year of national census (year5n)}$$

$$\mathrm{B_w(year5n + 5,\ age)}\text{: Number of own-children by mother's age } (\alpha_{\mathrm{age}}) \text{ and employment (industrial sector) } (w) \text{ based on year of national census 5 years later (year5n + 5)}$$

Numbers of births obtained by linear interpolation

Starting from the numbers of births at two time points, numbers of births at other time points can be calculated by linear interpolation (Lw) using the following formula.

$$\begin{aligned}
\mathrm{L_w}(\mathrm{year5n}+1, \alpha_{\mathrm{age}}, \beta_{\mathrm{age}}) &= \mathrm{B_w}(\mathrm{year5n}, \alpha_{\mathrm{age}}, \beta_{\mathrm{age}}) \\
\mathrm{L_w}(\mathrm{year5n}+1, \alpha_{\mathrm{age}}, \beta_{\mathrm{age}}) &= \mathrm{B_w}(\mathrm{year5n}, \alpha_{\mathrm{age}}, \beta_{\mathrm{age}}) \times 4/5 \\
&\quad + \mathrm{B_w}(\mathrm{year5n}+5, \alpha_{\mathrm{age}}, \beta_{\mathrm{age}}) \times 1/5 \\
\mathrm{L_w}(\mathrm{year5n}+2, \alpha_{\mathrm{age}}, \beta_{\mathrm{age}}) &= \mathrm{B_w}(\mathrm{year5n}, \alpha_{\mathrm{age}}, \beta_{\mathrm{age}}) \times 3/5 \\
&\quad + \mathrm{B_w}(\mathrm{year5n}+5, \alpha_{\mathrm{age}}, \beta_{\mathrm{age}}) \times 2/5 \\
\mathrm{L_w}(\mathrm{year5n}+3, \alpha_{\mathrm{age}}, \beta_{\mathrm{age}}) &= \mathrm{B_w}(\mathrm{year5n}, \alpha_{\mathrm{age}}, \beta_{\mathrm{age}}) \times 2/5 \\
&\quad + \mathrm{B_w}(\mathrm{year5n}+5, \alpha_{\mathrm{age}}, \beta_{\mathrm{age}}) \times 3/5 \\
\mathrm{L_w}(\mathrm{year5n}+4, \alpha_{\mathrm{age}}, \beta_{\mathrm{age}}) &= \mathrm{B_w}(\mathrm{year5n}, \alpha_{\mathrm{age}}, \beta_{\mathrm{age}}) \times 1/5 \\
&\quad + \mathrm{B_w}(\mathrm{year5n}+5, \alpha_{\mathrm{age}}, \beta_{\mathrm{age}}) \times 4/5 \\
\mathrm{L_w}(\mathrm{year5n}+5, \alpha_{\mathrm{age}}, \beta_{\mathrm{age}}) &= \mathrm{B_w}(\mathrm{year5n}+5, \alpha_{\mathrm{age}}, \beta_{\mathrm{age}})
\end{aligned}$$

Proportion ratio

The proportion ratio is calculated using the numbers of births linearly interpolated.

$$\mathrm{R_w(year5n + i,\ age)}\text{: i year later } (\mathrm{i} = 1 - 4)\text{, by industrial sector (w), proportion ratio for mothers' age (age)}$$

$$\mathrm{R_w(year5n + i,\ age)} = \mathrm{L(year5n + i,\ age)} / \sum_{\mathrm{cat}} \mathrm{L(year5n + i,\ age)}$$

Estimating numbers of births

Using the proportion ratio for mother's industrial sector (Rw) and age, the estimate for the number of births is calculated by the following formula.

Q_w(year5n + i, age): i year later (i = 1 − 4), Number of births for mother's age(age) and industrial sector (w)

T_w(year5n + i, age): Number of births by mother's age (age) i years later (i = 1 − 4) calculated retroactively from Life Table 5 years later

$$Q_w(\text{year5n} + i, \text{age}) = T_w(\text{year5n} + i, \text{age}) * R(\text{year5n} + i, \text{age})$$

7. The female population at each age is estimated retroactively from the female population at each age in the national census using the Life Table, as follows:

g(year, age): Retroactive population estimate by age (age) for calendar year (year)

SR(year, age): Female survival rate by age (age) based on Life Table for calendar year (year)

P(year, age): Female population by age (age) in calendar year (year)

Female population in the previous year

$$g(\text{year} - 1, \text{age} - 1) = P(\text{year}, \text{age})/SR(\text{year} - 1, \text{age} - 1)$$

Female population 2 years before

$$g(\text{year} - 2, \text{age} - 2) = P(\text{year}, \text{age})/SR(\text{year} - 1, \text{age} - 1)/SR(\text{year} - 2, \text{age} - 2)$$

Female population β years before

$$g(\text{year} - \beta, \text{age} - \beta) = P(\text{year}, \text{age})/SR(\text{year} - 1, \text{age} - 1)/SR(\text{year} - 2, \text{age} - 2)/\cdots/SR(\text{year} - \beta, \text{age} - \beta)$$

8. The proportion of women employed in a particular industrial sector, by age, is calculated from the entire female population of that age according to their employment status in the census.

L_w: Proportion of women employed by industrial sector and age (α_{age}) of the census year (year5n)

$$L_w(\text{year5n}, \alpha_{age}) = G_w(\text{year5n}, \alpha_{age})/G(\text{year5n}, \alpha_{age})$$

$G_w(\text{year5n}, \alpha_{age})$: Female population by industrial sector and age (α_{age}) in census year (year5n)

$G(\text{year5n}, \alpha_{age})$: Female population by age (α_{age}) in census year (year5n)

9. The proportions of females employed by industrial sector and by age for the four years following the national census year can be found by interpolating the proportion ratios of the various industrial sectors as follows:

$$L_w(\text{year5n}+1, \alpha_{age}) = L_w(\text{year5n}, \alpha_{age}) \times 4/5 + L_w(\text{year5n}+5, \alpha_{age}) \times 1/5$$
$$L_w(\text{year5n}+2, \alpha_{age}) = L_w(\text{year5n}, \alpha_{age}) \times 3/5 + L_w(\text{year5n}+5, \alpha_{age}) \times 2/5$$
$$L_w(\text{year5n}+3, \alpha_{age}) = L_w(\text{year5n}, \alpha_{age}) \times 2/5 + L_w(\text{year5n}+5, \alpha_{age}) \times 3/5$$
$$L_w(\text{year5n}+4, \alpha_{age}) = L_w(\text{year5n}, \alpha_{age}) \times 1/5 + L_w(\text{year5n}+5, \alpha_{age}) \times 4/5$$

The number of births by year: (year), and by mother's employment status (w) and age (α, age), and age in the year when the child is aged zero, (β, age) Bw, (see **2**, above), can then be found.

10. The number of women employed in a particular industrial sector each year is calculated by multiplying the female population of each age for that year by the proportion of women of that age employed in that sector.

For numbers of employees on parenting leave, g_w by age (α_{age}) each year (year)

$$g_w(\text{year}, \alpha_{age}) = g(\text{year}, \alpha_{age}) \times L_w(\text{year}, \alpha_{age})$$

11. If the estimate of the number of births, for the mother's employment status and age, and for the year when the child is aged zero, as shown in **9**, is now divided by the female population based on the same employment status, age, and year, as calculated in **10**, fertility rate estimates for these sets of conditions can be obtained. The calculation begins from age. The value for this is obtained by dividing the retroactive estimate of the number of births based on mother's age by the total number of the female population, again obtained retroactively based on age.

f(age): Numbers of births by mother's age

g(age): Numbers of women by age

$$\text{Fertility rate FR (age)} = \frac{\text{f(age)}}{\text{g(age)}}$$

$$\text{FR}_{\text{w}}(\text{year}, \alpha_{\text{age}}) = \frac{\text{f}_{\text{w}}(\text{year}, \alpha_{\text{age}})}{\text{g}_{\text{w}}(\text{year}, \alpha_{\text{age}})}$$

$$\text{TFR} = \sum_{\text{age}=15}^{49} \text{FR(age)}$$

$$\text{TFR(age5n)} = \sum_{\text{age}=\text{age5n}}^{\text{age5n}+4} \text{FR(age)}$$

12. Total fertility rates (TFR) for industrial sectors are calculated on a basis of the total fertility rate and age.

$$\text{TFR}_{\text{w}} = \sum_{\alpha_{\text{age}}=15}^{49} \text{FR}_{\text{w}}(\text{year}, \alpha_{\text{age}})$$

TFR_{w}: Total fertility rate of employed women by industrial sector (w) and age (α_{age}) for each year (year)

2.6 Results of Total Fertility Rate Estimates by Industrial Sector in Japan and the 47 Prefectures

2.6.1 Evaluation of TFR Estimate Results for a National Census Year

In this section, estimates are reported for total fertility rates (TFRs) by industrial sector in Japan and its 47 prefectures. These estimates are compared with the TFR values from the vital statistics, and the results are evaluated.

Estimates of the numbers of births by industrial sector and of the female population employed in each sector were made for the four census years 2000, 2005, 2010 and 2015. From this, data were then estimated for the non-census years 2001–2004, 2006–2009, and 2011–2014. Tables 2.4, 2.5, 2.6 and 2.7 show the TFR estimates for the whole of Japan by industrial sector for the census years covered. The data used are the numbers of births and the female populations in the time series before linear interpolation. The reason for the differences in the industry classifications each census year is that changes are made in the category standards used for statistic gathering (Japan Standard Industrial Classification). Table 2.9 shows the time-series data estimates. Estimates are offered up to 2015, but on the industrial sector classification base of 2000, which was the census year with fewest sector divisions. However, data which do not match the 2000 divisions may be reallocated.

Table 2.3 shows a comparison of the overall estimates obtained in this study with the values as calculated from vital statistics. However, as the national census shows the state of things on October 1 and the vital statistics data run from January 1 to December 31 of the same year, the contents presented are not identical. Looking at Table 2.3, the difference between the TFR estimates and the values obtained from the vital statistics was 0.008 (0.6%) in 2000, – 0.006 (– 0.5%) in 2005, 0.009 (0.6%) in 2010, and 0.012 (– 0.7%) in 2015. Comparing between 5-year age segments (15–19, etc.), the difference in the "age segment fertility rate" (ASFR) was larger in age segments up to 25–29 and smaller in age segments above that, but in every case less than ± 0.7%. For the purposes of this study, an estimate of this closeness is considered usable.

The census definition of an employed worker is as follows: "A person who during the week of the census survey has done remunerated work, including work at home, where "remuneration" may take the form, for example, of a wage or salary, an allowance, an earning or commission, or a payment in-kind. A person who has not done any remunerated work in the week of the survey will still count as an employed worker if either of the following conditions applies: (1) the person receives a wage or salary while absent from work due to illness or leave, or is entitled to a basic childcare leave benefit or care leave benefit in accordance with the Employment Insurance Act; (2) in the case of a person running a business, fewer than 30 days have elapsed since the person began an absence from work due to illness or for vacation, or a family member has been helping with the running of the business (agricultural concern, factory/retail business, etc.), even without remuneration."[10] Therefore, part-time and casual workers are to be counted as employed workers if they meet the definition during the survey period, and are to be included accordingly in the various totals of employed workers by industrial sector.

Looking at the TFR of employed persons, it was 0.48 in 2000 (Table 2.4, second column), 0.45 in 2005 (Table 2.5), 0.62 in 2010 (Table 2.6), and 0.80 in 2015 (Table 2.7). The TFR for non-employed persons (last column) was 2.89 in 2000, 2.78 in 2005, 3.06 in 2010, and 3.42 in 2015. Comparing these data, the situation for non-employed women was that the TFR was above sustainability level. For employed women, it was well below that level, but rising. By age segments, the TFR in 2000 for employed women was 0.14 for ages 25–29, 0.20 for 30–34, 0.08 for 35–39, and 0.01 for 40–44. In 2010, it was 0.16 for ages 25–29, 0.24 for 30–34, 0.13 for 35–39, and 0.03 for 40–44. In 2015, it rose to 0.19 for ages 25–29, 0.32 for 30–34, 0.19 for 35–39, and 0.04 for 40–44. There is also a trend toward later marriage, and broadly similar patterns are found among non-employed women.

---

[10] The 2010 census has the following additional condition for the definition of an employed person. http://www.stat.go.jp/data/kokusei/2010/users-g/word4.htm (accessed Feb. 7, 2022).

In addition, if a housewife who is employed part-time or at home does not do any remunerated work during the survey period (for the 2015 census survey, September 24–30), she is not to be counted in the category of "on leave from work," but in the category "housework."

Source: http://www.stat.go.jp/data/kokusei/qa-6.htm#f1 (accessed Feb. 7, 2022).

Table 2.3 Comparison of TFR estimates as calculated in this study and the values obtained from vital statistics

Mother's age	Vital statistics (A)				Estimates (B)				Differences (A)–(B)			
	2000	2005	2010	2015	2000	2005	2010	2015	2000	2005	2010	2015
15–19	0.027	0.025	0.023	0.021	0.015	0.014	0.011	0.009	0.012	0.012	0.012	0.011
20–24	0.197	0.182	0.178	0.148	0.161	0.162	0.147	0.121	0.035	0.020	0.031	0.026
25–29	0.497	0.423	0.436	0.422	0.471	0.398	0.410	0.394	0.026	0.025	0.026	0.028
30–34	0.462	0.429	0.479	0.517	0.493	0.456	0.498	0.542	− 0.031	− 0.027	− 0.019	− 0.025
35–39	0.157	0.176	0.232	0.286	0.184	0.208	0.261	0.321	− 0.027	− 0.032	− 0.029	− 0.034
40–44	0.019	0.024	0.039	0.056	0.026	0.035	0.051	0.072	− 0.006	− 0.011	− 0.012	− 0.017
45–49	0.001	0.001	0.001	0.002	0.001	0.002	0.002	0.003	− 0.001	− 0.001	− 0.001	− 0.001
TFR	**1.360**	**1.260**	**1.387**	**1.450**	**1.352**	**1.266**	**1.379**	**1.462**	**0.008**	**− 0.006**	**0.009**	**− 0.012**

Source The data (A) used are from the Main Statistical Table of the Annual Vital Statistics Report of the Ministry of Health, Labor and Welfare. The data (B), (A)–(B) are as estimated by the author

https://www.mhlw.go.jp/toukei/saikin/hw/jinkou/kakutei15/index.html (January 31, 2022)

Note The figures for each 5-year age segment of mothers are the total fertility rate for each age group. 15–19 includes 14 years old and younger. Similarly, 45–49 includes 50 years old and over

Bold indicates data of TFR.

Table 2.4 Total fertility rates by industrial sector in Japan, 2000

Age segment	Total	Employed	Agriculture and forestry	Agriculture	Fisheries	Mining and Quarrying of Stone and Gravel	Construction	Manufacturing
15–19	0.01	0.01	0.03	0.00	0.09	0.00	0.02	0.01
20–24	0.16	0.04	0.25	0.06	0.41	0.03	0.07	0.05
25–29	0.47	0.14	0.53	0.26	0.45	0.20	0.21	0.17
30–34	0.49	0.20	0.37	0.30	0.32	0.19	0.25	0.19
35–39	0.18	0.08	0.10	0.08	0.07	0.11	0.10	0.07
40–44	0.03	0.01	0.01	0.03	0.02	0.02	0.01	0.01
45–49	0.00	0.00	0.00	0.00	0.00	0.00	0.00	0.00
TFR	**1.35**	**0.48**	**1.29**	**0.73**	**1.37**	**0.56**	**0.67**	**0.51**
Age segment	Electricity, gas, heat supply and water	Transport and postal activities	Wholesale and retail trade	Finance and insurance	Real estate	Services	Government	Non employed
15–19	0.00	0.01	0.01	0.09	0.08	0.01	0.00	0.02
20–24	0.06	0.03	0.03	0.04	0.02	0.03	0.05	0.49
25–29	0.19	0.10	0.10	0.11	0.09	0.15	0.26	1.14
30–34	0.27	0.14	0.13	0.15	0.15	0.23	0.36	0.86
35–39	0.10	0.06	0.05	0.07	0.09	0.11	0.13	0.32
40–44	0.01	0.01	0.01	0.01	0.01	0.02	0.02	0.05

(continued)

Table 2.4 (continued)

Age segment	Electricity, gas, heat supply and water	Transport and postal activities	Wholesale and retail trade	Finance and insurance	Real estate	Services	Government	Non employed
45–49	0.00	0.00	0.00	0.00	0.00	0.00	0.00	0.00
TFR	**0.63**	**0.35**	**0.33**	**0.47**	**0.44**	**0.55**	**0.81**	**2.89**

Source Data as calculated by the author. *Note* The industrial sectors are the English term for the Japan Standard Industrial Classification (JSIC) and Japan Census categories.
Bold indicates data of TFR.

Table 2.5 Total fertility rates by industrial sector in Japan, 2005

Age segment	Total	Employed	Agriculture	Forestry	Fisheries	Mining and Quarrying of Stone and Gravel	Construction	Manufacturing	Electricity, gas, heat supply and water	Information and communications
15–19	0.01	0.01	0.02	0.00	0.11	0.00	0.03	0.01	0.00	0.00
20–24	0.16	0.04	0.19	0.06	0.54	0.07	0.10	0.06	0.04	0.02
25–29	0.40	0.12	0.42	0.22	0.53	0.07	0.22	0.15	0.20	0.06
30–34	0.46	0.18	0.32	0.34	0.36	0.25	0.25	0.18	0.31	0.15
35–39	0.21	0.09	0.12	0.14	0.09	0.08	0.12	0.08	0.15	0.11
40–44	0.04	0.02	0.02	0.02	0.02	0.03	0.02	0.01	0.03	0.02
45–49	0.00	0.00	0.00	0.00	0.00	0.01	0.00	0.00	0.00	0.00
TFR	**1.27**	**0.45**	**1.07**	**0.79**	**1.59**	**0.51**	**0.74**	**0.49**	**0.73**	**0.38**

Age segment	Transport and postal activities	Wholesale and retail trade	Finance and insurance	Real estate	Accommodation, eating and drinking services	Medical, health care and welfare	Education, learning support	Combined services	Services	Government	Non employed
15–19	0.00	0.00	0.00	0.00	0.00	0.00	0.00	0.00	0.01	0.00	0.02
20–24	0.04	0.03	0.05	0.02	0.04	0.04	0.01	0.05	0.03	0.05	0.45
25–29	0.09	0.09	0.11	0.09	0.10	0.19	0.10	0.19	0.08	0.20	1.03
30–34	0.12	0.12	0.17	0.16	0.10	0.25	0.28	0.25	0.12	0.35	0.85
35–39	0.06	0.06	0.08	0.10	0.05	0.11	0.17	0.10	0.08	0.16	0.37
40–44	0.01	0.01	0.02	0.02	0.01	0.02	0.03	0.01	0.02	0.02	0.07

(continued)

Table 2.5 (continued)

Age segment	Transport and postal activities	Wholesale and retail trade	Finance and insurance	Real estate	Accommodation, eating and drinking services	Medical, health care and welfare	Education, learning support	Combined services	Services	Government	Non employed
45–49	0.00	0.00	0.00	0.00	0.00	0.00	0.00	0.00	0.00	0.00	0.00
TFR	**0.33**	**0.32**	**0.47**	**0.40**	**0.32**	**0.62**	**0.59**	**0.61**	**0.34**	**0.79**	**2.78**

Source Data as calculated by the author. *Note* The industrial sectors are the English term for the Japan Standard Industrial Classification (JSIC) and Japan Census categories.
Bold indicates data of TFR.

Table 2.6 Total fertility rates by industrial sector in Japan, 2010

Age segment	Total	Employed	Agriculture and forestry	Agriculture	Fisheries	Mining and Quarrying of Stone and Gravel	Construction	Manufacturing
15–19	0.01	0.00	0.01	0.01	0.03	0.00	0.02	0.01
20–24	0.15	0.04	0.19	0.19	0.33	0.07	0.09	0.08
25–29	0.41	0.16	0.39	0.39	0.61	0.09	0.24	0.17
30–34	0.50	0.24	0.38	0.38	0.44	0.35	0.31	0.23
35–39	0.26	0.13	0.16	0.16	0.16	0.13	0.17	0.12
40–44	0.05	0.03	0.03	0.03	0.01	0.04	0.03	0.02
45–49	0.00	0.00	0.00	0.00	0.00	0.00	0.00	0.00
TFR	**1.38**	**0.62**	**1.17**	**1.18**	**1.58**	**0.69**	**0.86**	**0.64**
Age segment	Electricity, gas, heat supply and water	Information and communi-cations	Transport and postal activities	Wholesale and retail trade	Finance and insurance	Real estate and goods rental and leasing	Scientific research, professional and technical services	Accommodation, eating and drinking services
15–19	0.00	0.01	0.01	0.00	0.00	0.00	0.00	0.00
20–24	0.06	0.01	0.05	0.03	0.04	0.03	0.02	0.04
25–29	0.20	0.10	0.13	0.11	0.17	0.12	0.11	0.12
30–34	0.37	0.23	0.17	0.17	0.27	0.21	0.24	0.13
35–39	0.17	0.17	0.09	0.09	0.14	0.14	0.18	0.06
40–44	0.03	0.04	0.02	0.02	0.03	0.03	0.04	0.01
45–49	0.00	0.00	0.00	0.00	0.00	0.00	0.00	0.00
TFR	**0.82**	**0.57**	**0.46**	**0.43**	**0.66**	**0.53**	**0.60**	**0.37**

(continued)

Table 2.6 (continued)

Age segment	Living-related and personal services and amusement services	Education, learning support	Medical, health care and welfare	Combined services	Services, others	Government, except elsewhere classified	Industries, unclassifiable	Non employed
15–19	0.00	0.00	0.01	0.00	0.00	0.00	0.02	0.01
20–24	0.03	0.01	0.04	0.07	0.04	0.04	0.10	0.40
25–29	0.12	0.14	0.23	0.25	0.14	0.23	0.20	1.09
30–34	0.17	0.32	0.32	0.35	0.21	0.41	0.24	0.98
35–39	0.10	0.21	0.15	0.18	0.12	0.23	0.15	0.48
40–44	0.02	0.04	0.03	0.02	0.02	0.04	0.03	0.10
45–49	0.00	0.00	0.00	0.00	0.00	0.00	0.00	0.00
TFR	**0.45**	**0.72**	**0.78**	**0.87**	**0.53**	**0.95**	**0.74**	**3.06**

Source Data as calculated by the author. *Note* The industrial sectors are the English term for the Japan Standard Industrial Classification (JSIC) and Japan Census categories.
Bold indicates data of TFR.

Table 2.7 Total fertility rates by industrial sector in Japan, 2015

Age segment	Total	Employed	Agriculture and forestry	Agriculture	Fisheries	Mining and Quarrying of Stone and Gravel	Construction	Manufacturing
15–19	0.01	0.01	0.00	0.00	0.07	0.00	0.01	0.01
20–24	0.12	0.05	0.15	0.15	0.47	0.14	0.12	0.07
25–29	0.39	0.19	0.42	0.43	0.63	0.29	0.28	0.20
30–34	0.54	0.32	0.44	0.45	0.57	0.38	0.39	0.31
35–39	0.32	0.19	0.22	0.22	0.17	0.24	0.23	0.18
40–44	0.07	0.04	0.04	0.04	0.02	0.03	0.05	0.04
45–49	0.00	0.00	0.00	0.00	0.00	0.00	0.00	0.00
TFR	**1.46**	**0.80**	**1.29**	**1.30**	**1.93**	**1.08**	**1.08**	**0.81**
Age segment	Electricity, gas, heat supply and water	Information and commu-nications	Transport and postal activities	Wholesale and retail trade	Finance and insurance	Real estate and goods rental and leasing	Scientific research, professional and technical services	Accommodation, eating and drinking services
15–19	0.01	0.00	0.01	0.00	0.06	0.00	0.00	0.00
20–24	0.05	0.01	0.05	0.04	0.05	0.03	0.02	0.04
25–29	0.29	0.12	0.16	0.14	0.23	0.15	0.13	0.15
30–34	0.44	0.34	0.24	0.23	0.44	0.31	0.33	0.17
35–39	0.22	0.28	0.14	0.14	0.25	0.21	0.26	0.09
40–44	0.04	0.08	0.03	0.03	0.05	0.05	0.07	0.02
45–49	0.00	0.00	0.00	0.00	0.00	0.00	0.00	0.00
TFR	**1.05**	**0.85**	**0.63**	**0.58**	**1.09**	**0.76**	**0.82**	**0.48**

(continued)

Table 2.7 (continued)

Age segment	Living-related and personal services and amusement services	Education, learning support	Medical, health care and welfare	Combined services	Services, other	Government, except elsewhere classified	Industries, unclassifiable	Non employed
15–19	0.01	0.00	0.01	0.00	0.01	0.00	0.02	0.01
20–24	0.04	0.01	0.05	0.06	0.04	0.03	0.10	0.34
25–29	0.15	0.16	0.25	0.27	0.15	0.24	0.22	1.13
30–34	0.25	0.41	0.39	0.39	0.27	0.48	0.32	1.13
35–39	0.16	0.28	0.21	0.21	0.18	0.30	0.21	0.64
40–44	0.04	0.06	0.04	0.04	0.04	0.06	0.05	0.16
45–49	0.00	0.00	0.00	0.00	0.00	0.00	0.00	0.01
TFR	**0.65**	**0.93**	**0.96**	**0.97**	**0.69**	**1.11**	**0.92**	**3.42**

Source Data as calculated by the author. *Note* The industrial sectors are the English term for the Japan Standard Industrial Classification (JSIC) and Japan Census categories.

Bold indicates data of TFR.

Comparing TFRs by industrial sectors, sectors with high TFRs are the primary industries, followed by government, construction, finance and insurance, utilities (electricity, etc.), combined services, and medical, etc. Sectors showing low TFRs are accommodation, etc., wholesale and retail, and transportation, etc. Comparing the TFRs for the age segments and industrial sectors in Tables 2.4, 2.5, 2.6 and 2.7, rises appear everywhere in the age segments 30–34 and above for the years 2010 and 2015, as compared with 2000 or 2005.

Looking at the various industries, Fig. 2.6, shows the numbers of female employees up to age 49 by industrial sector according to the 2010 census. Figure 2.7 shows corresponding numbers for the 2015 census. We have already seen that women working in wholesale and retail trade have low TFRs in 2010 and 2015. But this is the industrial sector employing the second largest numbers of women. A policy of facilitating childbirth in a sector like this with a large workforce and a low TFR could be one key to developing effective measures against the decline in the number of births. The sector with the third highest female employment is manufacturing. After that comes accommodation, eating and drinking services, the sector with the lowest TFR. In these sectors too, therefore, it should be a priority to improve working environments and make it easier for women to have children. By comparison, medical, health care and welfare, the sector with the highest female workforce, has a relatively high TFR. But naturally, a further rise in this sector will also lead to a rise for the country as a whole (Tables 2.8 and 2.9).

2.6.2 *Evaluation of TFR Estimate Results for Japan and Its 47 Prefectures, 2000–2015*

Figure 2.8 shows national TFR estimates from this study for the 16 years 2000–2015 set alongside TFRs obtained from vital statistics. The variations in the values are approximately the same, but there are discrepancies in the period 2006–2008.

As was said earlier, the estimates for the non-census years are derived by linear interpolation from the firmer data of the census years. The discrepancies in Fig. 2.8 can be explained by supposing that the interpolations did not match the actual movements in some places. Table 2.10 shows the TFRs by industrial sectors for Japan as a whole, as estimated in this study for 2000–2015.

Next, Table 2.11 compares TFR estimates derived from this study for Japan and its 47 prefectures with the values obtained from vital statistics for the same period 2000–2015. The differences serve as indicators of the margin of error between the estimates and the findings of the census survey. The upper row error value each time is the RMSE (Root Mean Square Error) and the lower row value is the RMSPE (Root Mean Square Percentage Error). The RMSE for the whole country and its 47 prefectures is in the range 0.01–0.06, with an average value of 0.03. The RMSPE ranges from 0.89 to 4.49, with an average of 2.26. Values like these indicate that there is no problem with the results of this study.

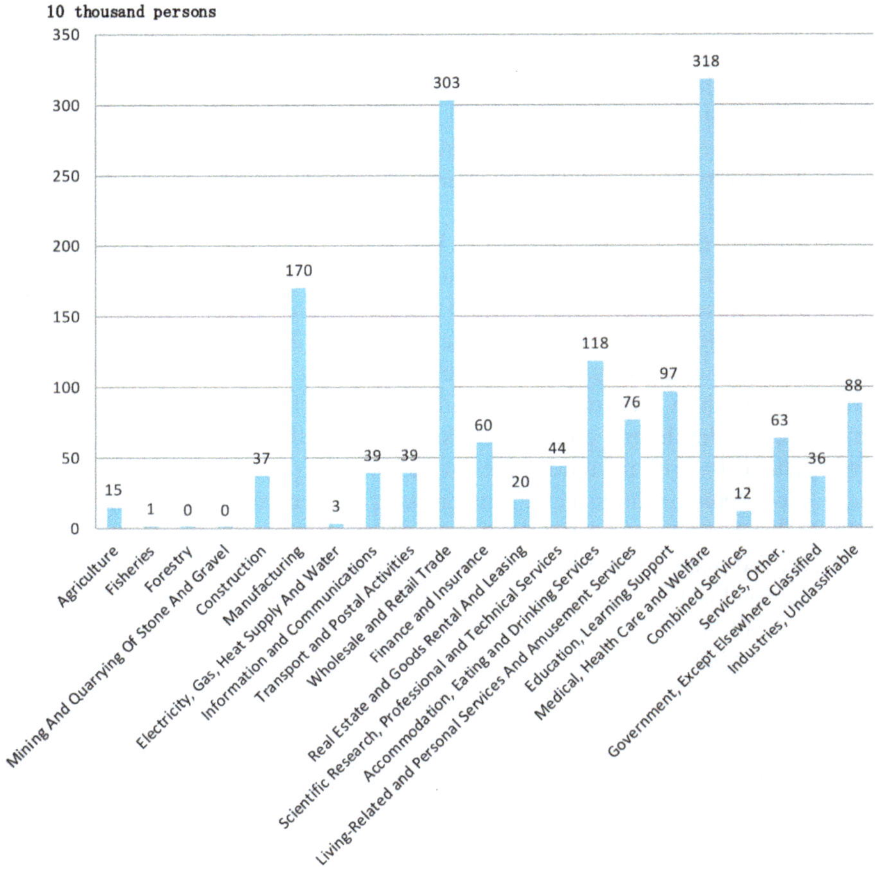

Fig. 2.6 Female workforces (ages 15–49) by industrial sectors in 2010. *Source* 2010 National Census, Basic Tabulation of Occupations (Statistics Bureau, Ministry of Internal Affairs and Communications), Table 21 Employment/non-employment, Industry (major categories), Marital Status (2 categories), Number of Own-children under Age 20 (5 categories), Age (in years) Japanese Female Population, Age 15–70—Based on Total Female Population Recorded in Japan and Prefectures, and on data by industrial sectors, created by the author

Figure 2.9 compares TFR values for Hokkaido (the first prefecture on the list) obtained from the vital statistics and from the estimates of this study and shows low differences on both the RMSE and the RMSPE measure. Figure 2.10 does the same for Gifu (21st on the list) but reveals higher error values for both RMSE and RMSPE. In fact, Gifu is the prefecture showing the largest differences between the TFR results calculated in this study and the values obtained from the vital statistics. The estimates do not fit the movements actually occurring in Gifu during the period of linear interpolation.

Table 2.12, finally, shows TFR estimates across the whole area of female private and public employment by prefecture, excluding agriculture, forestry and fisheries.

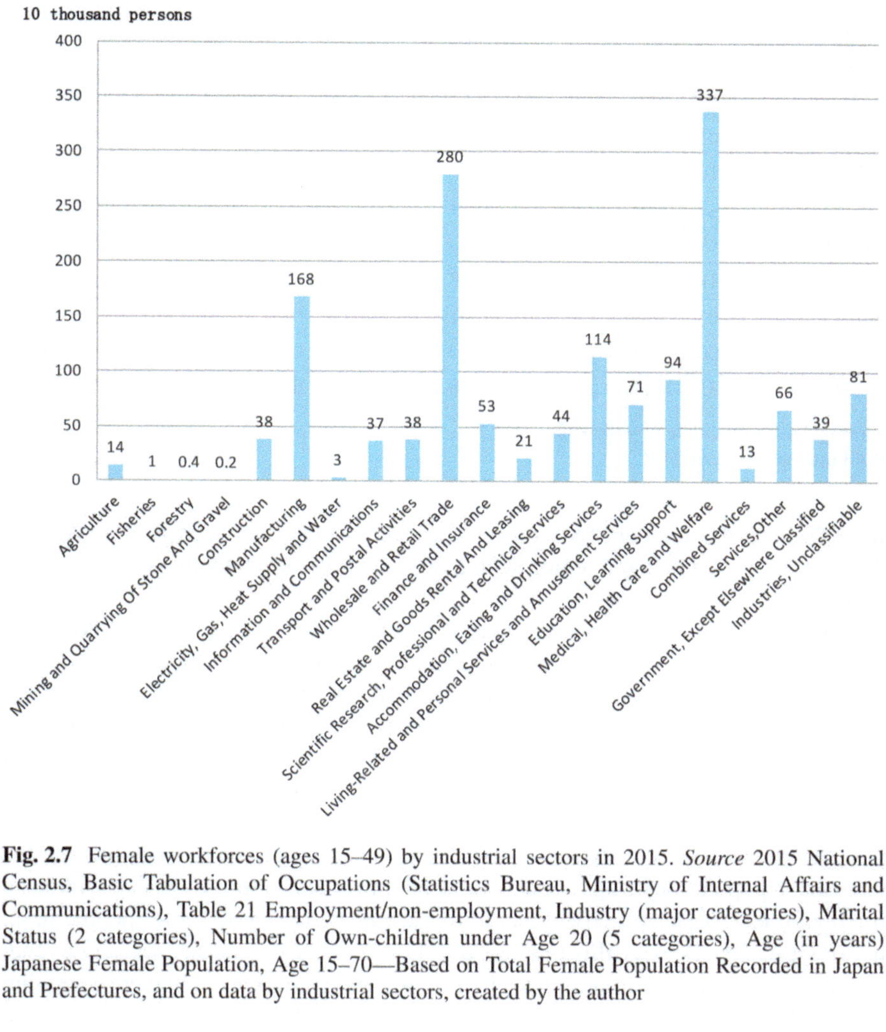

Fig. 2.7 Female workforces (ages 15–49) by industrial sectors in 2015. *Source* 2015 National Census, Basic Tabulation of Occupations (Statistics Bureau, Ministry of Internal Affairs and Communications), Table 21 Employment/non-employment, Industry (major categories), Marital Status (2 categories), Number of Own-children under Age 20 (5 categories), Age (in years) Japanese Female Population, Age 15–70—Based on Total Female Population Recorded in Japan and Prefectures, and on data by industrial sectors, created by the author

2.7 Analysis Results: Total Fertility Rate and Its Relationship with Regions

2.7.1 Background of Analysis

In this section, I will examine the relationship of Total Fertility Rate (TFR) with regional economy, and especially with regional agglomeration, using TFR analysis data for prefectures as a basis for the discussion.

Recent literature on TFR and agglomeration includes Zhang (2002), Sato and Yamamoto (2005), Sato (2007), and Morita and Yamamoto (2014). These studies show that TFRs are lower in densely populated than in less densely populated areas.

Table 2.8 Total fertility rates for employed and non-employed women

Age segments	Total				Employed				Non-employed			
	2000	2005	2010	2015	2000	2005	2010	2015	2000	2005	2010	2015
15–19	0.01	0.01	0.01	0.01	0.01	0.01	0.00	0.01	0.02	0.02	0.01	0.01
20–24	0.16	0.16	0.15	0.12	0.04	0.04	0.04	0.05	0.49	0.45	0.40	0.34
25–29	0.47	0.40	0.41	0.39	0.14	0.12	0.16	0.19	1.14	1.03	1.09	1.13
30–34	0.49	0.46	0.50	0.54	0.20	0.18	0.24	0.32	0.86	0.85	0.98	1.13
35–39	0.18	0.21	0.26	0.32	0.08	0.09	0.13	0.19	0.32	0.37	0.48	0.64
40–44	0.03	0.04	0.05	0.07	0.01	0.02	0.03	0.04	0.05	0.07	0.10	0.16
45–49	0.00	0.00	0.00	0.00	0.00	0.00	0.00	0.00	0.00	0.00	0.00	0.01
TFR	**1.35**	**1.27**	**1.38**	**1.46**	**0.48**	**0.45**	**0.62**	**0.80**	**2.89**	**2.78**	**3.06**	**3.42**

Source Data as calculated by the author.
Bold indicates data of TFR.

In addition, as the number of companies is greater in areas of high population density, this generally means that a region with a large number of companies will also have a low TFR.

Sato (2007)[11] offers theoretical reasons to show why wage levels will generally be higher in regions with agglomerated economies, where the number of younger employees with children is relatively higher than elsewhere. Put briefly: In a state of equilibrium, a region with a more agglomerated economy and a higher population density will offer higher wages and have a lower TFR. The background of this is as follows. Considering a balanced TFR as being one which combines two functions of utility levels and wage rates, areas with more agglomerated economies will attract younger people and, consequently, pay higher local wage rates. Subsequently, the increase in population brings about an uneconomical concentration which will make the region less attractive. Given that utility levels are the same for all people in all regions, differences in fertility rates are due more to the differences in wage rates and, in conditions of equilibrium, TFRs will thus be lower in regions of higher population density. Further, in more densely populated areas, women are also likely to opt for fewer children. In search of more settled living conditions, some people who grew up in areas of lower population density will later migrate to high density areas, resulting in still greater imbalance. Moreover, the greater this concentrating effect already is, the stronger will be the future pull that continues to draw further migrants. This can be shown using actual data.

In this study, these previous findings are verified from the study data. In addition, relationships between the agglomeration economy and fertility rates are examined and confirmed using indicators appropriate to an agglomeration economy.

[11] The summary below is based on Sato (2007), pp. 381–383.

Table 2.9 Full list of TFRs by industrial sectors across four censuses

Years	2000		2005		2010		2015	
	Industrial sector	TFR	Industrial sector	TFR	Industrial sector	TFR	Industrial sector	TFR
1	Fisheries	1.37	Fisheries	1.59	Fisheries	1.58	Fisheries	1.93
2	Agriculture	1.29	Agriculture	1.07	Agriculture	1.18	Agriculture	1.30
3	Forestry	0.73	Forestry	0.79				
4	Mining	0.56	Mining	0.51	Mining and quarrying of stone and gravel	0.69	Mining and quarrying of stone and gravel	1.08
5	Manufacturing	0.51	Manufacturing	0.49	Manufacturing	0.64	Manufacturing	0.81
6	Government	0.81	Government	0.79	Government	0.95	Government	1.11
7	Construction	0.67	Construction	0.74	Construction	0.86	Construction	1.08
8	Electricity, gas, heat supply and water	0.63	Electricity, gas, heat supply and water	0.73	Electricity, gas, heat supply and water	0.82	Electricity, gas, heat supply and water	1.05
9	Finance and insurance	0.47	Finance and insurance	0.47	Finance and insurance	0.66	Finance and insurance	1.09
10	Real estate	0.44	Real estate	0.40	Real estate and goods rental and leasing	0.53	Real estate and goods rental and leasing	0.76
11	Wholesale and retail trade, eating and drinking services	0.33	Retail trade	0.32	Wholesale and retail trade	0.43	Wholesale and retail trade	0.58
12	Transport and postal activities	0.35	Transport and postal activities	0.33	Transport and postal activities	0.46	Transport and postal activities	0.63
13			Compound services	0.61	Compound services	0.87	Compound services	0.97
14	Services	0.55	Services	0.34	Services, other	0.53	Services, other	0.69
15			Welfare	0.62	Medical, health care and welfare	0.78	Medical, health care and welfare	0.96

(continued)

Table 2.9 (continued)

Years	2000		2005		2010		2015	
	Industrial sector	TFR	Industrial sector	TFR	Industrial sector	TFR	Industrial sector	TFR
16			Education, learning support	0.59	Education, learning support	0.72	Education, learning support	0.93
17					Scientific research, professional and technical services	0.60	Scientific research, professional and technical services	0.82
18			Information and communications	0.38	Information and communications	0.57	Information and communications	0.85
19					Living-related and personal services and amusement services	0.45	Living-related and personal services and amusement services	0.65
20			Accommodation, eating and drinking services	0.32	Accommodation, eating and drinking services	0.37	Accommodation, eating and drinking services	0.48
21							Industries, unclassifiable	0.92

Source Data as calculated by the author

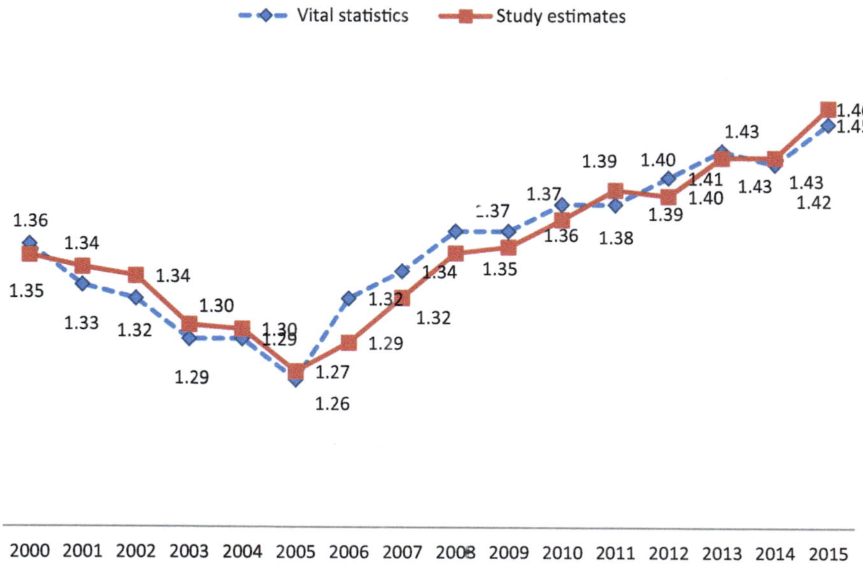

Fig. 2.8 Comparison of TFR estimates as calculated in this study with those obtained from vital statistics. *Source* Created by the author based on the calculated estimates of this study

2.7.2 *Indicators of an Agglomeration Economy*

Sato (2007), and Morita and Yamamoto (2014) use population density as an indicator of an agglomeration economy. In addition, Sato (2007) also uses data of net movement resulting from population migration.

The same kinds of statistical data were used in this study, selected to match the analysis period. In addition, this study also uses data relating to an agglomeration economy, obtained from the following two papers. First, Nakamura (2008)[12] defines agglomeration to include both concentration and specialization, and offers seven indicators, based on discussions in existing papers, as direct measures of regional economic agglomeration. Konishi and Saito (2012) used a census of manufacturing in Japan to obtain three indicators of the specialization effects of agglomeration on manufacturing production, which could then be used as a basis for analysis. These effects were in the areas of manufacturing and urbanization agglomeration. They also added a fourth special indicator of their own, as will be explained below.

The nature of the agglomeration indicators proposed by Nakamura (2008) and by Konishi and Saito (2012) can be summed up as follows. This study more particularly follows Konishi and Saito.

1. Relative concentration index of industry i in region j.

   Geographical concentration of employment is the expression of a spatial distribution of economic activity. Thus, an industrial specialization in a region indicates

[12] This formulation is based on Nakamura (2008), p. 103, line 11; p. 108, line 10.

Table 2.10 TFR estimates for Japan by industrial sectors, 2000–2015 (from this study)

	Total	Employed	Agriculture forestry, fisheries	Construction	Manufacturing	Electricity, gas, heat supply and water	Transport	Wholesale and retail trade, eating	Finance and insurance	Real estate	Services, other	Government, except elsewhere classified	Private government employed	Non employed
2000	1.352	0.478	1.281	0.670	0.507	0.635	0.354	0.332	0.466	0.441	0.549	0.809	0.467	2.890
2001	1.343	0.477	1.259	0.688	0.512	0.653	0.355	0.331	0.720	0.451	0.538	0.806	0.466	2.891
2002	1.337	0.474	1.237	0.707	0.511	0.674	0.355	0.331	0.680	0.433	0.527	0.806	0.464	2.895
2003	1.301	0.463	1.181	0.712	0.499	0.683	0.349	0.323	0.653	0.415	0.509	0.792	0.453	2.830
2004	1.297	0.464	1.155	0.734	0.500	0.712	0.351	0.324	0.559	0.410	0.503	0.799	0.453	2.835
2005	1.266	0.455	1.105	0.741	0.491	0.726	0.346	0.319	0.473	0.401	0.487	0.788	0.444	2.781
2006	1.287	0.485	1.124	0.767	0.518	0.744	0.378	0.338	0.515	0.429	0.517	0.816	0.471	2.834
2007	1.320	0.522	1.147	0.793	0.551	0.772	0.415	0.362	0.553	0.461	0.554	0.855	0.505	2.908
2008	1.354	0.558	1.177	0.824	0.585	0.795	0.451	0.386	0.597	0.489	0.591	0.892	0.538	2.989
2009	1.358	0.583	1.180	0.837	0.608	0.803	0.479	0.403	0.623	0.504	0.616	0.912	0.561	3.009
2010	1.379	0.616	1.196	0.860	0.638	0.823	0.512	0.426	0.656	0.526	0.650	0.946	0.593	3.062
2011	1.401	0.656	1.229	0.910	0.675	0.869	0.558	0.456	0.798	0.574	0.705	0.981	0.640	3.138
2012	1.396	0.683	1.237	0.940	0.698	0.900	0.593	0.479	0.918	0.611	0.750	0.998	0.677	3.159
2013	1.425	0.726	1.273	0.994	0.737	0.953	0.646	0.514	1.033	0.664	0.814	1.041	0.731	3.252
2014	1.425	0.755	1.284	1.027	0.762	0.985	0.686	0.538	1.095	0.702	0.863	1.062	0.771	3.289
2015	1.462	0.804	1.329	1.084	0.806	1.048	0.744	0.577	1.177	0.759	0.938	1.113	0.834	3.415

Source Created by the author based on the calculated estimates of this study
Note Private Government Employed excludes Agriculture, Forestry and Fisheries

Table 2.11 Comparison of TFR estimates from this study for Japan and its 47 prefectures with results from Vital statistics

		2000	2001	2002	2003	2004	2005	2006	2007	2008	2009	2010	2011	2012	2013	2014	2015	RMSE RMSPE
Japan	V	1.36	1.33	1.32	1.29	1.29	1.26	1.32	1.34	1.37	1.37	1.39	1.39	1.41	1.43	1.42	1.45	0.01
	S	1.35	1.34	1.33	1.30	1.30	1.27	1.29	1.32	1.35	1.36	1.38	1.40	1.40	1.43	1.43	1.46	0.99
Hokkaido	V	1.23	1.21	1.22	1.20	1.19	1.15	1.18	1.19	1.20	1.19	1.26	1.25	1.26	1.28	1.27	1.31	0.01
	S	1.21	1.22	1.24	1.20	1.20	1.15	1.17	1.20	1.21	1.21	1.25	1.25	1.26	1.27	1.29	1.30	0.89
Aomori	V	1.47	1.47	1.44	1.35	1.35	1.29	1.31	1.28	1.30	1.26	1.38	1.38	1.36	1.40	1.42	1.43	0.02
	S	1.46	1.48	1.45	1.39	1.38	1.30	1.32	1.30	1.34	1.30	1.37	1.37	1.37	1.38	1.44	1.39	1.71
Iwate	V	1.56	1.52	1.50	1.45	1.43	1.41	1.39	1.39	1.39	1.37	1.46	1.41	1.44	1.46	1.44	1.49	0.03
	S	1.54	1.54	1.53	1.46	1.45	1.42	1.41	1.44	1.43	1.44	1.46	1.41	1.44	1.45	1.44	1.49	1.94
Miyagi	V	1.39	1.33	1.31	1.27	1.24	1.24	1.25	1.27	1.29	1.25	1.30	1.25	1.30	1.34	1.30	1.36	0.03
	S	1.39	1.37	1.35	1.31	1.29	1.25	1.24	1.27	1.31	1.26	1.31	1.20	1.32	1.38	1.34	1.41	2.49
Akita	V	1.45	1.40	1.37	1.31	1.30	1.34	1.34	1.31	1.32	1.29	1.31	1.35	1.37	1.35	1.34	1.35	0.03
	S	1.45	1.41	1.40	1.36	1.33	1.33	1.34	1.35	1.37	1.33	1.33	1.34	1.35	1.32	1.34	1.35	2.00
Yamagata	V	1.62	1.58	1.54	1.49	1.47	1.45	1.45	1.42	1.44	1.39	1.48	1.46	1.44	1.47	1.47	1.48	0.04
	S	1.61	1.63	1.60	1.52	1.50	1.46	1.47	1.46	1.49	1.44	1.45	1.52	1.45	1.47	1.48	1.46	2.39
Fukushima	V	1.65	1.60	1.57	1.54	1.51	1.49	1.49	1.49	1.52	1.49	1.52	1.48	1.41	1.53	1.58	1.58	0.03
	S	1.63	1.63	1.61	1.55	1.54	1.48	1.50	1.50	1.51	1.49	1.50	1.46	1.35	1.45	1.53	1.55	2.25
Ibaraki	V	1.47	1.40	1.38	1.34	1.33	1.32	1.35	1.35	1.37	1.37	1.44	1.39	1.41	1.42	1.43	1.48	0.03
	S	1.46	1.45	1.44	1.39	1.40	1.33	1.35	1.38	1.40	1.40	1.42	1.43	1.42	1.44	1.44	1.49	2.48
Tochigi	V	1.48	1.43	1.40	1.38	1.37	1.40	1.40	1.39	1.42	1.43	1.44	1.38	1.43	1.43	1.46	1.49	0.03
	S	1.44	1.47	1.45	1.41	1.41	1.39	1.40	1.39	1.45	1.45	1.44	1.44	1.43	1.48	1.45	1.52	2.18
Gunma	V	1.51	1.42	1.41	1.38	1.35	1.39	1.36	1.36	1.40	1.38	1.46	1.41	1.39	1.41	1.44	1.49	0.04

(continued)

Table 2.11 (continued)

		2000	2001	2002	2003	2004	2005	2006	2007	2008	2009	2010	2011	2012	2013	2014	2015	RMSE RMSPE
Gunma	S	1.49	1.46	1.46	1.43	1.41	1.38	1.38	1.40	1.44	1.46	1.43	1.48	1.41	1.44	1.46	1.49	3.05
Saitama	V	1.30	1.24	1.23	1.21	1.20	1.22	1.24	1.26	1.28	1.28	1.32	1.28	1.29	1.33	1.31	1.39	0.03
	S	1.28	1.27	1.26	1.24	1.23	1.21	1.24	1.26	1.29	1.29	1.31	1.33	1.30	1.36	1.36	1.39	2.02
Chiba	V	1.30	1.24	1.24	1.20	1.22	1.22	1.23	1.25	1.29	1.31	1.34	1.31	1.31	1.33	1.32	1.38	0.03
	S	1.28	1.27	1.27	1.24	1.24	1.21	1.23	1.26	1.30	1.33	1.36	1.37	1.34	1.36	1.35	1.40	2.16
Tokyo	V	1.07	1.00	1.02	1.00	1.01	1.00	1.02	1.05	1.09	1.12	1.12	1.06	1.09	1.13	1.15	1.24	0.03
	S	1.06	1.03	1.04	1.01	1.02	1.00	1.02	1.06	1.09	1.11	1.13	1.13	1.14	1.19	1.21	1.26	3.06
Kanagawa	V	1.28	1.22	1.22	1.21	1.20	1.19	1.23	1.25	1.27	1.28	1.31	1.27	1.30	1.31	1.31	1.39	0.02
	S	1.26	1.24	1.24	1.21	1.22	1.18	1.21	1.24	1.27	1.28	1.31	1.31	1.32	1.34	1.35	1.40	1.68
Niigata	V	1.51	1.45	1.38	1.34	1.34	1.34	1.37	1.37	1.37	1.37	1.43	1.41	1.43	1.44	1.43	1.44	0.02
	S	1.50	1.47	1.43	1.36	1.39	1.33	1.37	1.38	1.38	1.38	1.41	1.44	1.42	1.43	1.42	1.43	1.63
Toyama	V	1.45	1.40	1.41	1.35	1.37	1.37	1.34	1.34	1.38	1.37	1.42	1.37	1.42	1.43	1.45	1.51	0.02
	S	1.43	1.40	1.42	1.36	1.37	1.34	1.35	1.36	1.41	1.39	1.41	1.39	1.44	1.45	1.45	1.49	1.26
Ishikawa	V	1.45	1.40	1.37	1.38	1.35	1.35	1.36	1.40	1.41	1.40	1.44	1.43	1.47	1.49	1.45	1.54	0.02
	S	1.45	1.41	1.39	1.39	1.35	1.35	1.36	1.40	1.45	1.43	1.43	1.44	1.51	1.51	1.50	1.57	1.62
Fukui	V	1.60	1.52	1.51	1.47	1.45	1.50	1.50	1.52	1.54	1.55	1.61	1.56	1.60	1.60	1.55	1.63	0.04
	S	1.60	1.56	1.56	1.52	1.48	1.48	1.52	1.56	1.59	1.61	1.58	1.61	1.61	1.62	1.60	1.65	2.42
Yamanashi	V	1.51	1.42	1.39	1.37	1.36	1.38	1.34	1.35	1.35	1.31	1.46	1.41	1.43	1.44	1.43	1.51	0.05
	S	1.50	1.46	1.46	1.43	1.43	1.37	1.39	1.41	1.42	1.40	1.48	1.44	1.46	1.47	1.50	1.51	3.69
Nagano	V	1.59	1.50	1.47	1.44	1.42	1.46	1.44	1.47	1.45	1.43	1.53	1.50	1.51	1.54	1.54	1.58	0.04
	S	1.55	1.55	1.54	1.48	1.48	1.45	1.46	1.49	1.50	1.47	1.51	1.52	1.52	1.56	1.54	1.58	2.40

(continued)

Table 2.11 (continued)

		2000	2001	2002	2003	2004	2005	2006	2007	2008	2009	2010	2011	2012	2013	2014	2015	RMSE RMSPE
Gifu	V	1.47	1.37	1.38	1.36	1.31	1.37	1.35	1.34	1.35	1.37	1.48	1.44	1.45	1.45	1.42	1.56	0.06
	S	1.45	1.41	1.44	1.41	1.38	1.37	1.39	1.41	1.46	1.45	1.46	1.53	1.52	1.53	1.49	1.55	4.49
Shizuoka	V	1.47	1.40	1.41	1.37	1.37	1.39	1.39	1.44	1.44	1.43	1.54	1.49	1.52	1.53	1.50	1.54	0.03
	S	1.45	1.43	1.46	1.41	1.42	1.38	1.41	1.47	1.49	1.49	1.52	1.50	1.54	1.56	1.52	1.54	2.28
Aichi	V	1.44	1.36	1.34	1.32	1.34	1.34	1.36	1.38	1.43	1.43	1.52	1.46	1.46	1.47	1.46	1.57	0.05
	S	1.42	1.40	1.38	1.35	1.36	1.34	1.37	1.42	1.47	1.49	1.51	1.53	1.54	1.54	1.54	1.58	3.24
Mie	V	1.48	1.38	1.40	1.35	1.34	1.36	1.35	1.37	1.38	1.40	1.51	1.47	1.47	1.49	1.45	1.56	0.05
	S	1.44	1.43	1.44	1.40	1.39	1.35	1.39	1.43	1.47	1.49	1.50	1.53	1.53	1.54	1.49	1.54	3.63
Shiga	V	1.53	1.46	1.44	1.41	1.41	1.39	1.41	1.42	1.45	1.44	1.54	1.51	1.53	1.53	1.53	1.61	0.04
	S	1.51	1.49	1.49	1.45	1.44	1.40	1.42	1.46	1.49	1.48	1.52	1.55	1.56	1.61	1.57	1.62	2.53
Kyoto	V	1.28	1.20	1.17	1.15	1.14	1.18	1.19	1.18	1.22	1.20	1.28	1.25	1.23	1.26	1.24	1.35	0.05
	S	1.28	1.25	1.22	1.21	1.17	1.17	1.21	1.22	1.25	1.26	1.29	1.32	1.30	1.32	1.35	1.37	4.16
Osaka	V	1.31	1.24	1.22	1.20	1.20	1.21	1.22	1.24	1.28	1.28	1.33	1.30	1.31	1.32	1.31	1.39	0.04
	S	1.29	1.28	1.26	1.22	1.23	1.20	1.22	1.26	1.29	1.30	1.33	1.35	1.35	1.38	1.38	1.43	2.80
Hyogo	V	1.38	1.29	1.29	1.25	1.24	1.25	1.28	1.30	1.34	1.33	1.41	1.40	1.40	1.42	1.41	1.48	0.03
	S	1.35	1.33	1.32	1.28	1.28	1.25	1.28	1.31	1.36	1.36	1.40	1.43	1.43	1.46	1.46	1.50	2.13
Nara	V	1.30	1.22	1.21	1.18	1.16	1.19	1.22	1.22	1.22	1.23	1.29	1.27	1.32	1.31	1.27	1.38	0.03
	S	1.29	1.26	1.25	1.22	1.20	1.19	1.21	1.25	1.24	1.25	1.29	1.28	1.33	1.34	1.32	1.39	2.26
Wakayama	V	1.45	1.41	1.35	1.32	1.28	1.32	1.34	1.34	1.41	1.36	1.47	1.49	1.53	1.52	1.55	1.54	0.04
	S	1.43	1.42	1.38	1.39	1.31	1.31	1.35	1.34	1.42	1.42	1.44	1.47	1.50	1.49	1.48	1.55	2.51
Tottori	V	1.62	1.58	1.51	1.53	1.50	1.47	1.51	1.47	1.43	1.46	1.54	1.58	1.57	1.62	1.60	1.65	0.04

(continued)

Table 2.11 (continued)

		2000	2001	2002	2003	2004	2005	2006	2007	2008	2009	2010	2011	2012	2013	2014	2015	RMSE RMSPE
Tottori	S	1.58	1.62	1.53	1.56	1.54	1.45	1.52	1.50	1.52	1.52	1.51	1.60	1.57	1.62	1.56	1.62	2.51
Shimane	V	1.65	1.60	1.52	1.48	1.48	1.50	1.53	1.53	1.51	1.55	1.68	1.61	1.68	1.65	1.66	1.78	0.05
	S	1.63	1.66	1.61	1.57	1.53	1.52	1.57	1.56	1.59	1.55	1.64	1.66	1.66	1.67	1.71	1.77	3.25
Okayama	V	1.51	1.46	1.44	1.38	1.38	1.37	1.40	1.41	1.43	1.39	1.50	1.48	1.47	1.49	1.49	1.54	0.04
	S	1.47	1.48	1.47	1.41	1.40	1.37	1.40	1.43	1.47	1.44	1.49	1.52	1.53	1.54	1.55	1.58	2.59
Hiroshima	V	1.41	1.37	1.34	1.34	1.33	1.34	1.37	1.43	1.45	1.47	1.55	1.53	1.54	1.57	1.55	1.60	0.04
	S	1.37	1.40	1.37	1.36	1.36	1.34	1.37	1.44	1.47	1.51	1.55	1.59	1.61	1.62	1.64	1.61	2.62
Yamaguchi	V	1.47	1.43	1.41	1.36	1.36	1.38	1.40	1.42	1.43	1.43	1.56	1.52	1.52	1.56	1.54	1.60	0.03
	S	1.44	1.44	1.44	1.39	1.38	1.37	1.40	1.43	1.45	1.49	1.51	1.55	1.50	1.55	1.53	1.59	1.74
Tokushima	V	1.45	1.39	1.36	1.32	1.31	1.26	1.31	1.30	1.30	1.35	1.42	1.43	1.44	1.43	1.46	1.53	0.03
	S	1.44	1.39	1.41	1.35	1.34	1.28	1.31	1.33	1.34	1.37	1.40	1.46	1.48	1.46	1.45	1.55	2.08
Kagawa	V	1.53	1.43	1.46	1.42	1.43	1.43	1.42	1.48	1.47	1.48	1.57	1.56	1.56	1.59	1.57	1.63	0.02
	S	1.50	1.49	1.47	1.42	1.43	1.42	1.40	1.46	1.49	1.50	1.56	1.56	1.59	1.62	1.59	1.64	1.53
Ehime	V	1.45	1.40	1.35	1.36	1.33	1.35	1.37	1.40	1.40	1.41	1.50	1.51	1.52	1.52	1.50	1.53	0.04
	S	1.42	1.41	1.39	1.38	1.38	1.34	1.37	1.40	1.44	1.45	1.49	1.54	1.57	1.58	1.59	1.55	2.71
Kochi	V	1.45	1.42	1.38	1.34	1.30	1.32	1.33	1.31	1.36	1.29	1.42	1.39	1.43	1.47	1.45	1.51	0.03
	S	1.40	1.45	1.40	1.36	1.31	1.31	1.32	1.34	1.36	1.35	1.39	1.39	1.40	1.47	1.44	1.51	1.88
Fukuoka	V	1.36	1.31	1.29	1.25	1.25	1.26	1.30	1.34	1.37	1.37	1.44	1.42	1.43	1.45	1.46	1.52	0.03
	S	1.35	1.34	1.33	1.29	1.28	1.26	1.29	1.35	1.39	1.40	1.43	1.46	1.45	1.48	1.50	1.54	2.02
Saga	V	1.67	1.62	1.56	1.51	1.49	1.48	1.50	1.51	1.55	1.49	1.61	1.61	1.61	1.59	1.63	1.64	0.03
	S	1.64	1.66	1.57	1.52	1.54	1.49	1.48	1.54	1.59	1.54	1.59	1.64	1.60	1.61	1.63	1.64	1.77

(continued)

Table 2.11 (continued)

		2000	2001	2002	2003	2004	2005	2006	2007	2008	2009	2010	2011	2012	2013	2014	2015	RMSE RMSPE
Nagasaki	V	1.57	1.52	1.48	1.45	1.46	1.45	1.49	1.48	1.50	1.50	1.61	1.60	1.63	1.64	1.66	1.67	0.02
	S	1.57	1.53	1.51	1.49	1.48	1.45	1.48	1.50	1.52	1.54	1.59	1.60	1.64	1.64	1.66	1.67	1.35
Kumamoto	V	1.56	1.52	1.50	1.48	1.47	1.46	1.50	1.54	1.58	1.58	1.62	1.62	1.62	1.65	1.64	1.68	0.05
	S	1.54	1.54	1.54	1.49	1.50	1.47	1.49	1.53	1.58	1.58	1.62	1.49	1.53	1.58	1.58	1.62	3.14
Oita	V	1.51	1.48	1.42	1.41	1.40	1.40	1.45	1.47	1.53	1.50	1.56	1.55	1.53	1.56	1.57	1.59	0.02
	S	1.49	1.49	1.46	1.41	1.40	1.40	1.44	1.46	1.52	1.52	1.54	1.58	1.56	1.58	1.59	1.58	1.31
Miyazaki	V	1.62	1.60	1.56	1.49	1.52	1.48	1.55	1.59	1.60	1.61	1.68	1.68	1.67	1.72	1.69	1.71	0.02
	S	1.59	1.61	1.59	1.51	1.53	1.48	1.52	1.59	1.62	1.61	1.67	1.67	1.69	1.70	1.72	1.71	1.13
Kagoshima	V	1.58	1.53	1.52	1.49	1.46	1.49	1.51	1.54	1.59	1.56	1.62	1.64	1.64	1.63	1.62	1.70	0.02
	S	1.56	1.56	1.56	1.52	1.50	1.49	1.51	1.53	1.57	1.57	1.62	1.66	1.66	1.66	1.65	1.71	1.53
Okinawa	V	1.82	1.83	1.76	1.72	1.72	1.72	1.74	1.75	1.78	1.79	1.87	1.86	1.90	1.94	1.86	1.96	0.02
	S	1.83	1.85	1.80	1.76	1.72	1.71	1.72	1.77	1.79	1.81	1.85	1.89	1.90	1.92	1.90	1.95	1.22

Source Created by the author based on the calculated estimates of this study
Note RMSE: root mean square error, RMSPE: root mean square percentage error. V in this table indicates vital statistics, S indicates study estimates

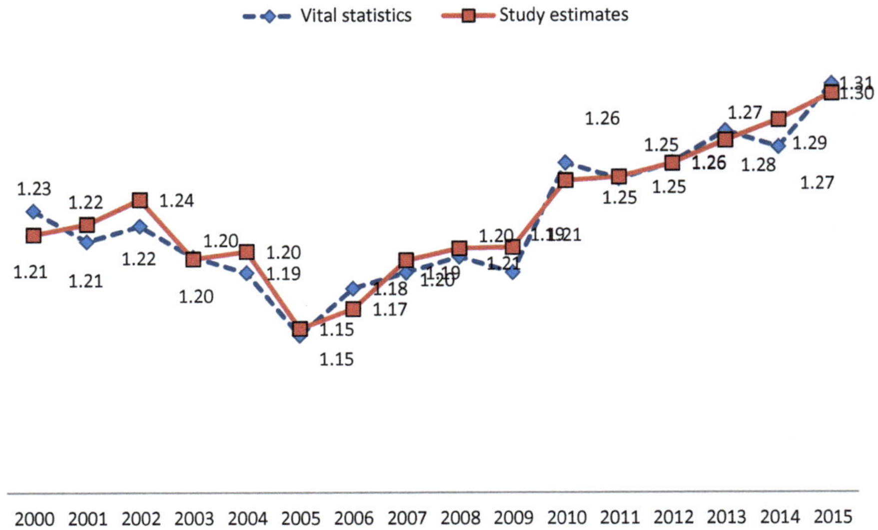

Fig. 2.9 Comparison of TFR estimates from this study for Hokkaido Prefecture with results from Vital statistics. *Source* Created by the author based on the calculated estimates of this study

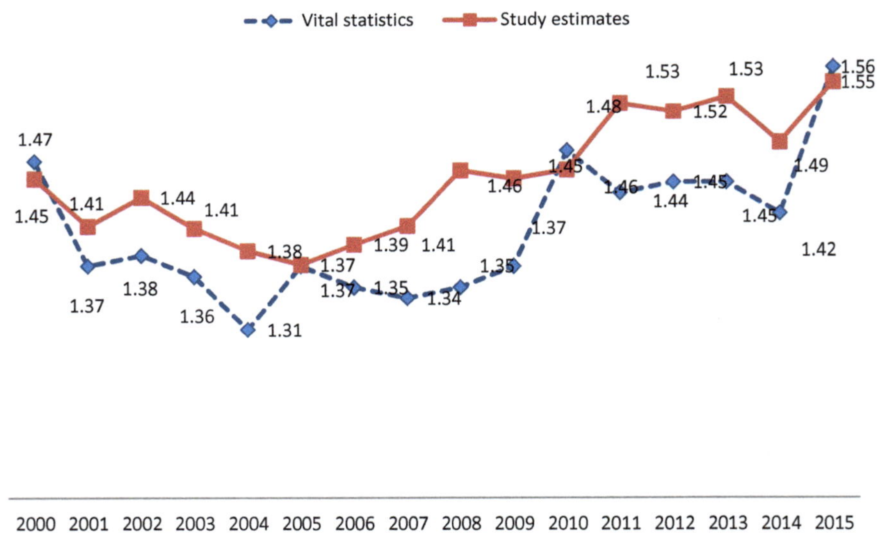

Fig. 2.10 Comparison of TFR estimates from this study for Gifu Prefecture with results from Vital statistics. *Source* Created by the author based on the calculated estimates of this study

Table 2.12 TFR estimates (private and public sector, excluding agriculture, forestry and fisheries sector), by prefecture

	2000	2001	2002	2003	2004	2005	2006	2007	2008	2009	2010	2011	2012	2013	2014	2015
Hokkaido	0.32	0.33	0.34	0.34	0.35	0.35	0.37	0.39	0.41	0.42	0.45	0.49	0.53	0.57	0.61	0.66
Aomori	0.68	0.71	0.71	0.72	0.75	0.66	0.70	0.71	0.76	0.75	0.78	0.82	0.86	0.91	0.98	1.00
Iwate	0.77	0.77	0.77	0.74	0.73	0.73	0.71	0.72	0.71	0.70	0.71	0.85	0.92	0.97	1.00	1.07
Miyagi	0.61	0.60	0.60	0.59	0.58	0.57	0.57	0.59	0.61	0.60	0.62	0.65	0.71	0.76	0.77	0.83
Akita	0.82	0.80	0.80	0.79	0.78	0.79	0.75	0.73	0.71	0.63	0.61	0.78	0.85	0.91	1.02	1.12
Yamagata	1.03	1.04	1.01	0.96	0.95	0.91	0.93	0.94	0.97	0.96	0.98	1.06	1.06	1.12	1.18	1.20
Fukushima	0.85	0.85	0.84	0.81	0.80	0.77	0.78	0.77	0.78	0.77	0.77	0.87	0.83	0.91	0.99	1.03
Ibaraki	0.56	0.55	0.55	0.53	0.53	0.51	0.53	0.56	0.58	0.59	0.62	0.65	0.68	0.72	0.75	0.81
Tochigi	0.57	0.58	0.57	0.56	0.55	0.55	0.57	0.58	0.62	0.63	0.64	0.67	0.68	0.73	0.74	0.79
Gunma	0.49	0.49	0.49	0.49	0.49	0.48	0.51	0.54	0.57	0.60	0.62	0.67	0.68	0.73	0.78	0.83
Saitama	0.36	0.36	0.36	0.36	0.37	0.37	0.40	0.43	0.46	0.49	0.52	0.56	0.57	0.63	0.66	0.70
Chiba	0.38	0.38	0.38	0.38	0.38	0.38	0.41	0.44	0.48	0.52	0.55	0.59	0.60	0.65	0.67	0.72
Tokyo	0.37	0.37	0.39	0.39	0.40	0.40	0.44	0.48	0.52	0.56	0.60	0.63	0.67	0.74	0.78	0.85
Kanagawa	0.35	0.36	0.36	0.36	0.37	0.37	0.40	0.44	0.48	0.51	0.56	0.59	0.63	0.67	0.71	0.77
Niigata	0.75	0.74	0.71	0.68	0.69	0.66	0.69	0.72	0.73	0.75	0.78	0.83	0.86	0.90	0.93	0.97
Toyama	0.67	0.66	0.69	0.68	0.71	0.64	0.66	0.68	0.73	0.74	0.77	0.79	0.85	0.89	0.93	1.00
Ishikawa	0.69	0.67	0.67	0.67	0.65	0.66	0.68	0.72	0.76	0.77	0.79	0.82	0.90	0.94	0.96	1.09
Fukui	0.82	0.80	0.80	0.78	0.77	0.76	0.80	0.84	0.88	0.91	0.92	0.97	1.01	1.06	1.09	1.17
Yamanashi	0.54	0.52	0.52	0.51	0.51	0.49	0.52	0.55	0.57	0.59	0.64	0.65	0.69	0.72	0.78	0.81
Nagano	0.47	0.47	0.47	0.45	0.45	0.45	0.47	0.50	0.53	0.54	0.58	0.61	0.64	0.69	0.72	0.77
Gifu	0.44	0.43	0.44	0.43	0.42	0.42	0.44	0.46	0.50	0.52	0.54	0.59	0.62	0.66	0.67	0.73
Shizuoka	0.46	0.47	0.48	0.47	0.48	0.48	0.51	0.55	0.58	0.60	0.63	0.66	0.70	0.74	0.76	0.80

(continued)

Table 2.12 (continued)

	2000	2001	2002	2003	2004	2005	2006	2007	2008	2009	2010	2011	2012	2013	2014	2015
Aichi	0.40	0.40	0.40	0.39	0.40	0.39	0.42	0.46	0.50	0.53	0.56	0.61	0.64	0.68	0.71	0.76
Mie	0.49	0.49	0.48	0.47	0.47	0.45	0.49	0.52	0.56	0.59	0.61	0.65	0.69	0.72	0.72	0.78
Shiga	0.52	0.52	0.53	0.52	0.53	0.52	0.54	0.57	0.59	0.60	0.64	0.68	0.72	0.78	0.81	0.87
Kyoto	0.46	0.45	0.44	0.44	0.43	0.44	0.47	0.49	0.52	0.55	0.57	0.62	0.64	0.69	0.73	0.78
Osaka	0.36	0.36	0.37	0.36	0.37	0.37	0.40	0.43	0.46	0.49	0.52	0.56	0.60	0.65	0.68	0.75
Hyogo	0.40	0.40	0.40	0.39	0.39	0.39	0.41	0.45	0.48	0.51	0.54	0.59	0.62	0.66	0.70	0.75
Nara	0.39	0.39	0.39	0.39	0.39	0.39	0.41	0.44	0.45	0.48	0.51	0.54	0.59	0.63	0.65	0.72
Wakayama	0.42	0.42	0.42	0.42	0.40	0.40	0.43	0.43	0.47	0.49	0.50	0.55	0.60	0.64	0.67	0.74
Tottori	0.80	0.83	0.79	0.81	0.82	0.76	0.81	0.81	0.86	0.86	0.87	1.00	1.04	1.14	1.15	1.29
Shimane	0.85	0.86	0.84	0.83	0.81	0.81	0.86	0.89	0.92	0.93	1.01	1.09	1.16	1.25	1.37	1.51
Okayama	0.56	0.57	0.57	0.55	0.56	0.56	0.58	0.61	0.65	0.66	0.70	0.76	0.81	0.85	0.90	0.97
Hiroshima	0.46	0.48	0.48	0.48	0.48	0.48	0.51	0.55	0.57	0.61	0.63	0.69	0.74	0.79	0.85	0.88
Yamaguchi	0.49	0.49	0.49	0.48	0.48	0.48	0.50	0.52	0.55	0.58	0.60	0.66	0.70	0.77	0.81	0.89
Tokushima	0.66	0.65	0.67	0.65	0.65	0.62	0.65	0.68	0.69	0.72	0.75	0.81	0.86	0.89	0.93	1.04
Kagawa	0.60	0.59	0.61	0.59	0.61	0.60	0.62	0.65	0.69	0.71	0.76	0.79	0.85	0.91	0.94	1.00
Ehime	0.46	0.47	0.47	0.47	0.49	0.48	0.50	0.52	0.55	0.56	0.59	0.65	0.71	0.76	0.82	0.85
Kochi	0.70	0.72	0.69	0.67	0.65	0.64	0.67	0.70	0.73	0.75	0.79	0.83	0.90	0.99	1.03	1.14
Fukuoka	0.47	0.47	0.47	0.46	0.46	0.46	0.48	0.53	0.56	0.58	0.62	0.67	0.70	0.76	0.80	0.87
Saga	0.72	0.73	0.69	0.69	0.70	0.66	0.66	0.71	0.75	0.74	0.79	0.87	0.91	0.98	1.05	1.13
Nagasaki	0.67	0.66	0.65	0.65	0.65	0.64	0.67	0.70	0.73	0.75	0.79	0.85	0.92	0.98	1.05	1.12
Kumamoto	0.66	0.67	0.67	0.66	0.67	0.66	0.70	0.73	0.78	0.80	0.84	0.85	0.92	0.99	1.06	1.17
Oita	0.54	0.54	0.53	0.51	0.50	0.50	0.53	0.57	0.62	0.64	0.67	0.73	0.77	0.83	0.89	0.94

(continued)

Table 2.12 (continued)

	2000	2001	2002	2003	2004	2005	2006	2007	2008	2009	2010	2011	2012	2013	2014	2015
Miyazaki	0.65	0.66	0.66	0.64	0.65	0.63	0.68	0.73	0.77	0.78	0.85	0.90	0.98	1.06	1.15	1.22
Kagoshima	0.51	0.53	0.54	0.54	0.55	0.55	0.57	0.60	0.64	0.67	0.71	0.77	0.83	0.88	0.92	1.01
Okinawa	0.85	0.86	0.84	0.82	0.81	0.81	0.83	0.88	0.91	0.94	0.99	1.07	1.13	1.22	1.27	1.37

Source As estimated by the author

a regional concentration of a particular industry. The geographical space distribution of employees for industry i in region j can be expressed as a proportion ratio, s_{ij}^{c}, relative to the distribution in the country as a whole[13]:

$$s_{ij}^{c} = \frac{x_{ij}}{\sum_{l=i}^{n} x_{ij}} = \frac{x_{ij}}{x_{i*}} \quad i = 1, 2, \ldots, n, \quad j = 1, 2, \ldots, m \tag{2.1}$$

A high value here indicates that industry i is relatively concentrated in region j. In general, the distribution of employment for any industry in region j, s_{*j}, will be in the form:

$$s_{*j} = \frac{\sum_{i=1}^{m} x_{ij}}{\sum_{i=1}^{m} \sum_{j=1}^{n} x_{ij}} = \frac{x_{*j}}{x_{**}}. \tag{2.2}$$

s_{*j} indicates the size of the regional economy as measured by the number of employees. Equation (2.1) divided by Eq. (2.2) gives Eq. (2.3), which can be regarded as the relative concentration index of industry i in region j.

$$LQ_{ij}^{c} = \frac{s_{ij}^{c}}{s_{*j}} = \frac{x_{ij}/x_{i*}}{x_{*j}/x_{**}} \tag{2.3}$$

2. Relative specialization index toward industry i in region j as compared to other industries.

   Next, the difference between Eqs. (2.1) and (2.2) can be used to indicate whether there is a relative specialization in industry i in region j in comparison to other industries. A positive value will indicate relative specialization.

$$s_{ij}^{c} - s_{*j} \tag{2.4}$$

3. Location index (number of employees and scale of operation locations).

   The next index has to do with whether there is an accumulation of business locations (e.g., factories) in a particular area. If y_{ij} is the number of locations (e.g., factories) for industry i in region j, the specialization coefficient, $LQ_{ij}^{s(p)}$, will be:

$$LQ_{ij}^{s(p)} = \frac{y_{ij}/y_{*j}}{y_{i*}/y_{**}}. \tag{2.5}$$

For the number of employees, the specialization coefficient will be:

$$LQ_{ij}^{s(E)} = \frac{x_{ij}/x_{*j}}{x_{i*}/x_{**}}. \tag{2.6}$$

The ratio of Eqs. (2.5)–(2.6) is as follows

[13] Author removed K and instead added i and j in Eq. (1) in Nakamura (2008), p. 103.

$$\frac{LQ_{ij}^{s(E)}}{LQ_{ij}^{S(P)}} = \frac{x_{ij}/x_{*j}}{x_{i*}/x_{**}} / \frac{y_{ij}/y_{*j}}{y_{i*}/y_{**}} = \underbrace{\frac{x_{ij}/y_{ij}}{x_{*j}/y_{*j}}}_{\substack{\text{Relative scale}\\ \text{of industry } i\\ \text{in region } j}} / \underbrace{\frac{x_{i*}/y_{i*}}{x_{**}/y_{**}}}_{\substack{\text{Relative scale}\\ \text{of industry } i \text{ in}\\ \text{the whole country}}} . \quad (2.7)$$

If the "relative scale of industry *i* in region *j* is larger than in Japan as a whole," this means that the degree of agglomeration measured by the number of employees is greater than the degree measured by the number of business locations, so the companies located in the region are relatively large. This shows in turn that industry *i* exists in an environment tending toward a regional monopoly. If it is "smaller than in Japan as a whole," the specialization is distributed among a number of smaller-scale locations, which indicates a more competitive regional situation.

4. Specialization-type and urbanization-type agglomeration index.
   In addition to the above three indices first proposed by Nakamura (2008), this study also adopts the specialization-type and urbanization-type agglomeration index devised by Konishi and Saito (2012). Konishi and Saito (2012)[14] use The Census of Manufactures[15] to estimate their agglomeration index for manufacturing locations. This index is not based on statistics kept by administrative units, but on estimates of the distances between individual business locations, and can thus reflect differences in agglomeration density within the same administrative area.
   A further feature of the data created in this way is that they can be presented without spatial correlation bias by dividing the administrative units. Furthermore, two distinct types of agglomeration index can be obtained, "specialization type" and "urbanization type," using the information from the main and sub-classifications in JSIC, respectively.
   Konishi and Saito (2012) assume that the effects (merits and demerits) of agglomeration as felt at the business location will be different in each case. But irrespective of this, the distances between each location and all other locations are cumulatively calculated in every case, and the agglomeration (density) index is estimated using the following five equation formulas.
   emp_j is the number of employees in each business location, j, ind_j is the industrial classification of the location j, and d_{ij} is the distance between business location *i* and business location j.

[14] This explanation step is based on Konishi and Saito (2012), pp. 6–7, "3. Creation of agglomeration index.".

[15] This census is data of Japan Standard Industrial Classification (JSIC). See note 5.

$$Agglomeration\_index_i^{5\,\mathrm{km}} = \sum_{j \in S_i^{5\,\mathrm{km}}} \mathrm{emp}, \mathrm{S}_\mathrm{i}^{5\,\mathrm{m}} = \{j : d_{ij} \le 5\,\mathrm{km}, ind_j = ind_j\} \quad (2.8)$$

$$Agglomeration\_index_i^{10\,\mathrm{km}} = \sum_{j \in S_i^{10\,\mathrm{km}}} \mathrm{emp}, \mathrm{S}_\mathrm{i}^{10\,\mathrm{m}} = \{j : d_{ij} \le 10\,\mathrm{km}, ind_j = ind_j\} \quad (2.9)$$

$$Agglomeration\_index_i^{20\,\mathrm{km}} = \sum_{j \in S_i^{20\,\mathrm{km}}} \mathrm{emp}, \mathrm{S}_\mathrm{i}^{20\,\mathrm{m}} = \{j : d_{ij} \le 20\,\mathrm{km}, ind_j = ind_j\} \quad (2.10)$$

$$Agglomeration\_index_i^{potential} = \sum_{j \in S_i^{potential}} \frac{emp_j}{d_{ij}}, \mathrm{S}_\mathrm{i}^{\mathrm{potential}} = \{j : ind_j = ind_j\} \quad (2.11)$$

$$Agglomeration\_index_i^{potential2} = \sum_{j \in S_i^{potential2}} \frac{emp_j}{d_{ij}^2}, \mathrm{S}_\mathrm{i}^{\mathrm{potential2}} = \{j : ind_j = ind_j\} \quad (2.12)$$

Equations (2.8)–(2.10) indicate the numbers of employees for each distance range as measured from a superposed mesh, meaning in this case the numbers of workers employed in business locations of the same industrial classification type as the one being considered, within ranges of 5, 10, and 20 km.

Equations (2.11) and (2.12) are data decay calculations that allow for a diminution in the impact of agglomeration on business locations as a function of distance. The distance decay function is the reciprocal of the distance in Eq. (2.11) and the reciprocal of the square of the distance in Eq. (2.12). In addition, JSIC information[16] is used to calculate two distinct agglomeration indexes of a "specialization" and "urbanization" type. If the 4-digit numbers of the JSIC coding are the same for two locations, it is a case of specialized agglomeration. Otherwise, provided the other location produces goods and can be classed as manufacturing, this counts as agglomeration of the urbanization type. In this study, I have used the data calculated by Konishi and Saito (2012) for the average values of the agglomeration costs of specialization and urbanization by region.

2.7.3 Analysis Results Obtained with TFR and Agglomeration Economy Indexes

The first table of results, Table 2.13, presents correlation coefficients between the logarithms of TFRs (grand totals) in the various industrial sectors of Japanese prefectures and population densities (in the same prefectures) for the years 2000, 2005, 2010, and 2015. Figures 2.11 and 2.12 show the same results in a scatter plot form.

From similar results, using TFR data from vital statistics, Morita and Yamamoto (2014) show that agglomerations of companies and diversity of consumer goods are reflected in gaps in fertility between regions. In addition, agglomerations of

[16] This is taken from Konishi and Saito (2012), p. 12, Table 5.

Table 2.13 Correlation coefficients between TFR by industry and population density, both at the prefectural level

	2000–2015	2000	2005	2010	2015
Total	– 0.473**	– 0.591**	– 0.568**	– 0.468**	– 0.391**
Employed	– 0.303**	– 0.456**	– 0.434**	– 0.330	– 0.184
Agriculture, forestry, and fisheries	– 0.131**	– 0.227	– 0.104	– 0.145	– 0.128
Construction	– 0.041	– 0.299	– 0.220	– 0.048	– 0.044
Manufacturing	– 0.243**	– 0.357	– 0.338*	– 0.281	– 0.120
Electricity, gas, heat supply and water	0.036	– 0.201	– 0.056	0.100	0.260
Transport and information and communications	– 0.089*	– 0.317*	– 0.183	– 0.014	0.142
Finance and insurance	– 0.129**	– 0.257	– 0.265	– 0.222	0.029
Real estate business	– 0.086*	– 0.168	– 0.151	– 0.007	0.096
Wholesale and retail trade	– 0.251**	– 0.341*	– 0.324*	– 0.264	– 0.113
Services	– 0.315**	– 0.467*	– 0.468**	– 0.342	– 0.413**
Government	0.111	0.026	0.039	0.095	0.420**
Private and public sectors, excluding agriculture, forestry and fisheries	– 0.292**	– 0.445**	– 0.425**	– 0.312*	– 0.293*
Private sector, excluding agriculture, forestry and fisheries	– 0.279**	– 0.444**	– 0.424**	– 0.312*	– 0.300*
Non employed	– 0.385**	– 0.540**	– 0.463**	– 0.362	– 0.373**
Number of samples	752	47	47	47	47

Source As estimated by the author
Note ** is significant at a level of 0.01%, * is significant at a level of 0.05%

workplaces contribute to rises in regional nominal income. Employees choose to work longer hours, at the cost of having fewer children, while the cost of child-rearing also rises. Sato (2007), also taking TFR data from vital statistics, shows theoretically why areas with stronger agglomeration economies have higher population densities and wage rates but lower TFRs.

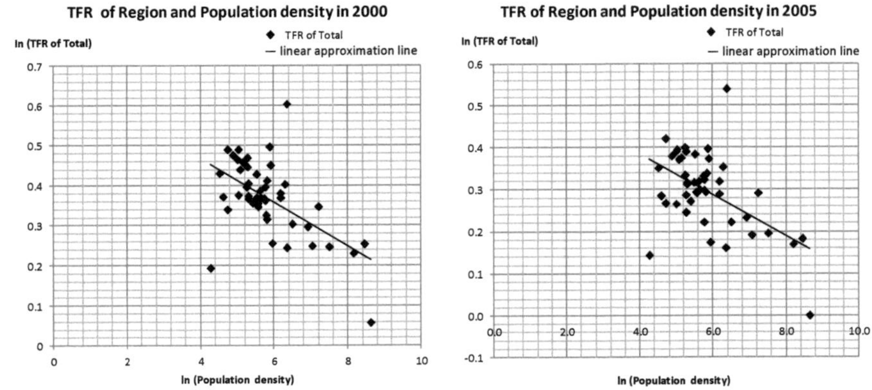

Fig. 2.11 Scatter plot of regional TFR (grand totals) and population density for 2000 and 2005. *Source* Created by the author based on the calculated estimates of this study

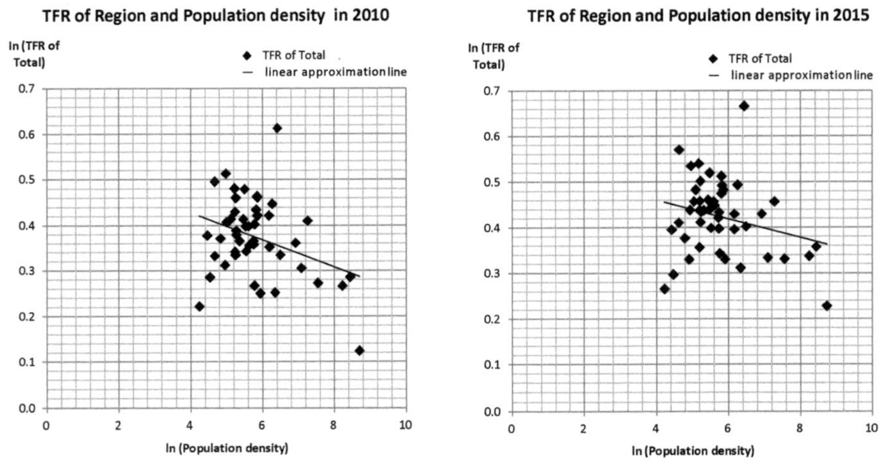

Fig. 2.12 Scatter plot of regional TFR (grand totals) and population density for 2010 and 2015. *Source* Created by the author based on the calculated estimates of this study

Looking at Table 2.13, most correlation coefficients between TFR and population density are negative, with exceptions for Electricity, etc. (2010, 2015), Government, and Transport, etc. (2015), Finance and Insurance (2015), and Real estate (2015). These results are similar to ones in Sato (2007) and Morita and Yamamoto (2014). The coefficients are at high levels of significance in many industrial sectors.

Sato (2007) shows that the differences in fertility rates are affected by wage rate differences, and that, in the equilibrium state, TFRs are lower in areas with higher population densities. Further, the average number of children born to the current generation of women is smaller in more populated areas. This is shown in Table 1 of Sato (2007)[17] with average and median values for prefectural TFRs (2000 rates) divided into three categories according to the prefecture's population density.

The TFRs by industrial sectors from 2000 to 2015 used in this study are shown in Tables 2.14 and 2.15. In these Tables, the 17 prefectures with the lowest population densities are ranked as "Low," the 15 with the highest densities are ranked as "High," and the remaining 15 are ranked as "Medium." The highlighted results are ones in which the relation between population density and TFR is different from what was theoretically expected. The population density and the TFR are either both high together, or both low together. As already mentioned, population density is divided into three categories. Looking for patterns in particular industrial sectors, the TFRs in Agriculture, forestry and fisheries tend to be high in areas with low population density, which matches the theory, but Electricity, gas, heat supply, water, Real estate, and Government all diverge from the theory. Also, starting around 2011, there are some diverging years in the Construction, Transport, and Finance and insurance sectors. Regarding these divergences, it seems to make no significant difference whether averages or medians are used for the categories of population density.

In the private sector overall, then, TFRs were close to what was theoretically expected. In other words, areas with a high population density have a low TFR, and areas with a high population density have a high TFR. The TFR in the government sector is unlikely to be affected by agglomeration economy factors because there are no significant regional differences in wage rates and the ease of taking childcare leave is similar everywhere.

For the economy to remain in a steady state, some people born in lower-density areas have to move to higher-density ones. Overall, this shows as a net movement of population from low to high, as people more often move out of sparsely populated areas into densely populated ones. Evidence for this in this study is shown in Table 2.16. For every year shown, densely populated areas have a large surplus of migrants coming in, and low-density areas have a surplus moving out.

Next, Table 2.17 shows correlations between eight commonly cited indicators of an agglomeration economy, TFRs in manufacturing, and TFRs in other private employment sectors (excluding agriculture, forestry, and fisheries). The eight indicators are (1) relative concentration of manufacturing, (2) relative regional specialization in manufacturing compared to other sectors, (3) specialization within manufacturing in each region, (4) number and scale of manufacturing locations, (5) number and scale of service locations, (6) number of manufacturing employees per habitable unit area, (7) specialization-type agglomeration index, and (8) urbanization-type ag-glomeration index. (For details, refer back to Sect. 2.7 2, above.)

The correlation coefficients found for four of these indicators matched what was theoretically expected for an agglomeration economy. These indicators were the number and scale of manufacturing locations, the number of manufacturing employees per habitable unit area, the specialization-type agglomeration index, and the urbanization-type agglomeration index.

---

[17] See Sato (2007), p. 375.

Table 2.14 Prefectural population density and TFR by industry (average for each population density level)

Year	Population density level	Total fertility rate							
		Total	Employed	Agriculture, etc.	Construction	Manufacturing	Electricity, etc.	Transport, etc.	Finance and insurance
2000	Low	1.51	0.70	1.35	0.85	0.73	0.81	0.54	0.58
	Medium	1.46	0.55	1.18	0.72	0.56	0.69	0.44	0.47
	High	1.38	0.47	1.13	0.66	0.48	0.67	0.36	0.42
2001	Low	1.51	0.70	1.33	0.89	0.72	0.76	0.53	0.62
	Medium	1.46	0.56	1.17	0.72	0.58	**0.78**	0.45	0.48
	High	1.36	0.47	1.13	0.68	0.47	0.68	0.37	0.43
2002	Low	1.49	0.69	1.30	0.91	0.71	0.76	0.52	0.63
	Medium	1.44	0.56	1.15	0.74	0.57	**0.81**	0.42	0.49
	High	1.35	0.47	1.12	0.70	0.48	0.69	0.37	0.44
2003	Low	1.44	0.68	1.23	0.87	0.69	0.77	0.51	0.65
	Medium	1.41	0.55	1.10	0.75	0.55	**0.81**	0.40	0.50
	High	1.32	0.47	1.10	0.71	0.48	0.69	0.37	0.45
2004	Low	1.43	0.68	1.20	0.86	0.69	0.80	0.50	0.71
	Medium	1.39	0.55	1.08	0.78	0.55	**0.85**	0.40	0.51
	High	1.31	0.47	**1.09**	0.75	0.48	0.71	0.38	0.47
2005	Low	1.39	0.66	1.16	0.86	0.67	0.81	0.49	0.73
	Medium	1.37	0.54	1.04	0.79	0.55	**0.87**	0.38	0.52
	High	1.29	0.47	**1.06**	0.77	0.48	0.71	0.37	0.48
2006	Low	1.42	0.69	1.09	0.88	0.70	0.83	0.51	0.72
	Medium	1.39	0.56	1.04	0.81	0.57	0.84	0.40	0.55
	High	1.31	0.50	**1.10**	0.79	0.51	0.75	0.40	0.52
2007	Low	1.43	0.72	1.10	0.89	0.72	0.84	0.53	0.80
	Medium	1.41	0.59	1.04	0.85	0.60	0.82	0.43	0.59
	High	1.35	0.54	**1.13**	0.82	0.54	0.79	**0.44**	0.57
2008	Low	1.45	0.75	1.11	0.92	0.75	0.86	0.54	0.79
	Medium	**1.46**	**0.63**	1.07	0.89	0.64	0.81	0.46	0.64
	High	1.38	0.57	**1.17**	0.85	0.57	**0.82**	**0.48**	0.61
2009	Low	1.44	0.76	**1.09**	0.92	0.76	0.87	0.56	0.80
	Medium	**1.46**	**0.65**	**1.12**	0.92	0.67	0.72	0.49	0.68
	High	1.38	0.59	**1.14**	0.87	0.58	**0.89**	0.49	0.65
2010	Low	1.48	0.79	1.14	0.98	0.89	0.83	0.58	0.82
	Medium	1.48	**0.68**	1.11	0.95	0.69	0.65	0.51	0.72
	High	1.42	0.63	**1.18**	0.90	0.62	**0.94**	**0.53**	0.70
2011	Low	1.49	0.82	1.17	1.01	0.92	0.82	0.62	0.86
	Medium	**1.50**	**0.71**	1.14	1.00	0.71	0.74	0.55	0.76
	High	1.43	0.66	**1.18**	0.94	0.66	**0.99**	**0.56**	**0.81**
2012	Low	1.49	0.84	1.18	1.02	0.94	0.81	0.64	0.89

(continued)

Table 2.14 (continued)

Year	Population density level	Total fertility rate							
		Total	Employed	Agriculture, etc.	Construction	Manufacturing	Electricity, etc.	Transport, etc.	Finance and insurance
2012	Medium	**1.51**	**0.74**	**1.19**	**1.04**	0.74	0.80	0.59	0.81
	High	1.43	0.69	1.18	0.97	0.69	**1.02**	0.59	**0.90**
2013	Low	1.50	0.87	1.20	1.04	0.98	0.81	0.68	0.94
	Medium	**1.53**	0.77	**1.24**	**1.08**	0.76	0.86	0.63	0.85
	High	1.46	0.73	**1.20**	1.01	0.72	**1.08**	**0.64**	**1.00**
2014	Low	1.51	0.89	**1.22**	1.05	1.01	0.81	0.70	0.98
	Medium	**1.52**	0.85	**1.23**	**1.12**	0.79	**0.86**	**0.71**	0.90
	High	1.46	0.76	**1.19**	1.04	0.76	**1.10**	0.66	**1.05**
2015	Low	1.54	0.92	1.24	1.02	1.04	0.80	0.74	1.10
	Medium	**1.56**	0.83	**1.31**	**1.17**	0.79	**0.99**	0.71	0.97
	High	1.50	0.80	1.23	1.10	0.79	**1.18**	0.72	**1.14**

Year	Population density level	Total fertility rate						
		Real estate business	Wholesale and retail trade	Services	Government	Privately/publicly employed	Privately employed	Non employed
2000	Low	0.61	0.53	0.74	0.80	0.69	0.69	3.30
	Medium	0.38	0.38	0.65	0.79	0.55	0.54	3.17
	High	**0.51**	0.34	0.54	**0.85**	0.47	0.46	2.87
2001	Low	0.60	0.53	0.73	0.82	0.69	0.66	3.33
	Medium	0.42	0.38	0.64	0.80	0.56	0.55	3.21
	High	**0.53**	0.34	0.53	**0.85**	0.47	0.46	2.88
2002	Low	0.57	0.52	0.73	0.83	0.68	0.66	3.32
	Medium	0.45	0.38	0.63	0.81	0.56	0.55	3.21
	High	**0.47**	0.33	0.53	**0.84**	0.47	0.46	2.89
2003	Low	0.55	0.51	0.72	0.82	0.67	0.65	3.23
	Medium	0.47	0.38	0.61	0.80	0.54	0.54	3.17
	High	0.45	0.33	0.51	**0.83**	0.47	0.46	2.86
2004	Low	0.54	0.51	0.72	0.83	0.67	0.65	3.22
	Medium	0.50	0.38	0.60	0.81	0.55	0.54	3.17
	High	0.44	0.33	0.51	**0.83**	0.47	0.46	2.89
2005	Low	0.52	0.49	0.70	0.83	0.65	0.65	3.16
	Medium	**0.53**	0.37	0.58	0.82	0.53	0.53	3.15
	High	0.44	0.33	0.50	0.82	0.47	0.46	2.87
2006	Low	0.56	0.51	0.72	0.86	0.68	0.67	3.22
	Medium	0.53	0.39	0.60	0.84	0.56	0.55	3.19
	High	0.45	0.35	0.53	0.86	0.49	0.48	2.92
2007	Low	0.59	0.52	0.73	0.88	0.70	0.69	3.25
	Medium	0.53	0.41	0.63	0.87	0.58	0.57	**3.26**
	High	0.48	0.38	0.57	**0.91**	0.53	0.52	3.00
2008	Low	0.59	0.55	0.75	0.91	0.72	0.66	3.29

(continued)

Table 2.14 (continued)

Year	Population density level	Total fertility rate						
		Real estate business	Wholesale and retail trade	Services	Government	Privately/ publicly employed	Privately employed	Non employed
2008	Medium	0.53	0.43	0.67	0.91	0.62	0.61	**3.35**
	High	0.50	0.40	0.60	**0.95**	0.56	0.55	3.07
2009	Low	0.59	0.56	0.76	0.92	0.73	0.67	3.26
	Medium	0.53	0.45	0.70	**0.93**	0.64	0.63	**3.36**
	High	0.51	0.41	0.62	**0.96**	0.58	0.57	3.09
2010	Low	0.60	0.59	0.78	0.96	0.76	0.74	3.33
	Medium	0.54	0.47	0.73	0.96	0.67	0.66	**3.42**
	High	0.53	0.43	0.66	**1.00**	0.61	0.60	3.16
2011	Low	0.63	0.61	0.91	0.96	0.83	0.82	3.40
	Medium	0.58	0.49	0.79	**1.00**	0.72	0.71	**3.47**
	High	0.58	0.46	0.70	**1.03**	0.65	0.64	3.20
2012	Low	0.65	0.62	0.98	0.96	0.87	0.87	3.41
	Medium	0.60	0.51	0.86	**1.02**	0.76	0.75	**3.55**
	High	**0.63**	0.49	0.75	**1.05**	0.69	0.68	3.22
2013	Low	0.68	0.64	1.08	0.97	0.93	0.93	3.48
	Medium	0.64	0.54	0.93	**1.05**	0.81	0.80	**3.64**
	High	**0.69**	0.52	0.81	**1.08**	0.74	0.73	3.30
2014	Low	0.71	0.66	1.17	0.98	0.98	0.98	3.52
	Medium	0.65	0.58	0.97	**1.06**	0.86	0.85	3.47
	High	**0.72**	0.54	0.84	**1.09**	0.77	0.77	3.30
2015	Low	0.75	0.69	1.29	0.99	1.06	1.06	3.62
	Medium	0.69	0.60	1.09	**1.10**	0.92	0.91	**3.80**
	High	**0.79**	0.58	0.92	**1.14**	0.83	0.83	3.41

Source As estimated by the author
Note Agriculture in Table 2.14 is inclusive of Forestry and Fisheries. Electricity is inclusive of Gas, Heat Supply and Water. Transport is inclusive of Information and Communications. Privately employed women's TFR is excluding agriculture, forestry and fisheries. Privately/publicly employed women's TFR is excluding agriculture, forestry and fisheries
Bold indicates data of TFR.

Regarding the specialization-type and urbanization-type agglomeration indexes, Konishi and Saito (2012) give average values for 1995, 2000, and 2005 by prefecture. For this study, therefore, it was possible to calculate the TFR correlation coefficients for these indexes for the years 2000 and 2005. In addition, as the agglomeration index in Table 2.17 was created using data from the manufacturing sector, the relationships with TFRs in the manufacturing industry could be obtained.

Table 2.18 shows average and median TFR values in different industrial sectors for the three agglomeration levels as identified respectively in the specialization-type index (agglomeration for the production of one kind of good) and the urbanization-type index (agglomeration for the production of various goods). The results obtained with both types of agglomeration index were in line with what was theoretically expected. Areas with high specialization-type agglomeration economies had low

Table 2.15 Prefectural population density and TFR by industry (median for each population density level)

Year	Population density level	Total fertility rate							
		Total	Employed	Agriculture, etc.	Construction	Manufacturing	Electricity, etc.	Transport, etc.	Finance and insurance
2000	Low	1.54	0.70	1.35	0.79	0.72	0.87	0.57	0.65
	Medium	1.44	0.52	1.08	0.73	0.51	0.75	0.42	0.47
	High	1.35	0.41	**1.11**	0.64	0.40	0.56	0.33	0.37
2001	Low	1.54	0.72	1.29	0.83	0.73	0.76	0.58	0.67
	Medium	1.44	0.52	1.03	0.72	0.51	**0.77**	0.43	0.47
	High	1.33	0.40	**1.12**	0.65	0.40	0.58	0.34	0.38
2002	Low	1.53	0.71	1.22	0.82	0.73	0.70	0.56	0.67
	Medium	1.44	0.53	1.01	0.74	0.53	**0.80**	0.42	0.47
	High	1.32	0.40	**1.08**	0.67	0.41	0.62	0.35	0.41
2003	Low	1.46	0.68	1.16	0.80	0.70	0.81	0.55	0.66
	Medium	1.40	0.52	0.97	0.76	0.53	0.78	0.39	0.46
	High	1.28	0.39	**1.03**	0.69	0.42	0.66	0.36	0.41
2004	Low	1.45	0.69	1.15	0.84	0.72	0.81	0.54	0.68
	Medium	1.38	0.52	0.98	0.75	0.54	0.80	0.40	0.46
	High	1.28	0.40	**1.01**	0.72	0.43	0.70	0.36	0.43
2005	Low	1.42	0.66	1.13	0.81	0.70	0.78	0.50	0.67
	Medium	1.37	0.52	0.99	0.76	0.54	**0.81**	0.37	0.50
	High	1.25	0.40	0.97	0.75	0.44	0.73	0.35	0.44
2006	Low	1.44	0.69	1.10	0.84	0.74	0.81	0.52	0.72
	Medium	1.39	0.54	0.95	0.78	0.56	0.77	0.40	0.52
	High	1.28	0.44	**1.01**	0.78	0.47	0.77	0.38	0.49
2007	Low	1.46	0.72	1.14	0.86	0.76	0.81	0.53	0.75
	Medium	1.41	0.57	0.94	0.83	0.60	**0.78**	0.42	0.57
	High	1.31	0.49	**1.08**	0.81	0.52	0.80	0.41	0.54
2008	Low	1.49	0.75	1.12	0.96	0.77	0.82	0.54	0.83
	Medium	**1.45**	0.60	1.04	0.86	0.64	0.80	0.45	0.64
	High	1.36	0.53	**1.13**	0.84	0.56	**0.82**	0.44	0.59
2009	Low	1.44	0.75	1.10	0.94	0.79	0.81	0.53	0.82
	Medium	**1.45**	0.62	1.05	0.91	0.69	0.71	0.48	0.65
	High	1.36	0.57	**1.16**	0.85	0.58	**0.92**	0.44	0.61
2010	Low	1.48	0.80	1.12	1.00	0.85	0.76	0.56	0.87
	Medium	**1.49**	0.66	1.06	0.95	0.71	0.67	0.51	0.70
	High	1.40	0.60	**1.24**	0.88	0.63	**0.92**	0.47	0.67
2011	Low	1.46	0.82	1.11	0.99	0.87	0.77	0.58	0.88
	Medium	**1.53**	0.68	1.02	**1.01**	0.69	0.73	0.57	0.76
	High	1.43	0.64	**1.18**	0.92	0.67	**0.99**	0.52	0.73
2012	Low	1.46	0.83	1.12	1.01	0.87	0.75	0.59	0.87
	Medium	**1.52**	0.70	1.09	**1.06**	0.73	0.73	**0.60**	0.81

(continued)

Table 2.15 (continued)

Year	Population density level	Total fertility rate							
		Total	Employed	Agriculture, etc.	Construction	Manufacturing	Electricity, etc.	Transport, etc.	Finance and insurance
2012	High	1.42	0.66	**1.18**	0.93	0.68	**1.04**	0.56	0.83
2013	Low	1.47	0.86	1.17	1.02	0.91	0.77	0.64	0.95
	Medium	**1.54**	0.74	1.11	**1.09**	0.77	**0.89**	**0.64**	0.86
	High	1.44	0.69	**1.20**	0.97	0.71	**1.06**	0.61	0.90
2014	Low	1.50	0.91	1.19	1.03	0.92	0.78	0.69	0.99
	Medium	1.50	0.80	**1.21**	**1.10**	0.78	**0.86**	**0.70**	0.89
	High	1.44	0.73	1.18	1.00	0.73	**1.02**	0.64	0.95
2015	Low	1.55	0.93	1.21	1.07	0.94	0.77	0.73	1.01
	Medium	1.55	0.79	**1.26**	**1.18**	0.78	**0.93**	**0.74**	0.97
	High	1.49	0.78	**1.22**	1.05	0.76	**1.08**	0.69	**1.03**

Year	Population density level	Total fertility rate						
		Real estate business	Wholesale and retail trade	Services	Government	Private/ publicly employed	Privately employed	Non employed
2000	Low	0.54	0.51	0.81	0.76	0.70	0.69	3.32
	Medium	0.33	0.35	0.66	**0.78**	0.52	0.52	3.13
	High	**0.36**	0.29	0.50	**0.83**	0.40	0.40	2.74
2001	Low	0.58	0.53	0.80	0.79	0.72	0.71	3.34
	Medium	0.37	0.35	0.62	0.78	0.52	0.52	3.17
	High	**0.38**	0.28	0.49	**0.81**	0.40	0.39	2.73
2002	Low	0.55	0.52	0.79	0.80	0.71	0.69	3.33
	Medium	0.39	0.35	0.61	0.79	0.53	0.52	3.20
	High	**0.39**	0.29	0.48	**0.82**	0.40	0.39	2.78
2003	Low	0.52	0.50	0.76	0.82	0.68	0.67	3.22
	Medium	0.42	0.33	0.59	0.79	0.52	0.51	3.14
	High	0.38	0.29	0.46	**0.81**	0.39	0.38	2.75
2004	Low	0.53	0.52	0.77	0.84	0.69	0.64	3.26
	Medium	0.47	0.33	0.59	0.81	0.53	0.52	3.15
	High	0.40	0.29	0.45	**0.82**	0.40	0.39	2.79
2005	Low	0.50	0.50	0.73	0.83	0.66	0.65	3.19
	Medium	0.47	0.33	0.57	0.82	0.52	0.51	3.15
	High	0.40	0.29	0.44	0.81	0.40	0.39	2.76
2006	Low	0.56	0.53	0.73	0.85	0.69	0.68	3.28
	Medium	0.48	0.35	0.59	**0.87**	0.54	0.53	3.17
	High	0.43	0.31	0.47	0.85	0.44	0.42	2.82
2007	Low	0.61	0.57	0.76	**0.87**	0.72	0.71	3.31
	Medium	0.50	0.38	0.62	**0.88**	0.57	0.56	**3.28**
	High	0.47	0.32	0.50	**0.90**	0.48	0.47	2.88
2008	Low	0.63	0.59	0.78	**0.87**	0.73	0.70	3.31

(continued)

Table 2.15 (continued)

Year	Population density level	Total fertility rate						
		Real estate business	Wholesale and retail trade	Services	Government	Private/ publicly employed	Privately employed	Non employed
2008	Medium	0.54	0.42	0.64	**0.90**	0.59	0.58	**3.31**
	High	0.49	0.34	0.53	**0.93**	0.52	0.51	2.99
2009	Low	0.60	0.60	0.77	**0.87**	0.75	0.72	3.32
	Medium	0.54	0.45	0.66	**0.95**	0.61	0.60	**3.42**
	High	0.49	0.37	0.56	**0.95**	0.55	0.53	3.01
2010	Low	0.60	0.61	0.75	**0.93**	0.77	0.76	3.38
	Medium	0.55	0.46	0.69	**0.97**	0.63	0.63	**3.50**
	High	0.51	0.39	0.61	**0.99**	0.57	0.56	3.09
2011	Low	0.65	0.65	0.92	**0.93**	0.83	0.82	3.43
	Medium	0.60	0.47	0.76	**1.02**	0.67	0.66	**3.54**
	High	0.55	0.42	0.63	**1.02**	0.62	0.61	3.10
2012	Low	0.67	0.64	0.97	**0.94**	0.86	0.85	3.46
	Medium	0.59	0.51	0.82	**1.02**	0.71	0.71	**3.66**
	High	0.59	0.45	0.68	**1.04**	0.64	0.63	3.11
2013	Low	0.70	0.67	1.04	**0.95**	0.91	0.91	3.52
	Medium	0.65	0.53	0.90	**1.07**	0.77	0.76	**3.72**
	High	0.65	0.48	0.72	**1.08**	0.69	0.68	3.17
2014	Low	0.71	0.69	1.18	**1.00**	0.99	0.99	3.52
	Medium	0.65	0.55	0.97	**1.07**	0.82	0.82	**3.68**
	High	**0.70**	0.51	0.76	**1.09**	0.73	0.73	3.20
2015	Low	0.75	0.71	1.26	**1.02**	1.04	1.04	3.55
	Medium	0.71	0.56	1.02	**1.14**	0.88	0.87	**3.81**
	High	**0.75**	0.54	0.83	**1.14**	0.78	0.77	3.32

Source As estimated by the author
Note Agriculture in Table 2.15 is inclusive of Forestry and Fisheries. Electricity is inclusive of Gas, Heat Supply and Water. Transport is inclusive of Information and Communications. Privately employed women's TFR is excluding agriculture, forestry and fisheries. Privately/publicly employed women's TFR is excluding agriculture, forestry and fisheries
Bold indicates data of TFR.

TFRs, but the same was true of areas with agglomeration economies of the more varied urbanization-type. Conversely, too, irrespective of the agglomeration type, TFRs were higher in areas where agglomeration levels were low. In the Government sector, in contrast, TFR values were independent of agglomeration levels and uniformly higher than in manufacturing.

Table 2.16 Population density, surplus of migrants coming in (minus values: surplus of migrants moving out)

Year	Population density level	Average	Median	Year	Population density level	Average	Median
2000	Low	– 1956	– 1734	2009	Low	– 5868	– 4434
	Medium	– 1313	– 1168		Medium	– 2606	– 2691
	High	3530	1660		High	9256	– 1395
2001	Low	– 3108	– 2974	2008	Low	– 4090	– 3757
	Medium	– 2156	– 2172		Medium	– 2904	– 2634
	High	5678	617		High	7539	801
2002	Low	– 3256	– 2956	2010	Low	– 3072	– 2147
	Medium	– 2206	– 2249		Medium	– 1996	– 1902
	High	5896	568		High	5478	416
2003	Low	– 3345	– 2558	2011	Low	– 3370	– 1377
	Medium	– 1839	– 1564		Medium	– 1681	– 1250
	High	5630	– 1072		High	5501	3114
2004	Low	– 3460	– 2611	2012	Low	– 3368	– 2165
	Medium	– 1687	– 2169		Medium	– 1450	– 1370
	High	5608	– 806		High	5268	1115
2005	Low	– 4424	– 4215	2013	Low	– 3427	– 2690
	Medium	– 2161	– 2103		Medium	– 2150	– 2505
	High	7174	– 240		High	034	31
2006	Low	– 5257	– 3963	2014	Low	– 3483	– 3185
	Medium	– 2487	– 2625		Medium	– 2293	– 2639
	High	8445	– 591		High	6241	– 391
2007	Low	– 5919	– 4752	2015	Low	– 3735	– 2934
	Medium	– 2599	– 2866		Medium	– 2995	– 2924
	High	9307	– 1808		High	7229	16

Source As estimated by the author

2.8 Conclusions

In this chapter, use has been made of the Own-Children Method to arrive at industry-specific estimates of total fertility rates (TFRs) in Japan and its 47 prefectures for the 16 years from 2000 to 2015. The TFRs published in the Vital statistics of the Ministry of Health, Labor and Welfare do not include separate values for each industrial sector, so calculating these values was the crux of the problem.

The TFR of employed women was 0.48 in 2000, 0.45 in 2005, 0.62 in 2010, and 0.80 in 2015. For non-employed women, the TFR was 2.89 in 2000, 2.79 in 2005, 3.06 in 2010, and 3.42 in 2015. Comparing these data, it can be seen that birth rates

Table 2.17 Correlations between agglomeration indexes and TFRs by industry

	Original data results				Results using logarithms				Number of samples
	Manufacturing TFR	Privately employed TFR	Wholesale and retail trade TFR	Services TFR	Manufacturing TFR	Privately employed TFR	Wholesale and retail trade TFR	Services TFR	
Relative concentration of manufacturing	– 0.112**	– 0.118**	–	–	– 0.062	– 0.112**	–	–	752
Relative regional specialization in manufacturing over other sectors	– 0.019	0.032	–	–	–	–	–	–	752
Specialization within manufacturing in each region	– 0.199**	– 0.240**	–	–	– 0.148**	–0.214**	–	–	752
Number and scale of manufacturing locations	– 0.122**	– 0.086*	–	–	– 0.124**	– 0.085*	–	–	752
Number and scale of service locations	–	–	– 0.080*	– 0.103*	–	–	0.210**	0.234**	752
Number of manufacturing employees per habitable unit area	– 0.381**	– 0.417**	–	–	– 0.396**	– 0.414**	–	–	752
Specialization-type agglomeration index	– 0.430**	– 0.576**	–	–	– 0.408**	– 0.594**	–	–	94

(continued)

Table 2.17 (continued)

	Original data results				Results using logarithms				Number of samples
	Manufacturing TFR	Privately employed TFR	Wholesale and retail trade TFR	Services TFR	Manufacturing TFR	Privately employed TFR	Wholesale and retail trade TFR	Services TFR	
Urbanization-type agglomeration index	− 0.433**	− 0.569**	–	–	− 0.401**	− 0.573**	–	–	94
Relative concentration of manufacturing	− 0.112**	− 0.118**			− 0.062**	− 0.112**	–	–	752

Source As estimated by the author
Note Privately employed TFR is excluding agriculture, forestry and fisheries

Table 2.18 Specialization-type/urban-type agglomeration index and industry-specific TFR

YEAR	Level of each type of agglomeration index	Total TFR	Employed women's TFR	Manufacturing TFR	Wholesale and retail trade TFR	Services TFR	Government TFR	Privately employed TFR	Non employed TFR
2000 Average	Specialization-type low	1.52	0.66	**0.66**	0.48	0.74	**0.77**	0.65	3.24
	Specialization-type medium	1.45	0.62	0.68	0.47	0.66	**0.87**	0.61	3.12
	Specialization-type high	1.38	0.45	0.44	0.30	0.53	**0.81**	0.44	2.99
2000 Average	Urbanization-type low	1.51	0.67	0.70	0.52	0.71	**0.80**	0.66	3.23
	Urbanization-type medium	1.49	0.62	0.65	0.44	0.71	**0.83**	0.61	3.24
	Urbanization-type high	1.35	0.43	0.42	0.29	0.51	**0.82**	0.42	2.88
2005 Average	Specialization-type low	1.42	0.66	0.65	0.50	0.70	**0.81**	0.64	3.15
	Specialization-type medium	1.34	0.56	0.58	0.40	0.61	**0.83**	0.56	3.05
	Specialization-type high	1.29	0.44	0.46	0.29	0.47	**0.82**	0.43	2.98
2005 Average	Urbanization-type low	1.40	0.64	0.64	0.48	0.69	**0.82**	0.63	3.14
	Urbanization-type medium	1.38	0.59	0.61	0.42	0.64	**0.83**	0.58	3.15
	Urbanization-type high	1.27	0.43	0.45	0.28	0.46	**0.82**	0.42	2.89

(continued)

Table 2.18 (continued)

YEAR	Level of each type of agglomeration index	Total TFR	Employed women's TFR	Manufacturing TFR	Wholesale and retail trade TFR	Services TFR	Government TFR	Privately employed TFR	Non employed TFR
2000 Median	Specialization-type low	1.54	0.68	**0.72**	0.50	0.75	**0.76**	0.67	3.28
	Specialization-type medium	1.45	0.60	0.74	0.42	0.66	**0.88**	0.59	3.11
	Specialization-type high	1.44	0.45	0.47	0.31	0.54	**0.80**	0.44	3.07
2000 Median	Urbanization-type low	1.54	0.68	0.72	0.50	0.75	**0.77**	0.67	3.28
	Urbanization-type medium	1.47	0.60	0.64	0.45	0.66	**0.76**	0.59	3.31
	Urbanization-type high	1.35	0.41	0.39	0.29	0.50	**0.82**	0.40	2.74
2005 Median	Specialization-type low	1.45	0.66	0.69	0.51	0.70	**0.80**	0.65	3.20
	Specialization-type medium	1.34	0.56	0.55	0.40	0.60	**0.82**	0.55	3.09
	Specialization-type high	1.35	0.44	0.45	0.29	0.47	**0.82**	0.43	3.10
2005 Median	Urbanization-type low	1.42	0.65	0.68	0.50	0.70	**0.80**	0.64	3.19
	Urbanization-type medium	1.35	0.60	0.60	0.40	0.66	**0.83**	0.59	3.12
	Urbanization-type high	1.25	0.40	0.43	0.28	0.44	**0.82**	0.39	2.76

Source As estimated by the author
Note Privately employed TFR is excluding agriculture, forestry and fisheries
Bold indicates data of TFR.

have been sustained among non-employed women over this period. Regarding the "employed" figures, women of 25–44 accounted for 0.43 of the TFR in 2000 (25–29: 0.14, 30–34: 0.20, 35–39: 0.08, 40–44: 0.01), increasing to 0.56 in 2010 (25–29: 0.16, 30–34: 0.24, 35–39: 0.13, 40–44: 0.03), and 0.74 in 2015 (25–29: 0.19, 30–34: 0.32, 35–39: 0.19, 40–44: 0.04). This shows that late marriage and parenthood is progressing. Similar trends are obtained for non- employed women.

Comparing TFRs by industrial sector in Japan as a whole, rates are highest in the primary industries, followed by the Government sector, Construction, Finance and insurance, Electricity, gas, heat supply and Water, Combined services, and Medical, health care and welfare. They are lowest in Accommodation, eating and drinking services, Wholesale and retail trade, and Transportation and postal activities. In 2015, Accommodation, eating and drinking services, Wholesale and retail trade, and Manufacturing showed low TFRs. These were sectors employing many women. Wholesale and retail were in second place for the number of female employees, Manufacturing third, and Accommodation, eating and drinking services, the sector with the lowest TFR, was fourth. On the other hand, Medical, health care and welfare, the sector with the largest number of women employees, showed a relatively high TFR. An increase in the number of births in this sector can contribute greatly to Japan's national TFR.

Specific challenges facing measures to reverse falling birthrates may be made more apparent by comparing the wages, work rules, and working environment in industrial sectors with high and low TFRs. Sector-specific data are of vital importance, therefore, when considering improvements in working conditions for women in each industrial sector, women's work choices more broadly, and the overall problem of birthrate decline.

A further of the research was to investigate relations between TFR and the agglomeration economy using TFR data drawn from different regions. Sato (2007) and Morita and Yamamoto (2014) have shown that areas with stronger agglomeration economies have higher population densities. And as wage rates are higher in areas with agglomerated economies, it can be theoretically argued that costs of obtaining child-rearing opportunities will be high and TFRs will be low.

The results of this study confirmed a negative correlation between TFR and population density in most industrial sectors, with exceptions in 2015 for Electricity, gas, heat supply and water, Government, Transport, and Real estate. This is similar to what was found by Sato (2007) and by Morita and Yamamoto (2014).

The dependence of the low fertility rate on the higher wage rate, and the reasons why TFRs, in an equilibrium state, are lower in areas of higher population density, are set out in Sato (2007). Sato also concludes that populated areas favor fewer children per woman. From the examination of TFRs by industrial sectors in the period 2000–2015, this study has confirmed that rates are higher in less populated, and lower in more populated areas so far as concerns the private sector. However, TFRs in the government sector are unlikely to be affected by economy of agglomeration as there are no significant regional differences in wage rates and the ease of taking childcare leave is the same.

Sato (2007) shows that some people born in less populated areas will later move to more populated ones. In other words, there is a net movement of people from lower density to higher density population areas. Overall, areas of low population density will have a surplus of people moving out, and areas of high population density a surplus moving in. Year after year, sparsely populated areas have a net loss of population through migration, while densely populated areas have a net gain.

Finally, the study also investigated TFRs in various industrial sectors in relation with 8 different indicators of agglomeration economies. Indicators that proved to be consistent with the predictions of agglomeration economy theory were the number and scale of employment locations (in Manufacturing), the number of employees per habitable unit area (in Manufacturing), and the agglomeration level, whether of the specialization or of the more general urbanization type.

An agglomeration index will have its own characteristics depending on the data creation process. Analyzing relations between TFRs by industrial sector and agglomeration indexes shows that TFRs for the Government sector are different from those for other industries. This might indicate that regional differences in TFRs could be reduced by bringing the working environment in private companies closer to what is usual in public employment.

References

Abe, M. (2005). The effects of a deteriorating employment and income environment on birth behavior (in Japanese). In Y. Higuchi (Ed.), *Declining birthrate and Japanese Economy and Society* (pp. 115–134). Policy Research Institute, Ministry of Finance, Nippon Hyoron Sha, Tokyo.

Abe, M., & Higuchi, Y. (1999). Economic fluctuations and the timing of women's marriage, childbirth, and employment—Analysis of fixed and variable factors. In Y. Higuchi & M. Iwata (Eds.), *Modern women from the viewpoint of panel data: Marriage, childbirth, employment, consumption, savings* (pp. 25–66). Toyo Keizai Shimposha, Tokyo. (in Japanese).

Adsera, A. (2005). Vanishing children: From high unemployment to low fertility in developed countries. *The American Economic Review, 95*(2), 189–193. https://doi.org/10.1257/000282805774669763

Adsera, A. (2011). Where are the babies? Labor market conditions and fertility in Europe. *European Journal of Population/Revue Européenne de Démographie, 27*(1), 1–32. https://doi.org/10.1007/s10680-010-9222-x

Albæk, K., & Larsen, M. (2014). The public-private sector fertility gap and the choice of occupation. In *The SFI Advisory Research Board Conference*, Copenhagen, 2–3 June 2014, p. 28.

Atoh, M., Itoh, T., & Kojima, H. (1986). An analysis of the relationship between marriage and fertility in Japan, 1961–2000 through macro-simulation. *Journal of Population Problems, 179*, 16–34. in Japanese.

Avery, C., St. Clair, T., Levin, M., & Hill, K. (2013). The 'Own Children' fertility estimation procedure: A reappraisal. *Population Studies, 67*(2), 171–183. https://doi.org/10.1080/00324728.2013.769616

Begall, K., & Mills, C. (2013). The influence of educational field, occupation, and occupational sex segregation on fertility in The Netherlands. *European Sociological Review, 29*(4), 720–742. https://doi.org/10.1093/esr/jcs051

Beine, A., Docquier, F., & Schiff, M. (2009). International migration, transfers of norms and home country fertility. World Bank Policy Research Working Paper No. 4925. https://doi.org/10.1596/1813-9450-4925

Berthoud, R. (2001). Teenage births to ethnic minority women. *Population Trends, 104*(Summer), 12–18. https://repository.essex.ac.uk/8731/. Accessed September 25, 2023.

Bratti, M., Bono, D., & Vuri, D. (2005). New mothers' labour force participation in Italy: The role of job characteristics. *Labour, 19*(1), 79–121. https://doi.org/10.1111/j.1467-9914.2005.00324.x

Butz, W., & Ward, M. (1979). The emergence of countercyclical U.S. fertility. *American Economic Review, 69*(3), 318–28. https://www.jstor.org/stable/1807367. Accessed September 25, 2023.

Cabinet Office, Government of Japan. (2005). White paper on the declining birthrate : Current state of measures against declining birthrate and associated issues. Gyosei, Tokyo. (in Japanese).

Cho, J., & Feeney, G. (1978). *Fertility estimation by the own-children method: A methodological elaboration. Reprint Series—Laboratories for Population Statistics* (20). Blackwells.

Cho, L. J., Retherford, R. D., & Choe, M. K. (1986). *The own-children method of fertility estimation.* University of Hawaii Press.

Cho, L. (2021). *Demography of incomplete data: Own child methodology, past and present.* University of Hawaii at Manoa, University of Hawai'i Press.

Coleman, A., & Dubuc, S. (2010). The fertility of ethnic minorities in the UK, 1960s–2006. *Population Studies, 64*(1), 19–41.

Coleman, A., & Smith, M. (2005). The projection of ethnic minority populations: problems and data needs. OXPOP Working Paper no. 13, Oxford.

Conti, M., & Sette, E. (2013). Type of employer and fertility of working women: Does working in the public sector or in a large private firm matter? *Cambridge Journal of Economics, 37*(6), 1303–1333.

Date Y., & Shimizutani, S. (2004). Why has Japan's fertility rate declined? An empirical literature survey with an emphasis on policy implications. ESRI Discussion Paper Series, 94. (in Japanese).

De la Rica, S., & Iza, A. (2005). Career planning in Spain: Do fixed-term contracts delay marriage and parenthood? *Review of Economics of the Household, 3*(1), 49–73. https://doi.org/10.1007/s11150-004-0979-8

Dubuc, S. (2009). Application of the own-child method for estimating fertility of women by ethnic and religious groups in the UK. *Journal of Population Research, 26*(3), 207–225. https://doi.org/10.1007/s12546-009-9020-7

Dubuc, S. (2012). Immigration to the UK from high-fertility countries: Intergenerational adaptation and fertility convergence. *Population and Development Review, 38*(2), 353–368. http://www.jstor.org/stable/41857383. Accessed September 25, 2023.

Dubuc, S., & Haskey, J. (2010). Ethnicity and fertility in the United Kingdom. In J. Stillwell & M. Ham (Eds.), *Population Trends and Processes Series. Vol. 3: Ethnicity and integration* (pp. 63–81). Springer. https://doi.org/10.1007/978-90-481-9103-1_4

Easterlin, R. (1969). Towards a socioeconomic theory of fertility: Survey of recent research on economic factors in American fertility. In S. Behrman, L. Corsajr, & R. Freedman (Eds.), *Fertility and family planning: A world view* (pp. 127–156). University of Michigan Press.

Goto, H., & Minamimura, K. (2015). Geography and demography: New economic geography with endogenous fertility. Discussion Paper Series from Research Institute for Economics and Business Administration, Kobe University, DP2015.33.

Hotz, J., Klerman, J., & Willis, R. (1996). The economics of fertility in developed countries. In *Handbook of population and family economics* (Vol. 1A, pp. 275–347), North Holland. https://doi.org/10.1016/S1574-003X(97)80024-4

Ito, T. (1980). Note on the expansibility and accuracy of the own-children method. The accuracy of the own-children method (population analysis note 4). *Journal of Population Problems, 15*, 63–70. (in Japanese). https://www.ipss.go.jp/syoushika/bunken/data/pdf/14193206.pdf. Accessed September 25, 2023.

Ito, T. (1985). Marriage duration specific birth rates based on the 1974 welfare survey using own-children method. *Journal of Population Problems, 175*, 48–58. (in Japanese). https://www.ipss.go.jp/syoushika/bunken/data/pdf/14191905.pdf. Accessed September 25, 2023.

Ito, T., & Bando, R. (1985). Fertility change of the year of "Hinoe-uma". *Journal of Population Problems, 181*, 31–43. (in Japanese). https://www.ipss.go.jp/syoushika/bunken/data/pdf/14167803.pdf. Accessed September 25, 2023.

Ito, T., & Yamamoto, C. (1977). Estimating current differential fertility from data on own-children for Japan: 1960–1975. *Journal of Population Problems, 142*, 16–36. (in Japanese). https://www.ipss.go.jp/syoushika/bunken/data/pdf/14214802.pdf. Accessed September 25, 2023.

Ihara, H. (2008). Estimation of fertility rates by industrial sector for 2005 based on the own-children method. The Population Association of Japan. Report Abstracts from the 60th Annual Meeting. (in: Japanese).

Ihara, H. (2011). Results of own-children method estimation of the total fertility rate in working households (1961–2005). *Research Memoir of the Statistics, 68*(Mar 2011), 69–115. (in Japanese). https://www.stat.go.jp/training/2kenkyu/ihou/68/pdf/2-2-683.pdf. Accessed September 25, 2023.

Ihara, H. (2012). Results of own-children method estimation of the total fertility rate by female workers occupation. *Research Memoir of the Statistics, 69*(Mar 2012), 83–144. (in Japanese). https://www.stat.go.jp/training/2kenkyu/ihou/69/pdf/2-2-694.pdf. Accessed September 25, 2023.

Ihara, H. (2013). Results of own-children method estimation of the total fertility rate by female labor status. *Research Memoir of the Statistics, 70*(Mar 2013), 103–158. (in Japanese). https://www.stat.go.jp/training/2kenkyu/ihou/70/pdf/2-2-704.pdf. Accessed September 25, 2023.

Imai, H. (1996). Application of Butz-Ward type models to fertility in Japan. *Journal of Population Problems, 52*(2(219)), 30–35. (in Japanese). https://warp.da.ndl.go.jp/info:ndljp/pid/285185/www.ipss.go.jp/syoushika/bunken/data/pdf/16896303.pdf. Accessed September 25, 2023.

Iwasawa, M. (2002). Influences of marriage and childbearing behavior changes on recent variations in total fertility rates of Japan. *Journal of Population Problems, 58*(3), 15–44. (in Japanese). https://www.ipss.go.jp/syoushika/bunken/data/pdf/16749503.pdf. Accessed September 25, 2023.

Kato, H. (1997). Time series analysis of fertility change in postwar Japan. *Jinkogaku Kenkyu (Journal of Population Studies), 20*, 23–25. https://doi.org/10.24454/jps.20.0_23

Kato, H. (2001). *Introduction to demographic economics*. Nippon Hyoron Sha. (in Japanese).

Kawasaki, S. (1985). Estimation results of fertility based on 1980 census table for own-children. *Research Memoir of the Statistics, 44*(Nov 1985), 1–17. (in Japanese).

Konishi, Y., & Saito, Y. (2012). Effects of specialization-type and urbanization-type agglomeration on productivity: Empirical data analysis at the business location level. RIETI Discussion Paper Series, 12-J-006 (Mar 2012), pp. 1–28. (in Japanese). https://www.rieti.go.jp/jp/publications/dp/12j006.pdf. Accessed September 25, 2023.

Krapf, S., & Kreyenfeld, M. (2015). Fertility assessment with the own-children-method: A validation with data from the German micro-census. MPIDR Technical Report TR-2015-003. Rostock, Max Planck Institute for Demographic Research. https://doi.org/10.4054/MPIDR-TR-2015-003

Krapf, S., & Wolf, K. (2015). Persisting differences or adaptation to German fertility patterns? First and second birth behavior of the 1.5 and second generation Turkish migrants in Germany. *KZfSS Kölner Zeitschrift für Soziologie und Sozialpsychologie, 67*(1), 137–164. https://doi.org/10.1007/s11577-015-0331-8

Macunovich, D. (1995). The Butz-Ward fertility model in the light of more recent data. *Journal of Human Resources, 30*(2), 229–255. https://doi.org/10.2307/146118

Macunovich, D. (1998). Fertility and the Easterlin Hypothesis: An assessment of the literature. *Journal of Population Economics, 11*(1), 53–111. https://www.jstor.org/stable/20007569. Accessed September 25, 2023.

Matsumura, M. (1980). Estimating the birth rate in Japan based on the own-children method: Results applied to the 1975 census. *Research Memoir of the Statistics, 34*, 65–79 (in Japanese). https://www.stat.go.jp/training/2kenkyu/ihou/68/pdf/2-2-683.pdf. Accessed September 25, 2023.

Matsumura, M. (2011). Parity-based population estimates based on the own-children table in the National Census, and recent trends in cohort birth rates. *Statistics and the Japanese Economy, 1*(1), 112–141. (in Japanese).

Mincer, J. (1963). Market prices, opportunity costs, and income effects. In C. F. Christ & Y. Grunfeld (Eds.), *Measurement in economics: Studies in mathematical economics and econometrics in memory of Yehuda Grunfeld* (pp. 67–82). Stanford University Press.

Moriizumi, R. (2005). The spread in atypical employment and declining birthrate. *Journal of Population Problems, 61*(3), 2–19. (in Japanese). https://www.ipss.go.jp/syoushika/bunken/data/pdf/13629002.pdf. Accessed September 26, 2023.

Morita, T., & Yamamoto, K. (2014). Economic geography, endogenous fertility, and agglomeration. RIETI Discussion Paper Series, 14-E-045 (July 2014). http://www.rieti.go.jp/en/. Accessed September 26, 2023.

Morita, Y. (2004). Analysis of child rearing costs and childbirth behavior. *JCER Economic Journal, 48*, 34–57. in Japanese.

Nakamura, J., & Ueda, A. (1999). On the determinants of career interruption by childbirth among married women in Japan. *Journal of the Japanese and International Economies, 13*(1), 73–89.

Nakamura, R. (2008). Measurement of economic agglomeration in urban/regional areas (1). *Journal of the Association of Economics Association of Okayama University, 39*(4), 99–121. (in Japanese).

National Institute of Population and Social Security Research. (2010). The 14th basic survey on birth trends, summary of results of marital survey (National Survey) on marriage and childbirth. (in Japanese). http://www.ipss.go.jp/site-ad/index_Japanese/shussho-index.html. Accessed March 25, 2016.

Ogawa, N., & Mason, A. (1986). An econometric analysis of recent fertility in Japan: An application of the Butz-Ward Model. *Jinkogaku Kenkyu (Journal of Population Studies), 9*, 5–15.

Ohbuchi, H. (1982). Empirical tests of the Chicago model and the Easterlin hypothesis: A case study in Japan. *Jinkogaku Kenkyu (Journal of Population Studies), 5*, 8–16.

Okun, S., Oliver, L., & Khait-Marelly, O. (2007). The public sector, family structure, and labor market behavior of Jewish mothers in Israel. *Work and Occupations, 34*(2), 174–204.

Oobayashi, S. (1979). Estimation of fertility during the period by own-children method. *Research Memoir of the Statistics, 33*, 1–16. in Japanese.

Retherford, R., Ogawa, N., Matsukura, R., & Ihara, H. (2004). *Trends in fertility by education in Japan, 1966–2000*. Nihon University Population Research Institute, East-West Center.

Sato, Y. (2007). Economic geography, fertility and migration. *Journal of Urban Economics, 61*(2), 372–387. https://doi.org/10.1016/j.jue.2006.08.002

Sato, Y., & Yamamoto, K. (2005). Population concentration, urbanization, and demographic transition. *Journal of Urban Economics, 58*(1), 45–61.

Schultz, T. P. (1985). Changing world prices, women's wages, and the fertility transition: Sweden, 1860–1910. *Journal of Political Economy, 93*(6), 1126–1154.

Shigeno, Y. (1996). Fertility and female labor supply behavior. *The Economic Review of Osaka University, 45*(3, 4), 65–74. (in Japanese).

Shigeno, Y., & Ohkusa, Y. (2001). Impact of childcare support measures on marriage, childbirth, and employment. In Y. Iwamoto (Ed.), *Social welfare and family economics*. Toyo Keizai Shinhosha. (in Japanese).

Simon, C. J., & Tamura, R. (2009). Do higher rents discourage fertility? Evidence from US cities, 1940–2000. *Regional Science and Urban Economics, 39*(1), 33–42.

Takayama, N., Ogawa, H., Yoshida, H., Arita, F., Kaneko, Y., & Kojima, K. (2000). The cost of marriage and child care and its effect on fertility: A note on the economic factors of below-replacement fertility in Japan. *Journal of Population Problems, 56*(4), 1–18. (in Japanese). https://www.ipss.go.jp/syoushika/bunken/data/pdf/15648401.pdf. Accessed September 26, 2023.

Tamura, R., Simon, C., & Murphy, M. (2012). Black and white fertility, differential baby booms. MPRA, p. 80. https://mpra.ub.uni-muenchen.de/40921/1/MPRA_paper_40921.pdf. Accessed September 26, 2023.

Toda, A. (2007). Empirical analysis of fertility rates—Focus on its relationship with the state of economic activity and family policy. RIETI Discussion Paper Series, 07-J-007, pp. 1–21. (in Japanese). https://www.rieti.go.jp/jp/publications/dp/07j007.pdf. Accessed September 26, 2023.

Tsukahara, Y. (1995). The effect of childcare support policy on childbearing behavior; Quantitative analysis of birth probability by employment type using experimental vignette approach. *JCER Economic Journal, 28*, 148–161. (in Japanese). https://dl.ndl.go.jp/info:ndljp/pid/11590070/1. Accessed September 26, 2023.

Tsutani, N., & Higuchi, Y. (2009). *Population decline and the Japanese economy: The future of the labor, pension, and medical care systems.* Nihon Keizai Shimbun Publications. (in Japanese).

United Nations. (1986). Manual X: Indirect techniques for demographic estimation, population studies, 1983, No. 81, New York. https://unstats.un.org/unsd/demographic/standmeth/handbooks/Manual_X-en.pdf. Accessed September 26, 2023.

Wada, K. (2015). *Demographic theory and its application to estimation.* Ohmsha. (in Japanese).

Waller, L., Berrington, A., & Raymer, J. (2014). New insights into the fertility patterns of recent Polish migrants in the United Kingdom. *Journal of Population Research, 31*(2), 131–150.

Willis, R. (1973). A new approach to the economic theory of fertility behavior. *Journal of Political Economy, 81*(2, Part II), S14–S64. https://www.jstor.org/stable/1840411. Accessed September 26, 2023.

Yamaguchi, K. (2005). Determining factors and countermeasures for the declining birthrate: The roles of the husband, the workplace, the government, and society. *Japanese Journal of Research on Household Economics. Institute for Research on Household Economics*, 66, 57–67. (in Japanese). https://kakeiken.jp/old_kakeiken/jp/journal/jjrhe/pdf/66/066_07.pdf. Accessed September 26, 2023.

Yamagami, T. (1999). The compatibility between childbirth, childcare and female employment. *Journal of Social Security Research, 35*(1), 52–64. (in Japanese). http://www.ipss.go.jp/syoushika/bunken/data/pdf/14358111.pdf. Accessed September 26, 2023.

Yamauchi, M. (2014). An empirical analysis of the effect of fertility measurement choice on subnational population projections: A case study of 47 prefectures in Japan. *Journal of Population Problems, 70*(2), 120–136. (in Japanese).

Yamashige, S., Kato, H., & Oguro, K. (2013). *Vital statistics and policy: Invitation to an economic approach.* Nippon Hyoronsha. (in Japanese).

Zhang, J. (2002). Urbanization, population transition, and growth. *Oxford Economic Papers, 54*(1), 91–117. https://www.jstor.org/stable/3488654

Zuberi, T., & Sibanda, A. (1999). *Fertility differentials in sub-Saharan Africa: Applying own-children methods to African censuses.* University of Pennsylvania. http://www.acap.upenn.edu/WorkingPaper/Papers/ACAPWP0001.pdf. Accessed September 26, 2023.

Chapter 3
Analysis of the Impact of Overtourism in Japan: The Effects of Congestion Phenomena

3.1 Introduction

The increase in international tourism gives rise to large movements of people around the world, creating economic effects of production and employment in a wide range of sectors such as air and rail transportation, accommodation, travel, food and drink services, and retailing. The tourism industry has become a major player in international trade, generating transfers of income from tourists' home countries to the destination countries that they travel to.

On the other hand, like any other industry, tourism is dogged by problems such as environmental damage and free riding on public goods and services which are harmful to the destination country's economy outside of the tourism industry. Examples of free riding include tourists' use of energy and water resources, the cost of which has to be borne by domestic taxpayers. Environmental damage might mean problems such as garbage, harm to the natural environment, or noise and smell, all of which are generated by overseas tourists as much as by native inhabitants. In addition, increased tourism will also lead to road congestion and crowding on public transportation due to the rise in the volume of traffic, and to greater loads on the environment due to the direct effects of tourist development. Conditions like these in tourist areas can lead to conflicts between efforts to bring in tourists and the interests of local residents. In some cities, problems of this kind have led to the emergence of protest actions which have come to be offered as evidence of a negative attitude towards visitors on the part of the residents there. With the growth of tourism development in frequently visited areas, land prices and rents will be driven up. These land price and congestion problems, combined with other causes, may have adverse effects on the lives of residents. In recent years, this tendency has developed into an international issue known as "overtourism."

S. Asahi, *Econometric Analysis of Regional Economy*,
https://doi.org/10.1007/978-981-99-8707-8_3

Between 2020 and 2022, it is a fact that there has been a dramatic decrease in tourist numbers worldwide due to the influence of Covid-19.[1] But once this disconcerting factor disappears, it seems likely that the number of tourists in the world will increase again, as in the years preceding 2020.[2] In that sense, overtourism remains a future issue.

In recent years, the number of international travelers visiting Japan has shot up sharply. Cities such as Kyoto and Kamakura have encountered overtourism problems already, and both cities are taking measures. Kyoto City had laid out its Kyoto Tourism Promotion Plan 2020 ("A Tourist City that the World will Aspire to") for the period 2014 to the end of 2020. "Overtourism" is one of the issues addressed. The plan was specifically adopted at the 6th Management Meeting for the "Kyoto Tourism Promotion Plan 2020" Management Conference.[3] Kamakura City also agreed in 2019 to provide marketing information on tourist behavior. The city has announced that it will conduct a visualization survey of tourist behavior with a view to eliminate overtourism. And like Kyoto, the Kamakura City Tourism Association has drawn up a Kamakura City Tourist Area Master Plan, "Toward a Sustainable Tourist Destination," as a discussion basis for measures against "damage due to tourist congestion (overtourism)."[4]

The chapter will begin by summarizing trends in the number of international visitors to Japan in recent years. This will be followed by an overview of the research on congestion phenomena related with tourism. Next, the model to be used in this study will be introduced. The purpose of the model is to estimate the demand function of international visitors to Japan, taking account of variables that indicate congestion phenomena. An analysis will then be performed to estimate the effect that these variables are likely to have on the numbers of international tourists visiting Japan in the future. Finally, based on these results, estimates for future variations in congestion phenomena will be displayed and summarized.

---

[1] This represents a view of the situation in February 2022.

[2] As announced in the UNWTO outlook for 2022. In the latest UNWTO Panel of Experts, a majority (64%) does not expect visitors from overseas to return to 2019 levels until 2024.

https://www.unwto.org/news/tourism-grows-4-in-2021-but-remains-far-below-pre-pandemic-levels (February 12, 2022).

[3] The 6th Management Meeting was held on Friday, January 19, 2018.

https://www.city.kyoto.lg.jp/sankan/page/0000186495.html (19, February, 2022).

https://www.city.kyoto.lg.jp/templates/shingikai_kekka/cmsfiles/contents/0000231/231298/tekiroku.pdf (19, February, 2022).

[4] The basic idea is to consider the introduction of "road pricing," i.e., charges on vehicles using particular stretches of road. (Nihon Keizai Shimbun Electronic Edition, News Senbo-tenbo, 6/10/2019, 8:00 p.m.)

3.2 Trends in the Number of International Visitors to Japan in Recent Years

The number of International visitors[5] to Japan in recent years has increased significantly compared to rates of increase in international tourism around the world. The average growth rate in numbers of international tourists for countries around the world from 2010 to 2019 was 5.1%, while the average rate in Japan was 19%.

There are several factors behind this. Economic conditions in neighboring Asian countries remain strong, visa requirements for visitors from several countries have recently been relaxed, and consumption tax exemption systems for international visitors have been expanded. Other background factors include growth in air traffic due to the entry of LCCs on the travel market, the resulting falls in airfares, the increasing use of SNS and blogs in marketing, and easier access to travel information.[6]

Figure 3.1 shows the changes in the number of international visitors to Japan since 2000. In the 22 years since 2000, the Ministry of Land, Infrastructure, Transport and Tourism (MLIT) has increased its promotion efforts, along with other related ministries, the private sector, and industries from outside the travel field. The MLIT "Global Tourism Strategy" was launched in 2000. Following this, a MLIT "Headquarters for the Promotion of the Global Tourism Strategy" was set up, headed by the Minister. The government also created a post of Minister Responsible for the Establishment of Tourism, to be held concurrently by the MLIT Minister. The Basic Act for Promoting a Tourism-Oriented Country was passed in 2006. This is a law that specifies tourism as an important pillar of Japanese policy. A Cabinet meeting of the Japanese government then approved a Basic Plan for Promoting a Tourism-Oriented Country, in which measures, goals and plans for the realization of this tourism-oriented nation were set out.

The Japan Tourism Agency (JTA) was established in 2008. The issuing of Chinese individual tourist visas began soon afterward, in 2009.[7]

Four revisions were made to the Basic Plan for Promoting a Tourism-Oriented Country in 2017: (1) Establishment of attractive tourist areas with a high degree

---

[5] The term "international visitors" is used by UNWTO and the Japan Tourism Agency (JTA). In other literature and media articles, "foreign visitors" is used in the same way.

[6] Reference 1: Ministry of Land, Infrastructure, Transport and Tourism (2017) "Promotion of LCC Business Development" 2016 Policy Review Results (Evaluation Report) https://www.mlit.go.jp/common/001179271.pdf (November 22, 2019).

Reference 2: Ministry of Land, Infrastructure, Transport and Tourism and Tourism Agency (March, 2017) "White Paper on Tourism" 2010–2018 edition, the state of tourism in 2018: Tourism measures in the year Reiwa 1, referring to the year Reiwa 1.

[7] Reference 1: Ministry of Land, Infrastructure, Transport and Tourism (2002) "Global Tourism Strategy" December 2002, http://www.mlit.go.jp/kisha/kisha02/01/011224_3/011224_3.pdf (November 22, 2019).

Reference 2: Watanabe T. (2004) Part 4: Research on the increase in internatioanl tourists visiting Japan: Development of inbound policies in modern Japan: From the opening of the country to the "global tourism strategy": Independent Research Report 2004, pp. 67–72, the Japan Travel Bureau Foundation.

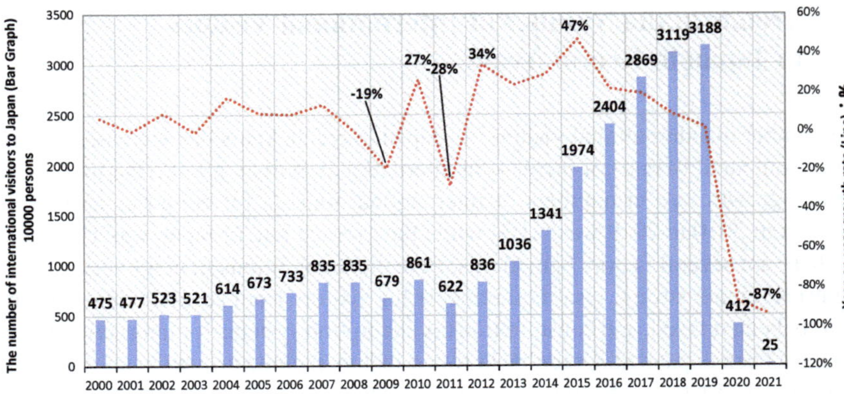

Fig. 3.1 Changes in the number of international visitors to Japan. *Source* Compiled by the author based on the number of international visitors to Japan released by the Japan National Tourist Organization (JNTO)

of international competitiveness, (2) stronger international competitiveness in the tourism industry and development of human resources to contribute to the promotion of tourism, (3) promotion of international tourism, and (4) measures such as environmental enhancement that have a promotional impact on tourist travel. In addition, the national government affirmed its commitment to the promotion of tourism to Japan.[8] As a result, the number of foreign visitors to Japan increased every year except 2009, the year of the global financial crisis, and 2011 due to the sharp appreciation of the yen and the Great East Japan Earthquake.

In 2019, the number of international visitors to Japan reached 31.88 million. However, in 2020 and 2021, tourist numbers dropped all around the world under the effects of novel coronavirus (Covid-19) infections. In Japan as elsewhere, the government has placed prohibitions on entries of travelers for purposes of tourism and numbers have therefore decreased.

Figure 3.2 shows changes in the total number of overnight stays for international visitors[9] in Japan, from the "Overnight Travel Statistics Survey" compiled by the JTA. The total number of overnight stays by foreign visitors to Japan increased steadily from 27.5 million in 2010 to 115.65 million in 2019. In other words, the total for 2018 was 4.2 times as large. According to figures from the JNTO (Japan National Tourism Organization), the number of international visitors to Japan rose from 8.61 million in 2010 to 31.88 million in 2019, which is 3.7 times higher. On this Chapter, the international visitors" describe foreign visitors to Japan, and "the international visit or overnight guests" describe those foreign- visitors to Japan checked in accommodations, etc. The correlation coefficient between the total number of foreign guests

[8] Japan Tourism Agency (2016) "Revision of 'Plan for Promoting a Tourism-Oriented Country," April 25, 2017 https://www.mlit.go.jp/common/001182997.pdf (October 22, 2019).

[9] Overnight stays for international visitors is a term used by the Tourism Agency and means foreign guests staying in overnight accommodation

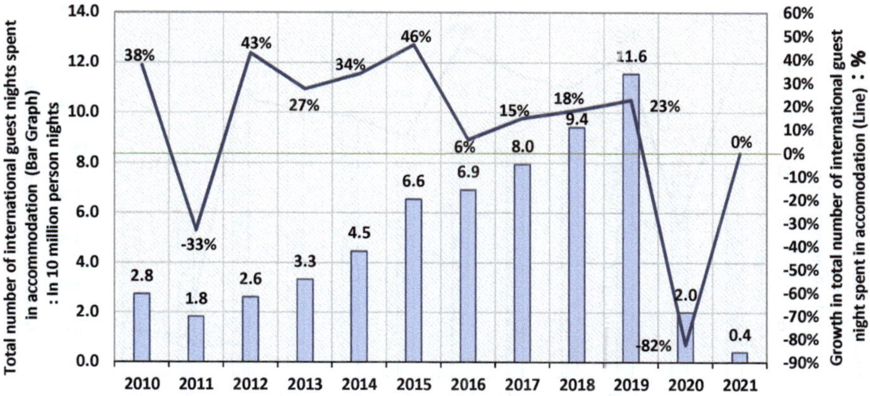

Fig. 3.2 Changes in the total number of international visitor as overnight guests. *Source* Created by the author based on the "Overnight Travel Statistics Survey" (JTA 2009–2021). *Note* For 2010, the growth rate in the total number of overnight guests was not included in the JTA's data for accommodation facilities employing 9 staff or less. Therefore, the proportion of the total number of overnight guests in facilities with 9 or less employees to the total number for all facilities was found for the year 2011 and used as a substitute to calculate the 2009 figures (in order to obtain year-on-year changes). The title of this figure "international visitor as overnight guests" mean foreign visitors using overnight accommodation "international visitor as overnight guests" is sometimes indicated in the JTA

staying in overnight accommodation in the "Overnight Travel Statistics Survey" and the total number of international visitors for the same ten years in the JNTO data is 0.98.

The input data used in this study for trends of international visits to Japan are for the total number of overnight stays by foreign visitors from the "Overnight Travel Statistics Survey." However, there is hardly any difference regardless which set of numerical values is used. The trends in both sets are essentially the same.

Figure 3.3 shows changes in total numbers of stays by domestic travelers[10] and visitors from overseas. The low figures for 2020 and 2021 are due to the effects of the novel coronavirus (Covid-19) pandemic. As there are special factors in play here, discussion will be confined to the total numbers of stays up to 2019. In 2019, domestic travelers accounted for 80.5% of the total number of stays, and international visitors for only 19.5%. The domestic travel share is very large.

Figure 3.4 shows changes in total numbers of accommodation stays for international visitors between the two years 2010 and 2019, for the 20 prefectures most often visited in 2019. In 2019, the number of international visitors staying was highest in Tokyo, followed by Osaka, Kyoto, Hokkaido, Okinawa, and Chiba. Comparing the numbers in 2010 and 2019, the number of stays in Okinawa prefecture has increased 15-fold compared with the data for 2010, in Kyoto, the number is 7.2 times higher and in Osaka, 4.4 times. The top 9 prefectures accounted for 79% of the total in 2109,

[10] This is indicated people of Japanese nationality or other people resident in Japan.

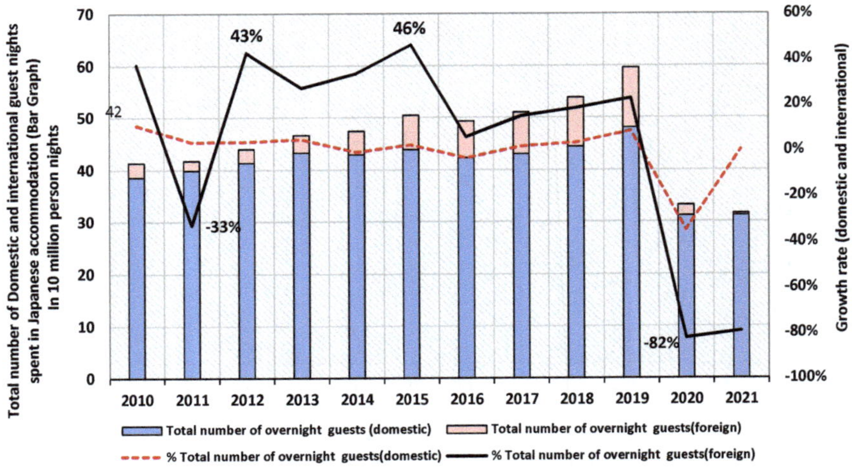

Fig. 3.3 Changes in total numbers of stays by Japanese travelers and visitors from overseas. *Source* Created by the author based on the "Overnight Travel Statistics Survey" (JTA 2009–2021)

and the top 6 prefectures for 69%. It is evident that the regional bias is extremely large.

As described above, it is very conspicuous that, in spite of some diversification, international visitors to Japan are still over-concentrated in a limited number of areas due to the increase in the total number of international visitors to Japan. This seems to be the main cause behind overtourism.

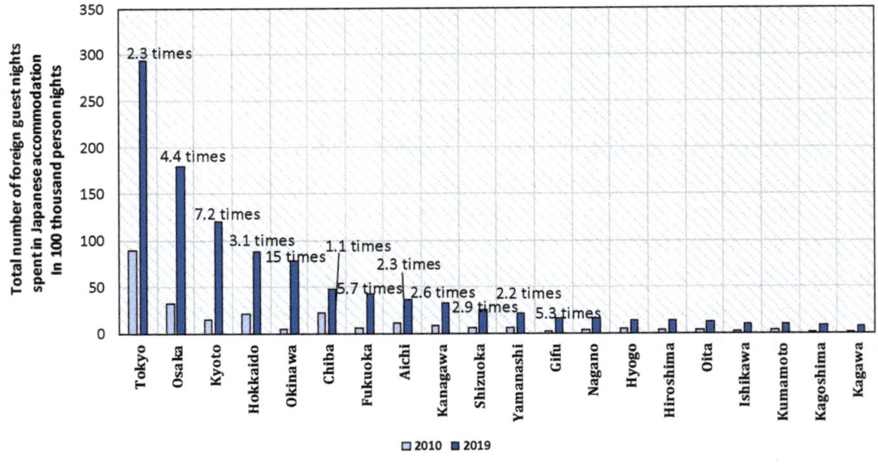

Fig. 3.4 Changes in numbers of international visitors making stays in Japan by prefecture in 2010 and 2019. *Source* Created by the author based on the "Overnight Travel Statistics Survey" (JTA 2010, 2019)

Total numbers of international visitors making stays in Japan in the two years 2010 and 2019 are shown by country or region of origin in Fig. 3.5. Looking at these data, visitors from China make up the highest number in both 2010 and 2019, and their share of the total has increased by 5%. The most frequent countries or regions after China in both years are South Korea, Taiwan, Hong Kong, the United States, Thailand, Australia, and Singapore. In 2019, these eight countries or regions accounted for 65% of international visitors staying in Japan. In 2010, their dominance was greater still but over these years it decreased by 7%.

Figure 3.6 shows changes in numbers of foreign visitors making stays in Japan by country. The increase for Chinese visitors in 2018 and 2019 is remarkable.

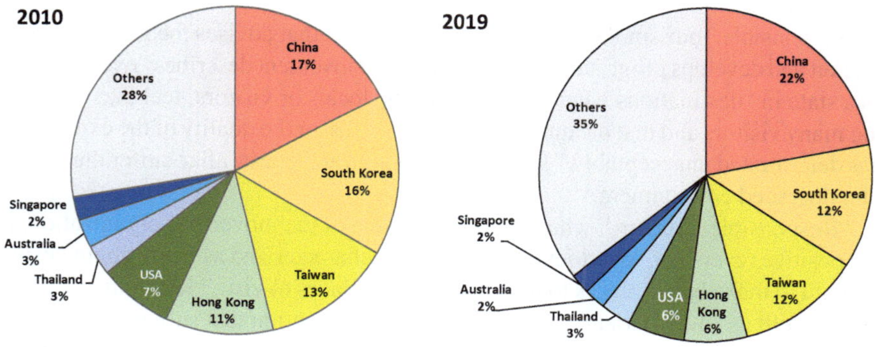

Fig. 3.5 Changes in shares of total numbers of international visitors making stays in Japan by country in 2010 and 2019. *Source* Created by the author based on the "Overnight Travel Statistics Survey" (JTA 2010, 2019)

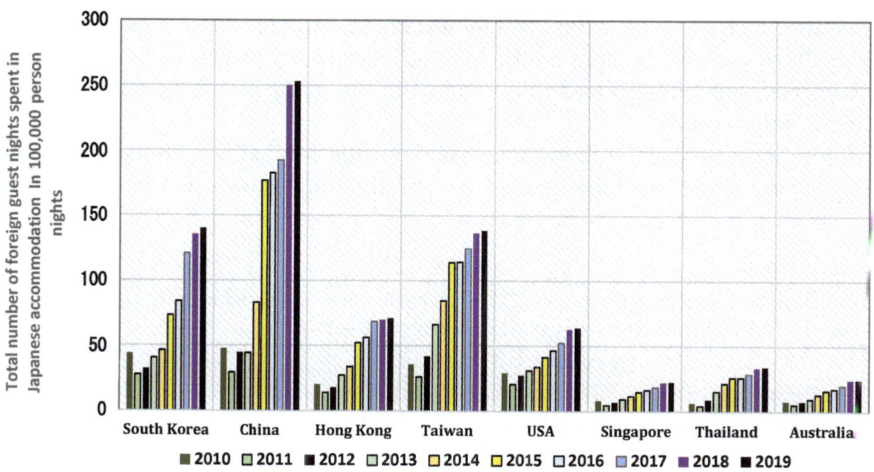

Fig. 3.6 Changes in numbers of international visitors making stays in Japan by country. *Source* Created by the author based on the "Overnight Travel Statistics Survey" (JTA 2010–2019)

3.3 Research by Means of a Tourism Demand Model Including Congestion Phenomena

3.3.1 *Definition of Overtourism*

In this section, I will first explain how "overtourism" has been dealt with in previous research.

UNWTO (2018) draws on Ali (2016), and in particular on his use of Skift's term "overtourism."[11] Universities cooperating in the UNWTO (2018) project define overtourism as "the impact of tourism on a destination, or parts thereof, that excessively influences perceived quality of life of citizens and/or quality of visitors experiences in a negative way."[12]

Responsible Tourism Partnership[13] is a movement that advises the global tourism market and develops programs for its growth. The movement describes "overtourism" as a state in "destinations where hosts or guests, locals or visitors, feel that there are too many visitors and that the quality of life in the area or the quality of the experience has deteriorated unacceptably." In addition, visitors and guests alike suffer the effects of a degraded environment.[14]

"Responsible Tourism," which is also the name of the movement organization, is the positive reverse of "overtourism" and can be characterized as being about "using tourism to make better places to live in and better places to visit." Richardson (2017) further defines "overtourism" as describing "any destination that suffers the strain of tourism". Destination UK (2017) explains "overtourism" as follows. "Over the last year or more, the word overtourism has increasingly been used to describe a situation where destinations feel either that there are too many tourists, or where the impact of tourist development is negatively affecting their home without providing enough benefits in return."[15] The explanation given by the Japan Tourism Agency (2018) is: "In a specific tourist destination, a significant increase in the number of visitors will bring about negative impacts on the lives of citizens, the natural environment, and landscapes, and will also lead to a situation in which the satisfaction of tourists is significantly reduced."[16]

From these sources, it is apparent that "overtourism" as a term has come into frequent use in just these few years. However, there are also some papers that show

---

[11] Overtourism is introduced in Ali, R. (2016), with reference to Sheivachman, A. "Iceland and the Trials of 21st Century Tourism" (https://skift.com/iceland-tourism/).

[12] UNWTO (2018), p. 4, right column, l. 20.

[13] The organization is called RTM: Responsible Tourism Movement.

[14] https://responsibletourismpartnership.org/overtourism/ (January 31, 2020).

[15] Richardson, D. (2017), p. 1.

[16] JTA (2018), p. 111. The Japan Tourism Agency has also compiled a report "Towards a Sustainable Advanced Tourism Country" (June 12, 2019), summarizing problems currently faced by Japanese regions as a result of rapid environmental changes due to tourism and the effects of overtourism.

that this phenomenon is not new.[17] Indeed, the debate about the harmful effects of tourism, and about problems of tourist congestion in particular, has been around since the 1960s.[18] Research surveys began in the 1970s on ways of putting pressure on regions to increase tourist numbers, and researchers were also discussing the ensuing risks of saturation that these moves might lead to for some destinations.

In addition, congestion has also been widely studied in the past because of its role as an indicator of mismanagement in the area of transportation economics.

[19]The World Tourism Organization (2004) deals with issues of practical guidance in the effective management of congestion in natural and cultural tourist destinations.

In particular, in its International Tourism Code of Conduct 3, the UNWTO calls for concerted efforts to protect and preserve resources of natural and cultural heritage through close collaboration within communities as well as between communities and visiting travelers, in order to ensure a sustainable future for the destination's resources and the tourist activities based on them. The World Commission on Protected Areas (WCPA), a joint initiative of the World Tourism Organization (UNWTO) and the United Nations Environment Program (UNEP), has developed planning and management guidelines for sustainable tourism in protected areas in an attempt to deal with this problem. The objective is to minimize negative impacts of tourism on the environment of protected natural areas while also providing practical advice and suggestions for more effective management. Seraphin et al. (2018) also points out the need to develop management strategies in tourism as a measure against overtourism.

3.3.2 *Life Cycle (TALC) Analysis of Tourist Destinations*

Tourism demand research has been undertaken for many years now against the backdrop of a general expansion of international tourism. Tourism demand models have been considered as a way of influencing analyses that cover a diverse range of research contents, theories, and methodologies and bring in a variety of determinant factors.[20] Congestion is the subject of this study, and clearly it is one of the determinants that can be included in tourism demand models.

One of the concepts frequently figuring in the study of tourism demand is "TALC," standing for Tourist Area Life Cycle" (or more recently "the life cycle of tourist destinations"), devised by Butler (1980), (2006).[21] Nakazaki (1998) regards the concept of TALC as "a way of indicating the principal dynamic potential of a tourist area at each stage in its life cycle as a function of the relationship between its elements of

[17] This is shown in Perkumienė and Pranskuunienė (2019).

[18] This is mentioned in Peeters et al. (2018).

[19] In public and environmental economics, it is shown as external diseconomy.

[20] Li et al. (2005) conducted a literature search for econometric studies of international tourism demand undertaken worldwide since 1961. This paper summarizes 81 models and empirical studies on prediction published between 1990 and 2004.

[21] Cole (2012) showed that more than 1500 works of research had appeared on TALC at that time.

capacity for drawing tourists and actual tourism demand."[22] Cole (2012) also includes a survey of research using TALC in his study of synergy and congestion. The "life cycle" of a tourist destination is thus the process of development and decline it passes through from exploration, involvement, development, and consolidation, to stagnation ending in either rejuvenation or decline. This is represented in Butler's (1980)[23] "basic S-shaped life cycle curve."

As "carrying capacity"[24] is the central point of this TALC concept, TALC is widely used in studies of tourism capacity.[25] Brougham and Butler (1981) define "carrying capacity" as the "maximum number of visitors" to a destination. The highest point of the S-shaped curve shown by Butler (1980) is the "critical range of elements of capacity," which represents the "peak in the number of visitors."

3.3.3 Research on Congestion Phenomena in Tourism

Popular resort areas and tourist attractions may end up drawing too many tourists into spaces that are too narrowly confined. In particular, this may come to have a negative impact of congestion in areas of high tourism demand and environmental abundance or in areas having cultural facilities or a high concentration of cultural assets. Congestion can also have an adverse effect on landscape and on the conservation of archaeological and historic sites, on natural habitats of flora and fauna, and on increases in waste discharge and local area water and air pollution. Problems like these then greatly diminish the satisfaction felt by visitors, resulting not only in a fall-off in the effect of the quality of tourism offered, but also in an actual fall in the number of visitors not to mention the great rise in stress for the local tourist area community. In a word, tourism has always had to coexist with the issue of sustainability.

From an economic point of view, the supply and demand sides of the local area tourism market both need to be kept in balance. The supply side has to be balanced in such a way as to achieve a more even distribution of the benefits of tourist visits, while any accompanying excess in the number of tourists in the area has to be kept to a minimum. Furthermore, more is required than a simple year-on-year balance. It is also vital to go on developing future tourism strategies for cities and regions with these aims in mind.

Here, I give an overview of research on congestion phenomena in tourism in recent years. Cruz and Zaragoza (2019) is an analysis in which tourism demand, in

---

[22] Nakazaki (1998), pp. 1–3. TALC is called a "CONCEPT" in the title of Butler 1980.

[23] Brougham was work on forecasting the development of tourism by Butler and Brougham (1972).

[24] Van der Borg et al. (1996) explain that it is more commonly known as capacity, that is, it is related to the maximum limits of tourism development.

[25] Shelby and Heberlein (1984), p. 62, see carrying capacity as the point from which visitors begin to feel crowded as the scale of tourism exceeds what can be accommodated. In addition, the number of accommodation spaces per 100 residents or per km^2 can be used as an index of tourism density, which has the potential for being felt as social or environmental pressure.

terms of congestion variables, is related to tourist satisfaction. There are numerous other similar studies concerned with congestion. Cruz and Zaragoza (2019) compare tourism demand and tourist satisfaction in order to determine an optimal accommodation density for tourist destinations. Taking the saturation level of the Canary Islands tourist area as an index, it is shown that there is no correlation between the number of tourist beds and the degree of tourist satisfaction.

Eliat and Einav (2004) is a study of relations between tourist attractiveness and congestion in three areas of natural appeal offering similar characteristics: Caribbean beaches, Spanish coasts and the island of Bali. It is found, however, that no simple comparison can be drawn between these areas as research subjects. The finding proposed is that the attractiveness of tourist destinations has to be evaluated in terms of the inherent natural values of the localities concerned. The study analyzes the tourist area characteristics of five islands belonging to the Canaries group using econometric panel data obtained from a standard trade model based on relative factors between regions.

Santana-Jiménez et al. (2011) offers an analysis of the effects of felt overcrowding on the attractiveness of a tourist destination. The measure of overcrowding used is the population density of each of the islands covered, and the panel data analysis makes use of a tourism demand model. As a result, the authors create an index for the maximum capacity of each island and discuss policies for limiting the numbers of tourists accordingly. Marrocu and Paci (2013) examine the combined effects of supply and demand on the domestic tourism flow among all 107 Italian provinces in 2009, using a spatial interaction model of origins and destinations (OD). This paper evaluates the relative roles of factors determining the attractiveness of each province to tourists. The dependent variables considered include both pull and push effects in addition to distance. It is found that the distance to be traveled and population density, as calculated by a gravity model, have a negative influence on the readiness of tourists to select a specific destination.

In a study of visitor perceptions, Cole (2009) analyzed visitor perceptions of resort congestion using a Logistic Tourism Model (LTM) and carrying capacity coefficients. In a study based on regional capacity, Jurado and Fernández-Morales (2013) analyzed the Costa del Sol tourist region in Spain, using a social capacity model. The results provide an indicator for the proportion of prospective tourist visitors who feel that a destination is overcrowded. Recent studies dealing with congestion in tourism analysis are summarized in Table 3.1. Various analytical methods are used.

3.3.4 Research Using a Tourism Demand Model

Research on tourism demand models has been continuously underway for many years. Studies involving variables such as congestion include the following.

Papatheodorou (2001), in a study of destination development, brings together facilities and locations as defining categories of tourism production functions and analyzes the effects of other factors such as price, advertising and agglomeration.

Table 3.1 Contents and analytical methods of recent tourism congestion studies

Author(s)	Research content	Analytical method
Jakus and Shaw (1997)	Analysis of customer reactions to congestion and policies that control congestion	Probit analysis
Yoon et al. (2001)	Analysis of the impact of tourism impact factors on the entire region and the support of local residents for tourism development	Confirmatory factor analysis
Timmins and Murdock (2007)	An evaluated analysis of a large recreational fishing ground in Wisconsin (Lake Winnebago)	GMM
Riganti and Nijkamp (2008)	Analyzing the difference between tourists' willingness to pay and factors of tourist background or attribute information for cultural destinations	Hierarchical multiple regression analysis
Tchetchik et al. (2011)	Analysis examining the optimal size of rural tourist villages affected by agglomeration and congestion	GMM
Eugeni-Martin (2011)	Analysis of the elasticity of the probability of visiting a destination for increased congestion using a random parameter logit model	Multinominal logistic regression analysis
Cole (2012)	Analysis of synergies and congestion for Caribbean islands	OLS using logistic equations for synergistic potential of congestion
Navarro Jurado et al. (2013)	Analysis of tourists' perceptions of overcrowding, socio-economic characteristics of tourists, and factors of capacity threshold	Cluster analysis
Brinkman (2016)	Analysis with a spatial model of urban structure that includes both congestion costs and agglomeration externalities	GMM

Source Created by the author

Zhang et al. (2007) conduct a panel analysis based on trade theory, and conclude that the question of whether there is a local cultural or natural attraction plays a major role in deciding how many tourists will be drawn to the destination. In studies making use of tourism demand theory, Li et al. (2005) and Witt and Song (2000) analyze the impact of various factors on the appeal of a destination. Tourist demand is explained in terms of exogenous or demand variables such as price indicators, exchange rates, incomes in the visitors' countries of origin, and transportation costs.

Albaladejo et al. (2016) perform an analysis based on the dynamic econometric model of tourism demand in TALC theory, which depends on the delayed impact of reputation and congestion effects on tourism demand. This study uses panel data from Spanish regions for the period 2000–2013. Separate estimates are conducted for domestic and international tourists using a dynamic demand model that includes persistence and reputation effects. From the analysis, the coefficients of reputation and congestion are found to be negative for both domestic and international tourists. However, it is also shown that the influence of reputation is not constant for domestic and international tourists, and that the effects of congestion more strongly deter international tourists visiting Spain. Albaladejo and González-Martínez (2019) also conducted a similar analysis for Spanish Mediterranean destinations using data from 2001 to 2015. The results show a strong persistence in the tourism demand, the effect of which is positive. In contrast, the reputation/congestion effect, which is the ratio of the capacity of a destination to the number of tourists, is negative. Lim (2007) analyzes tourism demand with a focus on habit persistence.

Santana-Jiménez et al. (2011) conducted a panel data analysis based on a survey covering numerous resorts in the Canary Islands. An estimate of the effect of over-crowding on demand is essential for tourist planning because it makes it possible to define the capacity of a destination. In addition, this research also allowed for the inclusion of population density among the dependent variables of tourist demand and offered an index for the recognition of tourist overcrowding.

3.3.5 Variables of Congestion in Tourism Research

Table 3.2 is a list of variables used to indicate congestion in tourism research.

In addition, UNWTO (2004) also mentions many other measures developed to indicate congestion in cultural facilities. Variables frequently used include the ratio of the local population to peak and off-peak visitors, the number of tourists per square meter at the destination, and the ratio of visitors who think the destination is crowded. Other variables include the amount of time spent waiting for transportation, the number of people overall per unit of space at the destination, and the amount of excess waste generated in densely crowded areas.

3.4 Analysis Method and Data Used

3.4.1 Tourism Demand Function Including Congestion Variables

This study is an analysis of tourism demand among international visitors to Japan, including variables of congestion. For this discussion, I refer first to Albaladejo et al. (2016), Albaladejo and González-Martínez (2019). In these papers, the tourism demand function includes variables of demand from a certain period before, which allows the effect of a destination's existing reputation to be taken into account. The content of this analysis makes use of TALC (Tourism Area Life Cycle Model) theory, and tourism congestion is used as the dependent variable. There has been no previous empirical study using variables of tourism congestion in Japanese economic research. My choice of this content was for that reason. This tourism demand function is assumed to be non-linear. The estimate period is from 2010 to 2018, and the figures for international tourists visiting Japan are obtained from panel data of the

Table 3.2 Research on tourism congestion and variables used to indicate it

Author(s)	Variable indicating congestion	Remarks
Defert (1967)	Number of hotel and other accommodation rooms per 100 inhabitants	Index of tourist function
UNWTO (1983)	2–4 accommodation spaces per 100 inhabitants	Now generally accepted ratio
Shelby and Heberlein (1984)[26]	Number of accommodation spaces per 100 people per km^2	Tourist density used as an index of the number of accommodation spaces
Machado-Carrillo (1990)	Number of beds per 2 local residents, or number of beds per km^2	Officially limited to 0.5 max per 2 local residents or 20 max per km^2[27]
Lundtorp and Wanhill (2001, 2006)	Ratio of visitors to capacity	
Lise and Tol (2002)	Population density	
Cole (2009)	Average annual number of surplus rooms, transport capacity parameters, distance to the beach	Variation in per visitor income due to the variation in accommodation rooms per km^2 (this figure decreases at a certain stage)
Santana-Jiménez and Hernández (2011)	Population density	
Fernández-Latorre and del Olmo (2011)	Room accommodation for 1000 people (max limit) per km^2	The pressure index for social environment tourism is set at this maximum value
Papatheodorou (2002) Rigall-I-Torrent and Fluvià (2011), Saló et al. (2014)	Congestion (measured as number of rooms per population or per km^2)	
Hernández et al. (2016)	Number of hotel rooms offering a good view	
Peeters et al. (2018)	Visitor density (number of beds/km^2)	The saturation level for the accommodation is set by a saturation benchmark
Cruz and Zaragoza (2019)	Capacity and crowding of tourist facilities	

Source Created by the author

total number of stays by international visitors in the "Statistical Survey of Overnight Travel" (JTA). Morley (2009) shows that tourism demand is likely to be influenced

[26] Shelby and Heberlein (1984), p. 62, see carrying capacity as the point from which visitors begin to feel crowded as the scale of tourism exceeds what can be accommodated. In addition, the number of accommodation spaces per 100 residents or per km^2 can be used as an index of tourism density, which has the potential for being felt as social or environmental pressure.

[27] Machado-Carrillo (1990), p. 88.

by dynamic factors. Therefore, a dynamic panel analysis is used here. As the data for the analysis have a relatively large number of cross sections for a small number of time series, the Arellano-Bond estimator as introduced by Takahashi (2013) seems appropriate. Here, Arellano-Bond instrumental variables and the generalized product factor method (GMM) are used.

The model used in the study is as explained in Albaladejo et al. (2016). The standard model is as follows.

$$T_t = \beta_0 + \beta_1 T_{t-1} + \gamma' X_t + \varepsilon_t \tag{3.1}$$

The output to be explained T_t is a variable indicating tourism demand, the explanatory variable T_{t-1} is a dependent variable with a lag in tourism demand, X_t is a variable relating to other factors of tourism demand, and ε_t is a regression error term.

X_t can be shown in the following way as a vector of price, income, or suchlike.

$$X_t = \left(X_t^1, X_t^2, \ldots, X_t^k\right) \tag{3.2}$$

Equations (3.1) and (3.3) assume that the lag in demand has a constant effect on current demand. In other words, the elasticity of current tourism demand with respect to demand "one period" ago is constant, and the persistence of tourism demand and the effects of reputation and congestion are constant as well.

$$\frac{\partial \mathrm{y}_t}{\partial \mathrm{x}_t} = \beta_1 \; is \; constant \tag{3.3}$$

However, there are many papers that point out that this elasticity may not be constant.[28] Morley (2000, 2009) proposes an equation using variables that show the effects of various other characteristics on tourism demand.[29] In addition, Lundtorp and Wanhill (2001, 2006) offer a relation approximating to a logistic growth model where parameter σ is the intrinsic rate of tourism growth, assumed as positive, and CC refers to the carrying capacity.

$$T_t - T_{t-1} = \sigma T_{t-1}\left(1 - \frac{T_{t-1}}{CC}\right) \tag{3.4}$$

σ in Eq. (3.4) is the pace of tourism growth and is considered to be a positive value CC is a variable indicating the carrying capacity. A rearrangement of Eq. (3.4) then gives Eq. (3.5).

$$T_t = \beta_1 T_{t-1} + \beta_2 \frac{T_{t-1}^2}{CC} \tag{3.5}$$

[28] As explained in Albaladejo et al. (2016), p. 133.

[29] As explained in Cruz and Zaragoza (2019), p. 10.

Here, β_1 is positive and β_2 is negative. Rewriting this into the form of a Riccati differential equation gives Eq. (3.6) below.

$$\frac{\partial T_t}{\partial T_{t-1}} = \beta_1 + 2\beta_2 \frac{T_{t-1}}{CC} \tag{3.6}$$

This shows the marginal negative effect handed down from the typical past traveler T_{t-1} to the current traveler T_t. In other words, this second term T_t includes the effect of a drop in reputation, and the ratio of new visitors to the past tourism capacity will decrease. This means that the persistence or reputation effect is not constant, but is affected by the second term.

When tourist destinations are too crowded, the number of visitors decreases due to the resultant lowering in their reputation. From the point of view of the tourist area life cycle (TALC), this means that if the tourist capacity in a resort remains constant, the pace of tourism growth will decrease as the number of tourists increases. To provide an analysis of this tourist demand, the right side of the equation makes use of the following model incorporating TALC theory and the dynamic capacity of the tourism area. Assuming that Eq. (3.6) has been calculated logarithmically, the calculation for returning it to its antilog form is as shown in Eq. (3.7) below. Since this equation is for the square of the lagged demand, it has to be divided by the timed independent variable and expressed in a quadratic form as follows.

$$T_t = \beta_0 + \beta_1 T_{t-1} + \beta_2 \frac{T_{t-1}^2}{CC} + \gamma' x_t + \varepsilon_t \tag{3.7}$$

3.4.2 Variables Indicating Tourism Demand

Variables used in the analysis of tourism demand include things such as the amount consumed by visitors at a tourist destination or the number of visitors. As the focus here is on the effects of congestion, tourist demand will be expressed through the number of visitors. As shown in Sect. 3.2 above, estimates of the number of visitors can be obtained from the total number of stays by international visitors recorded in the "Statistical Survey of Overnight Travel" by the Japan Tourism Agency (JTA) and from the number of foreign visitors to Japan according to the Japan National Tourism Organization (JNTO). Comparing these two sets of data, the yearly variation from 2010 to 2019 is the same. The correlation coefficient between the two sets over the 10 years is 0.97. Given this high correlation, the total numbers of stays by international visitors are taken in this study as input data indicating trends among international visitors traveling in Japan. That is to say, these data exclude the numbers of visitors arriving in the area on day trips only.

Other data sets exist that take in the total numbers of visitors arriving in a tourist area, but the data from the "Overnight Travel Statistics Survey" are preferred in this study as allowing a more accurate grasp of the numbers of tourists actually staying in the area. The "Statistical Survey of Overnight Travel" also stands out among tourism statistics as being conducted in accordance with Article 33 of the Statistics Act (Act No. 53 of 2007) on the basis of information gathered through survey forms. From these raw statistics, finer details can be obtained, for example, about total numbers of stays by international visitors by countries of origin, or by the prefectures stayed in. Thus, the survey covers accommodation facility locations (47 prefectures), total numbers of overnight guests, and within this, total numbers of international visitor overnight guests, capacity occupancy rates, numbers of rooms used, and room occupancy rates. For facilities with 10 or more employees, the coverage also extends to total numbers of international visitor overnight guests by country or citizenship (21 categories: 20 specified countries and "others"). Data for the total numbers of stays by overnight guests by countries of origin in the survey were only collected from accommodation facilities with 10 or more employees. For this study, it is therefore necessary to estimate country-specific totals for facilities with under 10 employees in each prefecture by first finding the proportional shares among the 21 country-of-origin categories in facilities employing 10 staff or more, and then applying the same proportions to the total number of stays by international visitor overnight guests at all accommodation facilities in that prefecture.

The nationalities (or citizenships) used in this study were for eight countries (or territories): China, Taiwan, South Korea, Hong Kong, the United States, Thailand, Australia, and Singapore. These countries were chosen for analysis because they accounted together for 70–80% of stays in overnight accommodation facilities by international visitors to Japan.

3.4.3 Variables Indicating Tourism Congestion

In TALC theory, as explained above, the effect of reputation on the tourist area is used as an indicator of tourism congestion. The maximum number of tourists that can be accommodated in a tourist area is taken as the capacity of the local tourism industry, the denominator of the term indicating congestion in the explanatory variable of Eq. (3.7). Various variables are used for this in the research literature. This study follows Marrocu and Paci (2013),[30] and also Albaladejo et al. (2016), Albaladejo and González-Martínez (2019), in taking account of the effect of the number of "Puntos turísticos (tourism sites)"[31] in the vicinity of the tourist destination. The larger the number of tourism sites, the more areas there are that offer attractions to tourists. This means that the spatial dispersion of the area will increase. In surveys performed by the Japan Tourism Agency, tourist numbers are given separately for the

[30] Marrocu and Paci (2013) use the number of museums and recreational attractions.

[31] At that time, "puntos turísticos were cultural or natural assets of certified value similar to UNESCO heritage sites. This chapter uses the term "Tourism" sites, although "Tourist spots" or "Tourist sites" may be more appropriate.

47 prefectures. Therefore, these are the numbers of overnight stays used in dependent variable of this study. The number of tourism sites for each prefectures are used as one of the explanatory variables. The numerator of the reputation variable is the number of tourists visiting. Therefore, the variable of congestion in each tourist destination can be found by dividing the number of tourists by the number of tourism sites. In addition to the number of tourism sites, alternative estimates were also made by substituting other measures such as guest room occupancies or total guest room capacities. However, these did not prove to be statistically significant variables.

3.4.4 Other Variables Relating to Tourism Demand and Formulas Used for Analysis

Relative price variables between the host region (a Japanese prefecture) and the country of origin of a particular international visitor are calculated as follows.

The relative price is calculated using the consumer price index for the prefectural capital concerned, the consumer price index for the country of origin, and the nominal exchange rate between the currency of that country and the Japanese yen.

$$IP_{ijt} = \frac{CPI_{it}}{CPI_{Jt}.EXjt} \quad i = 1, \ldots, 47 \quad j = 1, \ldots, 8 \tag{3.8}$$

The basic equation used for the analysis is Eq. (3.9) below. Equation (3.10), for use with the two years 2011 and 2012 which were affected by the Great East Japan Earthquake (March 2011), includes an additional dummy variable to compensate for the disturbance in the analysis.

$$T_{ij,t} = \beta_0 + \beta_1 T_{ij,t-1} + \beta_2 \frac{T_{ij,t-1}^2}{CC} + \beta_3 GDP_{j,t} + \beta_4 IP_{ij,t} + \varepsilon_{ij,t} \tag{3.9}$$

$$T_{ij,t} = \beta_0 + \beta_1 T_{ij,t-1} + \beta_2 \frac{T_{ij,t-1}^2}{CC} + \beta_3 GDP_{j,t} + \beta_4 IP_{ij,t} + \beta_5 D2012_t + \varepsilon_{ij,t} \tag{3.10}$$

GDP stands for data indicating the economic situation in each particular country of origin. The variable used in this study for the economic situation of individual tourists was the GDP per capita. This per capita GDP calculation was initially performed in two currencies, dollars and yen, allowing for fluctuations in exchange rates in each case. Finally, the yen results were preferred, as supplying a better estimate.

3.4.5 Variables Indicating the Strength of Tourism Supply

Variables used in the analysis of tourism demand include some which serve to indicate the strength of tourism supply.

Referring again to the research of Albaladejo et al., on hotel tourism on the Mediterranean coasts of Spain, the dependent variable used for the strength of tourism supply in Albaladejo and González-Martínez (2019) is the number of hotel beds in each area divided by the length of the province's coastline measured in kilometers.

Since there are no data on the number of beds in accommodation facilities in the "Overnight Travel Statistics Survey," the total capacity had to be indirectly calculated for this study. The calculation was performed by finding the ratios of the reported numbers of stays to the total available accommodation capacities. Similar to Albaladejo and González-Martínez (2019), this study makes use of a numerical value called *LANK*[32] obtained by dividing the data for each prefecture by the average distance (i.e., by the square root of the area) of the prefecture in question. Equation (3.11) is the formula obtained by adding the variable *LANK* to Eq. (3.10).

In Albaladejo et al. (2016), however, no variables are used that indicate the strength of tourism supply. Accordingly, this study also estimates the case where this variable is not added.

$$T_{ij,t} = \beta_0 + \beta_1 T_{ij,t-1} + \beta_2 \frac{T^2_{ij,t-1}}{CC} + \beta_3 GDP_{j,t} + \beta_4 IP_{ij,t} + \beta_5 LANK_{ij,t} + \beta_6 D2012_t + \varepsilon_{ij,t} \tag{3.11}$$

3.5 Results of Analysis

3.5.1 Tourism Demand Among International Visitors to Japan, by Prefectures of Stay

This study involved a dynamic panel analysis[33] of tourism demand among international visitors from eight countries staying in various prefectures. Four analysis operations were performed for varying numbers of prefectures. Concerning the numbers of international visitors, the numbers of prefectures covered were the top 6 by frequency of stay, the top 9, the top 20, and finally all 47 prefectures. The dependent variables used were the number of international visitors traveling to Japan in the previous year to indicate persistence, the variable to indicate reputation, per

[32] Albaladejo and González-Martínez (2019) used the variable of the strength of tourism supply named BEDKM.

[33] As shown in Kitaoka (2008) and Takahashi (2013).

capita income (by countries of origin), relative prices, the total number of accommodation facilities, indicating the strength of tourism supply divided by the distance of the prefecture concerned the square root of the area, and dummy variables to correct for the disruption from the Great East Japan Earthquake in 2011.

The Arellano-Bond instrumental variable includes two component variables. One of them, in this case, is the number of international visitors coming to Japan the previous year, as an indicator of persistence as a destination, and the other is an indicator of reputation/congestion. As an additional instrumental variable, estimates were also made that took no account of the strength of tourism supply.

Estimates were made using a two-step generalized method of moments (GMM), as will be seen below at the top of Tables 3.3 and 3.4. The first step is for when the disturbance term has no serial correlation or local dispersion. The second step is for when serial correlation or local dispersion plays a part in the disturbance term.

First, a check of the model formulation was carried out to see whether the selected model was appropriate. The Arellano-Bond estimator itself requires two tests, first a test for the condition of "non-autocorrelation" that is assumed in the model settings, and then a test for the "overidentification of covariates" to ensure that the number of moment constraints imposed by the instrumental variables is not greater than the number of explanatory variables. Problems with sign conditions were discovered in 20 prefectures, and problems with model formulation in 47. This result is probably due to the uneven distribution of areas visited by international tourists in Japan.

The Arellano-Bond estimator works on an assumption that the disturbance term contains "no autocorrelation." Under this assumption, it covers the correlation for the first-order difference expressed in the disturbance term, that is, the first-order autocorrelation AR (1). But it does not provide coverage for second- or higher-order autocorrelations. Putting this another way, the null hypothesis for an Arellano-Bond autocorrelation estimate is that there is "no autocorrelation." Therefore, the null hypothesis will not be rejected in the case of first-order autocorrelation AR (1). It will be rejected, however, in the case of second-order autocorrelation AR (2).

Table 3.3 shows estimate results for the nine prefectures in which international visitors most often stayed. Named from north to south, these were: Hokkaido, Chiba, Tokyo, Kanagawa, Aichi, Kyoto, Osaka, Fukuoka, and Okinawa. In the AR (1) autocorrelation test for all of these results, the null hypothesis (that there is no autocorrelation) cannot be rejected. In the AR (2) test, autocorrelation of second-order differences is rejected. Thus, the results from this model satisfy both conditions of non-autocorrelation. As a test for overidentification of restrictions, the Hansen J test was performed. The null hypothesis for this test is that "the number of instrumental variables is not excessive." The J statistic from the two-step estimate has a P value of 0.311 for the 6 explanatory and 63 instrumental variables, if the variable for the strength of tourism supply is included in the estimation formula. If the variable for the strength of tourism supply is left out, the P value is 0.365 for 5 explanatory and 63 instrumental variables. Whether the variable for the strength of tourism supply is left out or included, (at a significance level of 10%) the null hypothesis cannot be rejected. Therefore, there is no problem with the instrumental variables. However, in the case of a one-step GMM estimator, the null hypothesis is rejected in both cases.

Table 3.3 Estimated results of 9 prefectures—result of using the number of stays by visiting international tourists as a variable for effects of reputation and congestion

Estimation method GMM	One-step	Two-step	One-step	Two-step
Tourism supply strength variable	Included	Included	Not included	Not included
Dependent variable	Coefficient	Coefficient	Coefficient	Coefficient
Number of international tourists visiting prefectures one year ago (log)	0.759*	0.775***	0.891**	0.922***
Squared number of international tourists visiting prefectures one year ago (log)	− 0.153	− 0.161***	− 0.185	− 0.201***
GDP per capita in the country of origin one year ago (log)	0.574***	0.567***	0.547***	0.524***
Relative price variable between host area and country of origin (log)	− 1.899***	− 1.902***	− 2.047***	− 2.039***
Total capacity ((Total number of overnight guests/occupancy rate) ÷ average distance) (log)	0.964***	0.956***		
Dummy variable (2012 = 1, other year = 0)	0.366***	0.368***	0.406***	0.399***
Dummy variable (Korea, Australia, 2019 = 1, other year = 0)			0.766***	0.785***
Root mean squared error	0.2534	0.2534	0.2752	0.2756
Variance of dependent variables	0.2488	0.2488	0.2488	0.2488
Residual sum of squares	36.9800	36.9961	43.6153	43.7541
Number of instrumental variables	80	72	80	72
Mean of explained variables	0.2428	0.2428	0.2428	0.2428
Standard error of regression	0.2547	0.2548	0.2766	0.2771
J statistic	369.3118	70.8280	344.982	69.3471
(J-statistic) probability of appearance of value	0	0.3199	0	0.3653
Sample size	576	576	504	504
Estimated period	2012–2019	2012–2019	2012–2019	2012–2019
Length of period	8 years	8 years	8 years	8 years
Cross section	72	72	72	72
Arellano-Bond serial correlation test				
AR (1) (p value)	0.000	0.005	0.000	0.006
AR (2) (p value)	0.674	0.706	0.728	0.733

Source As estimated by the author
Note *** indicates significance level of 1%, ** indicates significance level of 5%, * indicates significance level of 10%. Estimated by the author using EVews11
Average distance indicates the data for each prefecture by the average distance (i.e., square root of its area)

Table 3.4 Estimated results of 9 prefectures—result of using the total number of stays by overnight tourists as a variable for effects of reputation and congestion

Estimation method GMM	One-step	Two-step	One-step	Two-step
Tourism supply strength variable	Included	Included	Not included	Not included
Dependent variable	Coefficient	Coefficient	Coefficient	Coefficient
Number of international tourists visiting prefectures one year ago (log)	0.481***	0.483***	0.591***	0.592***
Squared number of international tourists visiting prefectures one year ago (log)	– 0.190**	– 0.186***	– 0.026	– 0.035***
GDP per capita in the country of origin one year ago (log)	0.450***	0.439***	0.358**	0.359***
Relative price variable between host area and country of origin (log)	– 2.074***	– 2.062***	– 2.058***	– 2.055***
Total capacity ((Total number of overnight guests/occupancy rate) ÷ average distance) (log)	0.989***	0.978***		
Dummy variable (2012 = 1, other year = 0)	0.366***	0.369***	0.408***	0.401***
Dummy variable (Korea, Australia, 2019 = 1, other year = 0)	0.437***	0.439***	0.801***	0.830***
Root mean squared error	0.253	0.253	0.280	0.281
Variance of dependent variables	0.249	0.249	0.249	0.249
Residual sum of squares	36.955	36.936	45.082	45.527
Number of instrumental variables	88	88	88	88
Mean of explained variables	0.243	0.243	0.243	0.243
Standard error of regression	0.255	0.255	0.281	0.283
J statistic	391.921	70.635	416.778	70.592
(J-statistic) probability of appearance of value	0	0.295	0	0.327
Sample size	576	576	576	576
Estimated period	2012–2019	2012–2019	2012–2019	2012–2019
Length of period	8 years	8 years	8 years	8 years
Cross section	72	72	72	72
Arellano-bond serial correlation test				
AR (1) (p value)	0.000	0.003	0.000	0.003
AR (2) (p value)	0.761	0.811	0.927	0.905

Source As estimated by the author
Note Same as Table 3.3

Therefore, the two-step estimates are statistically significant for all explanatory variables. Comparing the effect of the number of tourists one year before on the number in the current year, this is positive with a value of 0.775 if the variable indicating the strength of tourist supply is included in the estimate formula, and also positive, but with a value of 0.922, if it is not included. Thus, this variable has a persistently positive effect on the following year. The effect of the previous ratio between tourist numbers and the number of tourism sites is negative with a value of − 0.161 if the tourism supply strength variable is included in the estimation. If it is not included, this negative effect is − 0.201. In TALC theory in tourist destinations, this is what corresponds to reputation: any perception of congestion leads to a negative effect in the following year. As for elasticity of income in the country of origin, this is positive, indicating that the number of tourists visiting Japan will depend on the level of income in that country. Price elasticity, on the other hand, is estimated to be negative, indicating an inhibiting effect of price changes on the number of international visitors. The effect is estimated to be − 1.902 if the tourism supply strength variable is included in the calculation, or − 2.039 if it is not included. The coefficient of the variable indicating the strength of tourism supply is positive, at 0.956.

In Table 3.3, the left pair of columns show results if the tourism supply strength variable is included in the calculation, and the right pair show results if it is not included.

Figure 3.7 is a scatter plot of the total number of stays by international visitors to Japan in 9 prefectures in 2019 and the effect on persistence, reputation, and congestion. This is a calculation of persistence and the further effects of reputation and congestion in 2019 using a coefficient estimated using two-step GMM estimator including the above variable indicating the strength of tourism supply.

This figure suggests a positive relationship between the number of stays by international visitors to Japan and the estimated effect. The prefectures that receive more tourists are those with a higher reputation and persistence effect on average. There are prefectures moving away from this average behavior. Hokkaido has a comparatively high estimated reputation and persistence effect in relation to the number of tourists. In contrast, Okinawa has a slightly lower estimated effect.

One more general characteristic of tourism in Japan, however, is that domestic travel (by people living in the country) accounts for a large share of the total. To appreciate the effects of reputation and congestion in TALC theory in connection with Japan, therefore, it seems necessary in this study to consider the total numbers of tourists staying in Japanese prefectures, both international and domestic. For that purpose, a further variable is used that combines the numbers of overnight tourists living in Japan with the numbers of international visitors to Japan from overseas. The results are shown in Table 3.4.

In Table 3.4, the left pair of columns show results if the tourism supply strength variable is included in the calculation, and the right pair show results if it is not included.

As with Table 3.3, the null hypothesis cannot be rejected in the AR (1) autocorrelation test for any of these results. In the AR (2) test, second-order autocorrelation is rejected. Accordingly, these results, too, are shown to meet the two conditions of

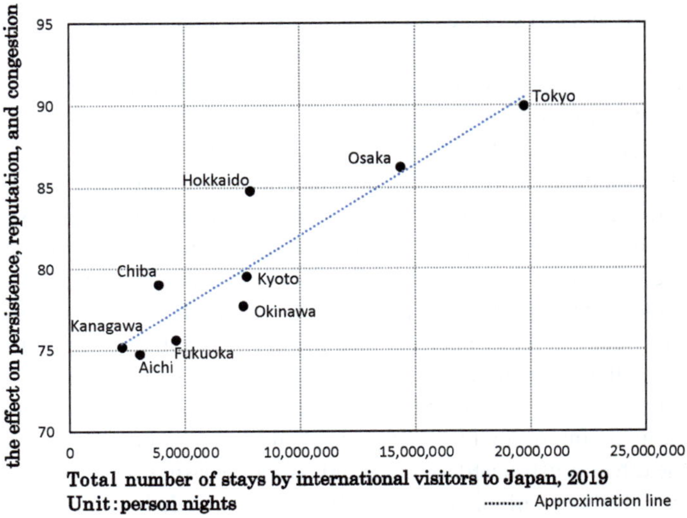

Fig. 3.7 Scatter plot of the total number of stays by international visitors to Japan in 9 prefectures in 2019 and the effect on persistence, reputation, and congestion. *Source* Created by the author using the estimate results

non-autocorrelation. Again, the Hansen J test was used as a test for overidentification of restrictions. The null hypothesis, again, was that "the number of instrumental variables is not excessive." In both of these cases, (in the two-step test, for a significance level of 10%) the null hypothesis cannot be rejected, showing that there is no problem with the instrumental variables.

The two-step estimates are statistically significant for all dependent variables. Again, the effect of the number of tourists one year previously on the number in the current year is positive with a value of 0.483 if the variable for the strength of tourist supply is included in the estimate. If it is not included, the effect is also positive, with a value of 0.592. As before, this variable has a persistent and positive effect on the following year.

The effect of the square (log) of the previous year's number of tourists is again negative with a value of − 0.186 if the tourism supply strength variable is included in the estimation. If it is not included, the effect is again negative, but the value is − 0.035. The coefficient of the variable indicating the strength of tourism supply is positive, at 0.978.

3.5.2 Tourism Demand Among International Visitors to Japan, in Six Prefectures

Here, the method of estimation is the same as described above, but the coverage is limited to the six prefectures most frequently stayed in by international visitors to Japan. Table 3.5 shows the analysis results from these prefectures: Hokkaido, Chiba, Tokyo, Kyoto, Osaka, and Okinawa. Also, this table displays the result of using the number of stays by visiting international tourists as a variable for effects of reputation and congestion and the result of using the total number of stays by overnight tourists as a variable for effects of reputation and congestion.

The null hypothesis in an Arellano-Bond autocorrelation estimate, as we have seen, is "no autocorrelation." This cannot be rejected for AR (1) (first-order autocorrelation). It can be rejected, however, for the second-order autocorrelation step AR (2). This model therefore satisfies the conditions of non-autocorrelation. In the test for overidentification of restrictions, the null hypothesis cannot be rejected at a significance level of 10% in the case of a two-step GMM estimator for the case including the above variable indicating the strength of tourism supply, showing that there is no problem with the instrumental variables. However, in the case of a one-step GMM estimator for the case including the tourism supply strength variable, and in two-step GMM estimator for the case in which it is not included, the null hypothesis is rejected. Therefore, it is necessary to reexamine the instrumental variables. Cases where the instrumental variables need to be reexamined irrespective of the kind of GMM estimator involved are not shown in Table 3.5.

In Table 3.5, the left pair of columns show results if the tourism supply strength variable is included in the calculation, and the right pair show results if it is not included.

The two-step estimates are statistically significant for all dependent variables. The effect of the number of tourists one year before on the number in the current year is again positive with a value of 1.039 if the variable for the strength of tourist supply is included. Here, too, the effect on the following year is persistently positive. The effects on reputation and congestion are − 0.325. The coefficients for elasticity of income (+) and for elasticity of price in the country of origin (−) show the same signs as in the results for the nine prefectures.

Thus Table 3.5, similarly to Table 3.4, once more shows the results of using the total number of stays by overnight tourists as a variable for effects of reputation and congestion. The Arellano-Bond test for autocorrelation and the test for overidentified restrictions give similar results to the ones for the number of stays by visiting international tourists already analyzed above for effects of reputation and congestion.

In the test for overidentification of restrictions, the null hypothesis cannot be rejected at a significance level of 10% in the case of a two-step GMM estimator for the case including the above variable indicating the strength of tourism supply, showing that there is no problem with the instrumental variables.

However, in the case of a one-step GMM estimator for the case including the tourism supply strength variable, and in the case of a two-step GMM estimator for

Table 3.5 Estimated results of 6 prefectures: result of using the number of stays by visiting international tourists as a variable for effects of reputation and congestion and result of using the total number of stays by overnight tourists as a variable for effects of reputation and congestion

	Result of using the number of stays by visiting international tourists		Result of using the total number of stays by overnight tourists	
Estimation method GMM	One-step	Two-step	One-step	Two-step
Dependent variable	Coefficient	Coefficient	Coefficient	Coefficient
Number of international tourists visiting prefectures one year ago (log)	1.041***	1.039***	0.535	0.528***
Squared number of international tourists visiting prefectures one year ago (log)	− 0.326*	− 0.325***	− 0.268***	− 0.280***
GDP per capita in the country of origin one year ago (log)	0.537***	0.533***	0.319	0.320***
Relative price variable between host area and country of origin (log)	− 1.603***	− 1.601***	− 2.106***	− 2.125***
Total capacity ((Total number of overnight guests/occupancy rate) ÷ average distance) (log)	1.048**	1.058***	1.070***	1.058***
Dummy variable (2012 = 1, other year = 0)			0.356***	0.354***
Root mean squared error	0.2996	0.2995	0.265	0.264
Variance of dependent variables	0.2518	0.2518	0.252	0.252
Residual sum of squares	34.4787	34.4508	26.953	26.853
Number of instrumental variables	77	48	88	48
Mean of explained variables	0.2526	0.2526	0.253	0.253
Standard error of regression	0.3016	0.3015	0.267	0.267
J statistic	284.8593	47.7638	317.796	45.463
(J-statistic) probability of appearance of value	0	0.2853	0	0.330
Sample size	384	384	384	384
Estimated period	2012–2019	2012–2018	2012–2019	2012–2018
Length of period	8 years	8 years	8 years	8 years
Cross section	48	48	48	48
Arellano-bond serial correlation test				
AR(1) (p value)	0.000	0.003	0.000	0.015
AR(2) (p value)	0.276	0.064	0.278	0.618

Source As estimated by the author
Note Same as Table 3.3

the case in which it is not included, the null hypothesis is rejected. Therefore, it is necessary to reexamine the instrumental variables. Cases where the instrumental variables need to be reexamined irrespective of the kind of GMM estimator involved are not shown in Table 3.5. The two-step estimate results for the case including the above variable indicating the strength of tourism supply estimates are statistically significant for all dependent variables.

The more detailed results from columns 4 and 5 in Table 3.5 are as follows. The persistence coefficient is 0.528, showing a positive effect. The effect on reputation and congestion is − 0.28. The income coefficient for the country of origin in the previous year is 0.32. Visits to Japan by international tourists are shown to be negatively affected by price changes. The coefficient of the variable indicating the strength of tourism supply is 1.058.

3.6 Conclusion

This study offers a summary of recent travel trends among international visitors to Japan and proposes a tourism demand function for estimates of future tourist numbers. Estimates of this kind make it more possible to analyze the ongoing impact of the congestion phenomenon and thus also contribute to the more general analysis of economic variables in this planning area.

The average growth rate in the number of international visitors coming to Japan in the ten years 2010–2019 was 19%. In 2019, the number of international visitors staying overnight was 31.88 million, ranking 12th in the world and 3rd in Asia. By prefectures, the number of overnight stays by visitors to Japan is highest in Tokyo, followed by Osaka, Kyoto, Hokkaido, Okinawa, and Chiba. In 2019, these six prefectures accounted for 69% of all overnight stays, while the top nine accounted for 79%. As Japan has 47 prefectures in all, this gives an idea of how extreme the regional bias in inbound tourism is. What is noticeable from these figures is that the recent rapid growth in the numbers of tourists coming in has led to greater concentrations in the same limited group of tourist areas. This suggests that conditions of overtourism are occurring. It is true that in 2020 and 2021, numbers of tourists fell worldwide with the novel coronavirus (COVID-19) pandemic. Once this external factor is removed, however, there is every chance that the demand for tourism will gradually reappear. If demand levels return to what they were in 2019, many tourist areas will soon face the problem of overtourism again.

With this in mind, the aim of this study was to arrive at an estimate of the demand function of tourists visiting Japan on the basis of the TALC (Tourist Area Life Cycle) model using data from the top nine, and more especially the top six, prefectures in terms of the number of overnight stays by international tourists. It was found that the ongoing effect of the current number of international visitors continuing to draw new visitors is persistent in the prefectures where tourists from overseas are already numerous. The subsequent effect of this on the reputation of these tourist areas, and on problems of congestion, will work out negatively in the following year. It was verified also that the effect of elasticity of income in the country of origin is positive, and that its influence on numbers will depend on the income level in each country. Further, visitor numbers were also affected by price changes.

The reputation of individual tourist areas will affect the future behavior of tourists visiting Japan. For that reason, national and local government, and the tourism industry in each tourist area, need to take measures to reduce congestion problems. This is not a tourism policy that focuses on numbers. Rather, what will increasingly count in future are efforts to enhance the image of destinations. In the case of Japan, geographical distributions of tourist operations so far have been uneven. In order to overcome this problem of unevenness, there is a vital need to build up local attractiveness area by area, to disseminate information, and to follow the tourism strategies that fit best locally.

References

Albaladejo, I. P., & González-Martínez, M. I. (2019). Non-constant reputation effect at Spanish Mediterranean destinations. In *Tourist destination management* (pp. 209–225). Springer. https://doi.org/10.1007/978-3-030-16981-7_12

Albaladejo, I. P., González-Martínez, M. I., & Martínez-García, M. P. (2016). Nonconstant reputation effect in a dynamic tourism demand model for Spain. *Tourism Management, 53*, 132–139. https://doi.org/10.1016/j.tourman.2015.09.018

Ali, R. (2016). Exploring the coming perils of overtourism. Skift, August 23, 2016 (Online). Available at https://skift.com/2016/08/23/exploring-the-coming-perils-of-overtourism/. Accessed October 7, 2023.

Brinkman, J. C. (2016). Congestion, agglomeration, and the structure of cities. *Journal of Urban Economics, 94*, 13–31. https://doi.org/10.1016/j.jue.2016.05.002

Brougham, J. E., & Butler, R. W. (1972). The applicability of the asymptotic curve to the forecasting of tourism development. Paper presented to the Research Workshop, Travel Research Association 4th Annual Conference, Quebec, July 1972.

Brougham, J. E., & Butler, R. W. (1981). A segmentation analysis of resident attitudes to the social impact of tourism. *Annals of Tourism Research, 8*(4), 569–590. https://doi.org/10.1016/0160-7383(81)90042-6

Butler, R. W. (1980). The concept of a tourist area cycle of evolution: Implications for management of resources. *Canadian Geographer, 24*(1), 5–12.

Butler, R. W. (2006). *The tourism area life cycle. Vol. 1, 2, 2: Conceptual and Theoretical Issues.* Channel View Publications.

Cole, S. (2009). A logistic tourism model—Resort cycles, globalization and Chaos. *Annals of Tourism Research, 36*(4), 689–714. https://doi.org/10.1016/j.annals.2009.07.004

Cole, S. (2012). Synergy and congestion in the tourist destination life cycle. *Tourism Management, 33*(5), 1128–1140. https://doi.org/10.1016/j.tourman.2011.11.018

Cruz, M. S., & Zaragoza, M. P. P. (2019). Analysis of the accommodation density in coastal tourism areas of insular destinations from the perspective of overtourism. *Sustainability, 11*(11), 1–19. https://doi.org/10.3390/su11113031

Defert, P. (1967). Le Taux de Fonction Touristique: Mise au Point et Critique. In *Les Cahiers du Tourisme. Série C-5*. Université d'Aix-Marseille.

Destination UK. (2017). WTM London's responsible tourism programme 2017. http://www.destination.uk.com/news/WTM-Londons-responsible-tourism-programme-2017-471. Accessed October 7, 2023.

Eliat, Y., & Einav, L. (2004). Determinants of international tourism: A three-dimensional panel data analysis. *Applied Economics, 36*, 1315–1327. https://doi.org/10.1080/000368404000180897

Eugenio-Martín, J. L. (2011). Assessing social carrying capacity of tourism destinations with random utility models. *Estudios de Economía Aplicada, 29–3*, 881–902.

Fernández-Latorre, F. M., & del Olmo, F. D. (2011). Huella ecológica y presión turística socio-ambiental: Aplicación en Canarias. *Boletín de la Asociación Geógrafos Españoles, 57*, 147–174.

Hernández, J. M., Suárez-Vega, R., & Santana-Jiménez, Y. (2016). The inter-relationship between rural and mass tourism: The case of Catalonia, Spain. *Tourism Management, 54*, 43–57. https://doi.org/10.1016/j.tourman.2015.10.015

Jakus, P., & Shaw, W. D. (1997). Congestion at recreation areas: Empirical evidence on perceptions, mitigating behaviour and management preferences. *Journal of Environmental Management, 50*(4), 389–401. https://doi.org/10.1006/jema.1997.0124

Japan Tourism Agency. (2018). 2018 White paper on tourism (in Japanese). Ministry of Land, Infrastructure, Transport and Tourism Agency, Tokyo.

Jurado, E. N., Damian, I. M., & Fernandez-Morales, A. (2013). Carrying capacity model applied in coastal destinations. *Annals of Tourism Research, 43*, 1–19. https://doi.org/10.1016/j.annals.2013.03.005

Kitaoka, T. (2008). Introduction to empirical analysis through EViews, applications (Chap. 2 GMM, pp. 65–94). In T. Kitaoka, H. Takahashi, & J. Yano (Eds.). Nihon Hyoronsha. (in Japanese).

Li, G., Song, H., & Witt, S. F. (2005). Recent developments in econometric modeling and forecasting. *Journal of Travel Research, 44*(1), 82–99. https://doi.org/10.1177/0047287505276594

Lim, C. (2007). A survey of tourism demand modelling practice Issues and implications. In L. Dwyer & P. Forsyth (Eds.), *International handbook on the economics of tourism* (pp. 45–72). Edward Elgar Publishing Ltd.

Lise, W., & Tol, R. S. (2002). Impact of climate on tourist demand. *Climatic Change, 55*(4), 429–449. https://doi.org/10.1023/A:1020728021446

Lundtorp, S., & Wanhill, S. (2001). The resort lifecycle theory: Generating processes and estimation. *Annals of Tourism Research, 28*(4), 947–964. https://doi.org/10.1016/S0160-7383(00)00080-3

Lundtorp, S., & Wanhill, S. (2006). Time path analysis and TALC stage demarcation. In W. R. Butler (Ed.), *The tourism area life cycle. Vol. 2: Conceptual and Theoretical Issues (Aspects of Tourism)* (pp. 138–149). Channel View Books.

Machado-Carrillo, A. (1990). Ecología, Medio Ambiente y Desarrollo Turístico en Canarias; Gobierno de Canarias Consejeria de la Presidencia: Santa Cruz de Tenerife.

Marrocu, E., & Paci, R. (2013). Different tourists to different destinations. Evidence from spatial interaction models. *Tourism Management, 39*, 71–83. https://doi.org/10.1016/j.tourman.2012.10.009

Morley, C. L. (2000). Demand modelling methodologies: Integration and other issues. *Tourism Economics, 6*(1), 5–19. https://doi.org/10.5367/000000000101297442

Morley, C. L. (2009). Dynamics in the specification of tourism demand models. *Tourism Economics, 15*(1), 23–39. https://doi.org/10.5367/000000009787536654

Nakazaki, S. (1998). R. W. Butler's "The concept of a tourist area cycle of evolution: Implications for management of resources" (1980). *Ryutsu Keizai University Faculty of Sociology,Department Bulletin Paper 8*(2), 97–111. (in Japanese). https://rku.repo.nii.ac.jp/records/1115. Accessed September 25, 2023.

Navarro Jurado, E., Damian, I. M., & Fernández-Morales, A. (2013). Carrying capacity model applied in coastal destinations. *Annals of Tourism Research, 43*, 1–19. https://doi.org/10.1016/j.annals.2013.03.005

Papatheodorou, A. (2001). Why people travel to different places. *Annals of Tourism Research, 28*(1), 164–179. https://doi.org/10.1016/S0160-7383(00)00014-1

Papatheodorou, A. (2002). Exploring competitiveness in Mediterranean resorts. *Tourism Economics, 8*(2), 133–150. https://doi.org/10.5367/000000002101298034

Peeters, P., Gössling, S., Klijs, J., Milano, C., Novelli, M., Dijkmans, C., Eijgelaar, E., Hartman, S, Heslinga, J., Isaac, R., Mitas, O., Moretti, S., Nawijn, J., Papp, B., & Postma, A. (2018).

Research for TRAN Committee—Overtourism: Impact and possible policy responses. European Parliament, Directorate General for Internal Policies, Policy Department B: Structural and Cohesion Policies, Transport and Tourism.

Perkumienė, D., & Pranskuunienė, R. (2019). Overtourism: Between the right to travel and residents' rights. *Sustainability, 11*, 21–38. https://doi.org/10.3390/su11072138

Richardson. D. (2017). Europe suffering the strain of tourism. https://www.ttgmedia.com/wtm/wtm-news/wtm-2017-europe-suffering-the-strain-of-tourism-12206. Accessed April 25, 2022.

Rigall-I-Torrent, R., & Fluvià, M. (2011). Managing tourism products and destinations embedding public good components: A hedonic approach. *Tourism Management, 32*(2), 244–255. https://doi.org/10.1016/j.tourman.2009.12.009

Riganti, P., & Nijkamp, P. (2008). Congestion in popular tourist areas: A multi-attribute experimental choice analysis of willingness-to-wait in Amsterdam. *Tourism Economics, 14*(1), 25–44. https://doi.org/10.5367/000000008783554785

Saló, A., Garriga, A., Rigall-I-Torrent, R., Vila, M., & Fluvià, M. (2014). Do implicit prices for hotels and second homes show differences in tourists' valuation for public attributes for each type of accommodation facility? *International Journal of Hospitality Management, 36*, 120–129. https://doi.org/10.1016/j.ijhm.2013.08.011

Santana-Jiménez, Y., & Hernández, J. M. (2011). Estimating the effect of overcrowding on tourist attraction: The case of Canary Islands. *Tourism Management, 32*(2), 415–425. https://doi.org/10.1016/j.tourman.2010.03.013

Seraphin, H., Sheeran, P., & Pilato, M. (2018). Over-tourism and the fall of Venice as a destination. *Journal of Destination Marketing & Management, 9*, 374–376. https://doi.org/10.1016/j.jdmm.2018.01.011

Shelby, B., & Heberlein, T. (1984). Social carrying capacity in recreation settings: Evolution, appraisal and application. *Leisure Sciences, 6*, 453–473.

Takahashi, S. (2013). A practical guide to dynamic panel analysis with EViews. *The Bulletin of Institute for Research in Business and Economics Meiji Gakuin University, 30*, 1–23. (in Japanese). https://econ.meijigakuin.ac.jp/research/nempo/pdf/30-1.pdf. Accessed September 25, 2023.

Tchetchik, A., Fleischer, A., & Finlkeshtain, I. (2011). An optimal size for rural tourism villages with agglomeration and congestion effects. *European Review of Agricultural Economics, 39*(4), 685–706. https://doi.org/10.1093/erae/jbr040

Timmins, C., & Murdock, J. (2007). A revealed preference approach to the measurement of congestion in travel cost models. *Journal of Environmental Economics and Management, 53*(2), 230–249. https://doi.org/10.1016/j.jeem.2006.08.002

UNWTO. (1983). *Risks of saturation of tourist carrying capacity overload in holiday destinations*. United Nations World Tourism Organization. https://doi.org/10.18111/9789284407545. Accessed October 7, 2023.

UNWTO. (2004). *Tourism congestion management at natural and cultural sites* (pp. 1–125). United Nations World Tourism Organization.

UNWTO. (2018). 'Overtourism'? Understanding and managing urban tourism growth beyond perceptions. UNWTO: Centre of Expertise Leisure, Tourism and Hospitality; NHTV, pp. 1–10. https://doi.org/10.18111/9789284420070. Accessed October 7, 2023.

Van der Borg, J., Costa, P., & Gootti, G. (1996). Tourism in European heritage cities. *Annals of Tourism Research, 23*(2), 306–321. https://doi.org/10.1016/0160-7383(95)00065-8

Witt, S. F., & Song, H. (2000). Advances in tourism research: Tourism demand modelling and forecasting. In *Modern econometric approaches. Advances in Tourism Research Series*. Routledge.

Yoon, Y., Dogan, G., & Chen, J. (2001). Validating a tourism development theory with structural equation modeling. *Tourism Management, 22*(4), 363–372. https://doi.org/10.1016/S0261-5177(00)00062-5

Zhang, J., Madsen, B., & Jensen-Butler, C. (2007). Regional economic impacts of tourism: The case of Denmark. *Regional Studies, 41*(6), 839–854. https://doi.org/10.1080/00343400701281733

Chapter 4
Analysis of Environmental and Economic Effectiveness of Wind Power Generation in Japan

4.1 Introduction

Many environmental problems result from economic activities, which affect not only the natural environment but also life in human societies in various environments. In some cases, emissions of hazardous substances have a direct once-off effect on the environment, in others the effect is cumulative over time and may extend to things that are not expected at all at first glance. In other words, there are many cases in which it is extremely difficult to identify the causal relationships behind the effects of environmentally hazardous substances. In this way, the resulting environmental problems are not only local in range but also global. Therefore, they need to be tackled within an international framework. In particular, various environmental problems, including global warming, acid rain and ocean pollution, have their root causes in human economic activities that consume large amounts of energy resources. In particular, the UN IPCC Sixth Assessment Report indicates that increases in greenhouse gas (GHG) concentrations, a prime cause of global warming, are clearly caused by human activities.[1] Carbon dioxide (CO_2), methane and nitrous oxide are the major GHGs. Others include hydrofluorocarbons, perfluorocarbons and sulfur hexafluoride.[2] CO_2 emissions, which account for 78%[3] of total GHG emissions, are particularly high when electric power is supplied from coal, oil and natural gas.

Reasons like these lay behind the initial adoption of the United Nations Framework Convention on Climate Change in Rio in 1992, the Third Conference of the Parties (COP3) to the Convention in Kyoto in 1997, and the twenty-first Conference of the

[1] IPCC Sixth Assessment Report Working Group 1: The Physical Science Basis, Summary for Policymakers, p.4 A1.1 (7th line up from the bottom). https://www.ipcc.ch/report/ar6/wg1/downloads/report/IPCC_AR6_WGI_SPM.pdf

[2] UN Environment Program (2022) "How do greenhouse gases actually warm the planet?". https://www.unep.org/news-and-stories/story/how-do-greenhouse-gases-actually-warm-planet (05 JAN 2022 STORY CLIMATE ACTION).

[3] AR5 Synthesis Report—Climate Change (2014), p. 46.

S. Asahi, *Econometric Analysis of Regional Economy*,
https://doi.org/10.1007/978-981-99-8707-8_4

Parties (COP21) in Paris in 2015. The IPCC Sixth Assessment Report (2022) has now also been published, and countries are considering measures in response.

In 2002, the Japanese government revised its "Climate Change Policy Program," originally decided in 1998, after the Kyoto Convention, in ways that spelled out more specific measures to achieve the quantitative targets. In addition, the Japanese government set a basic framework for measures to prevent global warming in Japan by passing the Act on the Promotion of Global Warming Countermeasures (Act No. 117 of 1998) and formulating basic policies based on it. In addition, the Act on the Rational Use of Energy (Act No. 49 of 1979) was amended and various domestic measures were implemented.[4] In 2013, a plan for global warming countermeasures was drawn up to replace the Kyoto Protocol Target Achievement Plan. In 2021, "The Plan for Global Warming Countermeasures," a comprehensive government plan based on the "Law Concerning the Promotion of the Measures to Cope with Global Warming," approved by the Cabinet in 2016 was revised. In April 2021, the Japanese government announced its aim to reduce greenhouse gases (carbon dioxide, etc.) from energy sources by 46% in 2030 (compared to 2013 levels), and to continue to strive for a further 50% reduction. These greenhouse gas measures involve the maximum possible changeover from carbon dioxide-based to renewable energy. The policy will be positively pursued while lightening the load on ordinary people and promoting inclusion for local communities.[5]

Renewable energy is obtained from many kinds of resources in the natural environment including biomass, solar energy, geothermal heat, hydropower, tides and waves, ocean thermal energy, and wind energy.[6]

The aim of this research is to analyze the effective use of the natural environment for wind power generation and to compare regional initiatives in this activity area, using existing survey results of wind power generation facilities in Japan and established research methods. In a study conducted in 2002, I estimated the amount of wind power generation in Japan. And, this study estimates the reduction effect of CO_2 against the amount of power generated, and the cost of generating power in Japan in 2002 and 2022. It also analyzes the ripple effect on the regional economy.

First, an overview is offered of the current state of wind power generation and of the purposes and challenges of moving into this new area. This is followed by an analysis of the amount of wind power currently generated, the CO_2 reduction effect, and the economic efficiency. In addition, the ripple effect of the construction of wind power generation plants on regional economies is analyzed, including the employment aspect.

[4] Global Warming Prevention Headquarters (2002), p. 6 (line 27).

[5] Ministry of the Environment (2021).

[6] IPCC (2011a, 2011b, 2011c), p. 178. Edenhofer et al.(2011).

4.2 The Present State of Wind Power Generation in Outline

4.2.1 Background to the Introduction of Renewable Energy

Against a backdrop of population growth and economic development, the world's energy consumption (primary energy) continued to increase at an average annual rate of 2.3% between 1965 and 2020, from a 1965 base of 3.7 billion tons (oil equivalent). In 2020, however, it decreased by 4.3% from the previous year to 13.3 billion tons (oil equivalent) due to the impact of the novel coronavirus pandemic. The world's largest energy consumer is China, with a share of 26.1%, followed by the United States with 15.8%, India with 5.7%, Russia with 5.1% and Japan with 3.1%.[7]

According to the World Energy Outlook 2021, 79% of energy was supplied from petrochemical resources in 2020, which has an impact on increases in carbon dioxide emissions that are a cause of global warming. Renewable energy accounted for 11.6% of total energy supply.[8] The breakdown for that was 2.2% for China, 1.8% for the EU, 1.7% for the United States, and 0.2% for Japan. Japan's share of the world's total supply of renewable energy in 2020 was less than 2%.

In terms of domestic supply, however, renewable energy (excluding hydropower) accounted for 7% of Japan's domestically supplied primary energy in FY2020. Figure 4.1 shows composition ratios of electric power generation sources in Japan for 2010 and 2020. Looking at this, renewable energy (excluding hydropower) accounted for 2.2% in FY2010, but this rose more than fivefold to 12% in FY2020. Looking at the breakdown for FY2020, solar power accounted for 7.9%, wind power 0.9%, geothermal energy 0.3%, and biomass 2.9%.

Figure 4.2 shows changes in the composition ratios of renewable energy (excluding hydropower) in Japan. Looking now at the composition ratio of supplies of renewable energy shares in this figure, in FY 2010 solar power accounted for 14%, wind power 15.8%, geothermal energy 10.4%, and biomass 59.8%; however, in FY 2020, the figures were 66% for solar power, 7.5% for wind power, 2.5% for geothermal power, and 24% for biomass, showing a significant increase in solar power generation. This is because the guaranteed purchase price was high after the introduction of the FIT (Feed-in Tariff) system in 2012. In addition, compared to wind and biomass power generation, solar power generation has a short development period, including installation, which is what favored the rapid increase in this area.[9]

Regarding wind power, the situation in Japan is as follows. According to the Global Wind Energy Council (GWEC), and as shown in Fig. 4.3, Japan's wind

---

[7] This is shown in BP (2021), p. 10.

[8] From World Energy Outlook 2021 in IEA (2021), p. 309 Annex A | Tables for scenario projections Table A.1d: World energy supply.

[9] As shown in the table comparing development periods for different types of renewable energy power generation facilities in Agency for Natural Resources and Energy (2015), p. 8.

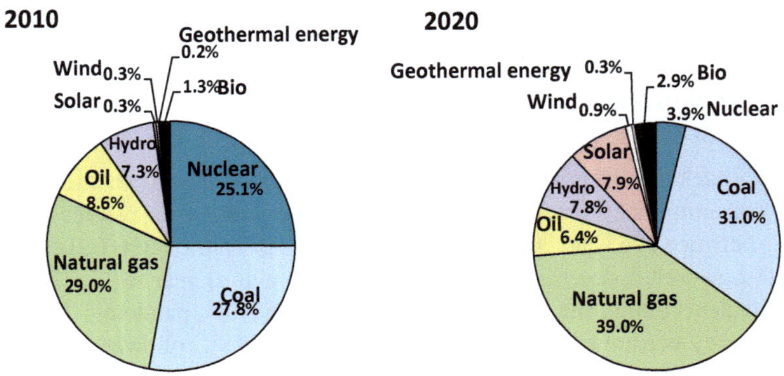

Fig. 4.1 The composition mix of renewable energy (excluding hydropower) in Japan in 2010 and 2020. *Source* Agency for Natural Resources and Energy, Ministry of Economy, Trade and Industry (2022a) Comprehensive Energy Statistics Time Series Table (reference table). BP (2021) Statistical Review of World Energy 2021 (70th edition) IEA

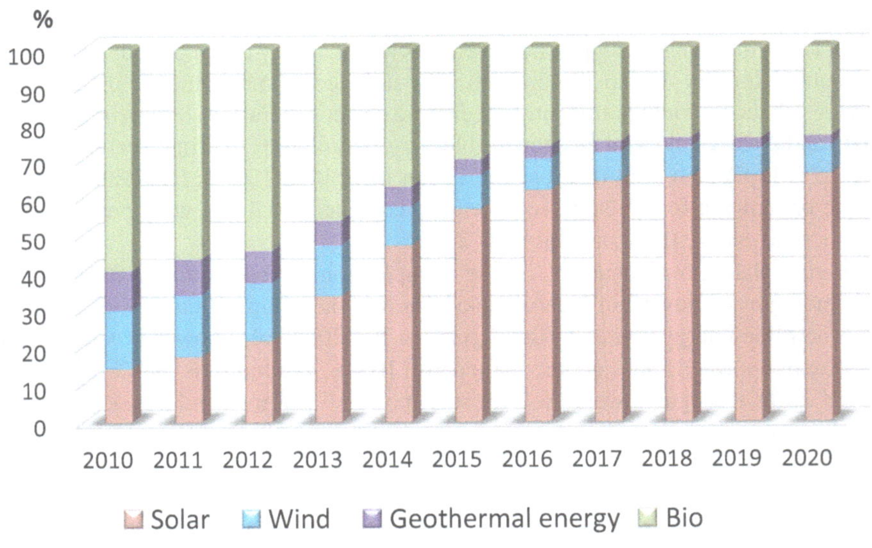

Fig. 4.2 The changes in the composition mix of renewable energy (excluding hydropower). *Source* Agency for Natural Resources and Energy, Ministry of Economy, Trade and Industry (2022a) Comprehensive Energy Statistics Time Series Table (reference table). BP (2021) Statistical Review of World Energy 2021 (70th edition)

power generation capacity was at the extremely low levels of 0.6% of the world's total in 2020 and 0.5% in 2021.

Figure 4.4 shows actual installed wind power generation capacity in Japan since 1989. Large increases can be seen in both the installed capacity and the number of bases. Capacity in 2021 had increased about 15-fold compared to 2001. However,

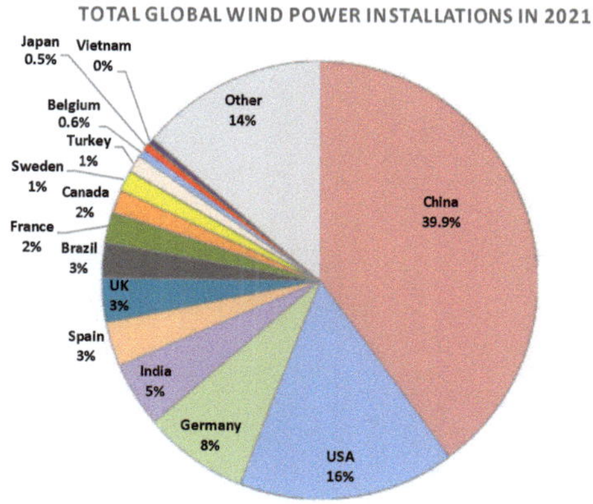

Fig. 4.3 Total global wind power installations in 2021. *Source* IRENA Renewable Energy Capacity Statistics 2022

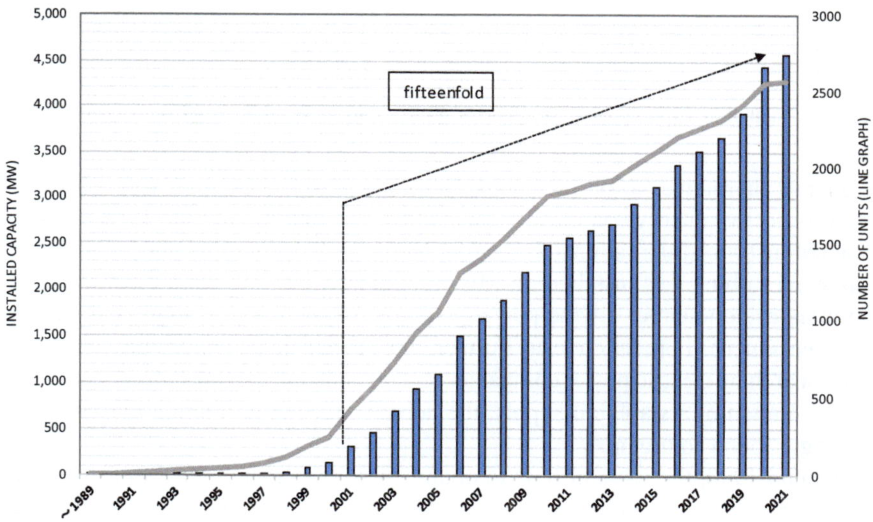

Fig. 4.4 Wind power installations in Japan. *Source* Global Wind Energy Council (GWEC)[10]

in the same period, total installed wind power capacity in the world increased about 35-fold. Thus, the increase elsewhere was much higher than in Japan (Fig. 4.5).

4.2.2 *Efforts to Introduce Wind Power Generation*

This section summarizes the policies and measures that lay behind the introduction of wind power generation in Japan. Subsequent to the oil crisis in the 1970s, interest

[10] At the time of this research, GWEC is data from the international trade association for the wind power industry and is delaied one year less than Japan's statistical data.

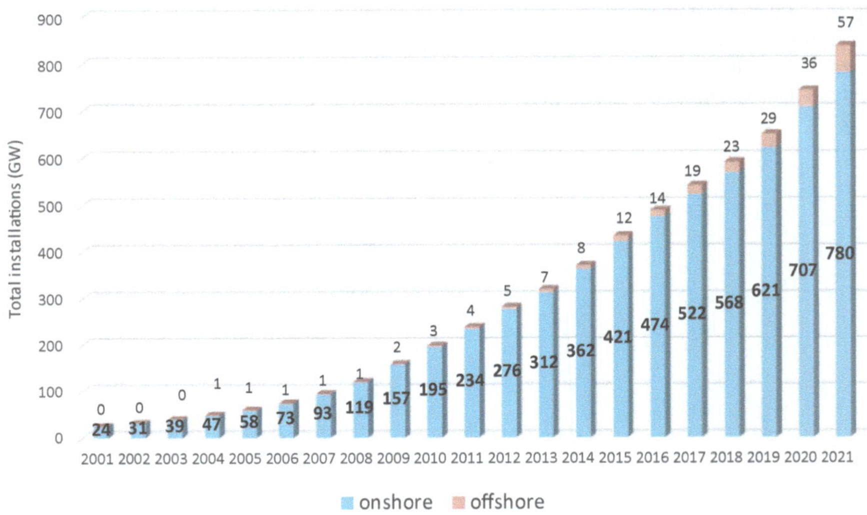

Fig. 4.5 Total global wind power installations. *Source* Global Wind Energy Council (GWEC)

in energy alternatives to oil increased, and wind power generation was selected as one prospective energy source, alongside other new energies, in the 1978 Sunshine Plan (Ministry of International Trade and Industry).[11] Under this plan, a horizontal axis wind turbine was installed on Miyakejima as a 100 kW class pilot plant, and the first development of a wind power generation system was inaugurated with the commencement of operation tests. Further, this opened up an opportunity for testing and research by electric power companies and manufacturers. But subsequently, with the restoration of a stable oil supply, the need for further promotion measures was no longer found so urgent.

Around 1990, the issue of how to obtain energy without an environmental load became extremely important with the need to address environmental problems such as global warming. In other words, wind power generation began to attract attention not only as an alternative to petroleum, but also as an energy source that was low on environmental loads such as carbon dioxide emissions and potentially unlimited with respect to resource availability. Accordingly, in 1990, the government simplified the installation procedure for wind power generation facilities through revision bills relating to the Electricity Business Act. Following this, in 1992, a surplus power purchase system was introduced to make it possible for excess energy generated from wind power to be sold to electric power companies. Guidelines for the technical requirements of the grid connections for this followed in 1993. Taken together, these measures opened the way to the introduction of wind power generation.

In 1995, the New Energy and Industrial Technology Development Organization (NEDO) initiated a subsidy policy for field test projects. In 1997, an Act on Special

[11] The Sunshine Plan included solar, geothermal, coal (but in the future after a liquefaction process) and hydrogen as new energies, but wind power was included among "other energies."

Measures Concerning Promotion of New Energy Use was passed and a subsidy system for businesses was introduced, also by NEDO. Then, from 1998 on, electric power companies were authorized to offer voluntary rates for wind power energy purchases.

Furthermore, a broad system was created in 2000 to promote the use of natural energy. This is a mutual self-help undertaking by all parties on the electrical energy supply side, such as power companies and renewable energy producers, and also on the demand side, such as consumers and corporate end users. This is known as the "Green Power System" and it is notable for not being mere a one-sided subsidy or support system under the control of the government or electric power companies. The 2003 Act on Special Measures Concerning Use of New Energies by Electricity Providers (the Renewables Portfolio Standard (RPS) Act) stipulates an obligatory minimum percentage share of new energies as sources for the amounts of electricity sold to electric power companies. This led to rapid acceleration in the introduction of new energies, and the share of electricity derived from new energies within the total amount sold increased about 3.7-fold in eight years since this law was introduced.[12]

Later, in 2009, a more drastic review of alternative energy policies was undertaken aimed at breaking away from dependence on oil. The Petroleum Alternative Energy Act was amended with an emphasis on using non-fossil energies such as renewables and nuclear power as alternatives to oil. This revised act came to be called the Act for Promoting the Development and Introduction of Alternative Energies. Another law enacted at the same time was the Act Concerning the Promotion of Uses of Non-Fossil Energy Sources by Energy Suppliers and Effective Uses of Fossil Energy Resources, a facilitating framework that further encouraged energy suppliers to move toward uses of renewable non-fossil energy. As for photovoltaic ("solar") power generation, the purchase of surplus electricity energy generated in this way at homes and offices became obligatory under the Excess Electricity Purchasing Scheme for Photovoltaic Power.[13]

Following the damage sustained by the Fukushima Number One Nuclear Power Station, operated by the Tokyo Electric Power Company, in the Great East Japan Earthquake of 2011, the Japanese government decided to review its energy policy and more actively promote the introduction of renewable energy.[14] 2012 saw the passing of an Act for Special Measures Concerning the Procurement of Electricity by Electrical Power Companies from Renewable Energy Sources and the establishment of a "Feed-in Tariff" (FIT) system obliging power companies to purchase energy at a fixed price from renewable sources, notwithstanding the higher generation costs

---

[12] These developments are shown in the source below.

150-year history of energy in Japan ⑤, Beginning of "The Global Warming Countermeasures" and "Electricity and gas liberalization." https://www.enecho.meti.go.jp/about/special/johoteikyo/history5heisei.html (2018-06-06).

[13] Details are shown in Ito (2009). The price for residential use was 48 yen/kWh, and for non-residential use 24 yen/kWh. Electric power companies were obliged to purchase privately generated power energy at 39 yen/kWh.

[14] The source for this is Agency for Natural Resources and Energy, Ministry of Economy, Trade and Industry (2022), p. 95.

compared with other energy sources, in order to compensate for the competitive cost weakness of the renewables. The costs necessary for these purchases were collected through higher charges borne by consumers and businesses end users. For solar power, the fixed price was set at 40 yen per kW/h plus tax for amounts of 10 kW or more with a procurement lead time of 20 years. For amounts of less than 10 kW, the price plus tax was 42 yen, over a 10-year lead time. The fixed prices plus tax for wind power were 22 yen per kW/h for amounts of 20 kW or more and 55 yen for amounts of less than 20 kW, both over a 20-year procurement period.[15] In the first three years after the start of this system, the share of renewable energies in total power sources, excluding hydroelectric, doubled from 1.4% in 2011 to 3.2% in 2014. In this sense, the introduction and expanded use of renewable energy was promoted with the introduction of the FIT system in 2012, but on the problematic side, the system became extremely biased toward solar power generation.

In 2017, the FIT system was revised in order to achieve both a maximum introduction of renewable energies and a reduction of the public financial burden. Thus, it became a system that adheres to business rather than facility planning. As a result, more appropriate amounts of maintenance and similar costs are now required of renewable energy operators. As of 2018, renewable energy power generation facilities had increased to approximately 2.3 times the number of 2012. Comparing the major renewable energy introduction targets for these years, based on the energy mix assumptions for March 2018, small- and medium-sized hydropower accounts came to approximately 87% of the 2018 target, solar accounts to about 70%, biomass ones to around 54%, geothermal ones to no more than 54%, and wind power accounts to a mere 35%. This shows that promotion of wind power generation has not been progressing in Japan nearly as rapidly as promotion of other renewables.

To promote the growth of competitiveness among energy resources, the government has now established a new "Feed-in Premium" (FIP) system for the a closer management of economic activities based on supply and demand and on actual prices in the current (2022) electricity market for operators engaged in renewable energy power generation. This system grants certain premiums based on latest market prices in addition to setting the basic tariffs as in the FIT system.[16] The background to this new system can be considered as follows. First, the potential of wind power generation in Japan is evaluated as extremely high.[17] Secondly, in recent years, the cost of wind power generation in the world has been declining rapidly. Japan therefore needs to make efforts to catch up. Finally, being surrounded by the sea, the potential for offshore wind power in particular is outstanding. Given this situation, the Port and Harbor Act was revised in 2016 to promote the introduction of offshore wind power generation and subsequently, in 2018, the Act on Promoting the Utilization

---

[15] This is from the purchase prices and lead periods (2012–2021) in "Nattoku Renewable Energies" on the following site. https://www.enecho.meti.go.jp/category/saving_and_new/saiene/kaitori/kakaku.html#h.

[16] This information comes from the Agency for Natural Resources and Energy, Ministry of Economy, Trade and Industry (2001).

[17] These arguments are set out in ITOCHU Techno-Solutions Corporation (2011) and Ministry of Environment (2011).

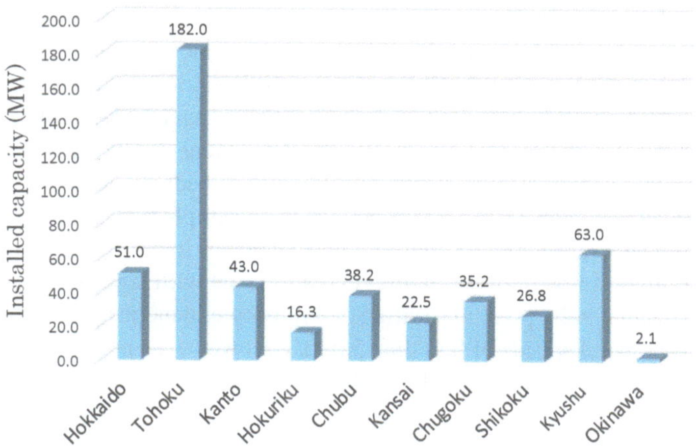

Fig. 4.6 Installed capacity of wind power generation in 10 regions (2022). *Source* JWPA

of Sea Areas for the Development of Marine Renewable Energy Power Generation Facilities was made law.[18] Late as this is, the promotion of offshore wind power is now underway.

4.3 Factual Situation of Wind Power Generation

4.3.1 Current Status of Wind Power Generation in Japan

Installed wind power capacity in Japan was reported to consist of 2622 wind power generation units with an output of approximately 4.80 million kW in December, 2022 [according to research by the Japan Wind Power Association (JWPA)]. The amount authorized under the Feed-in Tariff (FIT) system was reported to be 13.67 million kW, which is rapidly expanding. The breakdown of this FIT amount is 13.54 million kW for onshore units of 20 kW or more, 0.13 million kW for onshore units of less than 20 kW and 0.68 million kW for offshore units.[19]

The total installed capacities of wind power generation plants in the various regions of Japan up to the end of 2022 are shown in Fig. 4.6. The introduction of wind power has gone farthest in the Tohoku region, accounting for 38% of the national total, followed by Kyushu with 13.8% and Hokkaido with 10.6%.

---

[18] The details of the acts are from Ando and Nakamura (2018).

[19] The data used here is from the Act on Special Measures Concerning the Promotion of Uses of Electricity from Renewable Energies, Website, Table A: Amounts approved and installed by prefecture (as of the end of December 2021), Table section A④. https://www.fit-portal.go.jp/PublicInfoSummary. https://www.fit-portal.go.jp/servlet/servlet.FileDownload?file=0150K00000AyoEO.

The location choice of wind power generation facilities is affected by various regional characteristics. In particular, to ensure economic efficiency, the location is selected on a consideration of wind and weather conditions, topography, ground, and surrounding environment, and in each case must meet certain conditions. The Business Plan Formulation Guidelines (Wind Power Generation)[20] revised annually by the Agency for Natural Resources and Energy provides a summary of criteria to be observed for each of the above points in the implementation of renewable energy power generation projects and of "best endeavor items" to be recommended for appropriate business implementation in compliance with legal purposes. Natural conditions that generally preclude a siting of wind power generation facilities include annual average wind speeds of less than 5.5 m/s. However, in port areas this limit is set lower, at less than 5.0 m/s, and for offshore generation facilities higher, at less than 6.5 m/s.

The Business Plan Guidelines for (2022) are arranged in a way that allows the user to look up the wind speed from the Automated Meteorological Data Acquisition System (AMeDAS) operated by the Japan Meteorological Agency, the local wind map issued by the New Energy and Industrial Technology Development Organization (NEDO) and the map of wind conditions put out by the Ministry of the Environment.[21]

The first important stage of selection, therefore, is to find areas where suitable wind conditions can be expected based on these data. The Ministry of the Environment (2019)[22] is using the latest data to review calculation methods and numerical information used in past estimates of renewable energy sources, including wind. Other necessary criteria are that the terrain is flat, that the area used can be kept constant in size, and that there are no legal restrictions on the construction of wind power plants in the target area. For example, it has to be ensured that the site is not within a regulated area under the Natural Parks Act or the Civil Aeronautics Act, or in a regulated forest preserve area under the terms of The Forest and Forestry Basic Act. Also, the distance from the location to transmission lines, distribution lines, and electric power substations is very important. There are many areas that meet these conditions in the Tohoku and Hokkaido regions.

4.3.2 Issues in Introducing Wind Power Generation in Japan

There are many issues in promoting renewable energy and wind power generation in Japan's energy supply system. Ando and Nakamura (2018) point out the following

[20] The Agency for Natural Resources and Energy and the New Energy and Industrial Technology Development Organization (NEDO) are investigating future costs and prospects for the introduction of renewable energies.

[21] This can be seen from Agency for Natural Resources and Energy (2022), p. 7, l. 12–15.

[22] The Report on Entrusted Work Concerning the Development and Disclosure of Basic Zoning Information Concerning Renewable Energies being prepared by the Ministry of the Environment is at present under revision. The most recent state of information available as of November 2022 was that of March 2021.

four.[23] First, there is a need to bring generating costs down to international standard levels. Second, when introducing renewable energy and wind power generation facilities into an area for the first time, contractors will need to work in cooperation with local government and citizens. Similarly, after the completion of the work or at a later renewal stage, they will need to dispose of equipment in appropriate ways and plan for stable long-term operating conditions that are considerate of the environment. Third, for the whole electricity supply network from the generating facility down to the dependent consumer, there is a need to guard against outages resulting from a shortage of power capacity. And fourth, as also stressed by the Agency for Natural Resources and Energy (2018), there should be a sufficient adjustment capability to assure a sustained balance between supply and demand within the supply system. This will include a provision of high-performance storage batteries.[24]

Four further issues regarding offshore wind power generation have been raised by the Cabinet Office, Government of Japan (2021). First, current domestic regulations for civil engineering work and construction are not compatible with the construction of offshore wind power plants, making rapid development difficult. Second, government needs to pursue regulatory reforms to clear away needless obstacles to innovative wind power generation facilities by ensuring that the most advanced technologies and practices worldwide can be applied to their installation. Third, until domestic supply chains develop and catch up, there will be a need to make substantial use of overseas products for the time being. Fourth, since tasks that require supervising will extend across multiple ministries and agencies, responsibility for the promotion of offshore wind power generation will of necessity fall to the entire Japanese government.[25]

Finally, a further two "barriers" to the spread of offshore wind power in Japan are identified by Hiromachi (2019). Until recently, Japan did not have unified rules for exclusive uses of offshore sea areas in general. Prefectures could issue "exclusive use permits" by ordinance. However, the procedures for general sea areas differed from one prefecture to another. In addition, since the permit period was short, ranging from 3 to 10 years, it was difficult to offer medium- to long-term prospects for power generation operations. This posed problems for the procurement of funds as it was impossible to predict future outcomes. A further problem was the lack of a compensation framework for reaching settlements with prior users of the sea area, such as shipping and fishery operators.

The "Act on Promoting the Utilization of Sea Areas for the Development of Marine Renewable Energy Power Generation Facilities (Act on Promoting the Utilization of Sea Areas for Renewable Energy)" was passed in 2018.

Under the Act, the Japanese government was enabled to designate "promotion areas" for offshore wind power generation projects, and operators for these projects were to be selected through processes of "public offering." The operator selected

[23] Ando and Nakamura (2018), p. 65, l. 11–14.

[24] See Agency for Natural Resources and Energy (2018), 2017 Annual Report on Energy, p. 87–89.

[25] See Cabinet Office, Government of Japan (2021), p. 3. This document was in Japanese only, and some explicatory terms have been added to make it more understandable in English.

in this way was then entitled to exclusive use of the sea area for a period of up to 30 years. However, offshore wind power generation operations are limited to the designated areas, and operators other than those selected through public offering will not be able to enter the offshore wind power generation business.

4.4 Research on CO_2 Reduction Effect in Wind Power Generation

The reserch in this chapter estimates the amount of wind power generation in Japan, the reduction effect of CO_2 against the amount of power generated, and the cost of generating power in 2002 and 2022. It also analyzes the ripple effect on the regional economy. Since the 1990s, there have been many papers on CO_2 emission effects from various power generation systems and on CO_2 reduction effects from those based on natural energy.[26]

Uchiyama and Yamamoto (1992) and Yoshioka et al. (1994) are studies of greenhouse gases focusing on how they affect the construction and running costs of power plants in Japan. In particular, Yoshioka et al. (1994) surveyed construction data of coal-fired, oil-fired, and nuclear power plants using input–output analysis to estimate CO_2 emissions against the construction and normal running costs. Finally, the total effectiveness of each type of plant was calculated. Subsequent studies bringing in life cycle analysis include Uchiyama (1996) and Akai et al. (1997). As for research across multiple electric power generation systems, analyses of life cycle CO_2 emissions have been performed by Izuno et al. (2001) and similar estimates of life cycle nitric oxide and sulfur oxide emissions by Nomura et al. (2001).

Frequently cited papers include Hondo (2005) which shows results of life cycle greenhouse gas emission analyses across 9 different types of power generation systems, including wind power. In each case, the analysis begins from a survey of the generation system and then follows a method that combines process analysis with input–output analysis. Finally, an estimate is made of the life cycle greenhouse gas emissions per kWh of electricity generated.

Recent studies in other countries include research into the environmental impact of emissions in Ontario, Canada by Siddiqui and Dincer (2017) and in China by Wang et al. (2021). The former of these analyzes the environmental impact of power generation systems including wind power. The latter estimates CO_2, NO_X, and SO_2 emissions by region, using a life cycle evaluation method and based on the spatial distributions of various power sectors in China, including wind power.[27]

---

[26] For an analysis of the economic benefits of wind power in Japan, Ito et al. (2004), Nakata et al. (2005). Ziegelmann et al. (2000) analyzed the employment effects of investment in renewable energy expansion in Germany using an input-output table. Cosmi et al. (2003) optimize the investment system for renewable energy and evaluate the potential of using renewable energy resources on a regional scale according to the EU energy policy.

[27] Other similar studies in China include Wang et al. (2019) and Gao et al. (2019) and Gao et al. (2021).

Gao et al. (2019) makes use of a Chinese life cycle perspective to analyze the energy consumption and environmental impact of wind power plants. The results are further compared to those obtained for biomass power generation. Wind power plants in deserts have the lowest impact, suggesting that desert locations should be chosen as far as possible.

A study by Shao et al. (2020) presented a survey of existing papers on renewable energy power plants, including both onshore and offshore wind power plants. The survey covered 85 papers published between 2001 and 2018, assumed frequently used site selection standards, and used such methods as normalization of standard values, weighting of standards, and alternative evaluation to process the statistics and verify the results. An overview of these statistical methods is also included.

There are many investigations using industrial input–output (IO)-type tables as a basis for analysis. This is true of Lindner et al. (2013) that uses IO tables for China, and also of Kamidelivand et al. (2018) using them to analyze a range of renewable resources in Ireland, including wind power generation. Japanese research that can be applied to the analysis of renewable energy resources includes Hienuki et al. (2015) and Nakano and Washizu (2022). Of these, Hienuki et al. (2015) uses IO tables to analyze scenarios for the evaluation of the likely socioeconomic and environmental impacts of future combinations of power generation technology. Greenhouse gas emissions are estimated having regard for the difference between the lead time and the service life of each type of power generation technology. Nakano and Washizu (2022) proposes an IO Table for analyses of Next-Generation Energy Systems ("IONGES") making use of industrial reference tables compiled for the renewable energy sector by the Ministry of Internal Affairs and Communications. This research starts out from a consideration of the effect of introducing a carbon tax as a global warming countermeasure in the context of the existing energy-related tax system, and then goes on to analyze the changes in the tax burden that would result from more use of renewable energy. Both of these two industry-related IO tables lend themselves well to use in wind power research.

4.5 The CO_2 Reduction Effect of the Introduction of Wind Power Generation

4.5.1 Measurement of the Amount of Energy Supplied by Wind Power Generation

The amount of energy supplied by wind power is estimated from predictions based on the capacity of the generating equipment, annual average wind velocity and frequency, and the average activation rate of the equipment. The frequency of wind speeds can be approximated using the Weibull distribution.[28] As this requires a shape

[28] The frequency distribution for wind speeds can be approximated by the following Weibull distribution.

parameter, the distribution of occurrence frequencies can be estimated from average wind speeds using the Rayleigh distribution function obtained for cases where the distribution shape is set at 2.

The amount of energy obtained from a wind power generation system (i.e., the amount of power generated) is calculated using the output curve of the system and the wind speed frequency distribution for the site at the height of the turbines installed. From these data, the following formula is obtained.

$$\text{Annual amount of power generated (kWh)} = \Sigma(V_i \times F_i) \times 8760(\text{h}) \qquad (4.1)$$

V_i: Power output for wind speed class i (kW),

f_i: Occurrence frequency of wind speed class i.

The number of hours in a 365-day calendar year: $8760(\text{h}) = 365(\text{days}) \times 24(\text{h})$.

The amount of energy generated was estimated on the basis of annual average wind speeds and capacity utilization rates as obtained for the 2002 analysis. Data prior to 2002 were taken from a national questionnaire survey. The estimates for 2022 were based on data contained in government committee documents or published by relevant authorities.[29]

The total power generation can be estimated from the wind speed class, the wind speed at the start, the wind speed at the finish, and the wind speed distributions and frequencies for the mean wind speed class. A notable feature of the 2002 analysis, therefore, is its use of power generation figures not previously available but specially compiled and calculated from survey data. This was because the data required for analysis could not be obtained from all generating plants. Hence the need to arrive at the unavailable parts of the calculation input by using the method described above approximation method. A further requirement was that it was necessary to specify the shape of the power generation curve at each plant. This accounts for why the power output has to be based each time on an assumed annual average calculated from the mean annual wind speed indicated in the Wind Power Installation Guidebook and the average utilization factor obtained in the analysis.

The Weibull distribution $f(V) = (K/C)(V/C)^{k-1}\exp[-(V/C)]^K$

$f(V)$: The occurrence frequency distribution of wind speed V; K: The shape of the distribution; C: The coefficient of scale.

The probability that the wind speed V will be less than or equal to $V_x f\left(V \leqq V_x\right)$ can be formulated as $f\left(V \leqq V_x\right) = 1 - \exp\{-(V_x/C)\}$.

The average wind speed is given by the following formula.

$$V = C\Gamma(1 + (1/K)) \quad \Gamma: \text{ gamma function.}$$

The shape of the Weibull distribution ranges from about 0.8 to 2.2 in Japan according to the "Investigation on preparation of data relating to development of new energy technology (wind power generation). Research report in the fiscal year 1999" and is ascertained to lie between values of about 1.5 and 2.2 where the average wind speed is 5 m/s. The Rayleigh distribution is obtained by setting this value at 2.

[29] These figures come from the Agency for Natural Resources and Energy, Ministry of Economy, Trade and Industry (2023), p. 41 and 82nd Meeting of the Procurement Price Calculation Committee, Document 2 on Wind Power Generation, 2023, p. 24.

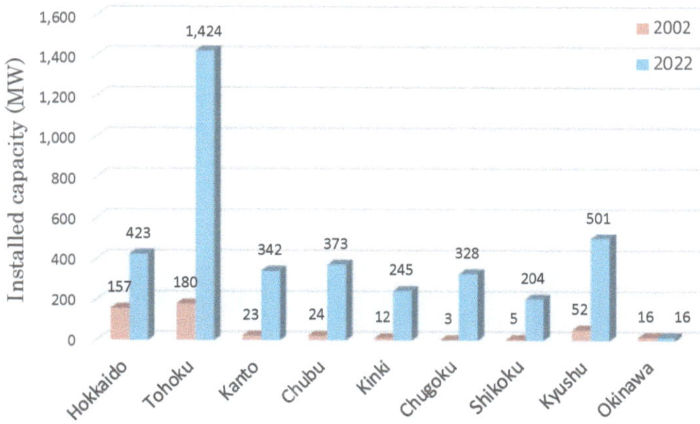

Fig. 4.7 Installed capacity of wind power generation by regions (years 2002, 2022). *Source* JWPA

The data used for the 2002 analysis were obtained from a national survey that I conducted.[30] As for the annual amount of energy supplied from each particular wind power operator or electric utilities company, which does not directly appear in the 2002 survey, it has to be calculated by multiplying the amount of generating capacity by the average rate of utilization and then by the number of hours (8760) in a 365-day calendar year.

According to the 2022 report of the Procurement Price Calculation Committee,[31] the average rate of equipment utilization was 25.6% in 2021, and 26.8% in 2022. The annual amount of wind power energy generated is now included in current Electric Power Survey Statistics by the Agency for Natural Resources and Energy. Therefore, the input figure for the 2022 analysis no longer needs to be estimated as it did for 2002. The annual amounts thus obtained are shown in Figs. 4.7 and 4.8 and in Tables 4.1 and 4.2.

4.5.2 *The Effect of Wind Power Generation in Reducing CO_2 Emissions*

An important motive for the introduction of wind power generation is that it is a clean energy source that involves no environmental burden. This study compares wind power generation in 2002 and 2022 by estimating how much reduction would

---

[30] I conducted a "The Fact-Finding Survey on Wind Power Generation" for wind power generation facilities in Japan. The following is a summary of the survey. Survey Period: March 30, 2004 - April 30, 2004, survey object: Organizations that had installed wind power generation by the end of March 2002, as surveyed by NEDO, and organizations participating in the National Council of Wind Power Promotion Municipalities (data from the National Wind Summit). Questionnaire method: mail, Questionnaire collection: sent, 170 collected, 85 collection rate: 50%.

[31] Same as 27 above.

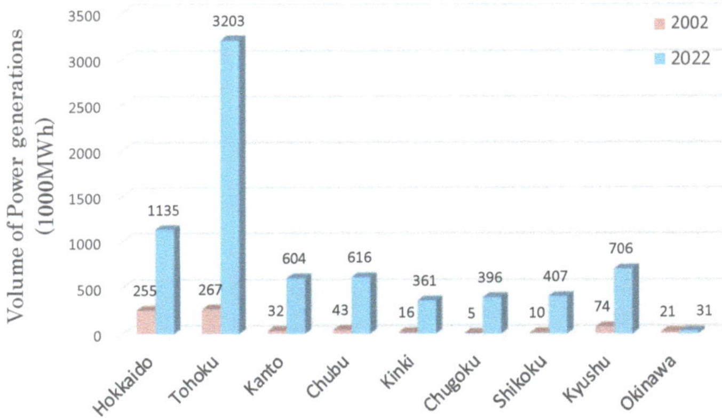

Fig. 4.8 Volume of wind power generation by regions (2002, 2022). *Source* Created by the author using estimate results of this study and data by the Japan Wind Power Association (JWPA)

result in CO_2 emissions if wind power energy were used to generate the same amount of electricity as in various types of thermal plants. Thus, it shows the reduction equivalence in CO_2 emissions over the same period of 20 years. The reduction effect on CO_2 emissions can thus be calculated by comparing the 2002 and 2022 emission figures for wind power generation with the equivalent emission estimates for the same energy outputs using thermal power. Three thermal power fuel sources are considered: oil, coal and LNG. The CO_2 emission equivalence compared with wind power is different in each case.

In Japan, oil, coal, and LNG are among the fuels most often used in thermal power generation. The calculation principle for the comparison, in each case, is that the resulting weight of CO_2 emissions has to be estimated on the assumption that the amount of energy generated from wind power had been generated instead from either oil, coal, or LNG thermal power. In Eq. (4.2), X is the reduction in CO_2 achieved by using wind power instead of oil (or coal, or LNG), and Y is the amount of energy generated. The thermal capacity per kWh is 860 kcal. This is then reconverted to a per liter rate through dividing by 9250, the amount of thermal energy in kcal per liter of crude oil. If the generating efficiency obtained in a primary energy exchange is 0.4, then

$$X = Y \times 980 \times (1/9250) \div (0.4 \times 0.001)/1000 \tag{4.2}$$

The base unit equivalents for CO_2 reduction as calculated by the Central Research Institute of the Electric Power Industry (1995) were 166.3 g-C/kWh for oil-fueled thermal power, 236.3 g-C/kWh for coal-fueled, and 144.3 g-C/kWh for LNG-fueled. The 2022 results obtained in various regions using these base values are shown in Table 4.1.

Table 4.1 CO_2 emission reductions from wind power generation in 2002

	Number of units	Installed capacity (kW)	Electric power generated, 2002 (MWh)	Oil-fueled as base unit (kl/h)	Reduction in CO_2 emissions t-CO_2/year		
					Equivalent oil-fueled thermal power	Equivalent coal fueled thermal power	Equivalent LNG fueled thermal power
Hokkaido	182	157,435	254,913	59,250	155,436	220,865	134,874
Tohoku	189	180,177	267,001	62,060	162,807	231,338	141,270
Kanto	44	22,877	32,482	7,550	19,806	28,143	17,186
Chubu	39	23,788	42,606	9,903	25,979	36,915	22,543
Kinki	15	11,820	15,652	3,638	9,544	13,561	8,281
Chugoku	7	3,324	4,795	1,115	2,924	4,155	2,537
Shikoku	10	4,830	9,942	2,311	6,062	8,614	5,260
Kyushu	69	51,875	74,344	17,280	45,332	64,414	39,335
Okinawa	34	15,715	20,821	4,839	12,696	18,040	11,016
Total	589	471,840	722,556	167,945	440,586	626,046	382,304

Source Created by the author using estimate results of this study and number of units and installed capacity of wind power generation is according to research by the Japan Wind Power Association (JWPA). Or the other data see Sects. 4.5.2 and 4.5.3.
Note 1 Oil-fueled reduction estimates are calculated as: wind power generation $\times$ (1/9250) $\div$ $(0.4 \times 0.001)/1000$
860 (kcal) is the amount of heat required per kWh, 9250 (kcal/ℓ) is the amount of thermal energy per liter of oil and 0.4 is the power generation efficiency in the case of a primary energy exchange.
Note 2 The CO_2 reduction intensity is a value taking in the manufacture, operation, fueling and disposal of the generation equipment as outlined in Uchiyama, Y. (1995a, 1995b) "Life Cycle Analysis of Power Generation Systems" 1995 issued by the Central Research Institute of the Electric Power Industry (CRIEPI). The base units for the reduction estimates are 166.3 g-C/kWh for oil-fueled thermal power plants, 236.3 g-C/kWh for coal-fueled, and 144.3 g-C/kWh for LNG-fueled. In this table, the carbon C equivalent is converted to CO_2 equivalent

The results for CO_2 reduction in 2022 as calculated by Imamura et al. (2016)[32] were 201.3 g-C/kWh for oil-fueled thermal generation, 257 g-C/kWh for coal fueled, and 163 g-C/kWh for LNG fueled, as shown in Table 4.2, Note 2. In both tables, the amounts for various types of carbon emissions are converted into their carbon dioxide equivalents.

In this chapter, the carbon C equivalent is converted to the CO_2 equivalent. It will be seen from Table 4.1 that the CO_2 reduction effect in 2002 was greatest (620 kt) in comparison with coal-fueled generation. Compared with oil, the reduction was 440 kt, and compared with LNG, 380kt. The CO_2 reduction effect in the Tohoku region from the use of wind power in place of coal was 231 kt-CO_2/year. This accounted

[32] Imamura et al. (2016), the Central Research Institute of the Electric Power Industry.

Table 4.2 CO_2 emission reductions from wind power generation in 2022

	Number of units	Installed capacity (kW)	Electric power generated, 2002 (MWh)	Oil-fueled as base unit (kl/h)	Reduction in CO_2 emissions t-CO_2/year		
					Equivalent oil-fueled thermal power	Equivalent coal-fueled thermal power	Equivalent LNG-fueled thermal power
Hokkaido	307	423,371	1,134,963	263,802	837,603	1,070,270	679,843
Tohoku	909	1,423,958	3,202,888	744,455	2,363,731	3,020,323	1,918,530
Kanto	262	341,690	603,938	140,375	445,706	569,514	361,759
Chubu	242	372,530	616,338	143,257	454,857	581,207	369,186
Kinki	151	244,740	360,719	83,843	266,211	340,158	216,071
Chugoku	188	327,620	395,971	92,037	292,227	373,401	237,187
Shikoku	158	203,870	407,081	94,619	300,426	383,877	243,841
Kyushu	380	500,957	705,540	163,990	520,689	665,324	422,619
Okinawa	25	16,180	30,504	7,090	22,512	28,765	18,272
Total	2622	3,854,916	7,457,942	1,733,468	5,503,961	7,032,840	4,467,307

Source Created by the author using estimate results of this study number of units and installed capacity of wind power generation is according to research by the Japan Wind Power Association (JWPA). And the other data see footnote 18 and Sect. 4.5.3.
Note 1 Same as in Table 4.1
Note 2 The CO_2 reduction intensity is based on data published in Imamura et al. (2016). The values come to 201.27 g-C/kWh for oil-fueled, 257 g-C/kWh for coal-fueled and 163 g-C/kWh for LNG-fueled. In this table, the carbon C equivalent is converted to CO_2 equivalent

for 36% of total CO_2 reductions (626 kt-CO_2/year) achieved that year in the whole of Japan.

In Table 4.2, it can again be seen that the CO_2 reduction effect was greatest (7032 kt) for wind power in place of coal. The effect as compared with oil-fueled generation was 5503 kt, and as compared with LNG, 4467 kt. The CO_2 equivalent reduction through the use of wind power as compared with coal in the Tohoku region was 3020 kt-CO_2/year, accounting for 43% of the total 7032 kt-CO_2/year reduction for the whole of Japan.

Initial proposals for a carbon tax within the Environmental Agency in August 2004 were for a low rate of about 3400 yen per carbon ton. But as a power development promotion tax was already being levied in the electric power industry, it could be assumed that the newly introduced tax would be equivalent to roughly a 3% rise in this, that is, 102 yen per carbon ton. The resulting CO_2 reduction effect is estimated at the same rates as above. On these assumptions, the economic benefits of CO_2 reduction would be 170.4 million yen compared with coal-fueled thermal power, 122.4 million yen compared with oil-fueled, or 106.2 million yen compared with LNG-fueled. Thus, a shift to wind power generation would certainly lead to a reduction in carbon tax payments.

Estimates for 2022 were calculated using the "Global Warming Tax" rate of 289 yen per ton of CO_2 emissions introduced by the Japanese government in 2012. This is 107 yen higher than the 102 yen assumed in 2002. On these assumptions, the economic benefits from CO_2 reductions will be 2.3 billion yen compared with coal-fueled thermal power, 1.59 billion yen compared with oil-fueled, or 1.29 billion yen compared with LNG-fueled.

4.5.3 Measuring the Costs of Wind Power Generation

This section will deal with the costs required to install a wind power plant in 2002 and 2022.

From the results of the 2002 survey referred to in Subsection 4.5.1, it appears that the average initial costs incurred by a company or organization installing a wind power facility were 436 million yen, with annual running costs of 0.12 billion yen. The initial cost per kW worked out at 341,000 yen, and the annual running costs per kW came to 9165 yen. This is based on cost data from 597 generators in Japanese wind power facilities for the year 2002. The data analyzed were for the initial installation outlay as based on the ratios of the various expense items to the total costs. For project support operations between local authorities and companies or organizations, in cases where no figure was available for initial installation costs, a rate of 257,000 yen per kW was assumed as shown in Table 4.3, and item costs were then calculated on the assumption that the weight of the various expense items in the total construction costs would on average be the same as indicated in the survey responses. Separate cost calculations for the ten Japanese regions assumed in this chapter are shown farther below in Table 4.4.

Wind power generation costs for 2022 are calculated using data from the Agency for Natural Resources and Energy (2022) prepared by the Procurement Price Calculation Committee. The average initial cost per kW in installing a wind power facility is now 355,000 yen, and average annual running costs per kW are 12,950 yen.

The great problem to be confronted for the introduction of wind power is the higher annual cost of supplying the energy compared with other generating methods. According to NEDO,[33] this can be calculated from the following set of Eqs. (4.3)–(4.5), where C is the total annual cost, Z is the cost of the plant construction, wind rotors, and other installation costs, P is the real interest rate for the borrowing of the money, and O stands for the operating and maintenance costs. Finally, G is the generating cost, while D is the total annual demand. The generating cost is found by dividing all of the annual costs by the total annual demand for electric power.

$$C = Z \times P + O \tag{4.3}$$

[33] This calculation was published in NEDO News, Vol. 19, No. 171 (August 1999).

Table 4.3 Costs of NEDO wind power generation equipment projects

	Operations supported by local authorities		Operations supported by businesses	
	¥10,000/kW	Composition (%)	¥10,000/kW	Composition (%)
Machinery	18.4	60.5	16.9	65.8
Design costs	0.5	1.6	0.3	1.2
Construction costs	7.7	25.3	6.4	24.9
Electricity support	2.4	7.9	0.9	3.5
Consumption tax	1.4	4.6	1.2	4.7
Total	30.4	100.0	25.7	100.0
Annual average wind speed (m/s)	6.1		6.1	
Scale of new installations (kW/location)	2000.0		5400.0	
Scale of generators (kW/generator)	650.0		1000.0	
Construction price (¥10,000/kW)	30.4		25.7	
Generating cost of wind energy (¥10,000/kWh)	12.7		9.8	

Note NEDO (New Energy and Industrial Technology Development Organization) (2000) "Data Survey for New Energy Technology Development (Wind Power Generation)", March 2000: p. 98

$$P = r/(1 - (1 + r)^{-n}) \tag{4.4}$$

$$G = C/D \tag{4.5}$$

For the calculation of P in (4.4), r is the interest rate, and n is the number of years of depreciation. For 2002, the interest rate is set at 3.6% and the depreciation period at 17 years. For 2022, the interest rate is 2.6% and the depreciation period 20 years.

The generating cost can then be calculated on the basis of electric power demand over the whole year. The results of the calculation are shown below in Tables 4.4 and 4.5 (Table 4.6).

From reports on renewable energy around 2001, it was known that the cost of wind power generation was 10–14 yen/kWh for a large-scale facility, and 18–24 yen/kWh for a medium or small facility. Even for large wind power generators supported by a subsidy policy, the cost envisaged for renewable energy was still 7–11 yen /kWh. This compares with 10.2 yen for oil-fueled thermal power, 6.5 yen for coal-fueled, and 6.4 yen for LNG-fueled. For other non-carbon sources, the figures were 5.9 yen for nuclear power and 13.6 yen for hydroelectric. The economic efficiency of wind power in 2001 was thus considerably inferior to that of other power supply systems.

Table 4.4 Measurement statistics of wind power generating costs by regions (2002)

Region	Hokkaido	Tohoku	Kanto	Chubu	Kinki	Chugoku	Shikoku	Kyushu	Okinawa	Total
No. of units	186	189	48	39	15	7	10	69	34	597
No. of units × unit output (kW)	160,485	180,177	25,277	23,788	11,820	3,324	4,830	51,875	15,715	477,290
Installation costs (×10,000 yen)	41,290	49,070	7,122	6,647	3,095	854	1,591	16,115	3,911	129,695
Annual running costs (×10,000 yen)	1,224	1,347	167	323	85	24	33	401	102	3,707
Annual cost (C) (×10,000 yen)	4,528	5,273	737	855	333	93	160	1,691	415	14,083
Total annual demand of wind energy (MWh)	254,913	267,001	32,482	42,606	15,652	4,795	9,942	74,344	20,821	722,556
Generating cost of wind energy (yen /kWh)	17.8	19.7	22.7	20.1	21.2	19.3	16.1	22.7	19.9	19.5

Source Created by the author using estimate results of this study and number of units and installed capacity of wind power generation is according to research by the Japan Wind Power Association (JWPA). And the other data see Sect. 4.5.3.
Note Annual running costs are included the operating and maintenance costs

Table 4.5 Measurement statistics of wind power generating costs by regions (2022)

Region	Hokkaido	Tohoku	Kanto	Chubu	Kinki	Chugoku	Shikoku	Kyushu	Okinawa	Total
Number of units	307	909	262	242	151	188	158	380	25	2622
No. of units × unit output (kW)	423,371	1,423,958	341,690	372,530	244,740	327,620	203,870	500,957	16,180	3,854,916
Installation costs (×10,000 yen)	150,297	505,505	121,300	132,248	86,883	116,305	72,374	177,840	5,744	1,368,495
Annual running costs (millions of yen)	5,483	18,440	4,425	4,824	3,169	4,243	2,640	6,487	210	49,921
Annual cost (C) (millions of yen)	15,215	51,174	12,280	13,388	8,795	11,774	7,327	18,003	581	138,538
Total annual demand of wind energy (MWh)	1,134,963	3,202,888	603,938	616,338	360,719	395,971	407,081	705,540	30,504	7,457,942
Generating cost of wind energy (yen /kWh)	13.4	16.0	20.3	21.7	24.4	29.7	18.0	25.5	19.1	20.9

Source Created by the author using estimate results of this study and Renewable Energy Institute (2022a, 2022b, 2022c).
Note Annual running costs are included the operating and maintenance costs

Table 4.6 Costs of wind power generation by regions (2022) (million yen)

Region	No. of units	No. of units × unit output (kW)	Installation costs (millions of yen)	Annual running costs (millions of yen)	Turbine costs	Construction costs	Local construction	Electrical work	Outsourced
Hokkaido	307	423,371	150,297	5,483	77,650	37,248	8,868	9,398	16,042
Tohoku	909	1,423,958	505,505	18,440	261,167	125,279	29,825	31,609	53,955
Kanto	262	341,690	121,300	4,425	62,669	30,062	7,157	7,585	12,947
Chubu	242	372,530	132,248	4,824	68,325	32,775	7,803	8,269	14,115
Kinki	151	244,740	86,883	3,169	44,888	21,532	5,126	5,433	9,273
Chugoku	188	327,620	116,305	4,243	60,088	28,824	6,862	7,273	12,414
Shikoku	158	203,870	72,374	2,640	37,392	17,936	4,270	4,526	7,725
Kyushu	380	500,957	177,840	6,487	91,880	44,074	10,493	11,120	18,982
Okinawa	25	16,180	5,744	210	2,968	1,424	339	359	613
Total	2,622	3,854,916	1,368,495	49,921	707,026	339,153	80,741	85,571	146,065

Source Created by the author using estimate results of this study and number of units and installed capacity of wind power generation is according to research by the Japan Wind Power Association (JWPA). Or the other data see footnote 18 and Sect. 4.5.3.
Note Annual running costs are included the operating and maintenance costs

These cost calculation results were similar to survey results from The Subcommittee on Grid Interconnection of Wind Power, New and Renewable Energy Subcommittee, The Subcommittee for Natural Resources and Energy (2001). In Table 4.4, for the year 2002, the lowest generating cost for wind power was 16.1 yen/kWh for Shikoku, followed by 17.81 yen for Hokkaido. The ranking order here may be skewed by the fact that there happened to be a comparatively abundant stock of survey data available from wind power generators in Shikoku. In Hokkaido, where wind farms tend to be large scale, the low cost can probably be attributed to scale efficiency. The results for 2022 in Table 4.5 show that the lowest cost for wind power has come down to 13.4 yen/kWh in Hokkaido. Next is 17.81 yen for Tohoku.

As already argued above, while the cost of wind power generation in 2002 was high, there are no associated releases of CO_2. If the cost of carbon tax per kW is added to the costs of the competing energy sources in line with the 2002 CO_2 differences calculated above, the cost rises to 24 yen/kWh for coal-fueled power generation, 14.7 yen/kWh for LNG-fueled, and 16.9 yen/kWh for oil-fueled. However, this still leaves out the problem of supply stability, and for overall energy policy it is important to plan for an electricity supply based on a variety of energy sources.

In 2021, the Power Generation Cost Verification Working Group in the Ministry of Economy, Trade and Industry estimated generation costs by power source for 2020 as follows[34]: Coal-fueled thermal generation in the range of 12.5–13 yen per kWh, LNG-fueled at around 10.5–11 yen, and oil-fueled at around 26.5–27 yen. Onshore wind power generation was found to be in the area of 19.5–20 yen per kWh. These values almost match the national estimates in the present research for 2022. This being so, if the new carbon tax is brought in for wind power, along with the benefits of feed-in tariffs (FITs) and feed-in premiums (FIPs), the cost issue may well be offset.

[34] Calculations from the report of the Power Generation Cost Verification Working Group, Ministry of Economy, Trade and Industry (2021), p. 5.

4.6 Regional Economic Effects of Wind Power Generator Plant Constructions

4.6.1 *Measurement of Economic Ripple Effects Using Data from Interregional Industrial Input–Output Tables*

The aim of this section is to analyze the economic effects of wind power plant construction projects in nine regions using inter-prefectural input–output tables[35] compiled by the Research Institute of Economy, Trade and Industry (RIETI) for all 47 Japanese prefectures for the year 2011.[36] First, the construction of the interregional input–output table will be explained this time comprising nine region, and the analysis method will be presented. Table 4.7 displays a part of the result, offering a compact competitive overview of interregional population and commodity inflows among the nine regions selected

The variable subscript i, j in X_{ij}^{rs} in Table 4.7 indicates a flow from sector i to sector j. The superscript r, s indicates a flow from region r to region s. Thus, putting i, j and r, s together, X_{ij}^{rs}, shows a flow from sector i in region r to sector j in region s.

The first horizontal row in Table 4.7 is structured as follows. Intermediate demands X in region 1, {reg. 1 $(x_{11}^{11}, x_{12}^{11}, \ldots, x_{1n}^{11})$} are transferred to region 2, becoming {reg. 2 $(x_{11}^{12}, x_{12}^{12}, \ldots, x_{1n}^{12})$}, and so on up to region 9, {reg. 9 $(x_{11}^{19}, x_{12}^{19}, \ldots, x_{1n}^{19})$}. Similarly, final demand F in region 1, {reg. 1 (F_1^{11})} is transferred to region 2, becoming {reg. 2 (F_1^{12})}, and so on up to region 9, {reg. 9 (F_1^{19})}. Then additionally, there are external exports (E_1^1) and imports (M_1^1) to be shown and accounted for.

As for the first vertical column in Table 4.7, it is structured: Intermediate industrial inputs X in region 1 $(x_{11}^{11}, x_{21}^{11}, \ldots, x_{n1}^{11})$, inputs by transfer from region 2 $(x_{11}^{21}, x_{21}^{21}, \ldots, x_{n1}^{21})$ and so on, down to inputs by transfer from region 9 $(x_{11}^{91}, x_{21}^{91}, \ldots, x_{n1}^{91})$. The gross value added $\left(V_1^1\right)$ is then shown as produced and input.

The inter-regional input coefficients for the nine regions are as follows.

$$a_{ij}^{rs} = x_{ij}^{rs} / X_j^s \quad i, j = 1, 2, 3, \ldots, n \quad r, s = 1, 2, 3, \ldots, 9 \tag{4.6}$$

---

35 The Ministry of Economy, Trade and Industry (METI) discontinued the production of interregional input-output table in 2005 after the last one. Therefore, in a recent RIETI discussion paper of Arai (2022), the 47 prefectures are grouped into nine regions in I-O tables, as follows. 1. Hokkaido, 2. Tohoku (Aomori, Iwate, Miyagi, Akita, Yamagata, Fukushima), 3. Kanto (Ibaraki, Tochigi, Gunma, Saitama, Chiba, Tokyo, Kanagawa, Niigata, Yamanashi, Nagano, Shizuoka), 4. Chubu (Toyama, Ishikawa, Gifu, Aichi, Mie), 5. Kinki (Fukui, Shiga, Kyoto, Osaka, Hyogo, Wakayama), 6. Chugoku (Tottori, Shimane, Okayama, Hiroshima, Yamaguchi), 7. Shikoku (Tokushima, Kagawa, Ehime, Kochi), 8. Kyushu (Fukuoka, Saga, Nagasaki, Kumamoto, Oita, Miyazaki, Kagoshima), 9. Okinawa.

36 The underlying data were obtained from an Inter-prefectural Input–Output Table for 2011 devised and described by Arai, S. and published by RIETI in 2022.

Table 4.7 The 9 regions interregional input–output table

		Region 1				Region 2					Region 3				Final demand				Export	Import	Regional production
		Sector 1	Sector 2		Sector n	Sector 1	Sector 2		Sector n		Sector 1	Sector 2		Sector n	Region 1	Region 2		Region9			
Region 1	Sector 1	x_{11}^{11}	x_{12}^{11}	…	x_{1n}^{11}	x_{11}^{12}	x_{12}^{12}	…	x_{1n}^{12}	…	x_{1n}^{19}	x_{1n}^{19}	…	x_{1n}^{19}	F_1^{11}	F_1^{12}	…	F_1^{19}	E_1^1	M_1^1	X_1^1
	Sector 2	x_{21}^{11}	x_{22}^{11}	…	x_{2n}^{11}	x_{21}^{12}	x_{22}^{12}	…	x_{2n}^{12}	…	x_{2n}^{19}	x_{2n}^{19}	…	x_{2n}^{19}	F_2^{11}	F_2^{12}	…	F_2^{19}	E_2^1	M_2^1	X_2^1
	⋮	⋮	⋮		⋮	⋮	⋮		⋮		⋮	⋮		⋮	⋮			⋮	⋮	⋮	⋮
	Sector n	x_{n1}^{11}	x_{n2}^{11}	…	x_{nn}^{11}	x_{n1}^{12}	x_{n2}^{12}	…	x_{nn}^{12}	…	x_{nn}^{19}	x_{nn}^{19}	…	x_{nn}^{19}	F_n^{11}	F_n^{12}	…	F_n^{19}	E_n^1	M_n^1	X_n^1
Region 2	Sector 1	x_{11}^{21}	x_{12}^{21}	…	x_{1n}^{21}	x_{11}^{22}	x_{12}^{22}	…	x_{1n}^{22}	…	x_{1n}^{29}	x_{1n}^{29}	…	x_{1n}^{29}	F_1^{21}	F_1^{22}	…	F_1^{29}	E_1^2	M_1^2	X_1^2
	Sector 2	x_{21}^{21}	x_{22}^{21}	…	x_{2n}^{21}	x_{21}^{22}	x_{22}^{22}	…	x_{2n}^{22}	…	x_{2n}^{19}	x_{2n}^{29}	…	x_{2n}^{29}	F_2^{21}	F_2^{22}	…	F_2^{29}	E_2^2	M_2^2	X_2^2
	⋮	⋮	⋮		⋮	⋮	⋮		⋮		⋮	⋮		⋮	⋮	⋮		⋮	⋮	⋮	⋮
	Sector n	x_{n1}^{21}	x_{n2}^{21}	…	x_{nn}^{21}	x_{n1}^{22}	x_{n2}^{12}	…	x_{nn}^{22}	…	x_{nn}^{29}	x_{nn}^{29}	…	x_{nn}^{29}	F_n^{21}	F_n^{22}	…	F_n^{29}	E_n^2	M_n^2	X_n^2
	⋮	⋮	⋮	⋮	⋮	⋮	⋮	⋮	⋮	⋮	⋮	⋮	⋮	⋮	⋮	⋮		⋮	⋮	⋮	⋮
Region n	Sector 1	x_{11}^{91}	x_{12}^{91}	…	x_{1n}^{91}	x_{11}^{92}	x_{12}^{92}	…	x_{1n}^{92}	…	x_{1n}^{99}	x_{1n}^{99}	…	x_{1n}^{99}	F_1^{91}	F_1^{92}	…	F_1^{99}	E_1^9	M_1^9	X_1^9
	Sector 2	x_{21}^{91}	x_{22}^{91}	…	x_{2n}^{91}	x_{21}^{92}	x_{22}^{92}	…	x_{2n}^{92}	…	x_{2n}^{99}	x_{2n}^{99}	…	x_{2n}^{99}	F_2^{91}	F_2^{92}	…	F_2^{99}	E_2^9	M_2^9	X_2^9
	⋮	⋮	⋮		⋮	⋮	⋮		⋮		⋮	⋮		⋮	⋮	⋮		⋮	⋮	⋮	⋮
	Sector n	x_{n1}^{91}	x_{n2}^{91}	…	x_{nn}^{91}	x_{n1}^{92}	x_{n2}^{92}	…	x_{nn}^{92}	…	x_{nn}^{99}	x_{nn}^{99}	…	x_{nn}^{99}	F_n^{91}	F_n^{92}	…	F_n^{99}	E_n^9	M_n^9	X_n^9
	Ferrous metal scrap	K_1^1	K_2^1	…	K_n^1	K_1^2	K_2^2	…	K_n^2	…	K_1^9	K_2^9	…	K_n^9							

(continued)

Table 4.7 (continued)

	Region 1				Region 2					Region 3				Final demand				Export	Import	Regional production
	Sector 1	Sector 2		Sector n	Sector 1	Sector 2		Sector n		Sector 1	Sector 2		Sector n	Region 1	Region 2		Region9			
Total value added	V_1^1	V_2^1	…	V_n^1	V_1^2	V_2^2	…	V_n^2	…	V_1^9	V_2^9	…	V_n^9							
Regional production	X_1^1	X_2^1	…	X_n^1	X_1^2	X_2^2	…	X_n^2	…	X_1^9	X_2^9	…	X_n^9							

$$X_{ij}^{rs} = a_{ij}^{rs} X_j^s \tag{4.7}$$

Thus, the demand balance formula is as follows.

$$\begin{aligned}
&a_{11}^{11}X_1^1 + a_{12}^{11}X_2^1+, \ldots, +a_{1n}^{11}X_n^1 + a_{11}^{12}X_1^2 + a_{12}^{12}X_2^2+, \ldots, \\
&+a_{1n}^{12}X_n^2+, \ldots, +a_{11}^{19}X_1^9 + a_{12}^{19}X_2^9+, \ldots, +a_{1n}^{19}X_n^9 + F_1^{11} \\
&+F_1^{12}+, \ldots, +F_1^{19} + E_1^1 - M_1^1 = X_1^1 \\
&a_{21}^{11}X_1^1 + a_{22}^{11}X_2^1+, \ldots, +a_{2n}^{11}X_n^1 + a_{21}^{12}X_1^2 + a_{22}^{12}X_2^2+, \ldots, \\
&+a_{2n}^{12}X_n^2+, \ldots, +a_{21}^{19}X_1^9 + a_{22}^{19}X_2^9+, \ldots, +a_{2n}^{19}X_n^9 + F_2^{11} \\
&+F_2^{12}+, \ldots, +F_2^{19} + E_2^1 - M_2^1 = X_2^1 \\
&\qquad \vdots \qquad\qquad \vdots \\
&a_{n1}^{11}X_1^1 + a_{n2}^{11}X_2^1+, \ldots, +a_{nn}^{11}X_n^1 + a_{n1}^{12}X_1^2 + a_{n2}^{12}X_2^2+, \ldots, \\
&+a_{nn}^{12}X_n^2+, \ldots, +a_{n1}^{19}X_1^9 + a_{n2}^{19}X_2^9+, \ldots, +a_{nn}^{19}X_n^9 + F_n^{11} \\
&+F_n^{12}+, \ldots, +F_{1n}^{19} + E_n^1 - M_n^1 = X_n^1 \\
&a_{11}^{21}X_1^1 + a_{12}^{21}X_2^1+, \ldots, +a_{1n}^{21}X_n^1 + a_{n1}^{22}X_1^2 + a_{12}^{22}X_2^2+, \ldots, \\
&+a_{1n}^{22}X_n^2+, \ldots, +a_{11}^{29}X_1^9 + a_{12}^{29}X_2^9+, \ldots, +a_{1n}^{29}X_n^9 + F_1^{21} \\
&+F_1^{22}+, \ldots, +F_1^{29} + E_1^2 - M_1^2 = X_1^2 \\
&a_{21}^{21}X_1^1 + a_{22}^{21}X_2^1+, \ldots, +a_{2n}^{21}X_n^1 + a_{21}^{22}X_1^2 + a_{22}^{22}X_2^2+, \ldots, \\
&+a_{2n}^{22}X_n^2+, \ldots, +a_{21}^{29}X_1^9 + a_{122}^{29}X_2^9+, \ldots, +a_{2n}^{29}X_n^9 + F_2^{21} \\
&+F_2^{22}+, \ldots, +F_2^{29} + E_2^2 - M_2^2 = X_2^2 \\
&\qquad \vdots \qquad\qquad \vdots \\
&a_{n1}^{91}X_1^1 + a_{n2}^{91}X_2^1+, \ldots, +a_{nn}^{91}X_n^1 + a_{n1}^{92}X_1^2 + a_{n2}^{92}X_2^2+, \ldots, \\
&+a_{nn}^{92}X_n^2+, \ldots, +a_{n1}^{99}X_1^9 + a_{n2}^{99}X_2^9+, \ldots, +a_{nn}^{99}X_n^9 + F_n^{91} \\
&+F_n^{92}+, \ldots, +F_{1n}^{99} + E_n^9 - M_n^9 = X_n^9
\end{aligned}$$

The series formula is as follows.

$$
\begin{bmatrix}
a^{11}_{11} & a^{11}_{12} & \cdots & a^{11}_{1n} & a^{12}_{11} & a^{12}_{12} & \cdots & a^{12}_{1n} & \cdots & a^{19}_{11} & a^{19}_{12} & \cdots & a^{19}_{1n} \\
a^{11}_{21} & a^{11}_{22} & \cdots & a^{11}_{2n} & a^{12}_{21} & a^{12}_{22} & \cdots & a^{12}_{2n} & \cdots & a^{19}_{21} & a^{19}_{22} & \cdots & a^{19}_{2n} \\
\vdots & \vdots & & \vdots & \vdots & \vdots & & \vdots & & \vdots & \vdots & & \vdots \\
a^{11}_{n1} & a^{11}_{n2} & \cdots & a^{11}_{nn} & a^{12}_{n1} & a^{11}_{n2} & \cdots & a^{19}_{n1} & \cdots & a^{19}_{n1} & a^{19}_{n2} & \cdots & a^{19}_{nn} \\
a^{21}_{11} & a^{21}_{12} & \cdots & a^{21}_{1n} & a^{22}_{11} & a^{22}_{12} & \cdots & a^{29}_{11} & \cdots & a^{29}_{11} & a^{29}_{12} & \cdots & a^{29}_{nn} \\
a^{21}_{21} & a^{21}_{22} & \cdots & a^{21}_{2n} & a^{22}_{21} & a^{22}_{22} & \cdots & a^{22}_{21} & \cdots & a^{29}_{21} & a^{29}_{22} & \cdots & a^{29}_{2n} \\
\vdots & \vdots & & \vdots & \vdots & \vdots & & \vdots & & \vdots & \vdots & & \vdots \\
\vdots & \vdots & & \vdots & \vdots & \vdots & & \vdots & & \vdots & \vdots & & \vdots \\
a^{91}_{n1} & a^{91}_{n2} & \cdots & a^{91}_{nn} & a^{92}_{n1} & a^{91}_{n2} & \cdots & a^{92}_{nn} & \cdots & a^{99}_{n1} & a^{99}_{n2} & \cdots & a^{99}_{nn}
\end{bmatrix}
\begin{bmatrix}
X^1_1 \\ X^1_2 \\ \vdots \\ X^1_n \\ X^2_1 \\ X^2_2 \\ \vdots \\ \vdots \\ X^9_n
\end{bmatrix}
+
\begin{bmatrix}
F^{11}_1 + F^{12}_1 + \cdots + F^{19}_1 \\
F^{11}_2 + F^{12}_2 + \cdots + F^{19}_2 \\
\vdots \quad \vdots \quad \vdots \\
F^{11}_n + F^{12}_n + \cdots + F^{19}_n \\
F^{21}_1 + F^{22}_1 + \cdots + F^{29}_1 \\
F^{21}_2 + F^{21}_2 + \cdots + F^{21}_2 \\
\vdots \quad \vdots \quad \vdots \\
\vdots \quad \vdots \quad \vdots \\
F^{91}_n + F^{92}_n + \cdots + F^{99}_n
\end{bmatrix}
+
\begin{bmatrix}
E^1_1 \\ E^1_2 \\ \vdots \\ E^1_n \\ E^2_1 \\ E^2_2 \\ \vdots \\ \vdots \\ E^9_n
\end{bmatrix}
$$

$$
=
\begin{bmatrix}
m^1_1 & 0 & \cdots & 0 & 0 & 0 & \cdots & \cdots & 0 \\
0 & m^1_2 & \cdots & 0 & 0 & 0 & \cdots & \cdots & 0 \\
\vdots & \vdots & \ddots & \vdots & \vdots & \vdots & \vdots & \vdots & \vdots \\
0 & 0 & 0 & m^1_n & 0 & 0 & \vdots & \vdots & 0 \\
0 & 0 & 0 & 0 & m^2_1 & 0 & \vdots & \vdots & 0 \\
0 & 0 & 0 & 0 & 0 & m^2_2 & \vdots & \vdots & 0 \\
\vdots & \vdots & \vdots & \vdots & 0 & 0 & \ddots & \vdots & \vdots \\
\vdots & \vdots & \vdots & \vdots & \vdots & \vdots & \vdots & \ddots & \vdots \\
0 & 0 & \cdots & 0 & 0 & 0 & \cdots & \cdots & m^9_n
\end{bmatrix}
\begin{bmatrix}
X^1_1 \\ X^1_2 \\ \vdots \\ X^1_n \\ X^2_1 \\ X^2_2 \\ \vdots \\ \vdots \\ X^9_n
\end{bmatrix}
+
\begin{bmatrix}
X^1_1 \\ X^1_2 \\ \vdots \\ X^1_n \\ X^2_1 \\ X^2_2 \\ \vdots \\ \vdots \\ X^9_n
\end{bmatrix}
\tag{4.8}
$$

The import coefficient is assumed to be $m^s_i = M^s_i / X^s_j$. Imports here are assumed to be proportionate to intra-regional demand only. As a result, it follows that:

$$
\begin{bmatrix} X_1^1 \\ X_2^1 \\ \vdots \\ X_n^1 \\ X_1^2 \\ X_2^2 \\ \vdots \\ \vdots \\ X_n^9 \end{bmatrix} = \begin{bmatrix} m_1^1 & 0 & \cdots & 0 & 0 & 0 & \cdots\cdots & 0 \\ 0 & m_2^1 & \cdots & 0 & 0 & 0 & \cdots\cdots & 0 \\ \vdots & \vdots & \ddots & \vdots & \vdots & \vdots & \vdots & \vdots & \vdots \\ 0 & 0 & 0 & m_n^1 & 0 & 0 & \vdots & \vdots & 0 \\ 0 & 0 & 0 & 0 & m_1^2 & 0 & \vdots & \vdots & 0 \\ 0 & 0 & 0 & 0 & 0 & m_2^2 & \vdots & \vdots & 0 \\ \vdots & \vdots & \vdots & \vdots & 0 & 0 & \ddots & \vdots & \vdots \\ \vdots & \vdots & \vdots & \vdots & \vdots & \vdots & \vdots & \ddots & \vdots \\ 0 & 0 & \cdots & 0 & 0 & 0 & \cdots\cdots & m_n^9 \end{bmatrix}
$$

$$
= \left(\begin{bmatrix} A_1^1 & 0 & \cdots & 0 & 0 & 0 & \cdots\cdots & 0 \\ 0 & A_2^1 & \cdots & 0 & 0 & 0 & \cdots\cdots & 0 \\ \vdots & \vdots & \ddots & \vdots & \vdots & \vdots & \vdots & \vdots & \vdots \\ 0 & 0 & 0 & A_n^1 & 0 & 0 & \vdots & \vdots & 0 \\ 0 & 0 & 0 & 0 & A_1^2 & 0 & \vdots & \vdots & 0 \\ 0 & 0 & 0 & 0 & 0 & A_2^2 & \vdots & \vdots & 0 \\ \vdots & \vdots & \vdots & \vdots & 0 & 0 & \ddots & \vdots & \vdots \\ \vdots & \vdots & \vdots & \vdots & \vdots & \vdots & \vdots & \ddots & \vdots \\ 0 & 0 & \cdots & 0 & 0 & 0 & \cdots\cdots & A_n^9 \end{bmatrix} \begin{bmatrix} X_1^1 \\ X_2^1 \\ \vdots \\ X_n^1 \\ X_1^2 \\ X_2^2 \\ \vdots \\ \vdots \\ X_n^9 \end{bmatrix} + \begin{bmatrix} F_1^1 \\ F_2^1 \\ \vdots \\ F_n^1 \\ F_1^2 \\ F_2^2 \\ \vdots \\ \vdots \\ F_n^9 \end{bmatrix} \right) \tag{4.9}
$$

A simplification of this is:

$$
AX + F + E = X + M'\left(A^* X + F^*\right) \tag{4.10}
$$

M′ is a diagonal matrix made up of the regional import coefficients as diagonal elements. Hence, X can be expressed as in Eq. (4.11). Lastly, the effect of final demand on production is given by Eq. (4.12).

$$
X = \left[I - \left(A - M'A^*\right)\right]^{-1}\left(F - M'F^* + E\right) \tag{4.11}
$$

$$
\Delta X = \left[I - \left(A - M'A^*\right)\right]^{-1}\left(\Delta F - M'\Delta F^*\right) \tag{4.12}
$$

For the purposes of this analysis, the effects of final demand on production are first multiplied by an employment income coefficient. Within this total, the second-or indirect ripple effects on consumption can then be calculated.[37]

[37] An increase in output leads to an increase in employment income. The subsequent effect of this rise in income on consumption was the point of the analysis.

4.6.2 Analysis of the Ripple Effects from Construction Investment

Ripple effects from construction investments in each region can be estimated using an input–output table to analyze transfers in the construction sector. The expenditure vector in the construction sector will vary depending on what is being built. The method adopted for this calculation is as follows. For intra-regional production as a whole, the formula used in the input–output table is set out in Eq. (4.13).

$$X = A \cdot X + F + E - M \tag{4.13}$$

Equation (4.14) then shows the formula used in sectors other than construction, while the formula for the construction sector is the one shown in Eq. (4.15)

$$A_{11}X_1 + A_{12}X_1 + F_1 + E_1 = M_1 + X_1 \tag{4.14}$$

$$A_{21}X_1 + A_{22}X_2 + F_2 + E_2 = M_2 + X_2 \tag{4.15}$$

For exports, imports and intermediate transfer stages, the account in the construction sector is zero, as shown in Eq. (4.16), which can be summed up as in Eq. (4.17).

$$A_{21} = 0 \quad A_{22} = 0 \quad E_2 = 0 \quad M_2 = 0 \tag{4.16}$$

$$F_2 = X_2 \tag{4.17}$$

When measuring the production-inducing effect of public works in an input–output analysis, it is necessary to examine sectors in which the amount of public investment depends on the nature of the project. The data for the investment sectors are then calculated using the input coefficients from the construction analysis input–output table. Here, the table for 2011 is used. The formula for measuring the inducing effect can be shown and summed up as follows,

$$\begin{aligned} \Delta X_1 = {} & \left[I - \left(A - M'A^*\right)\right]^{-1}\left(\Delta F_1 - M'\Delta F_1^*\right) \\ & + \left[I - \left(A - M'A^*\right)\right]^{-1}\left(\Delta F_2 - M'\Delta F_2^*\right) \end{aligned} \tag{4.18}$$

$$\Delta X_2 = F_2 \tag{4.19}$$

where X_1 is the vector of induced production growth for the non-construction sector, X_2 is the same vector in the construction sector, M is the diagonal matrix of import coefficients, N is the diagonal matrix of transfer coefficients, A is the input coefficient matrix, F_1 is the vector of final demand for the non-construction sector, F_2 is the

Table 4.8 Wind power construction costs by region (2022) (unit: ×10,000 yen)

	Local construction costs only		All-inclusive costs	
	Site development	Other civil engineering work	Site development	Other civil engineering work
Hokkaido	6,995	9,260	31,265	14,850
Tohoku	23,540	31,292	105,055	50,049
Kanto	4,805	6,650	25,746	11,472
Chubu	3,172	6,969	27,920	12,658
Kinki	3,826	5,052	18,271	8,387
Chugoku	5,237	7,186	24,115	11,570
Shikoku	3,254	4,474	15,008	7,199
Kyushu	8,005	11,385	36,595	17,972
Okinawa	259	357	1,192	570
Total	59,092	82,626	285,166	134,728

Source Created by the author using estimate results of this study

vector of final demand in the construction sector, K is the input coefficient matrix in the segmented construction sector. $*$ indicates transfers confined to the home-region.

The construction of a wind power electricity generation plant involves work first on access roads and site development, and then on structure foundations including both the plant structure and the wind turbines. For the purpose of the analysis, the construction investments need to be regarded as effectively including all of these preparation tasks. In this study, therefore, for the allocation of input coefficients within the Input–Output table in the construction sector analysis, a distinction is drawn between two categories of costs: for road and site development work on the one hand, and for structure foundations on the other. However, as the amount of road building will vary with the size of the plant, assumptions based on average cost rates can be made only for site development and foundation work. Here, it is assumed that site development will account for 43% of (intra-regional) construction work, and other civil engineering work (foundations) for the remaining 57%.[38] To provide a broad region-by-region analysis of all nine regions, two kinds of case analyses are considered: one in which the analysis is confined to within the home-region, and another for plants having buildings or structures that require construction investments transcending the region. This is shown in Table 4.8.

The former type of analysis can be said to apply for minimum scale investments in wind power construction, while the latter type applies for much larger-scale projects. The data used in these analyses are presented in Table 4.8. Note that these figures are for all construction investments in the wind power plants currently in operation. It should be noted that this is not an analysis of effects obtained in a single particular year; one-year effects have to be worked out later by dividing the total investments by 20, the number of years in the service life of a wind power installation.

[38] The proportion ratios used in the analysis were as assumed in Asahi (2005).

4.6.3 Results of Analysis

The ripple effects of wind power plant investments on the Japanese economy in 2022 are presented in Table 4.9 and in Figs. 4.9 and 4.10.

The figures for economic ripple effects within a region show that a direct investment of 141.717 billion yen results in a total output of 265.873 billion yen when indirect effects are counted in. For the purposes of this study, the increase in consumption once the induced production has fed through into employee incomes is also counted as a secondary indirect effect. The induced production coefficient including these indirect effects is 1.8. The areas showing the largest increases in primary and secondary indirect effects were scientific research, professional and technical services with 20.9 billion yen, followed by wholesale and retail trade with 12.7 billion yen. In the manufacturing sector, primary metals showed an increase of 12.2 billion yen and ceramic, stone and clay products an increase of 6.69 billion yen. The effects on employment are shown in the graph in Fig. 4.9. By sector, 17,562 jobs were added directly in construction. Indirectly, 3844 jobs were added in scientific research and professional and technical services, followed by 3479 in wholesale and retail trade. Overall, there was a gain of 6613 new jobs in the manufacturing sector.

Of course, the increase in production due to the construction of wind farms comes at the cost of an increase in energy consumption and therefore also in CO_2 emissions. The CO_2 emissions from this wind power construction investment amount to 233,901 tons. At an environmental tax rate of 289 yen/t-CO_2 in Japan,[39] this gives a tax liability of 0.676 billion yen, equivalent to a mere 0.25% of the economic ripple effects of the induced production. In other words, the carbon tax costs arising from the construction of wind power generation plants are not at a level to have any significant offsetting effect on the positive gains in production.

Table 4.10 presents a summary of the economic and employment effects of the construction of wind power generation plants in each of the 9 regions, along with the offsetting CO_2 emission effects. In the Tohoku region, the induced production benefits amount to 88.943 billion yen, and the number of jobs created is 6765. In Kanto, the corresponding figures are 36.589 billion yen for induced production and 4769 jobs. In Kyushu, the corresponding figures are 34.88 billion yen and 2966 jobs.

I next move on to analyses of very large-scale wind power construction projects, involving construction investments extending beyond a single region.

For the ripple effects of this region-transcending type of plant construction investment, the right side of the table shows that a direct investment of 419.894 billion yen produces a total output of 758.429 billion yen when indirect effects are counted in. The induced production coefficient including these indirect effects is 1.8. The largest increases, counting primary and secondary indirect effects together, were 568.7 billion yen in scientific research, and professional and technical services, followed by 35.4 billion yen in wholesale and retail trade. In manufacturing, primary

[39] In addition to the environmental tax, the introduction of a separate carbon tax is also currently under consideration.

Table 4.9 Economic ripple effects of investments in wind power plant construction (units: economic effects: billions of yen, emissions: CO_2-tons)

Sector	Home-region investments					Region-transcending investments				
	Direct effects	Primary indirect effects	Secondary indirect effects	Total	CO_2 emissions	Direct effects	Primary indirect effects	Secondary indirect effects	Total	CO_2 emissions
Agriculture, forestry and fishery	0	292	549	840	1,207	0	840	1,487	2,327	3,342
Mining	0	267	19	286	326	0	798	52	850	969
Beverages and foods	0	70	1,441	1,511	433	0	198	3,942	4,140	1,186
Textile products	0	80	66	146	73	0	226	180	406	203
Pulp, paper, paperboard, building paper	0	1,157	189	1,346	2,093	0	3,043	518	3,560	5,538
Chemical products, petroleum and coal products	0	4,015	807	4,822	11,105	0	11,205	2,224	13,428	30,924
Ceramic, stone and clay products	0	6,645	47	6,692	23,818	0	19,741	131	19,871	70,726
Primary metals	0	12,116	155	12,271	47,283	0	27,690	430	28,120	108,353
Metal products	0	5,509	85	5,594	1,097	0	11,175	235	11,410	2,237
Manufacture of general-purpose machinery	0	1,625	58	1,683	70	0	5,947	158	6,105	255
Electronic parts, devices and electronic circuits	0	244	36	280	35	0	749	101	849	107

(continued)

Table 4.9 (continued)

Sector	Home-region investments					Region-transcending investments				
	Direct effects	Primary indirect effects	Secondary indirect effects	Total	CO_2 emissions	Direct effects	Primary indirect effects	Secondary indirect effects	Total	CO_2 emissions
Electrical machinery	0	748	75	824	43	0	2,603	209	2,812	147
Manufacture of information and communication electronics equipment	0	132	56	188	6	0	431	156	587	18
Manufacture of transportation equipment	0	917	304	1221	145	0	2,490	871	3,361	398
Printing and allied industries	0	546	147	693	94	0	1,506	403	1,909	260
Miscellaneous manufacturing industries	0	2,456	316	2,773	535	0	7,009	872	7,881	1,520
Electricity, gas, heat supply and water	0	4,743	1,241	5,984	95,413	0	15,131	3,403	18,535	295,521
Construction	141,718	686	323	142,727	103	419,894	1,923	888	422,704	288
Wholesale and retail trade	0	9,772	2,929	12,701	769	0	27,378	8,026	35,403	2,145

(continued)

Table 4.9 (continued)

Sector	Home-region investments					Region-transcending investments				
	Direct effects	Primary indirect effects	Secondary indirect effects	Total	CO_2 emissions	Direct effects	Primary indirect effects	Secondary indirect effects	Total	CO_2 emissions
Transport and postal activities	0	6,885	1,195	8,080	43,915	0	19,147	3,281	22,428	121,897
Accommodations, eating and drinking services	0	1	1,348	1,349	547	0	2	3,709	3,711	1,506
Information and communications	0	1,813	1,155	2,968	24	0	5,056	3,158	8,214	67
Internet based services, image information, character information production and distribution	0	1,952	496	2,447	41	0	5,225	1,364	6,589	111
Finance and Insurance	0	3,509	1,751	5,260	53	0	9,863	4,804	14,667	148
Real estate and goods rental and leasing	0	1,428	5,133	6,561	106	0	3,997	14,095	18,092	292

(continued)

Table 4.9 (continued)

Sector	Home-region investments					Region-transcending investments				
	Direct effects	Primary indirect effects	Secondary indirect effects	Total	CO_2 emissions	Direct effects	Primary indirect effects	Secondary indirect effects	Total	CO_2 emissions
Scientific research, professional and technical services	0	18,903	2,020	20,923	1,563	0	51,333	5,542	56,875	4,248
Public administration	0	95	140	235	40	0	282	384	666	115
Education, learning support	0	106	552	658	116	0	301	1,526	1,827	322
Medical, health care and welfare	0	13	1120	1134	164	0	37	3,062	3,099	449
Others	0	3,419	1,932	5,351	2,683	0	10,054	5,294	15,348	7,694
Central office	0	6,522	1,805	8,327	–	0	17,711	4,942	22,653	–
Total	141,718	96,666	27,490	265,874	233,901	419,894	263,088	75,447	758,429	660,985

Source Created by the author using estimate results of this study

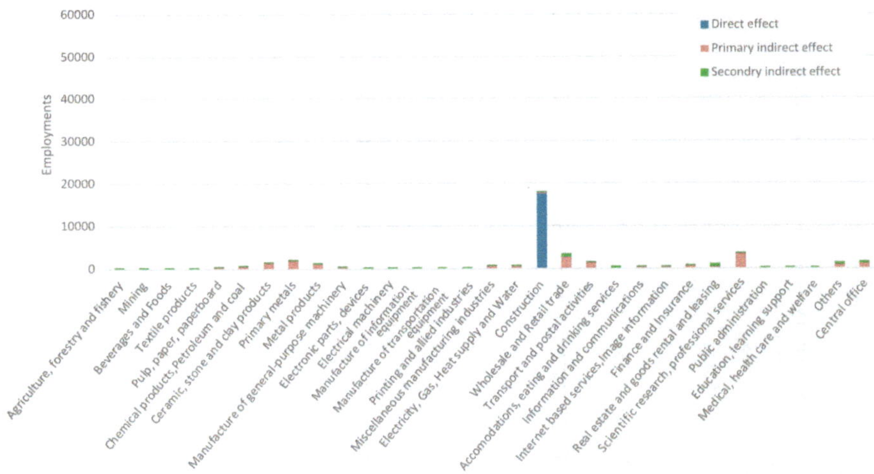

Fig. 4.9 Employment effects of home-region investments in wind power plant construction. *Source* Created by the author using estimate results of this study

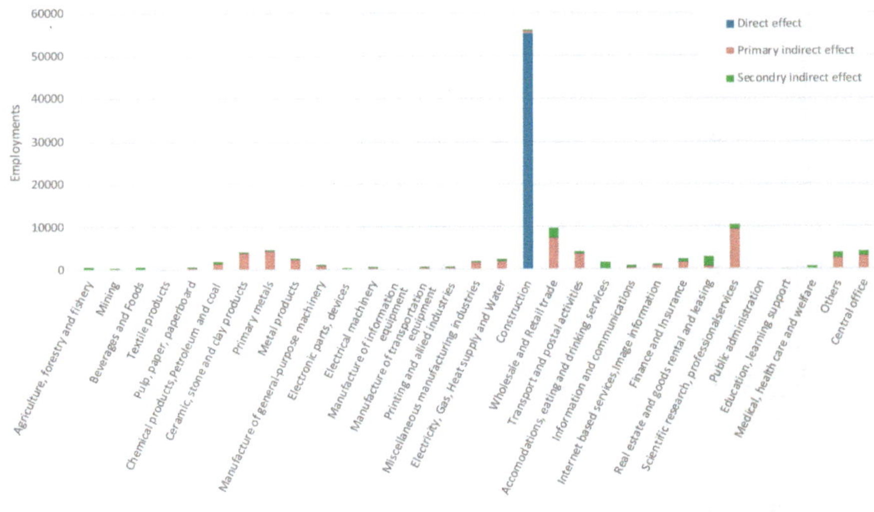

Fig. 4.10 Employment effects of region-transcending investments in wind power plant construction. *Source* Created by the author using estimate results of this study

metal products increased by 28.1 billion yen, and ceramic, stone and clay products by 19.8 billion yen.

Effects on employment can be seen from the graph in Fig. 4.10. The sector most affected was construction, with a direct gain of 55,302 jobs. Indirectly, 10,449 jobs were added in scientific research, and professional and technical services, followed

Table 4.10 Economic and employment effects and CO_2 emission costs by region (units: economic effects: millions of yen, employment: persons, emissions: CO_2-tons)

	Home-region investments						Region-transcending investments					
	Direct effects	Primary indirect effects	Secondary indirect effects	Total	Employment effects (indirect effect)	CO_2 emissions	Direct effects	Primary indirect effects	Secondary indirect effects	Total	Employment effects (indirect effect)	CO_2 emissions
Hokkaido	16,255	9,705	2,525	28,485	2,386	25,999	46,115	25,316	6,693	78,124	6,245	70,844
Tohoku	54,832	27,093	7,018	88,943	6,765	65,258	155,104	72,412	18,739	246,254	18,028	185,449
Kanto	11,454	17,958	7,177	36,589	4,769	35,504	37,218	50,437	20,048	107,704	13,379	101,612
Chubu	10,141	8,010	2,208	20,359	1,977	19,746	40,578	26,672	7,286	74,535	6,574	68,667
Kinki	8,878	8,125	2,322	19,325	2,031	19,218	26,658	22,152	6,415	55,225	5,549	53,376
Chugoku	12,423	8,683	1,903	23,009	2,016	23,897	35,686	22,655	5,078	63,418	5,279	63,912
Shikoku	7,727	4,634	1,118	13,479	1,138	11,637	22,206	11,171	2,724	36,101	2,732	29,145
Kyushu	19,390	12,076	3,122	34,588	2,966	31,610	54,566	31,306	8,242	94,114	7,708	85,078
Okinawa	616	383	97	1,096	102	1,078	1,762	1,014	268	3,044	253	2,946
Total	141,718	96,666	27,490	265,874	24,150	233,946	419,894	263,133	75,492	758,519	65,746	661,030

Source Created by the author using estimate results of this study

by 9696 in wholesale and retail trade. Overall, the manufacturing sector added 18,997 new jobs.

The CO_2 emissions from this wind power construction investment amount to 660,985 tons. At an environmental tax rate of 289 yen/t-CO_2, this gives a tax liability of 0.19 billion yen. Here again, tax costs like these are nowhere near large enough to have any significant offsetting effect on the economic production growth. Economic and employment effects by region are presented in Table 4.10. In the Tohoku region, the induced production resulting from the construction of wind power generation plants amounts to 155.1 billion yen, and the number of jobs created is 246,254. In Kanto, the corresponding figures are 107.7 billion yen and 13,379 jobs, and in Kyushu 94.1 billion yen and 7708 jobs.

Tables 4.11 and 4.12 show differences in the amounts of ripple effect (referring here to primary indirect effects from direct investments) spilling over into other regions. The direct effects are shown in the top row for the region named at the top of each column. In the rows below, the ripple effects from direct investments are shown in vertical order from Hokkaido (northernmost) down. To take examples for the Tohoku region, Table 4.11, for home-region investments, shows a direct investment of 54.832 billion yen in the "Tohoku" column bringing a spillover ripple effect of 0.3 billion yen to neighboring Hokkaido. Then comes the home-region ripple effect of 26.798 billion yen for Tohoku, followed by spillovers of 5.162 billion yen for Kanto, 0.9 billion yen for Chubu, and so on.

Table 4.12, on the other hand, for "region-transcending" projects requiring contractors from outside of the region, shows a direct construction investment of 155.104 billion yen for Tohoku having a ripple effect of 0.785 billion yen (spillover) on Hokkaido, then, after the home-region ripple effect of 71,596 billion yen within Tohoku, we find quite large spillovers of 13.544 billion yen for Kanto (which includes Tokyo), 2.498 billion yen for Kinki (including Osaka), etc. For projects involving construction investments contracted from outside the region, we see that induced production spillover effects tend to be higher in regions like Kanto than in the regions nearer at hand to where the investment is placed.

4.7 Conclusion

The present study has shown that there is a positive cost–benefit balance in favor of the expansion of wind power generation capacity in Japan. It began by summarizing the economic and social background and the steps that this expansion has taken so far. In particular, the rise in the amount of power generated, the resulting CO_2 reduction effect, the cost of generating wind power, and the ripple effects on regional economies were analyzed.

The amount of energy generated from wind power in 2022 was 7.45 m MWh. It can be calculated that the equivalent output from a coal-fired thermal plant would have resulted in 7032 kt of CO_2 emissions. In other words, supplying this energy from wind power instead of coal has an effect of eliminating virtually all of this

Table 4.11 Home-region construction investment effects and spillover to other regions (units: millions of yen)

		Hokkaido	Tohoku	Kanto	Chubu	Kinki	Chugoku	Shikoku	Kyushu	Okinawa	Total
Direct effect		16,255	54,832	11,454	10,141	8,878	12,423	7,727	19,390	616	141,718
Primary indirect effects	Hokkaido	9,276	302	33	25	17	14	11	27	1	9,706
	Tohoku	71	26,798	79	40	30	42	26	53	15	27,154
	Kanto	1,225	5,162	7,611	800	635	698	548	1,246	43	17,968
	Chubu	199	930	206	5,921	197	150	104	297	7	8,012
	Kinki	297	971	279	323	5,162	358	240	483	13	8,127
	Chugoku	154	406	132	143	204	7,069	188	373	15	8,684
	Shikoku	29	109	35	32	43	56	4,252	76	2	4,634
	Kyushu	104	365	118	110	95	213	101	10,957	14	12,076
	Okinawa	[illegible]	19	4	1	1	1	1	6	346	382
Total of primary indirect effects		11,358	35,063	8,498	7,394	6,384	8,601	5,470	13,518	455	96,742

Source Created by the author using estimate results of this study

Table 4.12 Spillovers to other regions in cases involving region-transcending construction investments (units: millions of yen)

		Hokkaido	Tohoku	Kanto	Chubu	Kinki	Chugoku	Shikoku	Kyushu	Okinawa	Total
Direct effect		46,115	155,104	37,218	40,578	26,658	35,686	22,206	54,566	1,762	419,894
Primary indirect effects	Hokkaido	24,180	785	96	80	44	35	25	67	3	25,316
	Tohoku	181	71,596	225	123	68	94	48	119	17	72,471
	Kanto	3121	13,544	22,781	2,801	1,750	1,833	1,298	3,212	104	50,445
	Chubu	494	2,359	599	21,288	529	386	243	755	18	26,669
	Kinki	729	2,498	803	1,080	14,338	912	559	1,197	33	22,149
	Chugoku	357	991	362	447	508	18,617	418	915	34	22,649
	Shikoku	73	287	102	110	116	148	10,128	197	4	11,165
	Kyushu	252	913	328	355	250	530	228	28,410	32	31,298
	Okinawa	5	52	13	4	4	3	3	15	903	1,002
Total of primary indirect effects		29,392	93,024	25,309	26,288	17,607	22,559	12,952	34,885	1,147	263,163

Source Created by the author using estimate results of this study

CO_2 load. Looking at individual regions, Tohoku stands out as saving the equivalent of 3020 kt-CO_2/year, accounting for 42% of the national total. The measured cost of wind power energy generation is found to lie between 13.4 and 29.7 yen/kwh, although this takes no account of the scale of the plant. Depending also on regional differences, there is no denying that wind energy can be more expensive than energy from other sources.

In Japan, the environmental tax on CO_2 emissions is only 289 yen per ton, so generating electricity from high-carbon energy resources has relatively little negative impact on the enterprise concerned, but once a more targeted carbon tax is introduced, as in other countries, the cost benefits of wind power electricity are likely to rise.

The economic ripple effects of investments in wind power plant construction, estimated only within the home-region, suggest that a direct investment of 141.718 billion yen results in a total output of 265.874 billion yen when indirect effects are counted in. The induced coefficient with these indirect effects included is 1.8. Increased production from this investment in plant construction also leads to the creation of 41,667 additional jobs. From my analysis of the ripple effects in the case of very large investment projects involving contractors outside the home-region, the direct benefit to the whole Japanese economy from the building of wind power generating plants can be evaluated at 419.8 billion yen, while the total induced rise in production value, including indirect effects, comes to 758.4 billion yen.

Increased production due to these investments in plant construction also results in the creation of 121,003 additional jobs. It is true that the construction of plants itself requires a certain cost of resource and energy consumption. But in view of the very small amounts of CO_2 involved, the carbon tax payable on this would come to no more than about 0.25% of the economic benefit from the increase in production. To conclude, then, wind energy results in very little release of CO_2, and the environmental loads of the plant construction and energy generation remain minimal.

Previous analyses of the economic effects of wind power abroad have revealed positive benefits in terms of production and employment, and the results of this study support that. In addition, if a targeted carbon tax is incorporated into the Japanese economic system, the advantages of new energy sources such as wind power could become highly competitive. At the same time, as it is not easy to tap new energy continuously as a base-load power source, Japan also needs to continue with its wider policy of finding the best mix of energies, which must certainly include the new energies.

References

Agency for Natural Resources and Energy. (2015, June 24). Current Situation and Issues Facing Systems for Promoting the Introduction of Renewable Energy (in Japanese). https://www.meti.go.jp/shingikai/enecho/kihon_seisaku/saisei_kano/pdf/001_02_00.pdf. Accessed October 7, 2023

Agency for Natural Resources and Energy, Ministry of Economy, Trade and Industry. (2021, September 17). Briefing materials on the revision of Act on Special Measures Concerning Procurement of Electricity from Renewable Energy Sources by Electricity Utilities (in Japanese). https://www.enecho.meti.go.jp/category/saving_and_new/saiene/kaitori/dl/fip_2020/fip_document01.pdf. Accessed October 7, 2023

Agency for Natural Resources and Energy, Ministry of Economy, Trade and Industry. (2022a). Comprehensive Energy Statistics Time Series Table (reference table) (in Japanese). https://www.enecho.meti.go.jp/statistics/total_energy/results.html#headline2. Accessed October 7, 2023

Agency for Natural Resources and Energy, Ministry of Economy, Trade and Industry. (2022b). Cabinet Decision Made on the FY2021 Annual Report on Energy (Japan's Energy White Paper 2022) (in Japanese). https://www.enecho.meti.go.jp/about/whitepaper/2022/html/. https://www.meti.go.jp/english/press/2022/pdf/0607_002a.pdf. Accessed October 7, 2023

Agency for Natural Resources and Energy, Ministry of Economy, Trade and Industry. (2022c, December 26). 82nd Meeting of the Procurement Price Calculation Committee (in Japanese). Document 2 on Wind Power Generation. https://www.meti.go.jp/shingikai/santeii/pdf/082_02_00.pdf. Accessed October 7, 2023

Agency for Natural Resources and Energy, Ministry of Economy, Trade and Industry. (2023, April 7). Report on procurement pricing (in Japanese). https://www.shugiin.go.jp/internet/itdb_gian.nsf/html/gian/gian_hokoku/20230407chotatsu.pdf/$File/20230407chotatsu.pdf. Accessed October 7, 2023

Akai, M., Nomura, N., Waku., H., & Inoue, M. (1997). Life-cycle analysis of a fossil-fuel power plant with CO_2 recovery and a sequestering system. *Energy, 22*(2–3), 249–255. https://doi.org/10.1016/S0360-5442(96)00094-1

Ando, T., & Nakamura, N. (2018). *Issues of renewable energy as viewed from the current status of wind power generation in Japan* (in Japanese) (Legislation and Surveys No. 407) (pp. 63–73). Planning and Coordination Office, House of Councillors, The National Diet of Japan. https://www.sangiin.go.jp/japanese/annai/chousa/rippou_chousa/backnumber/2018pdf/20181203063.pdf. Accessed October 7, 2023

Arai, S. (2022). *Inter-prefectural input-output table for 2011 in Japan: Construction method and main results* (RIETI Discussion Paper Series 22-J-003) (in Japanese). Research Institute of Economy, Trade and Industry (RIETI). https://www.rieti.go.jp/jp/publications/dp/22j003.pdf. Accessed October 7, 2023

Asahi, S. (2005). Evaluation of the potential for wind power generation in Japan, Wellington, In S. Pratt, & C. Davies (Eds.), *The Fifth Asia Pacific Conference on Sustainable Energy and Environmental Technologies*, Wellington, New Zealand, Massey University (pp. 150–156). https://natlib.govt.nz/records/21990244?search%5Bpath%5D=items&search%5Btext%5D=Small%252C+Clive. Accessed September 25, 2023

BP. (2021). *Statistical review of world energy 2021* (70th ed.). https://www.bp.com/content/dam/bp/business-sites/en/global/corporate/pdfs/energy-economics/statistical-review/bp-stats-review-2021-full-report.pdf. Accessed September 25, 2023

Cabinet Office, Government of Japan. (2021, September 21). General Inspection Task Force for Regulations Concerning Renewable Energy, etc. Document 3. RWE Renewables Japan. Issues in the Promotion of Offshore Wind Power. Cabinet Office. https://www8.cao.go.jp/kisei-kaikaku/kisei/conference/energy/20210921/210921energy04.pdf. Accessed September 25, 2023

Cosmi, C., Macchiato, M., Mangiamele, L., Marmo, G., Pietrapertosa, F., & Salvia, M. (2003). Environmental and economic effects of renewable energy sources use on a local case study. *Energy Policy, 31*(5), 443–457. https://doi.org/10.1016/S0301-4215(02)00073-3

Edenhofer, O., Pichs-Madruga, R., Sokona, Y., Seyboth, K., Kadner, S., Zwickel, T., & Matschoss, P. (Eds.). (2011). *Renewable energy sources and climate change mitigation: Special report of the intergovernmental panel on Climate change*. Cambridge University Press. https://archive.ipcc.ch/report/srren/

Gao, C., Na, H., Song, K., Dyer, N., Tian, F., Xu, Q., & Xing, Y. (2019). Environmental impact analysis of power generation from biomass and wind farms in different locations. *Renewable and Sustainable Energy Reviews, 102*, 307–317. https://doi.org/10.1016/j.rser.2018.12.018

Gao, C., Zhu, S., An, N., Na, H., You, H., & Gao, C. (2021). Comprehensive comparison of multiple renewable power generation methods: A combination analysis of life cycle assessment and ecological footprint. *Renewable and Sustainable Energy Reviews, 147*, 111–255. https://doi.org/10.1016/j.rser.2021.111255

Global Warming Prevention Headquarters. (2002). Climate Change Policy Programme. https://www.env.go.jp/earth/ondanka/taiko/all.pdf. Accessed September 25, 2023

Hienuki, S., Kudoh, Y., & Hondo, H. (2015). Establishing a framework for evaluating environmental and socio-economic impacts by power generation technology using an input-output table—a case study of Japanese future electricity grid mix. *Sustainability, 7*(12), 15794–15811. https://www.mdpi.com/2071-1050/7/12/15786

Hiromachi, Y. (2019). Why isn't offshore wind power spreading in Japan? What are the two barriers to entry? *Solar Journal, 28*(1), 20–21. https://solarjournal.jp/windpower/28527/, https://www.fujisan.co.jp/product/1281697181/b/1776267/

Hondo, H. (2005). Life cycle GHG emission analysis of power generation systems: Japanese case. *Energy, 30*(11–12), 2042–2056. https://doi.org/10.1016/j.energy.2004.07.020

IEA. (2021). World Energy Outlook 2021. https://iea.blob.core.windows.net/assets/4ed140c1-c3f3-4fd9-acae-789a4e14a23c/WorldEnergyOutlook2021.pdf. Accessed September 25, 2023

Imamura, E., Iuchi, M., & Bando, S. (2016). Comprehensive assessment of life cycle CO_2 emissions from power generation technologies in Japan (in Japanese). CRIEPI Socio-economic Research Center Report No. Y6. https://criepi.denken.or.jp/hokokusho/pb/reportDlConf?reportNoUkCode=Y06&tenpuTypeCode=30&seqNo=1. Accessed September 25, 2023

Institute of Energy Economics, Japan. (1998). The future cost of renewable energy, and the prospect of introduction. IEE-SR291, Report of Research investigation.

IPCC. (2011a). Renewable Energy Sources and Climate. Change Mitigation. Special Report of the Intergovernmental. Panel on Climate Change, Cambridge University Press.

IPCC. (2011b). Renewable Energy and Climate Change, Chapter 1, p. 178. 1.2 Summary of renewable energy resources. 1.2.1 Definition, conversion and application of renewable energy.

IPCC. (2011c). Renewable energy and climate change. https://archive.ipcc.ch/pdf/special-reports/srren/Chapter%201%20Renewable%20Energy%20and%20Climate%20Change.pdf. Accessed September 25, 2023

IPCC. (2014). IPCC Fifth Assessment Report—Synthesis Report. https://www.ipcc.ch/site/assets/uploads/2018/05/SYR_AR5_FINAL_full_wcover.pdf. Accessed September 20, 2023

IPCC. (2021a). Sixth Assessment Report, Working Group 1: The Physical Science Basis Summary for Policymakers. https://www.ipcc.ch/report/ar6/wg1/downloads/report/IPCC_AR6_WGI_SPM.pdf. Accessed September 20, 2023

IPCC. (2021b). IPCC Sixth Assessment Report—Working Group 1: The Physical Science Basis A (pp. 33−144). https://doi.org/10.1017/9781009157896.002. https://www.ipcc.ch/report/ar6/wg1/downloads/report/IPCC_AR6_WGI_TS.pdf. Accessed September 20, 2023

IPCC. (2021c). IPCC Sixth Assessment Report—Summary for Policymakers (pp. 3−32). https://doi.org/10.1017/9781009157896.001. https://www.ipcc.ch/report/ar6/wg1/downloads/report/IPCC_AR6_WGI_SPM.pdf. Accessed September 20, 2023

IRENA. (2022). Renewable capacity statistics 2022, (pp. 1–50). The International Renewable Energy Agency, Abu Dhabi.

ITOCHU Techno-Solutions Corporation. (2011, February 28). Basic Survey Project for Promoting the Introduction of New Energy (Fiscal 2010). (Survey on the amount of wind energy that can be introduced) Survey report, Ministry of Economy, Trade and Industry. https://warp.da.ndl.go.jp/info:ndljp/pid/9919854/www.meti.go.jp/meti_lib/report/2011fy/E001771.pdf. Accessed September 20, 2023

Ito, Y. (2009). Issues raised by the "new purchase system for solar power generation" and electricity business policy (in Japanese). *IEEJ*, 1–21.

Ito, Y., & Nakata, T. (2004). Input-output analysis for installing renewable energy systems. *Energy & Environment, 15*(2), 271–281.

Izuno, N., Akutsu, N., & Yamada, K. (2001). Life-cycle CO_2 analysis of various power generation systems in electric power utilities (in Japanese). In *Proceedings of the 17th Conference on Energy, Economy, and Environment* (Vol. 17, pp. 199–202).

Kamidelivand, M., Cahill, C., Llop, M., Rogan, F., & O'Gallachoir, B. (2018). A comparative analysis of substituting imported gas and coal for electricity with renewables—An input-output simulation. *Sustainable Energy Technologies and Assessments, 30*, 1–10. https://doi.org/10.1016/j.seta.2018.08.003

Lindner, S., Legault, J., & Guan, D. (2013). Disaggregating the electricity sector of China's input output table for improved environmental life-cycle assessment. *Economic Systems Research, 25*(3). https://doi.org/10.1080/09535314.2012.746646

Ministry of the Environment. (2011, March). Study of potential for the introduction of renewable energy (FY 2010). https://www.env.go.jp/earth/report/h23-03/full.pdf. Accessed September 20, 2023

Ministry of the Environment. (2019). Entrusted work concerning the development and disclosure of basic zoning information concerning renewable energies (FY 2019). https://www.renewable-energy-potential.env.go.jp/RenewableEnergy/dat/report/r01/r01_revision_history_1.pd. Accessed September 20, 2023

Ministry of the Environment. (2021, October 22). "The Plan for Global Warming Countermeasures" Approved by Cabinet. http://www.env.go.jp/earth/211022/mat01.pdf. Accessed September 20, 2023

Nakano, S., & Washizu, A. (2022). *Creation and application of the 2015 input-output table for analysis of next-generation energy systems: Analysis of the effects of introducing carbon tax* (Discussion Paper Series No. 2103). Research Institute for Environmental Economics and Management, Waseda University. https://www.waseda.jp/prj-rieem/dp/dp2103.pdf. Accessed October 12, 2023

Nakata, T., Kubo, K., & Lamont, A. (2005). Design for renewable energy systems with application to rural areas in Japan. *Energy Policy, 33*(2), 209–219. https://doi.org/10.1016/S0301-4215(03)00218-0

New Energy and Industrial Technology Development Organization. (2000). Investigation on preparation of data relating to development of new energy technology (wind power generation). Research report for fiscal year 1999.

New Energy and Industrial Technology Development Organization. (2000). Survey of data collection of technical renewable energy (wind generation). NEDO P-9908.

Nomura, N., Inaba, A., Tonooka, Y., & Akai, M. (2001). Life-cycle emission of oxidic gases from power-generation systems. *Applied Energy, 68*(2), 215–227. https://doi.org/10.1016/S0306-2619(00)00046-5

Power Generation Cost Verification Working Group, Ministry of Economy, Trade and Industry. (2020, September). Report on Power Generation Cost Verification to the Basic Policy Subcommittee, Document 1.

Renewable Energy Institute. (2022a). *Analysis of technology trends and costs of onshore wind power generation in Japan* (pp. 1–20). https://www.renewable-ei.org/pdfdownload/activities/REI_JapanOnshoreWindAnalysis2022.pdf. Accessed September 20, 2023

Renewable Energy Institute. (2022b, March). *Analysis of cost and technology trends for onshore wind power generation in Japan.* https://www.renewable-ei.org/pdfdownload/activities/REI_JapanOnshoreWindAnalysis2022. Accessed September 20, 2023

Renewable Energy Institute. (2022c, May). *Cost and technology trends for onshore wind power in Japan* (pp. 1–25). https://www.renewable-ei.org/pdfdownload/activities/REI_JapanOnshoreWindAnalysis2022_EN.pdf. Accessed September 20, 2023

Shao, M., Han, Z., Sun, J., Xiao, C., Zhang, S., & Zhao, Y. (2020). A review of multi-criteria decision making applications for renewable energy site selection. *Renewable Energy, 157*, 377–403. https://doi.org/10.1016/j.renene.2020.04.137

Siddiqui, O., & Dincer, I. (2017). Comparative assessment of the environmental impacts of nuclear, wind and hydro-electric power plants in Ontario: A life cycle assessment. *Journal of Cleaner Production, 164*, 848–860. https://doi.org/10.1016/j.jclepro.2017.06.237

Subcommittee on Grid Interconnection of Wind Power, New and Renewable Energy Subcommittee, Advisory Committee for Natural Resources and Energy. (2001). The Future Measure against Renewable Energy. The renewable energy meeting report (in Japanese). http://earthresources.sakura.ne.jp/er/Rene_SE_T2.html. Accessed September 20, 2023

Uchiyama, Y. (1995a). Life cycle analysis of power generation systems (in Japanese). CRIEPI Review Y94009. https://criepi.denken.or.jp/hokokusho/pb/reportDlConf?reportNoUkCode=Y94009&tenpuTypeCode=30&seqNo=1. Accessed September 25, 2023

Uchiyama, Y. (1995b). Life cycle analysis of electricity generation and supply systems. Net energy analysis and greenhouse gas emissions. In *Electricity, Health and the Environment: Comparative Assessment in Support of Decision Making. Proceedings of an International Symposium*, Vienna, October 16–19, 1995. ÔÎIS (Sil A, 16) (p. 279). https://pure.iiasa.ac.at/4411/1/28006115.pdf#page=293. Accessed September 25, 2023

Uchiyama, Y. (2001). *Greenhouse effect analysis of power generation plants* (pp. 1–200). CRIEPI.

Uchiyama, Y., & Yamamoto, H. (1992). *Analysis of greenhouse effect of power generation plants* (Report No. Y91005). Central Research Institute of Electric Power Industry (in Japanese). https://criepi.denken.or.jp/hokokusho/pb/reportDlConf?reportNoUkCode=Y91005&tenpuTypeCode=30&seqNo=1. Accessed September 25, 2023

UN Environment Programme. (2022, January 5). STORY CLIMATE ACTION How do greenhouse gases actually warm the planet? https://www.unep.org/news-and-stories/story/how-do-greenhouse-gases-actually-warm-planet. Accessed September 20, 2023

Wang, L., Wang, Y., Du, H., Zuo, J., Li, R. Y. M., Zhou, Z., Bi, F., & Garvlehn, M. P. (2019). A comparative life-cycle assessment of hydro-, nuclear and wind power: A China study. *Applied Energy, 249*, 37–45. https://doi.org/10.1016/j.apenergy.2019.04.099

Wang, M., Yao, M., Wang, S., Qian, H., Zhang, P., Wang, Y., Sun, Y., & Wei, W. (2021). Study of the emissions and spatial distributions of various power-generation technologies in China. *Journal of Environmental Management, 278*, 111401. https://doi.org/10.1016/j.jenvman.2020.111401

Yoshioka, K., Uchiyama, Y., Suga, M., & Hondo, H. (1994). An application of input–output approach in environmental analysis: estimating CO_2 emissions from fossil-fired and nuclear power generation. *Sangyo Renkan (Input-Output Analysis), 5*(1), 31–56 (in Japanese). https://doi.org/10.11107/papaios.5.31

Ziegelmann, A., Mohr, M., & Unger, H. (2000). Net employment effects of an extension of renewable-energy systems in the Federal Republic of Germany. *Applied Energy, 65*, 329–338. https://doi.org/10.1016/S0306-2619(99)00072-0

Chapter 5
Economic Ripple Effects of Choice Factors and Disaster-Related Investments at Nagoya Port

5.1 Introduction

In the greatest natural disaster of recent times, the Great East Japan Earthquake[1] of March 2011, vessels in many affected ports were washed ashore by tsunami, causing extensive damage to the whole port area. At the same time, congestion in supply chains also reduced the production capacity of companies.

This situation led to an 8.9% fall in year-on-year exports in April 2011, followed by a further 5.9% fall in May. In year-on-year terms, the year from April 2011 to March 2012 saw a decrease of 1.2%.[2] For comparison, the second worst recent disaster, the January 17 1995 Great Hanshin Earthquake, led to no drop in Japan's overall exports of the year January–December 1995, with exports actually increasing by 3.0% over1994.[3]

However, the value of exports from the Port of Kobe that year fell by 36.8% year-on-year, while the value of imports also fell by 40.3%. Major disasters such as earthquakes and tsunamis are expected to cause extensive damage in the central Pacific coast region of Tokai as well, where recurrent earthquakes in the Tokai (East), Tonankai (Southeast) and Nankai (Southern) trough systems are considered likely to strike soon. Therefore Nagoya, as the principal port in this part of Japan, needs to take precautionary measures to minimize damage to the port and to protect the living space of the 2,325,000 Nagoya residents in the immediate hinterland.

With this background in mind, the aim of this study is to understand changes likely to occur in choices of ports by companies using the port of Nagoya as a combined result of natural disasters and of the spillover effects of the port's disaster prevention projects on the local economy. And the way to do that is through a quantitative

---

[1] The Japanese name style Great East Japan Earthquake was assigned by a Cabinet decree.

[2] These figures were calculated from export amounts published in the Ministry of Finance Trade Statistics, adjusted to real values using the Bank of Japan's Export Price Index.

[3] These figures for exports and imports following the Great Hanshin-Awaji Earthquake are as estimated by Tanaka (2011).

S. Asahi, *Econometric Analysis of Regional Economy*,
https://doi.org/10.1007/978-981-99-8707-8_5

examination of the plain and latent factors that recommend Nagoya as a choice for shipping services. In addition, the study summarizes the results of a survey on choices of which port to depend on in the special conditions following natural disasters. This will make business users more clearly aware of the advantages and problems of depending on Nagoya and will also provide information to help the port's planners strengthen the advantages and respond to the problems. Finally, it will help to clarify the motivations of business people who opt for the use of this port during times of disaster.

More specifically, the study analyzes the regional economic ripple effects of projects that are intended to limit damage to the port from natural disasters. This is in response to the 2014 Basic Plan for National Resilience and the accompanying National Resilience Action Plan, also approved in 2014.[4] In plainer language, if natural disaster countermeasures are understood as measures for ensuring port security and creating a port and harborage resilient to disaster, the further aim here is to analyze the ripple effects that investments like these will also bring to the Nagoya area's regional economy.

This chapter is structured as follows. Section 5.2 first summarizes the impact of the Great East Japan Earthquake on ways in which ports were used. In particular, the uses that the port of Nagoya was put to after the Great East Japan Earthquake are examined. Section 5.3 provides a quantitative analysis of the concrete factors leading to these uses of the port and the latent factors that led port users to select Nagoya in the first place. This section then ends with a general summary of its findings on factors for port selection under special circumstances, such as natural disasters. Section 5.4 focuses on the safety investments being made by the Port of Nagoya to ensure the port's security and provide disaster prevention measures, and to build up an adequate response capability against major disasters including earthquakes. At the same time, it analyzes the ripple effects of these investments on the local economy of Aichi Prefecture within which the port is situated. As a framework for this, use is made of an interregional input–output table originally prepared by the author in 2005 for the analysis of ripple effects between construction sectors in Aichi Prefecture and the rest of the country. With the aid of this table, somewhat modified, the economic ripple effects of this recent port construction activity on the local area are identified and shown in detail.

[4] The Basic Act for National Resilience Contributing to Preventing and Mitigating Disasters for Developing Resilience in the Lives of the Citizenry was enacted in 2013 and, under this legislation, a Basic Plan for National Resilience was issued the following year as a blueprint for building up Japan as a more resilient country. The National Resilience Action Plan 2014 was also issued that year and has since been reviewed annually.

5.2 The Impact of the Great East Japan Earthquake on Port Logistics

5.2.1 The Impact of the Great East Japan Earthquake on Japanese Port Economies

Figure 5.1 shows that the total seaborne freight traffic in Japan in March 2011, the month of the Great East Japan Earthquake, was 22.2 million tons. This level dropped somewhat in the following three months, but was back to above the March level in July.

The more detailed year-on-year figures for seaborne freight movements in Fig. 5.2 show that exports fell fastest and farthest after the earthquake, followed by imports. Imports actually rose slightly in April 2011, but then also fell to a minimum in May, as did the total for imports and exports combined. Incoming domestic freight movements similarly fell slightly more than outgoing ones. Not all of these changes in Fig. 5.2 can be attributed to the earthquake and tsunami disaster, as there may have been influences from exchange rates or other factors. However, the sharp decline starting after the March 11 disaster and continuing up to September that year, appears to match the disruption in economic activity felt and widely reported by people at the time. The data from which Fig. 5.2 was created can be seen in numerical form in Table 5.1.

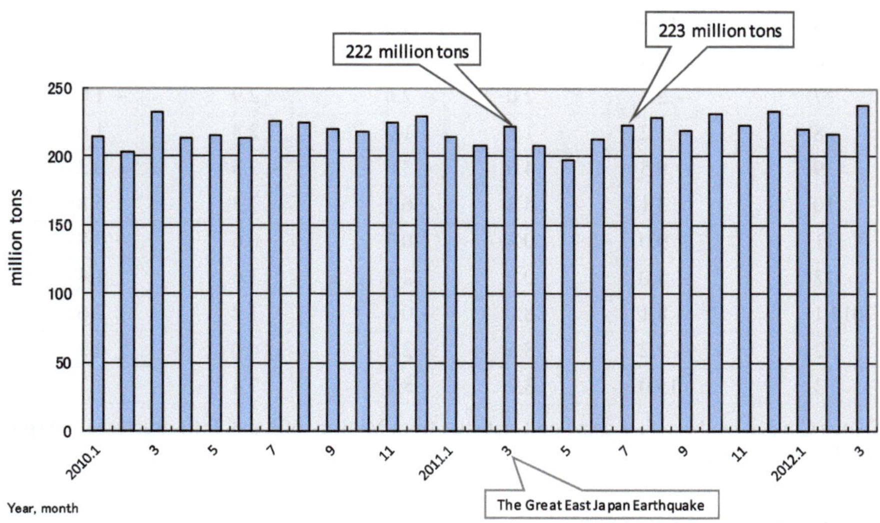

Fig. 5.1 Total amount of seaborne freight handled in Japan. *Source* Created by the author using port statistics from Ministry of Land, Infrastructure, Transport and Tourism

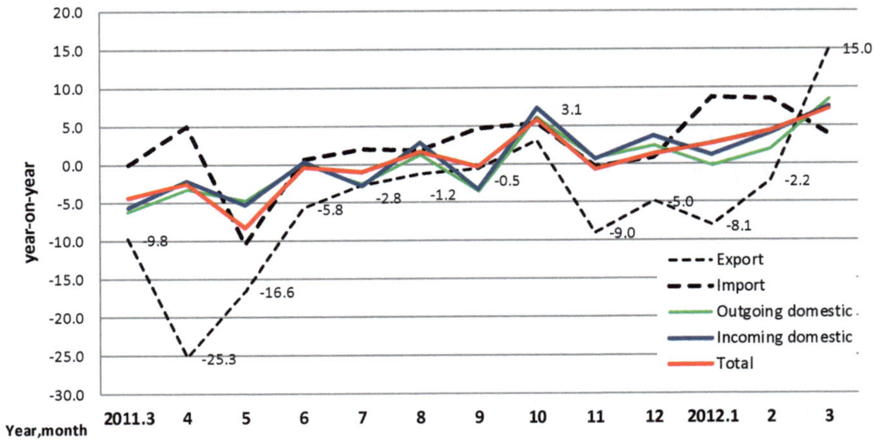

Fig. 5.2 Year-on-year trends in seaborne freight in Japan. *Source* Created by the author using port statistics from Ministry of Land, Infrastructure, Transport and Tourism

Table 5.1 Changes in year-on-year trends in seaborne freight traffic in Japan

Year month	International %		Domestic %		Total %
	Export	Import	Outgoing	Incoming	
2011 3	– 9.8	0.0	– 6.2	– 5.7	– 4.3
4	– 25.3	5.0	– 3.2	– 2.1	– 2.6
5	– 16.6	– 10.5	– 4.8	– 5.4	– 8.3
6	– 5.8	0.7	0.1	0.4	– 0.3
7	– 2.8	2.0	– 2.6	– 2.9	– 1.0
8	– 1.2	1.8	1.3	2.8	1.6
9	– 0.5	4.6	– 3.6	– 3.3	– 0.3
10	3.1	5.3	6.1	7.3	5.8
11	– 9.0	– 0.4	0.7	0.6	– 0.8
12	– 5.0	0.8	2.5	3.6	1.4
2012 1	– 8.1	8.6	– 0.3	1.2	2.6
2	– 2.2	8.5	2.0	4.0	4.3
3	15.0	3.9	8.4	7.4	7.1

Source Created by the author using port statistics from Ministry of Land, Infrastructure, Transport and Tourism

5.2.2 Freight Logistics at the Port of Nagoya

Nagoya was designated a super-hub port for Ise Bay in July 2004 through the enactment of a Partial Amendment of the Harbors Law Relating to Super-Hub Ports. This gave it a rank of outstanding preeminence among 'Designated Ports of Special

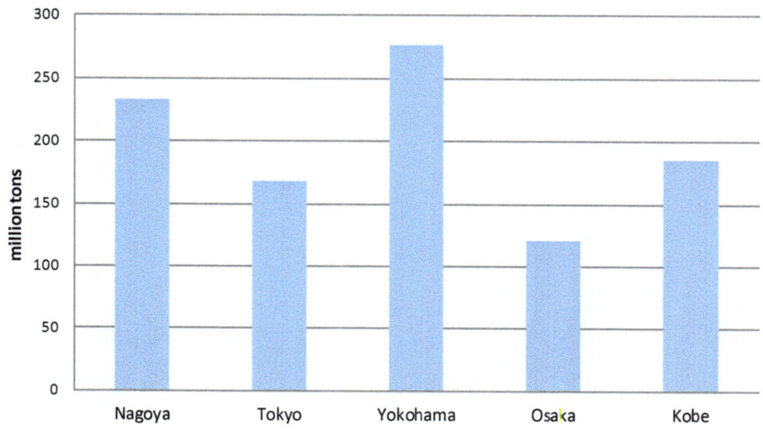

Fig. 5.3 Gross tonnage of vessels entering major ports in 2011. *Source* Created by the author using port statistics from Ministry of Land, Infrastructure, Transport and Tourism

Importance'.[5] This section evaluates the national significance of the Port of Nagoya compared with other major ports in Japan.

Figure 5.3 shows the gross tonnage of vessels entering major Japanese ports in 2011. Nagoya ranks second after Yokohama, with 232 million tons. The value of trade through Nagoya that year was 13,447.9 billion yen. Nagoya was in first place for the value of merchandise handled in both 2010 and 2011 (for value details, see below).

Figure 5.4 shows the volumes of freight handled by the same five ports from 2000 to 2020 and indicates Nagoya's unrivaled first position during this whole period. Looking more closely, Nagoya's volume and share showed a steadily increasing trend from 2001 to 2008, followed by a fall (of 53 million tons) in 2009. After that, the level partly recovered in 2010, and then held steady in the earthquake year 2011, neither rising nor falling. Since then, up to the disruption from the coronavirus pandemic, trends remained close to level.

Figure 5.5, for the span January 2010 to April 2012, shows rising and falling trends in monthly freight traffic through the port of Nagoya, including the month of the earthquake disaster (March 2011). Freight traffic decreased 12% that month compared with the month before.

Figure 5.6 shows the year-on-year changes, further broken down into inbound and outbound categories. Exports fell 34% in April 2011 and 31% in May. These falls are considerably greater than the ones in the national data (Fig. 5.2), indicating that the effects of the earthquake were temporarily very serious in this locality. However, exports then fell only 1% in June 2011, turned up 3% in July, and returned to a rising trend from there on. The total volume of freight handled similarly started to increase after June.

[5] See pp. 1 and 2 of the National Resilience Action Plan (2015) of the Cabinet Secretariat.

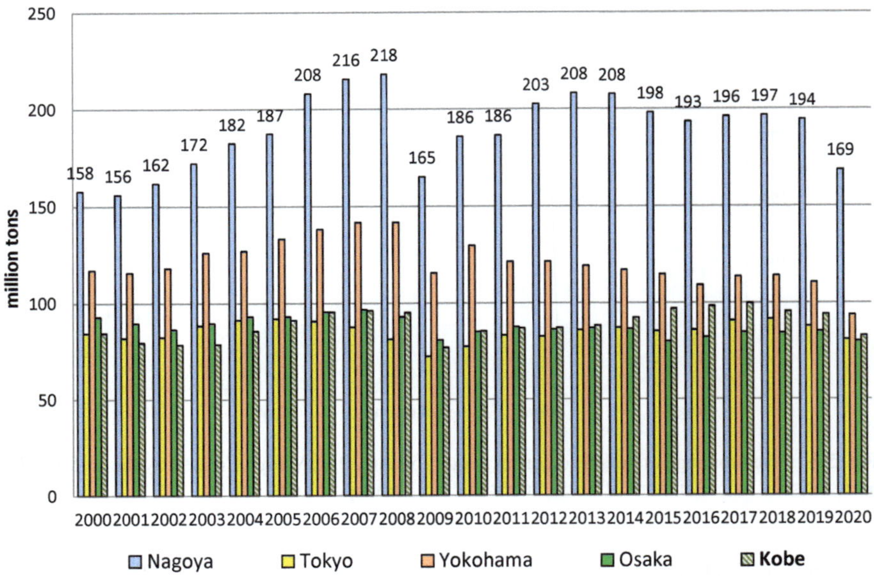

Fig. 5.4 Total amount of freight handled at the five major Japanese ports. *Source* Created by the author using Statistical Yearbook[6] of the Port of Nagoya

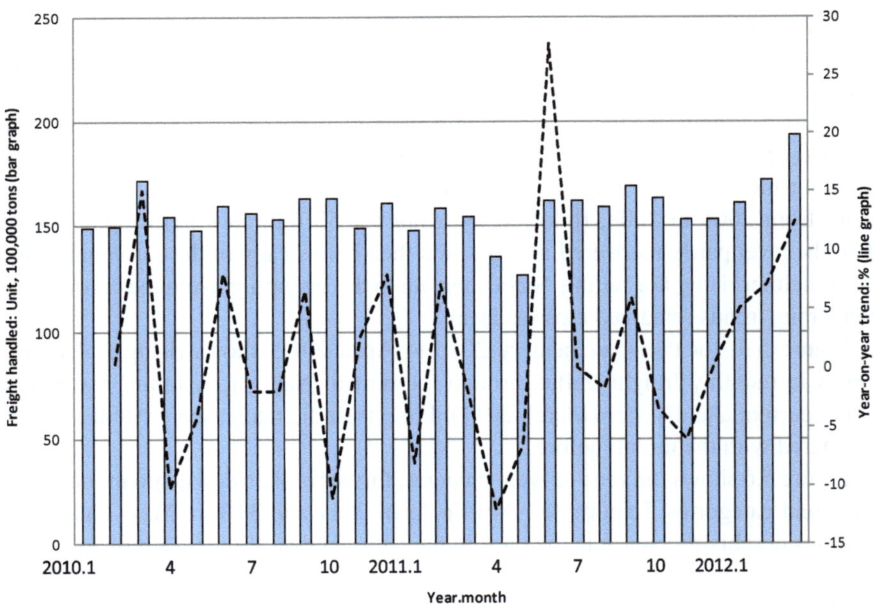

Fig. 5.5 Freight handled at the port of Nagoya. *Source* Created by the author using port statistics from Ministry of Land, Infrastructure, Transport and Tourism

[6] This Yearbook can be found online on the Nagoya Port Authority website. https://www.port-of-nagoya.jp/shokai/toukei/toukeinagoyako/index.html

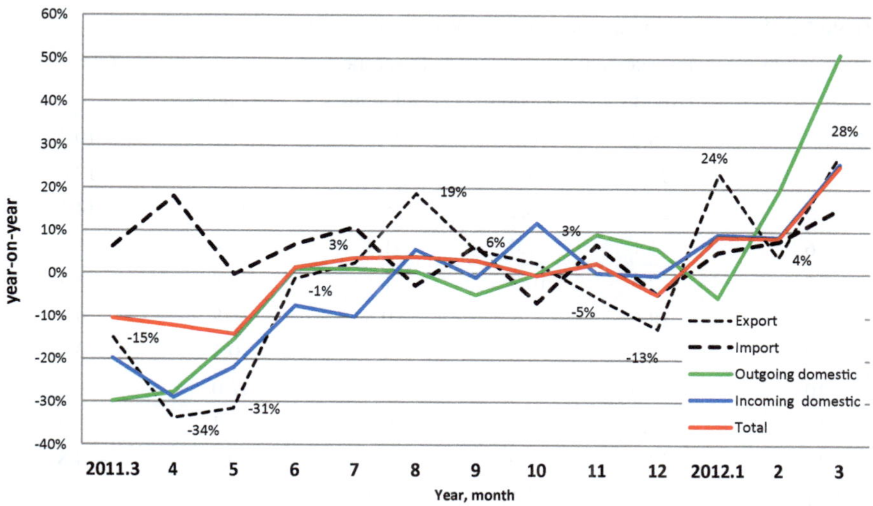

Fig. 5.6 Year-on-year trends in freight handled at the port of Nagoya. *Source* Created by the author using port statistics from Ministry of Land, Infrastructure, Transport and Tourism

Table 5.2 shows the same year-on-year data for freight traffic through Nagoya in numerical form. It can be seen that the port was greatly affected by the earthquake up until May 2011, not only in exports but also in its outgoing and incoming domestic freight operations.

5.3 Analysis of Factors Favoring the Choice of the Port of Nagoya

This section seeks to identify and quantify the concrete factors that cause companies to use the port of Nagoya and the latent factors that lead them to opt for it in preference to other solutions. This knowledge can help us to see the advantages and problems of this port's services from a user's viewpoint. In addition, it will cast light on areas in which the port should strive to exploit its strengths further and where possible also address and overcome weaknesses. And it will close with the results of a survey of the intentions of port users regarding alternative courses of action for the very exceptional contingency of the port of Nagoya being struck by a natural disaster.

Table 5.2 Year-on-year trends in freight handled at the port of Nagoya

Year month	International %		Domestic %		Total %
	Export	Import	Outgoing	Incoming	
2011 3	– 15.0	6.5	– 29.6	– 19.7	– 10.3
4	– 33.8	18.0	– 27.6	– 28.7	– 12.0
5	– 31.4	– 0.2	– 15.1	– 21.8	– 14.1
6	– 1.1	7.0	1.4	– 7.4	1.6
7	2.6	10.9	1.3	– 9.8	3.7
8	18.6	– 2.8	0.6	5.8	4.0
9	5.6	6.6	– 4.8	– 0.7	3.4
10	2.6	– 6.8	0.1	12.0	– 0.2
11	– 5.3	6.9	9.4	0.3	2.7
12	– 12.9	– 4.6	5.9	– 0.1	– 4.8
2012 1	23.6	5.1	– 5.3	9.4	8.8
2	3.9	7.7	19.5	8.9	8.7
3	27.8	15.3	51.2	26.0	25.3

Source Created by the author using port statistics from Ministry of Land, Infrastructure, Transport and Tourism

5.3.1 Previous Papers Regarding Port Choices

Previous papers on ports and port choices, including at times of disaster, include Akita and Kotani (2007), Okamoto (1999), Ishikawa and Katada (2004) and Chang (2000).

Akita and Kotani (2007) reported a survey of freight shipping companies etc. in western Japan in 2001 which aimed to assess the state of international freight traffic at Japanese container terminals at that time and to analyze the structure of attitudes regarding choices of ports. From this, they listed the concerns that were found to be most important and identified the latent factors behind the choices. The survey was sent to 2118 companies etc. sampled at random from a list of trading companies supplied by local governments. The form was to be completed by a person knowledgeable of the overall import/export operations of the company. Of the 2118 forms distributed, 234 were returned, a return rate of 11%. 70% of the responses were from companies in Hyogo and Osaka Prefectures. As Hyogo is the prefecture for Kobe and Osaka the one for Osaka, this study by Akita and Kotani can essentially be seen as examining the complementary relationship of Kobe and Osaka as neighboring major ports. The results show no great difference in concerns of importance for port selection between imports and exports. However, the latent factors, and the structures of the attitudes behind the choices, do differ for this import/export distinction. Viewing Kobe and Osaka as complementary partners, Kobe can offer "quality export services" and an "established reputation," while for imports, the larger and better-connected port of Osaka offers "speed" and "inland access." Through productive collaboration, these differential strengths contribute complementary benefits to this "Hanshin Port" relationship (Hanshin is an inclusive name for the greater Osaka-Kobe area). "Total cost," finally, is a differential factor driving competition for imports and exports alike. The paper therefore concludes on the point that "Hanshin Port" as a whole needs to work hard on reducing costs.

Okamoto (1999) has devised a container freight demand analysis method ("shipping port selection behavior model") as part of a procedure for evaluating the economic effects of port development. This paper also considers measures for increasing the freight aggregation potential at core ports through demand analysis and, finally, examines their effectiveness. The analysis covers incoming and outgoing freight traffic between Niigata, a designated port in northeast Japan, and terminals on the Tohoku and Hokuriku coasts considered to lie within its range of operations. The MNL ("Multinomial Logit Model") demand model in this study makes use of a disaggregate logit model and uses a time cost variable for freight transport. Its time transferability capacity is considered very high. However, when adding new data in response to increases in port or route options, or relating to relevant services at ports in neighboring countries, it becomes necessary to consider the timing constraints set for the updating of the model's parameters. As it is not possible to maintain an even export–import balance relying on core and regional ports alone, this paper also notes the recent tendency to include a number of smaller provincial ports on newly opened routes, or on routes connecting with Busan and China, to correct for gaps in the balance through the insertion of shoter two-way freight calls to serve as filler connections.

Ishikawa and Katada (2004) have analyzed the economic impact of naturally occurring disasters on directly affected and other areas and have created an interregional input–output table for estimates of the economic impacts of torrential rain and flooding in the Tokai area. This input–output table, which takes in the cities and towns with the highest data constraints as well as all 16 wards of the city of Nagoya, makes it possible not only to analyze the direct impact of a disaster, but also, as illustrated in the study, to estimate economic spillover effects in three time phases of "normal," "disrupted" and "post-recovery." As a first step for this ex-post analysis, a questionnaire survey was conducted among businesses to obtain usable data for a structural analysis of torrential rain and flood damage. Based upon this, an economic spillover analysis was performed, using estimates of the likely changes in production corresponding to changing patterns of private consumption during the disruption period, local function recovery and adoption of business emergency measures, and subsequent reconstruction demands for public and similar facilities.

In a study of the port of Kobe which was severely damaged in the 1995 Great Hanshin Earthquake, Chang (2000) analyzed the situation that existed before the earthquake, including that of other competing ports in the surrounding area. The study then went on to discuss the issues raised by the severe damage sustained by freight traffic within Japan. It showed that transshipment operations are particularly vulnerable to the effects of temporary but long-term rerouting diversions to competing ports.

5.3.2 *Factors for Port Selection with Regard to the Port of Nagoya*

The present study refers closely to the work of Akita and Kotani (2004), but focuses on selection factors for the port of Nagoya. The data for the analysis come from a questionnaire survey of business operations conducted among companies etc. in the nearby area.

5.3.2.1 Outline Summary of the Survey of Business Operations

This was a survey conducted by the Port of Nagoya Authority in 2011 in the course of a study of economic effectiveness. The surveying task was undertaken by the Mitsubishi Research Institute, using a questionnaire about business activities addressed to firms in the vicinity. An overview of the procedures used, including the distributing and retrieval methods, is given below.

The period of the survey was November to December 2011 and the year covered was 2010. On the port services side, questionnaires were sent out to 442 companies in the areas of marine transport, docking operations, port and harbor transportation, warehousing and cargo unloading. The valid response rate here was 43.21%. On the users' side, they were sent to 1576 corporate port users selected from the Nagoya Port Users Guide, the Aichi Trade-Related Companies Directory for 2010, and the Aichi Industrial Promotion Organization. Here, the valid response rate was 22.32%. Distribution was by post.

5.3.2.2 Factors Seen as Significant for Selecting the Port of Nagoya

Regarding reasons for the choice of Nagoya as a port, one question asked corporate users to pick out reasons that they saw as more, or less, important when choosing a port for their imports or exports. Five evaluation grades were offered: (1) Not at all important, (2) Not very important, (3) No opinion either way, (4) Somewhat important, and (5) Important. Data were compiled from the responses to this question item.

The results are shown in Figs. 5.7 and 5.9. These can be compared with Akita and Kotani's results for "Hanshin Port" (the ports of Kobe and Osaka taken together and evaluated by users in Hyogo and Osaka Prefectures), as shown in Figs. 5.8 and 5.10.

Groups of reasons covered in the survey and their relevance include: *Low import and export logistics costs*, as seen in: "Inexpensive inland transportation to or from port" and "Inexpensive total costs at port," *Smooth operations*, as in: "Reliable shipping companies," "Demand from related companies or local communities," and "Recommended by logistics companies," and *Promptness of service*, as in: "Road access to or from further inland," "Rapid cargo handling," "Reliable lead times", "Function as feeder port," and "Flexible handling of mixed cargoes." Reasons relating to

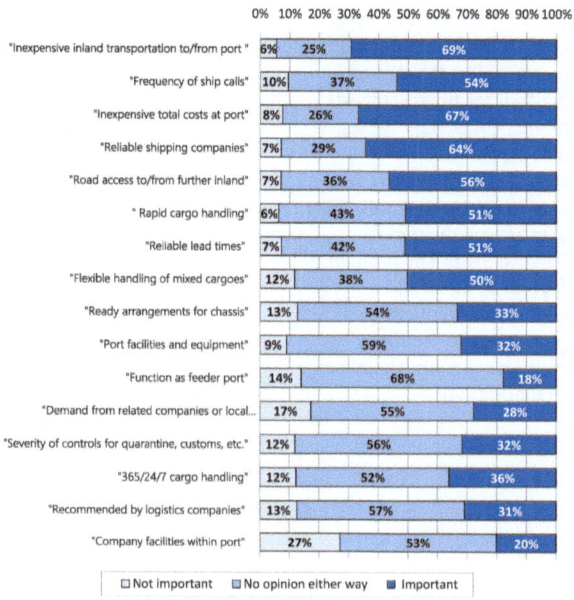

Fig. 5.7 Reasons prompting companies in the Nagoya area to select the port of Nagoya for freight exports. *Source* Created by the author using questions and data from a survey on the activities of companies in the area around the port of Nagoya. *Note* The original 5-point scale for the responses is reduced to 3 points here to facilitate comparison with Akita and Kotani (2004)

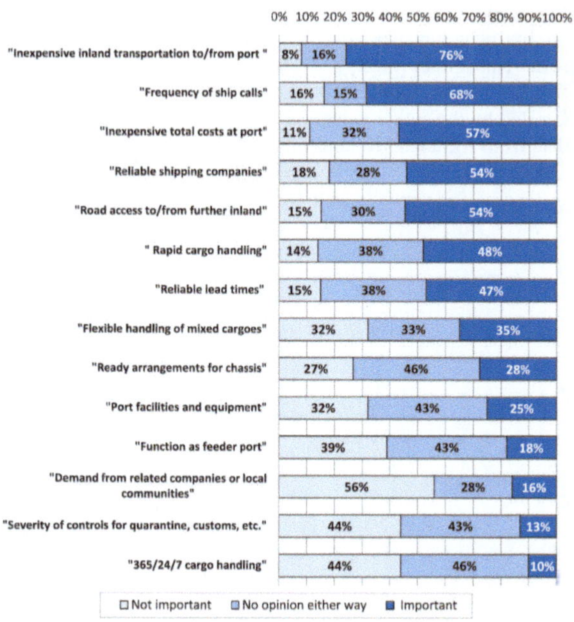

Fig. 5.8 Reasons prompting companies to select Hanshin Port for freight exports. *Source* Created by the author using data from Akita and Kotani (2004)

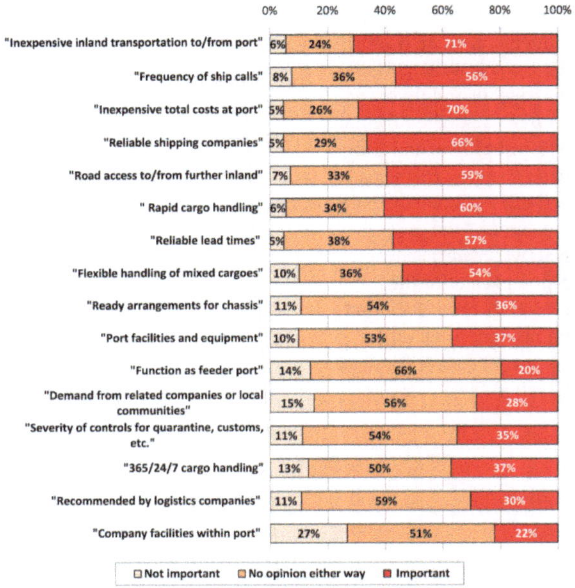

Fig. 5.9 Reasons prompting companies in the Nagoya area to select the port of Nagoya for freight imports. *Source* Created by the author using questions and data from a survey on the activities of companies in the area around the port of Nagoya. *Note* The original 5-point scale for the responses is reduced to 3 points here to facilitate comparison with Akita and Kotani (2004)

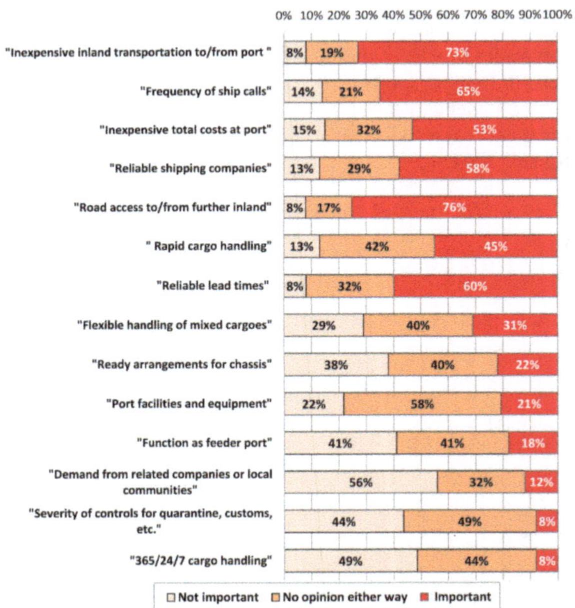

Fig. 5.10 Reasons prompting companies to select Hanshin Port for freight imports. *Source* Created by the author using data from Akita and Kotani (2004)

Enhanced port service include: "Frequent ship calls," "Severity of controls for quarantine, customs, etc.," "365/24/7 cargo handling," "Port facilities and equipment," "Ready arrangements for chassis," and "Company facilities within port."

For freight exports, the reasons most often seen as "important" for Nagoya (Fig. 5.7) are: "Inexpensive inland transportation to port," "Inexpensive total costs at port," "Reliable shipping companies," and "Road access from further inland."

Reasons of less regard are: "Function as feeder port," "Demand from related companies or local communities," "365/24/7 cargo handling," and "Port facilities and equipment." Looking at the same part of the "Hanshin Port" results (Fig. 5.9), the most important reasons are: "Inexpensive inland transportation to port" and "Frequent ship calls." The proportion of companies selecting "365/24/7 cargo handling" varied widely, between 36% in the Nagoya survey and 10% for "Hanshin Port." "Severity of controls for quarantine, customs, etc." had a similar low selection figure of only 13% for Hanshin Port.

Among the reasons of importance for freight imports, "Inexpensive inland transportation from port" and "Inexpensive total costs at port" were again most important for Nagoya (Fig. 5.8). Next came "Road access inland," a factor relating to promptness, and "Rapid cargo handling" and "Reliable lead times," two factors of enhanced port service. "Function as feeder port" was regarded as least important. For import-oriented Hanshin Port, Fig. 5.10 shows that the reasons of concern for freight imports have to do with *low logistics costs* and *promptness* through *smooth port operations*. As at Nagoya, the regard given to *enhanced port service* is lower.

5.3.3 Analysis of Selection Factors for the Port of Nagoya

This section presents a factor analysis that was performed to extract potential factors for the selection of Nagoya as a port. On the exports side (Table 5.3, left), three factors were extracted, accounting for a cumulative proportion of variance of 60%. Factor 1 can be called a factor of *low logistics costs*, including "Inexpensive total costs at port" and "Inexpensive inland transportation to/from port," as well as items related to *promptness* of service. Factor 2 has to do with *smoothness of operations*: and *enhanced port service*: "Demand from related companies or local communities," "Severity of controls for quarantine and customs, etc." Factor 3 is for selection reasons strongly relating to *port functions for easy handling of exports*, as seen from the high interest for the variable "Flexible handling of mixed cargoes" and the inclusion also of choices like "Rapid cargo handling" and "Port facilities and equipment."

For imports at Nagoya (Table 5.3, right), again three factors were extracted, explaining a cumulative proportion of variance of 59.5%. Factor 1 shows a high concern with choices for *low logistics costs* for imports, especially: "Inexpensive inland transportation to/from port" and "Inexpensive total costs at port." Factor 2 relates to *enhanced port service* and *promptness* for imports, as in "Port facilities and equipment" and "Ready arrangements for chassis." Factor 3 relates strongly to "Demand from related companies or local communities."

Table 5.3 Results of selection factor analysis for exports and imports at the Port of Nagoya

Reason for port selection	Exports (n = 201)				Imports (n = 201)			
	Factor 1	Factor 2	Factor 3	Communality	Factor 1	Factor 2	Factor 3	Communality
"Inexpensive inland transportation to/from port"	**0.82**	– 0.01	– 0.06	0.67	**0.85**	– 0.16	0.00	0.74
"Frequency of ship calls"	**0.52**	0.15	0.16	0.32	**0.46**	0.32	0.03	0.31
"Inexpensive total costs at port"	**0.87**	0.06	– 0.06	0.77	**0.86**	– 0.11	0.06	0.75
"Reliable shipping companies"	**0.55**	– 0.05	0.37	0.45	**0.58**	0.33	– 0.03	0.45
"Road access to/from further inland"	**0.44**	0.12	0.34	0.32	**0.53**	0.27	0.08	0.36
" Rapid cargo handling"	**0.40**	– 0.03	**0.51**	0.43	**0.59**	**0.42**	– 0.10	0.53
"Reliable lead times"	**0.50**	– 0.05	**0.49**	0.49	**0.68**	0.24	0.01	0.51
"Flexible handling of mixed cargoes"	0.22	– 0.06	**0.65**	0.48	0.30	**0.50**	– 0.01	0.33
"Ready arrangements for chassis"	0.07	0.37	**0.43**	0.33	0.08	**0.83**	– 0.04	0.69
"Port facilities and equipment"	0.02	**0.40**	**0.51**	0.42	0.02	**0.72**	0.17	0.55
"Function as feeder port"	– 0.02	**0.41**	**0.46**	0.38	– 0.08	**0.67**	0.24	0.51
"Demand from related companies or local communities"	– 0.05	**0.81**	– 0.03	0.66	0.06	**0.05**	**0.74**	0.56
"Severity of controls for quarantine, customs, etc."	0.05	**0.61**	0.25	0.44	0.09	**0.41**	0.37	0.31
"365/24/7 cargo handling"	0.15	**0.57**	0.16	0.38	0.14	**0.45**	0.22	0.27
"Recommended by logistics companies"	0.18	**0.63**	– 0.12	0.44	0.08	0.04	**0.66**	0.45
"Company facilities within port"	– 0.06	**0.55**	– 0.01	0.31	– 0.09	0.03	**0.47**	0.23
Variance explained	2.73	2.57	1.98	CPV 59.9	7.89	1.20	0.44	CPV 59.5
Proportion of variance explained (%)	49.47	8.13	2.34		49.30	7.52	2.74	

Source Results analyzed and presented by the author
Note The factors counted are defined as those with an eigenvalue of 0.81 or more, and values with factor loadings of 0.4 or more are shown in bold. The estimation uses the Principal axis method and the rotation method is Promax. CPV indicates cumulative proportion of variance explained

Table 5.4 Results of selection factor analysis for exports and imports at Hanshin Port

Reason for port selection	Exports (n = 79)			Imports (n = 79)			
	Factor 1	Factor 2	Factor 3	Factor 1	Factor 2	Factor 3	Factor 4
"365/24/7 cargo handling"	**0.61**	0.02	0.08	0.41	0.14	− 0.19	0.09
"Severity of controls for quarantine, customs, etc."	**0.55**	0.07	0.07	**0.49**	0.31	0.12	0.25
"Frequency of ship calls"	**0.54**	0.28	− 0.07	0.35	0.21	− 0.25	− 0.28
"Port facilities and equipment"	0.30	**0.67**	− 0.03	**0.44**	**0.40**	− 0.04	0.01
"Reliable shipping companies"	0.06	**0.63**	0.26	0.30	**0.56**	0.19	0.12
"Reliable lead time"	0.14	**0.61**	0.30	− 0.01	**0.76**	0.08	− 0.04
"Inexpensive inland transportation to/from port "	0.02	0.04	**0.77**	− 0.06	0.00	**0.57**	0.33
"Inexpensive total costs at port"	0.01	0.27	**0.59**	0.02	0.11	**0.77**	− 0.12
"Function as feeder port"	**0.47**	0.15	0.03	**0.74**	− 0.24	− 0.03	− 0.10
"Demand from related companies or local communities"	**0.47**	0.22	0.14	**0.43**	− 0.06	0.15	**0.52**
"Flexible handling of mixed cargoes"	0.27	**0.49**	0.18	0.32	0.32	− 0.16	0.05
"Road access to/from further inland"	0.33	0.22	**0.45**	− 0.02	0.32	− 0.05	**0.51**
"Rapid cargo handling"	0.39	0.27	0.34	0.06	**0.60**	− 0.04	0.13
"Ready arrangements for chassis"				**0.59**	0.18	0.10	0.04
Variance explained	14.27	13.93	11.47	14.37	13.46	8.03	6.04
Proportion of variance explained (%)	14.27	28.20	39.66	14.37	27.83	35.87	41.90

Source Summary by the author of analysis results obtained by Akita and Kotani (2004)
Note The factors counted are defined as those with an eigenvalue of at least 1.0, and values with factor loadings of 0.4 or more are shown in bold. The estimation uses the Principal axis method and the rotation method is Varimax. All factors with an eigenvalue above 1.0 are extracted

For exports through Hanshin Port (Table 5.4, left), Akita and Kotani (2004) also extracted three factors accounting for a cumulative proportion of variance of 39.7%. Factor 1 relates to the kind of *enhanced port service* required for exports, while Factor 2 relates to *port functions* for easy handling of exports, with high factor loadings going to "Port facilities and equipment," "Reliable shipping companies," and "Reliable lead times." Factor 3 is for the selections seeking to reduce logistics costs for exports, with high loadings for "Inexpensive inland transportation to/from port" and "Inexpensive total costs at port." In this case, for simplicity, the extraction process is halted here to exclude further factors with an eigenvalue of below 1.0. Comparing the results for exports through these two ports, it is clear that the contents for Factors 1 and 3 are reversed. Another difference is that the cumulative proportion of variance explained by the top three factors is lower in the case of Hanshin Port than in that of Nagoya. In fact, as we will next see, this is also true for imports.

For imports, four factors were extracted for Hanshin Port, with a cumulative factor contribution of 41.9%. Factor 1 can be summed up again as enhanced port service, but for imports, with high factor loadings for "Function as feeder port," "Ready arrangements for chassis," and "Severity of controls for quarantine and customs, etc." Factor 2 centers on how long it takes for freight to clear the unloading and port procedures, and high factor loadings appear for *promptness*, specifically: "Rapid cargo handling," "Reliable lead times," and "Reliable shipping companies." Factor 3 has to do with *low logistics costs*: "Inexpensive inland transportation to/from port" and "Inexpensive total costs at port." Factor 4, finally, relates to *promptness* and *smoothness in the logistics operations.*

5.3.4 Selection of Ports Other Than Nagoya During an Earthquake Situation

This next section reports the summarized results of the port users' thoughts and intentions in the event of a major earthquake - an additional question added to the 2011 'the questionnaire survey on business activities in the area behind the Port of Nagoya'[7] conducted by the Nagoya Port Authority. This time, companies around the port were asked about their corporate actions with regard to the hypothetical choice of a port in such special circumstances.

The survey opened with a lead in: In the Great East Japan Earthquake, as in the Hanshin Earthquake before it, ports suffered severe disruption to their various functions. The purpose of this questionnaire is to ask port users whether they are considering the possible use of alternative ports in the event of a major earthquake on the Tokai, Tonankai or Nankai scale that might leave Nagoya unusable.

[7] This questionnaire survey was carried out in cooperation between Senior Researchers Hachiya, K., Tsuchiya, K. and Oishi, M. of the Policy Evaluation Group, Social Systems Research Division, Mitsubishi Research Institute and the author Asahi, S., of Mie University.

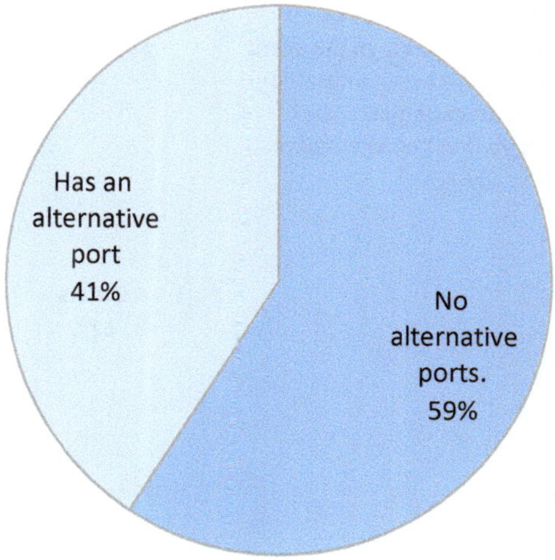

Fig. 5.11 Plans for an alternative port in the event of Nagoya being unusable after an earthquake, etc. (N = 330)

Respondents considering alternative ports were asked to name up to 3 choices in order of preference. They were also asked to evaluate their reasons for each choice by assigning points on a 1 to 5 scale for the importance they attached to a list of possible reasons. They had to enter separate answers for exports and imports in each case. The reason options offered were "cargo handling capacity," "port costs, etc.," "number of port calls," "reliability," "frequency of port calls," "safety," "convenience of access," "risk management," "handling times, etc.," "IT level," "freight charges," on account of the company's "existing business continuity plan (BCP)," and "other."

The results of this survey are as follows. First, in answer to whether alternatives to Nagoya were being considered (Fig. 5.11), 41% of companies said that they were, and 59% said they were not. Osaka was the port most frequently chosen as an alternative, followed by Kobe, Yokkaichi and Yokohama (Fig. 5.12, Table 5.5).

The next results concern the reasons for these choices of alternative ports. On the exports side (Table 5.6), Osaka was chosen for "cargo handling capacity," "number of port calls," "frequency of port calls," "handling times," or on account of "existing BCP." The second-choice port, Kobe, was chosen for "number of port calls" and "frequency of port calls," while Yokkaichi was chosen for "convenience of access" and "freight charges." For fourth-placed Yokohama, the reasons given are "cargo handling capacity," "number of port calls," "frequency of port calls," "reliability," "risk management," and "IT level." Some of the reasons mentioned came up only a few times in a small sample, however, and should therefore be treated with caution. This also applies to the reasons given for choosing alternative ports for imports, which will now follow.

On the imports side (Table 5.7), Osaka was chosen for "cargo handling capacity," "number of port calls," "frequency of port calls," "handling times," "port costs," "risk management," or on account of "existing BCP." Kobe, as with exports, was chosen for "number of port calls" and "frequency of port calls," and Yokkaichi for "number of port calls," "frequency of port calls," "port costs," "safety," "risk management,"

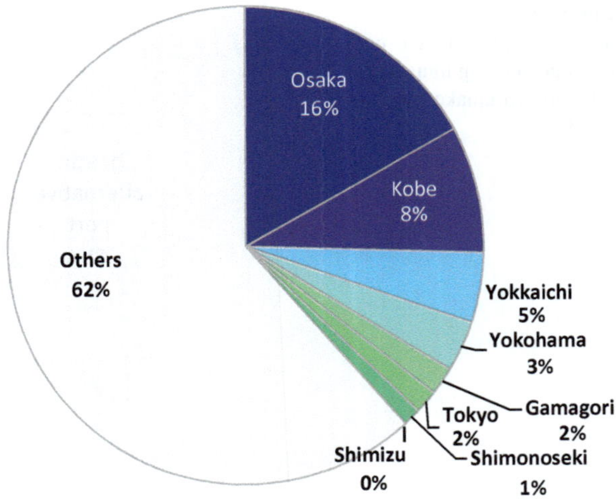

Fig. 5.12 Choices of alternative ports in the event of Nagoya being unusable after an earthquake, etc. (excluding "no alternative," N = 134)

"IT level," or on account of "existing BCP." Yokohama, finally, was chosen for its "number of port calls," "frequency of port calls," "handling times," "reliability," "safety," "risk management," and "IT level."

Table 5.8 shows the beneficiaries, activity concerns, and expected effects of examples of earthquake resilience projects for ports published by the Ministry of Land, Infrastructure, Transport and Tourism (1996). For example, port resilience projects in areas of transportation can be expected to result in reductions of cost for users of freight and mobility services. In the present study, this would correspond to the choices of "rapid cargo handling" and "inexpensive total costs at port" as the most important reasons for selecting an alternative port.

Table 5.9 then shows the frequencies of alternative port choices proportionately to the freight commodity concerned. This reveals, for example, a high proportion of metal and machinery exports being rerouted through Osaka. A factor analysis was accordingly performed of the reasons behind this choice of Osaka for metal and machinery exports, based on the 29 samples available. The results are presented in Table 5.10 although, due to the small sample size, the results should be treated with caution. The first factor extracted was for "Port costs, etc." and "Reliability" of shipping companies. The second was for reasons relating to "Convenience of access" and "Freight charges." The third had to do with the reliable discharge of port and shipping services required for exports: "Cargo handling capacity" and "Number of port calls." The cumulative proportion of variance accounted for by these factors is 78.75%.

Table 5.5 Choices of alternative ports in the event of Nagoya being unusable after an earthquake

Alternative port	Osaka	Kobe	Yokkaichi	Yokoha-ma	Gamagori	Tokyo	Shimo-noseki	Shimizu	Others	No alternative ports	Total
Choice 1	54	27	15	11	6	5	4	0	12	196	330
Choice 2	17	25	0	31	0	2	0	5	22	196	298
Choice 3	0	3	2	12	1	8	0	4	10	196	236

Source Results analyzed and presented by the author
Note Ports mentioned less than twice are included in "Others."

Table 5.6 Alternative ports for Nagoya (exports) and importance given to possible reasons

Choice 1 port	Sample Size	Cargo handling capacity	Number of port calls	Frequency of port calls	Convenience of access	Handling times	Freight charges	Port costs	Reliability	Safety	Risk management systems	IT level	Existing BCP
Osaka	71	3.9	4.0	4.0	4.0	3.9	4.0	3.9	3.8	3.9	3.6	3.6	3.5
Kobe	34	3.4	4.1	4.1	4.0	3.2	3.8	3.6	3.7	3.6	3.4	3.0	2.3
Yokkaichi	23	3.3	3.9	3.6	4.7	3.5	4.5	3.9	3.5	4.0	3.9	3.7	3.2
Yokohama	17	4.8	4.5	4.5	3.9	3.7	3.5	3.5	4.6	4.5	4.3	4.1	2.6
Tokyo	9	4.1	4.4	4.4	4.7	4.1	4.0	3.2	4.3	4.1	4.0	3.6	2.3
Toyohashi	4	3.0	3.0	2.0	3.5	3.0	2.0	4.0	**5.0**	**5.0**	4.0	4.0	4.0
Shimonoseki	2	**5.0**	**5.0**	**5.0**	**5.0**	**5.0**	**5.0**	**5.0**	**5.0**	**5.0**	**5.0**	**5.0**	**5.0**
Kinuura	2	2.0	2.0	2.0	4.0	3.0	**5.0**	**5.0**	**5.0**	**5.0**	3.0	3.0	3.0
Moji	1	4.0	4.0	4.0	4.0	4.0	4.0	4.0	**5.0**	4.0	4.0	3.0	3.0
Tsuruga	2	–	–	–	4.0	–	–	–	–	–	–	–	–
Yoshiura	1	–	–	–	**5.0**	–	–	–	–	–	–	–	–
Sample total/ average	166	3.7	3.9	3.7	4.3	3.7	4.0	4.0	4.4	4.3	3.9	3.7	3.2
Total sample size from Osaka to Toyohashi/ average	158	3.8	4.1	4.0	4.1	3.7	3.9	3.8	3.9	3.9	3.7	3.5	3.0

Source Results analyzed and presented by the author

Note In the table, the highest figure for each reason option is indicated in boldface, while figures higher than the average are underlined. These numbers include two decimal places and are compared to the average of sample total.

Table 5.7 Alternative ports for Nagoya (imports) and importance given to possible reasons

Choice 1 port	Sample Size	Cargo handling capacity	Number of port calls	Frequency of port calls	Convenience of access	Handling times	Freight charges	Port costs	Reliability	Safety	Risk management systems	IT level	Existing BCP
Osaka	56	4.2	4.2	4.0	4.2	3.8	4.2	3.9	3.8	3.9	3.7	3.4	3.2
Kobe	18	3.4	4.0	4.1	3.9	3.3	4.3	3.5	3.7	3.6	3.2	2.8	2.7
Yokkaichi	14	3.5	4.1	4.0	4.1	3.4	4.0	3.9	3.6	4.1	4.1	3.8	3.3
Yokohama	13	**4.7**	4.5	4.5	4.2	4.0	3.6	3.5	4.2	4.2	4.1	3.9	2.9
Tokyo	9	**4.7**	**4.7**	4.7	4.9	4.6	4.3	3.7	4.8	4.6	**4.4**	**4.0**	2.7
Mikawa	4	3.0	3.0	3.0	**5.0**	3.0	**5.0**	3.0	3.0	3.0	3.0	3.0	3.0
Shimizu	4	4.0	4.0	**5.0**	**5.0**	4.0	**5.0**	**5.0**	**5.0**	**5.0**	4.0	3.0	-
Kinuura	3	2.7	2.3	2.3	4.0	3.3	4.7	4.7	4.7	4.7	3.3	3.0	3.0
Gamagori	3	2.7	3.7	3.7	4.3	3.3	4.3	3.3	3.0	3.3	3.0	3.0	3.0
Tsuruga	3	4.0	3.0	3.0	4.8	3.0	**5.0**	3.0	3.0	3.0	3.0	3.0	3.0
Toyohashi	3	3.7	3.3	3.0	3.8	3.0	3.3	3.3	4.3	4.3	4.0	3.7	3.3
Kashima	2	3.0	4.0	3.0	4.0	3.0	3.0	3.0	3.0	3.0	3.0	–	–
Shimonoseki	1	3.0	3.0	4.0	4.0	**5.0**	**5.0**	**5.0**	**5.0**	**5.0**	4.0	**4.0**	**4.0**
Moji	1	4.0	4.0	4.0	4.0	4.0	4.0	4.0	**5.0**	4.0	4.0	3.0	3.0
Sample total/ average	134	3.6	3.7	3.7	4.3	3.6	4.3	3.8	4.0	4.0	3.6	3.4	3.1
Total sample size from Osaka to Toyohashi/ average	118	4.1	4.2	4.1	4.2	3.7	4.2	3.8	3.9	4.0	3.7	3.4	3.1

Source Results analyzed and presented by the author
Note In the table, the highest figure for each reason option is indicated in boldface, while figures higher than the average are underlined. These numbers include two decimal places and are compared to the average of sample total.

Table 5.8 Beneficiaries, concerns, and expected effects of earthquake resilience projects for ports

Beneficiaries and concerns		Effects
Port users	Freight/ mobility	Reduced transport costs
	Interaction	–
	Recreation	–
	Environment	–
	Safety	–
	Operations	–
The area served by Nagoya Port	Sense of security	Assuagement of anxiety about future damage
		Assuagement of fears for future livelihood
	Safety	Supporting the lives of local population
	Environment	Reduced emissions
	For the area served by Nagoya Port	Avoidance of reduction in local employment and income
		Increase in employment and income from construction work
		Support for port restoration and reconstruction
		Avoidance of reduced international competitiveness
Public sector	Taxes	Avoidance of shortfall in national and local tax revenues
	Cost reduction	Avoidance of damage to public facilities

Source Created by the author based on Ministry of Land, Infrastructure and Transport (December 1996). Earthquake Resilience Projects (in Japanese)
Note An empty space in the Effects column means that the Ministry did not supply an example of an earthquake resilience project targeting "Interaction," etc. But naturally, such projects exist and are important

5.4 Economic Ripple Effects of Port and Harbor Disaster Mitigation Projects on Local and Other Regional Economies

Investments in port development have a ripple effect on the regional economy, as indicated by Asahi (2003a, 2003b), and also lead to increased employment. This section analyses the regional economic ripple effects of disaster mitigation projects at ports such as Nagoya.

Japan has an urgent need to prepare for earthquakes as a way of ensuring port safety and developing ports to be capable of response to large-scale disasters. In what follows, I analyze the ripple effects that investments of this kind in the Port of Nagoya improvement budget for business year 2012 had on the home prefecture (Aichi) and beyond.

The analysis begins from an overview of the direct investments assigned for this project in the 2012 budget along with their uses. This is followed by an explanation of the methods used to create a two-region inter-industry input–output table between

Table 5.9 Alternative port choices proportionately to freight commodities

Exports			Imports		
Type of commodity	Port	Proportion of total (%)	Type of commodity	Port	Proportion of total (%)
Forestry products	Osaka	100	Agricultural and fishery products (n = 18)	Kobe	22
Mining products (n = 2)	Kobe	50		Shimizu	22
	Osaka	50		Osaka	17
Metals and machinery (n = 43)	Osaka	56		Yokkaichi	17
	Kobe	19		Yokohama	11
	Yokohama	16		Kashima	11
	Yokkaichi	9	Forestry products (n = 11)	Osaka	73
Chemicals (n = 16)	Osaka	38		Gamagori	9
	Kobe	31		Tsuruga	9
	Yokkaichi	13	Mining products (n = 1)	Kinuura	100
	Yokohama	6	Metals and machinery (n = 29)	Osaka	48
	Kinuura	6		Yokkaichi	14
Light industrial products (n = 8)	Osaka	38		Mikawa	14
	Kobe	25		Kobe	14
	Yokkaichi	13		Yokohama	10
	Yokohama	13	Chemicals (n = 10)	Osaka	30
	Tokyo	13		Tokyo	30
Miscellaneous industrial products (n = 8)	Tokyo	38		Yokkaichi	20
	Osaka	25		Kinuura	10
	Kobe	25		Yokohama	10
	Yokkaichi	13	Light industrial products (n = 6)	Osaka	67
				Yokohama	17
				Yokkaichi	17
			Miscellaneous industrial products (n = 31)	Osaka	48
				Yokkaichi	23
				Tokyo	10
				Kobe	10
				Tsuruga	6
				Shimonoseki	3

Source Results analyzed and presented by the author

Aichi Prefecture and the rest of Japan for the analysis, with reference to Yamada (1996a, 1996b) and Doi, Asari, and Nakano (1996). Finally, the calculated results

Table 5.10 Factor analysis accounting for the frequent choice of Osaka as an alternative port for metal and machinery exports

Reason options	Factor 1	Factor 2	Factor 3	Commonality
Cargo handling capacity	0.3545	– 0.0962	**0.5108**	0.40
Number of port calls	– 0.1557	0.3153	**0.8247**	0.80
Convenience of access	0.0095	**0.7279**	0.3864	0.68
Handling times	**0.4683**	0.3198	0.3635	0.45
Freight charges	– 0.1138	**0.8477**	0.0968	0.74
Port costs	**0.5292**	**0.7158**	– 0.2306	0.85
Reliability	**0.6423**	0.0809	0.2520	0.48
Risk management systems	**0.9442**	– 0.0907	0.2220	0.95
IT level	**1.0001**	– 0.1365	0.0735	1.02
Existing BCP	**0.8145**	0.0993	– 0.1900	0.71
Variance explained	3.63	2.01	1.44	7.08
Proportion of variance explained (%)	54.37	17.68	6.70	78.75

Source Results analyzed and presented by the author
Note The factors counted are defined as those with an eigenvalue of at least 1.0, and values with factor loadings of 0.4 or more are shown in bold. The estimation uses the Principal axis method and the rotation method is Varimax. All factors with an eigenvalue above 1.0 are extracted

are presented. For a previous study by the author of economic ripple effects from the Port of Nagoya, see Asahi (2003a, 2003b).[8]

5.4.1 Data and Analysis Methods

5.4.1.1 Data

The data used in this study relate to the contents of the 2012 Port of Nagoya port improvement project. For this reason, the presentation here follows the stated Measures of the project. Three Measures are highlighted:

The three key Measures of the port improvement project of the Port of Nagoya.

1. Development to ensure port safety and guard against damage to the local area in the event of a major disaster.
2. Development to raise the region's international and industrial competitiveness and create a port that can respond to changes in the port logistics business environment.

[8] Analysis of the economic ripple effects at Nagoya Port was conducted five times by the Nagoya Port Authority by 2,000 years. Please see Nagoya Port Authority (1991) and Arakawa (1991). Port Investment Evaluation Study Group (ed.) (2001) is indicated analysis of the social evaluation of Japanese ports.

3. Development leading to a more environmentally friendly and people-friendly port in which visions, fulfillments and lively activities can coexist.

Particular examples of development for enhanced safety for the port and disaster safeguards for the region at times of large-scale disaster include measures for strengthening the protective functions of breakwaters and seawalls against storm surges, further shore strengthening at Ote Pier (South), better dredging of mooring areas, repairs to port traffic systems, more seawall reinforcements, and security measures at port facilities generally.

As a port, Nagoya has functions that drive the Japanese economy. A situation in which they were to break down, or in which companies in the surrounding region were to cease operating due to earthquake or tsunami damage would deal a severe blow to the Japanese economy. One of the responsibilities of the port is to facilitate regional business through logistics. Another is to protect the lives and property of the numerous people living in the region or depending on its services. Hence, outside assistance was clearly needed to enable the port to move forward rapidly with this project for "strengthening its multiple protective functions."

Development to raise the region's international and industrial competitiveness and respond to changes in port logistics includes additions to the pier and portside transport facilities, channel improvements, and more fully equipped container and bulk freight facilities. The old Nagoya Garden Pier is now home to the Port Aquarium, the Nagoya Port Building, and the Portside Green Garden. This zone is also a port of call for cruise ships and hosts many events such as the Port Festival. With this in mind, the third key Measure for the 2012 port improvement project is to make the port more environmentally friendly and people-friendly. Redevelopment is thus needed to enhance this zone as a base and center for this lively meeting place of sea, land and visitors.

Measuring the production-inducing effect of a public works project with the aid of input–output analysis requires an examination of how much was actually invested in the project in each of the various sectors from which the investments came, and this has to be ascertained from the project content. The relevant investment (project cost) budget for Nagoya Port in business year 2012 was 13.721 trillion yen. If loans are excluded from this, the amount comes to 12.948 trillion yen, as detailed in Table 5.11.

Using input coefficients from a previous 2005 input–output table for an analysis of construction sectors, the costs were allocated among the various sectors in the table according to the content of each investment portion. The 2005 table includes general operation categories such as construction, architecture, civil engineering and public works, as well as more special ones such as erosion control, coastal works, sewerage, road transport works, port works, fisheries, aviation, environmental health, parks and disaster recovery. For the purposes of this study, the investment items in the 2012 Port of Nagoya improvements budget will be assigned in proportion to their input coefficients to the four sectors of port, fisheries, road, and parks. Costs beyond these, such as construction repairs, precision equipment, and other business services, will be reckoned into the relevant demand vector.

Table 5.11 List of Port of Nagoya budgets for 2012

Measures	Budgeted amount thousand yen	Main projects	Amount for project (thousand yen)		Content	Input–output table for analysis of construction sector
Developments to ensure port safety and guard against damage to the local area in the event of a major disaster	*3,952,000*	Port disaster prevention measures				
		Storm surge measures (e.g. revetment improvements)	374,800		Reinforcing seawalls and improving breastworks	Construction repairs
		Storm surge measures (Horikawa-guchi pumping station)	103,000		Removal of pumping installation	Construction repairs
		Tsunami and storm surge risk management measures	126,600		Land lock (tide gate) renewal	Construction repairs
		Seawall aging measures	16,200		Reinforcement of seawall functions	Port, Fisheries
		Improvements to protect seawalls from storm surges	635,500	(1,906,500)	Improvements to protect seawalls from storm surges	Construction repairs
		GPS wave meters	100,000	(300,000)	Setting wave meters	Precision instruments
		Other surveys, etc.	487,546		Disaster prevention plan reviews	Others, surveys, etc. (Construction repairs 2,249,179)
					Seismic surveys of port structures, etc.	
		Subtotal	***1,843,646***			
		Dredging of mooring areas Shounai River anchorage area)	***648,000***	***(1,440,000)***	Dredging work	Port, Fisheries
		Safety measures for port transport facilities (e.g. repair of vessel monitoring systems)	***507,779***		Maintenance and repairs	Construction repairs
			501,500		Inspection, maintenance	Construction repairs

(continued)

Table 5.11 (continued)

Measures	Budgeted amount thousand yen	Main projects	Amount for project (thousand yen)		Content	Input–output table for analysis of construction sector
		Safety measures for port transport facilities(e.g. security and monitoring services, security maintenance measures)	***451,075***		Security and monitoring services, maintenance and repair	Construction repairs
Developments to raise the region's international and industrial competitiveness and create a port that can respond well to changes in the port logistics environment	*6,783,000*	Development of wharf sites (e.g. revetment for waste landfill at Inanaga Wharf)	***269,0543***		Seawall construction	Port, Fisheries
		Development of road transport systems (e.g., Nabeta Pier Road)	***1,940,648***		Road development	Road transport works
		Improvements to channels (e.g., East Channel, etc.)	***648,000***	***(1,680,000)***	Dredging work	Port, Fisheries
		Development of road transport systems				
		Nabeta Pier channel, berths	***220,000***	***(660,000)***	Dredging work	Port, Fisheries
		Development of Nabeta Pier Container Terminal (loan), Nagoya Port Pier Corporation (provisional name) investment outlay, etc.	371,862		Loan	
		Subtotal	*591,862*			
		Development of bulk-related facilities (Preliminary soil survey at Kitahama Pier, etc.)	*260,000*		Soil survey (borings, etc.)	Other business services
		Other inspections of project planning, etc	*651,947*		Review of the revision history of the Port Plan, the management state of the Port Corporation, etc.	Other business services

(continued)

Table 5.11 (continued)

Measures	Budgeted amount thousand yen	Main projects	Amount for project (thousand yen)		Content	Input–output table for analysis of construction sector
Creation of ports with environmentally friendly, dreams, sense of contentment, liveliness and familiarity	*2,986,000*	Green areas within the port Development of the Nakagawa Canal from Horidome as a waterside green space	491,000		Bank strengthening work	Port, Fisheries, Park
		Maintenance of waterfront green areas, etc.	704,711		Maintenance of green areas, etc	Port, Fisheries Park
		Subtotal	***1,195,711***			
		Alternative development of waste disposal facility at Inae Pier	***974,471***		Bank strengthening work	Port, Fisheries
		Facilities to evoke maritime associations, etc. (Shinmaiko Boat Park development phase II, Nagoya Port Hall operations, etc.)	***551,718***		Maintenance of mooring facilities, publicity, maintenance and repairs	Construction repairs (half of cost)
		Aquarium Loan charges for living creatures. Exhibition and repair costs, etc.	***250,200***		Rental costs for living creatures, maintenance and repairs	Construction repairs (half of cost)
		Redevelopment and improvements (Garden Pier district)	***13,900***		Commissioned research, etc.	Other business services

Source Created by the author on the basis of a 2005 table for an input–output analysis of construction sectors, but using contents from the 2012 Port of Nagoya budget (Nagoya City)
Note Figures in parentheses for projects directly under state control show overall project cost

Table 5.12 Regional input–output table for Aichi Prefecture

	Intermediate demand	Final demand	Outflow	Inflow	Export	Import	Total output
Intermediate input	AX_1	F_1	N_2	N_1	E_1	M_1	X_1
Value added	V_1						
Total inputs	X_1						

Table 5.13 Input–output table for Japan

	Intermediate demand	Final demand	Export	Import	Total output
Intermediate input	AX_j	F_j	E_j	M_j	X_j
Value added	V_j				
Total inputs	X_j				

Table 5.14 Regional input–output table for all other prefectures excluding Aichi

	Intermediate demand	Final demand	Outflow	Inflow	Export	Import	Total output
Intermediate input	AX_2	F_2	N_1	N_2	E_2	M_2	X_2
Value added	V_2						
Total inputs	X_2						

5.4.1.2 Method of Preparing an Inter-Regional Input–Output Table Between Aichi Prefecture and the Rest of the Country

This analysis makes use of a two-region inter-regional input–output table (I-O table) for Aichi Prefecture and the rest of the country. This section describes how to create a table of this sort, based on the methods used by Yamada (1996a, 1996b) and Doi, Asari and Nakano (1996). For inter-regional input–output tables for three or more regions, Yamada (2015), Asari and Doi (2016) and Miller and Blair (2009) are useful.

First, as schematic examples, Table 5.12 shows a simplified input–output table for Aichi Prefecture only, Table 5.13 for Japan, and Table 5.14 for Japan excluding Aichi Prefecture. Table 5.15 presents an inter-regional input–output table for the two regions using sub-sections from the respective preceding tables.

Each of the variables in the I-O table for Japan (Table 5.13) can also be shown as the sum of the corresponding variables in the two regional I-O tables for Aichi Prefecture (Table 5.12) and for all other prefectures excluding Aichi (Table 5.14), as shown in the combined Table 5.15.

Formally, this gives the following matrix equations.

ADX_1 indicates intermediate demand in Aichi for commodities produced in the home prefecture, while ANX_1 indicates intermediate demand there for inflowing

Table 5.15 Example of a two-region inter-regional input–output table for the case off "Aichi" and "all other prefectures excluding Aichi (Rest of Japan)"

	Intermediate demand		Final demand			Import	Total output
	Aichi Prefecture	Rest of Japan	Aichi Prefecture	Rest of Japan	Export		
Aichi Prefecture	ADX_1	ANX_2	FD_1	FN_2	E_1	M_1	X_1
Rest of Japan	ANX_1	ADX_2	FN_1	FD_2	E_2	M_2	X_2
Value added	V_1	V_2					
Total inputs	X_1	X_2					

commodities from other prefectures; ADX_2 indicates intermediate demand in all other prefectures for (domestic) commodities produced anywhere other than in Aichi, while ANX_2 indicates intermediate demand in all those other prefectures for commodities inflowing from Aichi.

The following equations can be obtained for the variables in the I-O table for Aichi Prefecture (Table 5.12). Matrix of intermediate input for Aichi Prefecture: $AX_1 = (ADX_1 + AXN_1)$, matrix of final demand: $F_1 = (FD_1 + FN_1)$, export vector: E_1, import vector: M_1, production vector: X_1, matrix of value added: V_1, exports and outflows vector: $NM_2 = N_2 + E_1$, imports and inflows vector: $NM_1 = N_1 + M_1$.

The corresponding I-O table equations for all other prefectures excluding Aichi (Table 5.14) can similarly be found as: Matrix of intermediate input for all other prefectures excluding Aichi: $AX_2 = AX_j - AX_1$ (or its equivalent $(AX_2 = ADX_2 + ANX_2)$, matrix of final demand: $F_2 = F_j - F_1 (= FN_2 + FD_2)$, matrix of value added: $V_2 = V_j - V_1$, output vector: $X_2 = X_j - X_1$.

The transfer coefficients between two regions (NN_1, NN_2) are defined as follows. Note that the AX_1 and AX_2 rows can be aggregated into a vector i_x and the F_1 and F_2 rows into a vector i_f. The transpose of a matrix is indicated *delta*.

The transfer coefficients for each region are then

$$NN_1 = delta(N_1) \times delta(ADX_1 \times i_x + F_1 \times i_f)^{-1}$$

$$NN_2 = delta(N_2) \times delta(ADX_2 \times i_x + F_2 \times i_f)^{-1}$$

Using these inflow coefficients, a regional intermediate or final demand can be divided by either the intra-regional or the transfer demand.

$$\begin{aligned} ANX_1 &= NN_1 + AX_1 & FN_1 &= NN_1 + F_1 \\ ANX_2 &= NN_2 \times AX_2 & FN_2 &= NN_2 + F_2 \\ ADX_1 &= (I - NN_1) \times AX_1 & FD_1 &= (I - NN_1) \times F_1 \end{aligned}$$

Table 5.16 Estimated inter-industry input–output table for two regions and one sector (unit: billion yen)

Item/area	Intermediate demand		Intermediate demand total	Final demand		Exports	Imports	Total output
Intermediate input	Aichi Prefecture	Rest of Japan		Aichi Prefecture	Rest of Japan			
Aichi Prefecture	29,927	10,452	40,379	25,430	7,382	11,152	−5,271	79,071
Rest of Japan	12,981	412,781	425,762	5,831	463,876	62,617	−67,212	892,944
Intermediate input total	42,908	423,233	466,141	31,260	471,259	73,769	−72,483	972,015
Value added	36,163	469,711	505,874					
Total output	79,071	892,944	972,015					

Source Underlying I-O tables created and results obtained by the author

Table 5.17 Estimated input coefficients, value added coefficients, etc., for the data in Table 5.16

Item/area	Intermediate demand		Intermediate demand total	Final demand		Exports	Imports	Total output
Intermediate input	Aichi Prefecture	Rest of Japan		Aichi Prefecture	Rest of Japan			
Aichi Prefecture	0.38	0.01	0.04	0.81	0.02	0.15	0.07	0.08
Rest of Japan	0.16	0.46	0.44	0.19	0.98	0.85	0.93	0.92
Intermediate input total	0.54	0.47	0.48	1.00	1.00	1.00	1.00	1.00
Value added	0.46	0.53	0.52					
Total output	1.00	1.00	1.00					

Source Results calculated and analyzed by the author

$$ADX_2 = (I - NN_2) \times AX_2 \quad FD_2 = (I - NN_2) \times F_2$$

The above procedures were used to estimate values for the two-region inter-industry input–output table, using the 108 industrial sectors of the 2005 Japanese table and the 110 sectors of the 2005 Aichi Prefecture one to produce the final 108 sector list. Table 5.16 gives a schematic summary of the estimated two-region inter-industry input–output table for these two regions and just one sector, while Table 5.17 shows the input ratios.

5.4.2 Analysis of the Economic Ripple Effects of Public Investments in Nagoya Port

A formula for measuring induced-production effects can be expressed as follows.

$$X_1 = [I - (I - M - N)A]^{-1}(I - M - N)F_1 + [I - (I - M - N)A]^{-1}(I - M - N)KF_2 \tag{5.1}$$

$$X_2 = F_2 \tag{5.2}$$

Here, X_1 is the vector of induced production excluding the construction sector, X_2 is the vector of induced production in the construction sector, M is the diagonal matrix of import coefficients, N is the diagonal matrix of inflow coefficients, A is the input coefficient matrix, F_1 is the vector of final demand excluding the construction sector, F_2 is the vector of final demand in the construction sector, and K is the input coefficient matrix of the segmented construction sector.

Equations (5.1) and (5.2) are used to calculate induced production. Next, to analyze the effect of consumption on induced production, employment income is assumed to have a consumption propensity of 0.7 and calculated values are distributed among sectors following known demand distributions in private consumption. All calculations were performed for all 108 sectors, but the table of results summarized below is restricted to 34 sectors owing to space limitations. Finally, the number of employed persons affected by each production spillover is estimated using the employment coefficient from the Aichi Input–Output Table from 2005.

Three analyses are presented, corresponding to the three Measures of the 2012 Port of Nagoya Port Improvement Project (see Sect. 5.4.1.1). The three Measure are:

1. Development to ensure port safety and guard against damage to the local area in the event of a major disaster.
2. Development to raise the region's international and industrial competitiveness and create a port that can respond to changes in the port logistics business environment.
3. Development leading to a more environmentally friendly and people-friendly port in which visions, fulfillments and lively activities can coexist.

Since the production-inducing effects of investment lead to increases in employment income, which then spill over into consumption, this consumption effect is of relevance for this study. Calculated estimates of these ripple effects will presently be shown in Table 5.18. But starting first from the direct investments, in the case of Measure 1 of the Port Improvement Project, the total budgeted amount comes to 3.952 billion yen. For Measure 2, the total amount is 6.411 billion yen, and for Measure 3, it is 2.585 billion yen. These amounts were also shown in the second column of Table 5.11.

Table 5.18 Estimated results of economic effects (unit: million yen)

Economic effects/port improvement measures	Measure1. Development to ensure port safety and guard against damage to the local area in the event of a major disaster	Measure 2. Development to raise the region's international and industrial competitiveness and create a port that can respond to changes in the port logistics environment	Measure 3. Development leading to a more environmentally friendly and people-friendly port in which visions, fulfillments and lively activities can coexist
Aichi Prefecture direct effects	3,952	6,411	2,585
Aichi Prefecture primary (pri.) effects	5,689	10,400	4,442
Aichi Prefecture secondary (sec) effects	94	117	53
Aichi Prefecture (primary +secondary effects) total	5,782	10,516	4,495
Rest of Japan direct effects	0	0	0
Rest of Japan primary effects	1,524	1,107	677
Rest of Japan secondary effects	166	1,615	709
Rest of Japan (primary + secondary effects)	1,690	2,722	1,385
Aichi Prefecture + rest of Japan primary effects	7,212	11,507	5,119
Aichi Prefecture + eest of Japan secondary effects	259	1,732	762
Aichi Prefecture + rest of Japan (pri. + sec. effects) total	7,472	13,239	5,881
Aichi primary effects distribution ratios %	79%	90%	87%
Rest of Japan primary effects distribution ratios ratio %	21%	10%	13%
Aichi secondary effects distribution ratios %	36%	7%	7%

(continued)

Table 5.18 (continued)

Economic effects/port improvement measures	Measure1. Development to ensure port safety and guard against damage to the local area in the event of a major disaster	Measure 2. Development to raise the region's international and industrial competitiveness and create a port that can respond to changes in the port logistics environment	Measure 3. Development leading to a more environmentally friendly and people-friendly port in which visions, fulfillments and lively activities can coexist
Rest of Japan secondary effects distribution ratios %	64%	93%	93%
Aichi (primary + sec. effects) distribution ratios (%) total	77%	79%	76%
Rest of Japan (prim. + sec. effects) distribution ratios (%) total	23%	21%	24%
Aichi Prefecture production inducement coefficient	1.5	1.6	1.7
Rest of Japan production inducement coefficient	0.4	0.4	0.5

Source Results calculated and analyzed by the author

The direct effect of the public investments for Measure 1, port safety, is valued at 3.952 billion yen as already noted, and the total production effect expected from this is 7.1 billion yen, of which 5.6 billion yen occurs within Aichi Prefecture and 1.5 billion yen outside. The primary ripple effect is 79% within Aichi Prefecture and 21% outside, with approximately 20% of the value of the induced products also occurring outside. Secondary production inducement can be valued at 0.09 billion yen within, and 0.16 billion yen outside of Aichi, with a total economic impact of 250 million yen to be expected, 36% of it inside the prefecture and 64% outside. The total effect for the whole of Japan comes to 7.4 billion yen.

The primary ripple effect within Aichi Prefecture is largest in construction sector, with 2.94 billion yen, followed by 1.08 billion yen in personal services and 0.16 billion yen in freight transport. In contrast, the primary ripple effect generated outside of Aichi is largest for general machinery production at 0.2 billion yen, followed by commerce at 0.17 billion yen. The combined effect of primary and secondary rippling was also greatest for construction in Aichi Prefecture, at 2.94 billion yen. The overall inducement coefficient for Aichi is 1.5, while for Japan it is 1.9. All of this can be seen in Table 5.18.

In the area of the second project Measure, competitiveness and response to change, the direct effect of the budget investments is 6.411 billion yen. The primary production effect is 10.4 billion yen within Aichi Prefecture and 1.1 billion yen outside, for a total of 11.5 billion yen. The primary ripple effect appears 90% within, and 10% outside the prefecture. The secondary production inducement value is 110 million yen within Aichi and 1.6 billion yen outside, for a total economic impact of 1.7 billion yen. 7% of this is within the prefecture and 93% outside. The total national impact is 13.2 billion yen.

In Aichi prefecture, the primary ripple effect is greatest for the construction sector, at 5.5 billion yen, followed by 1.33 billion yen for personal services and 0.498 billion yen for freight transport. Outside of Aichi, the primary ripple is largest for metal products, at 0.1 billion yen, followed by business services at 0.09 billion yen. The combined effect of the primary and secondary ripple effects was again greatest in the construction sector in Aichi, with 5.5 billion yen. The inducement coefficient for Aichi Prefecture is 1.6, while for Japan it is 2.1.

For the third Measure, an environmentally and people-friendly port, the direct effect of the public investments is 2.585 billion yen, with 4.44 billion yen within, and 0.67 billion yen outside of Aichi Prefecture, for a total primary production effect of 5.1 billion yen. The primary ripple effect is 87% within Aichi and 13% outside, with approximately 10% of the induced production value generated outside the prefecture. Secondary production inducement comes to 0.5 billion yen in Aichi and 0.7 billion yen outside. The total economic impact for Japan is 0.76 billion yen, of which 7% is within, and 93% outside Aichi Prefecture. The total value for Japan is 5.8 billion yen.

The primary ripple effect in Aichi Prefecture is again greatest in construction, at 2.6 billion yen, far ahead of 390 million yen in business services and 219 million yen in freight transport. Outside of Aichi, the primary ripple effect is largest in the commerce sector at 0.07 billion yen, followed by general machinery at 0.05 billion yen. The combined effect of primary and secondary ripple effects in Aichi Prefecture was again greatest in the construction sector, with a value of 2.6 billion yen (Table 5.19).

Figure 5.13 shows the impact that these ripple effects have on employment. The analysis for Aichi Prefecture is estimated using the employment coefficients in the employment table for Aichi Prefecture, while the other analyses are estimated using the employment coefficients in the employment table for Japan. The total number of people likely to find employment due to the 2012 Port of Nagoya Improvements Plan is estimated to be 1616. The greatest number of these are in the construction sector (689), followed by personal services (351) and business services (104).

Table 5.19 Ripple effects on sectors in Aichi and rest of Japan (unit: million yen)

		Industrial sectors/ port improvement measures	Measure 1	Measure 2	Measure 3	Meas. 1. Primary ripple effects total	Secondary ripple effects total	Total	Meas. 2. Primary ripple effects total	Secondary ripple effects total	Total	Meas. 3. Primary ripple effects total	Secondary ripple effects total	Total	(Meas. 1 + Meas. 2 + Meas. 3) total
Aichi	01	Agriculture, forestry and fishery	0.0	0.0	0.0	2.1	1.9	4.0	9.1	3.3	12.3	12.3	3.6	15.9	32.2
	02	Mining	0.0	0.0	0.0	11.4	0.1	11.4	75.3	0.1	75.4	5.8	0.0	5.9	92.7
	03	Beverages and Foods	0.0	0.0	0.0	0.2	4.2	4.4	0.5	6.9	7.4	0.4	3.0	3.4	15.2
	04	Textile products	0.0	0.0	0.0	5.7	0.2	5.9	2.8	0.7	3.5	3.8	0.3	4.1	13.4
	05	Pulp, paper, paperboard, wooden products	0.0	0.0	0.0	53.4	0.6	54.0	20.0	1.1	21.1	18.6	0.5	19.1	94.2
	06	Chemical products	0.0	0.0	0.0	24.6	0.8	25.4	34.9	1.9	36.8	21.9	0.8	22.7	84.9
	07	Petroleum and coal products	0.0	0.0	0.0	5.7	0.4	6.1	5.5	0.9	6.4	9.4	0.4	9.8	22.4
	08	Ceramic, stone and clay products	0.0	0.0	0.0	75.6	1.7	77.2	213.5	3.6	217.2	77.2	1.6	78.8	373.2
	09	Iron and steel	0.0	0.0	0.0	73.3	0.2	73.4	429.8	0.4	430.2	136.7	0.2	136.9	640.5
	10	Non-ferrous metals	0.0	0.0	0.0	52.9	0.1	53.0	113.3	0.4	113.7	62.1	0.2	62.2	229.0
	11	Metal products	0.0	0.0	0.0	65.9	0.2	66.1	190.6	0.8	191.3	19.3	0.3	19.7	277.1
	12	General machinery	0.0	0.0	0.0	134.3	0.2	134.5	317.5	0.7	318.3	127.9	0.3	128.2	581.0
	13	Electrical machinery	0.0	0.0	0.0	167.8	0.6	168.4	70.0	1.6	71.6	54.6	0.7	55.3	295.2

(continued)

Table 5.19 (continued)

		Industrial sectors/ port improvement measures	Measure 1	Measure 2	Measure 3	Meas. 1. Primary ripple effects total	Secondary ripple effects total	Total	Meas. 2. Primary ripple effects total	Secondary ripple effects total	Total	Meas. 3. Primary ripple effects total	Secondary ripple effects total	Total	(Meas. 1 + Meas. 2 + Meas. 3) total
Aichi	14	Information · Communication equipment	0.0	0.0	0.0	7.2	0.1	7.3	4.6	0.6	5.2	9.3	0.3	9.5	22.0
	15	Electronic components	0.0	0.0	0.0	2.2	0.0	2.2	5.1	0.1	5.2	4.8	0.0	4.8	12.2
	16	Transportation equipment	0.0	0.0	0.0	14.4	1.2	15.6	9.9	2.7	12.6	17.7	1.2	18.8	47.0
	17	Precision instruments	100.0	0.0	0.0	0.0	1.2	1.2	0.0	4.6	4.6	0.0	2.0	2.0	7.8
	18	Miscellaneous manufacturing products	0.0	0.0	0.0	99.5	2.1	101.6	39.2	8.6	47.8	58.2	3.8	62.0	211.4
	19	Construction	2913.4	5499.2	2571.1	2940.0	1.4	2941.3	5575.7	1.3	5577.1	2602.2	0.6	2602.8	11,121.2
	20	Electricity · Gas and heat supply	0.0	0.0	0.0	30.7	2.1	32.9	71.8	2.1	73.9	32.0	0.9	32.9	139.7
	21	Water supply and waste disposal business	0.0	0.0	0.0	12.4	1.4	13.8	19.7	1.5	21.2	10.1	0.6	10.7	45.7
	22	Commerce	0.0	0.0	0.0	167.1	5.1	172.2	359.2	10.5	369.7	201.7	4.6	206.3	748.2
	23	Finance and insurance	0.0	0.0	0.0	34.1	9.0	43.1	135.1	7.4	142.6	30.3	3.3	33.6	219.2

(continued)

Table 5.19 (continued)

		Industrial sectors/ port improvement measures	Measure 1	Measure 2	Measure 3	Meas. 1. Primary ripple effects total	Secondary ripple effects total	Total	Meas. 2. Primary ripple effects total	Secondary ripple effects total	Total	Meas. 3. Primary ripple effects total	Secondary ripple effects total	Total	(Meas. 1 + Meas. 2 + Meas. 3) total
Aichi	24	Real estate	0.0	0.0	0.0	128.3	10.7	138.9	228.1	9.8	237.9	73.2	4.3	77.5	454.3
	25	Transport	0.0	0.0	0.0	168.8	19.5	188.3	498.8	17.9	516.8	219.4	7.9	227.2	932.3
	26	Information and communications	0.0	0.0	0.0	128.5	4.8	133.3	227.0	4.6	231.6	91.2	2.0	93.2	458.1
	27	Public administration	0.0	0.0	0.0	10.3	0.6	10.9	17.5	0.6	18.1	10.6	0.2	10.8	39.8
	28	Education and research	0.0	0.0	0.0	6.6	2.3	8.9	18.0	1.9	19.9	6.1	0.9	6.9	35.7
	29	Medical service, health, social security and nursing care	0.0	0.0	0.0	23.0	3.3	26.2	39.9	3.4	43.4	20.7	1.5	22.2	91.8
	30	Other public services	0.0	0.0	0.0	0.0	0.1	0.1	0.0	0.1	0.1	0.9	0.0	1.0	1.2
	31	Business services	938.6	911.9	13.9	152.7	3.8	156.5	315.8	4.2	319.9	391.2	1.8	393.0	869.5
	32	Personal services	0.0	0.0	0.0	1082.4	11.3	1093.7	1334.9	10.0	1344.9	91.6	4.4	96.0	2534.6
	33	Office supplies	0.0	0.0	0.0	2.8	2.2	5.0	5.4	1.9	7.4	2.3	0.9	3.1	15.5
	34	Activities not elsewhere classified	0.0	0.0	0.0	5.0	0.2	5.2	11.3	0.2	11.5	18.9	0.1	18.9	35.6

(continued)

Table 5.19 (continued)

		Industrial sectors/ port improvement measures	Measure 1	Measure 2	Measure 3	Meas. 1. Primary ripple effects total	Secondary ripple effects total	Total	Meas. 2. Primary ripple effects total	Secondary ripple effects total	Total	Meas. 3. Primary ripple effects total	Secondary ripple effects total	Total	(Meas. 1 + Meas. 2 + Meas. 3) total
Rest of Japan	01	Agriculture, forestry and fishery	0.0	0.0	0.0	22.4	4.4	26.8	66.0	34.8	100.7	16.4	15.3	31.7	159.2
	02	Mining	0.0	0.0	0.0	8.3	0.7	9.0	14.4	5.3	19.8	5.1	2.3	7.4	36.2
	03	Beverages and Foods	0.0	0.0	0.0	1.6	13.8	15.3	1.8	111.1	112.9	1.0	48.8	49.8	178.0
	04	Textile products	0.0	0.0	0.0	3.4	1.6	5.0	1.8	12.2	14.0	1.5	5.3	6.9	25.8
	05	Pulp, paper, paperboard, wooden products	0.0	0.0	0.0	57.5	2.4	59.8	30.1	19.7	49.8	24.8	8.6	33.5	143.0
	06	Chemical products	0.0	0.0	0.0	62.2	4.2	66.4	58.3	32.4	90.7	43.5	14.2	57.7	214.8
	07	Petroleum and coal products	0.0	0.0	0.0	24.2	2.6	26.7	16.7	19.3	35.9	11.2	8.5	19.6	82.3
	08	Ceramic, stone and clay products	0.0	0.0	0.0	88.8	6.8	95.6	89.8	52.6	142.5	53.1	23.1	76.2	314.2
	09	Iron and steel	0.0	0.0	0.0	80.9	0.6	81.5	39.5	4.6	44.1	20.9	2.0	22.9	148.5
	10	Non-ferrous metals	0.0	0.0	0.0	78.0	0.6	78.6	63.4	4.2	67.7	24.2	1.9	26.1	172.4
	11	Metal products	0.0	0.0	0.0	121.9	0.9	122.8	101.3	6.4	107.7	38.0	2.8	40.8	271.3
	12	General machinery	0.0	0.0	0.0	215.9	1.1	217.0	42.9	8.0	51.0	56.4	3.5	60.0	327.9
	13	Electrical machinery	0.0	0.0	0.0	56.5	1.6	58.1	22.6	12.5	35.1	35.0	5.5	40.5	133.7

(continued)

Table 5.19 (continued)

		Industrial sectors/ port improvement measures	Measure 1	Measure 2	Measure 3	Meas. 1. Primary ripple effects total	Secondary ripple effects total	Total	Meas. 2. Primary ripple effects total	Secondary ripple effects total	Total	Meas. 3. Primary ripple effects total	Secondary ripple effects total	Total	(Meas. 1 + Meas. 2 + Meas. 3) total
Rest of Japan	14	Information · Communication equipment	0.0	0.0	0.0	9.0	0.4	9.4	5.4	2.8	8.2	10.2	1.2	11.4	29.0
	15	Electronic components	0.0	0.0	0.0	6.7	0.4	7.1	1.9	3.2	5.1	3.2	1.4	4.6	16.7
	16	Transportation equipment	0.0	0.0	0.0	9.1	3.0	12.1	5.6	25.1	30.8	7.9	11.0	19.0	61.8
	17	Precision instruments	0.0	0.0	0.0	0.0	1.4	1.4	0.0	11.8	11.8	0.0	5.2	5.2	18.4
	18	Miscellaneous manufacturing products	0.0	0.0	0.0	25.5	4.3	29.8	23.0	33.1	56.0	28.8	14.5	43.3	129.1
	19	Construction	0.0	0.0	0.0	19.4	2.3	21.7	18.5	22.7	41.2	10.0	10.0	20.0	82.9
	20	Electricity · Gas and heat supply	0.0	0.0	0.0	27.3	3.5	30.8	23.2	35.3	58.4	13.9	15.5	29.3	118.6
	21	Water supply and waste disposal business	0.0	0.0	0.0	5.7	1.8	7.6	4.2	20.7	24.9	2.7	9.1	11.8	44.3
	22	Commerce	0.0	0.0	0.0	171.3	24.0	195.3	92.8	240.3	333.0	74.1	105.4	179.5	707.9
	23	Finance and insurance	0.0	0.0	0.0	56.2	9.6	65.9	42.0	104.5	146.5	24.3	45.9	70.2	282.6

(continued)

Table 5.19 (continued)

		Industrial sectors/ port improvement measures	Measure 1	Measure 2	Measure 3	Meas. 1. Primary ripple effects total	Secondary ripple effects total	Total	Meas. 2. Primary ripple effects total	Secondary ripple effects total	Total	Meas. 3. Primary ripple effects total	Secondary ripple effects total	Total	(Meas. 1 + Meas. 2 + Meas. 3) total
Rest of Japan	24	Real estate	0.0	0.0	0.0	36.3	20.7	57.0	53.1	242.0	295.2	18.9	106.2	125.1	477.3
	25	Transport	0.0	0.0	0.0	92.3	7.9	100.2	68.8	70.6	139.4	39.3	31.0	70.3	309.8
	26	Information and communications	0.0	0.0	0.0	61.9	9.2	71.0	58.5	91.5	149.9	29.6	40.1	69.7	290.7
	27	Public administration	0.0	0.0	0.0	15.0	1.9	16.9	17.8	16.2	34.0	10.3	7.1	17.4	68.3
	28	Education and research	0.0	0.0	0.0	3.8	2.8	6.6	3.4	33.8	37.1	1.8	14.8	16.7	60.3
	29	Medical service, health, social security and nursing care	0.0	0.0	0.0	16.2	5.0	21.1	10.0	57.1	67.1	8.9	25.0	33.9	122.1
	30	Other public services	0.0	0.0	0.0	0.0	0.2	0.2	0.0	2.6	2.6	0.0	1.1	1.1	3.9
	31	Business services	0.0	0.0	0.0	104.2	8.8	113.0	94.7	79.9	174.6	42.7	35.1	77.7	365.4
	32	Personal services	0.0	0.0	0.0	39.9	14.9	54.8	33.7	166.7	200.4	17.7	73.1	90.8	346.1
	33	Office supplies	0.0	0.0	0.0	0.7	2.4	3.1	0.6	29.4	30.1	0.3	12.9	13.3	46.4
	34	Activities not elsewhere classified	0.0	0.0	0.0	2.0	0.3	2.2	1.2	2.7	3.9	0.9	1.2	2.0	8.2
Aichi Prefecture Primary industry			0.0	0.0	0.0	2.1	1.9	4.0	9.1	3.3	12.3	0.0	0.0	0.0	16.4

(continued)

Table 5.19 (continued)

Industrial sectors/ port improvement measures	Measure 1	Measure 2	Measure 3	Meas. 1. Primary ripple effects total	Secondary ripple effects total	Total	Meas. 2. Primary ripple effects total	Secondary ripple effects total	Total	Meas. 3. Primary ripple effects total	Secondary ripple effects total	Total	(Meas. 1 + Meas. 2 + Meas. 3) total
Aichi Prefecture Secondary industry	3013.4	5499.2	2571.1	3733.8	15.3	3749.1	7108.2	37.2	7145.4	3229.7	16.3	3246.0	25,224.2
Aichi Prefecture Tertiary industry	938.6	911.9	13.9	1952.6	76.3	2028.9	3282.5	76.2	3358.7	1200.0	33.4	1233.5	8485.6
Aichi Prefecture total	3952.0	6411.1	2585.0	5688.5	93.5	5782.0	10,399.8	116.6	10,516.4	4429.7	49.7	4479.5	33,726.1
Rest of Japan Primary industry	0.0	0.0	0.0	22.4	4.4	26.8	66.0	34.8	100.7	16.4	15.3	31.7	159.2
Rest of Japan Secondary industry	0.0	0.0	0.0	868.8	48.5	917.2	537.1	387.0	924.1	375.0	169.8	544.8	2386.2
Rest of Japan Tertiary industry	0.0	0.0	0.0	632.8	113.0	745.8	504.0	1193.3	1697.3	285.2	523.6	808.8	3251.9
Rest of Japan total	0.0	0.0	0.0	1524.0	165.8	1689.8	1107.0	1615.2	2722.1	676.6	708.7	1385.3	5797.3
Total	3952.0	6411.1	2585.0	7212.5	259.3	7471.8	11,506.8	1731.8	13,238.6	5106.3	758.5	5864.8	39,523.4

Source Results calculated and analyzed by the author

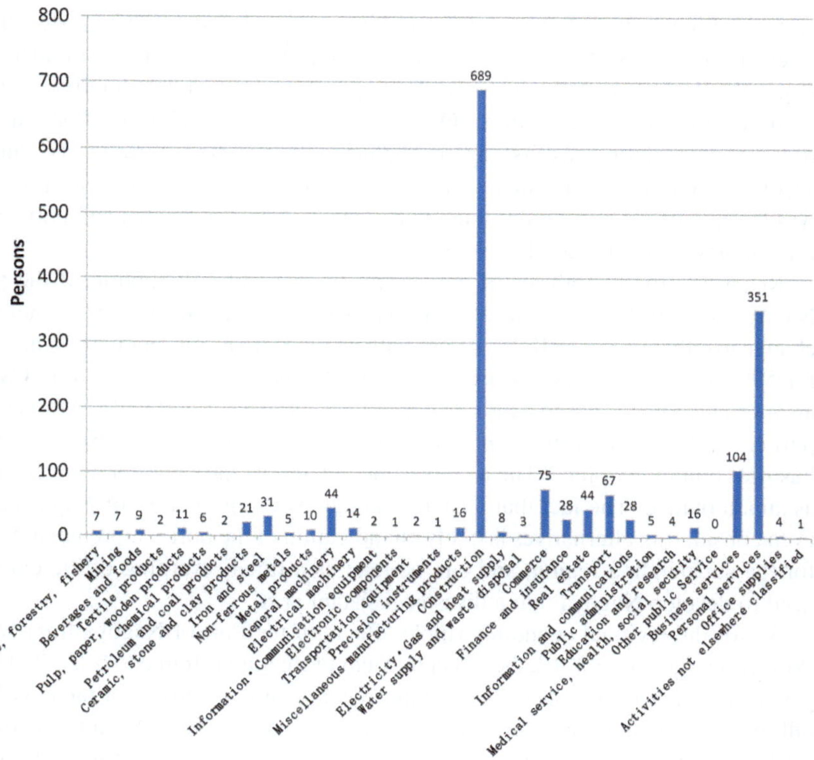

Fig. 5.13 Impacts of these ripple effects on employment (unit: persons). *Source* Created using results analyzed by the author

5.5 Conclusions

The study in this chapter has identified the factors that lead companies to use Nagoya as a port and has characterized ways in which this port choice may be assumed to change in a set of special circumstances such as a natural disaster. Where public investments are used to make the port more resistant to damage from large-scale disasters, the study has further analyzed the economic impact that such resilience measures have on the surrounding region.

Reasons emphasized for choosing Nagoya as a port for exports include "inexpensive inland transportation to port" and "inexpensive total costs at port." On the imports side, too, Nagoya offers the same advantage of low "total costs at port," along with time-saving considerations of good "road access to further inland," "rapid cargo handling," and "reliable lead times."

A comparison was next drawn with "Hanshin Port," the port partnership of Kobe and Osaka. Regarding exports, while the first factor of choice for Hanshin Port related to "enhanced port service required for exports," the second factor was "reputation" relating to "port functions for easy handling of exports." A third was "total logistics costs," taking in both "port costs" and "inland freight costs." The order of these interests differs from the order in Nagoya, above, where total costs and rapid handling come clearly first, with "port service for exports" second, and "reliability" (but here focused more on "speed") third. On the imports side, for Hanshin Port, the order of the choice factors was first, again, "enhanced port service for imports," and then second, "promptness." In Nagoya, as was just said, the first choice factor for imports was "total costs at port" (conjoined with "speed at port"). "Enhanced port services for imports" ranked second at Nagoya.

Regarding the hypothesis of an earthquake or similar disruption, if the port of Nagoya were to become unusable in that way, many companies were inclined to change to either Osaka or Kobe. Those with no plans for an alternative port accounted for 59% of all responses, however. For exports, the reasons for selecting Osaka as an alternative were "cargo handling capacity," "number of port calls," "frequency of port calls," "handling times," and other reasons, including the company's "existing business continuity plan." The results came out almost the same for choices of Kobe as an alternative. The fact that 59% of companies using the port of Nagoya are not even considering alternatives is likely an indication of the port's supreme importance for the surrounding region, and can be read as a timely warning of the existential need to develop Nagoya into a disaster-resistant port.

As for the regional economic ripple effects of the Port of Nagoya Improvement Projects budgeted for 2012, the effect in Aichi Prefecture is found to be 20.794 billion yen against a project cost of 12.948 billion yen, while the effect on Japan is 26.594 billion yen, with a production inducement coefficient of 1.6 for Aichi Prefecture and 2.1 for Japan. In terms of employment, there is an effect equivalent to 1616 jobs.

Looking at the three project Measures one by one, the effects were estimated as follows. It will be recalled that: Measure 1 aims to ensure port safety and guard against damage to the local area in the event of a major disaster. Measure 2 aims to raise the region's international and industrial competitiveness and create a port that can respond to changes in the port logistics environment. Measure 3 aims to lead to a more environmentally friendly and people-friendly port in which visions, fulfillments and lively activities can coexist.

In terms of their direct effects within Aichi Prefecture, Measure 1 is estimated to have a ripple effect of 3.9 billion yen, Measure 2 of 6.4 billion yen and Measure 3 of 2.5 billion yen. The total primary effect and secondary effects in Aichi come to 5.7 billion yen for Measure 1, 10.5 billion yen for Measure 2, and 4.4 billion yen for Measure 3. Finally, adding the amounts for smaller ripple effects outside Aichi Prefecture, the total for Japan as whole reaches 7.4 billion yen for Measure 1, 13.2 billion yen for Measure 2 and 5.8 billion yen for Measure 3. The induced coefficient for Aichi Prefecture is 1.5 for Measure 1, 1.6 for Measure 2 and 1.7 for Measure 3.

Considering the financial situation of Japan in recent years, it is difficult to use all public investments in a region for social capital. However, renewal investment is necessary to replace those parts of the country's social capital that are of highest importance. But in order to accurately assess the importance of a stock of social capital, it is necessary to conduct a thorough study not only of the elements at work in the capital *per se*, but also of the many other possible impacts there may be on regions rather remote from its home location.

References

Akai, N., Uemura, T., Sawano, K., Takemoto, T., & Yokomi, M. (2009). Financial analysis of efficient and effective maintenance and operation of ports and harbors: structural analysis of maintenance, regulation and operation (in Japanese). DP—RIETI Discussion Paper Series 09-J-010, Research Institute of Economy, Trade and Industry (RIETI). https://www.rieti.go.jp/en/publications/summary/09050012.html. Accessed September 27, 2023

Akita, N., & Kotani, M. (2007). Analysis of shipper's consciousness on port choice behavior. In *Proceedings of Infrastructure Planning* (in Japanese). JSCE Committee of Infrastructure Planning and Management, Japan Society of Civil Engineers. "Proceedings of 2007 Civil Engineering Planning Research Conference".

Arakawa, M. (1991). The structure of industrial linkage in Aichi Prefecture and the induced effects of outflow and export from the Port of Nagoya. Aichi University Chubu Sangyo Kenkyu Hokokusho (Chubu Industry Research Report), No. 44, Institute of Regional Research of Chubu, Aichi University (in Japanese)

Asahi, S. (2003a). Input-output table and economic structure of Nagoya City, research on methods for estimating and using regional input-output tables (in Japanese). Yamada, M. (Research Representative), (Grant-in-Aid number 12630030) Report of the Scientific Research Project of the Ministry of Education, Culture, Sports, Science and Technology.

Asahi, S. (2003b, March). *1995 Input-output table and economic structure of Nagoya City* (in Japanese). Discussion Paper Series 0210, 1–41, Chukyo University Institute of Economics.

Asari, I., & Doi, E. (2016). *Theory and practice of inter-regional input-output analysis* (in Japanese). Nippon Hyoronsha.

Cabinet Secretariat, Japan (2015, June 16). *Action plan for national resilience 2015* (in Japanese). https://www.cas.go.jp/jp/seisaku/kokudo_kyoujinka/pdf/ap2015.pdf. Accessed September 25, 2023

Chang, S. E. (2000). Disasters and transport systems: Loss, recovery and competition at the Port of Kobe after the 1995 earthquake. *Journal of Transport Geography, 8*(1), 53–65. https://doi.org/10.1016/S0966-6923(99)00023-X

Doi, E., Asari, I., & Nakano, C. (1996). *Introduction to regional input-output analysis (Hajimeyo Sangyo Renkan Bunseki)* (in Japanese). Nippon Hyoronsha.

Ishikawa, Y., & Katada, T. (2004). The economic impact of a disaster and inter-regional input-output analysis (in Japanese). Paper presented at the 15th Annual Conference (October 30–31, 2004) of the Pan Pacific Association of Input-Output Studies.

Katada, T. (1997). Changes in the multiplier effects of Japanese construction investment during the period 1965–1990 (in Japanese). *Sangyo Renkan (Input-Output Analysis), 7*(3), 42–54. https://doi.org/10.11107/papaios.7.42

Kobayashi, T., Sawa, K., Kagawa, M., & Yoshioka, H. (2001). Modern Japanese economy and ports (in Japanese). Seizando Shoten.

Miller, R. E., & Blair, P. D. (2009). *Input-output Analysis: Foundations and extensions*. Cambridge University Press.

Nagoya Port Authority. (1991, June). *Port of Nagoya and regional economy: Economic ripple effect analysis using the input-output table* (in Japanese).

Okamoto, N. (1999). Effects and future direction of a regional gateway port development (in Japanese). *Transport Policy Studies Review, 2*(3), 2–8. https://doi.org/10.24639/tpsr.TPSR_2R_10

Port Investment Evaluation Study Group (Ed.). (2001). *The role and socio-economic evaluation of ports* (in Japanese). Keizai Shinposha.

Tanaka, A. (2011, March 29). Special feature article: Great East Japan Earthquake—Challenges and policies for economic recovery (Column: No. 307). 'What impact will the earthquake have on international trade?'. Research Institute of Economy, Trade and Industry (RIETI). https://www.rieti.go.jp/jp/columns/a01_0307.html. Accessed September 25, 2023

Yamada, M. (1996a). An interregional input-output table of Mie Prefecture, Japan: Estimation and applications. *Journal of Applied Input-Output Analysis, 3*, 64–79. http://www.gakkai.ne.jp/papaios/en/img/jaia1996_3-4.pdf. Accessed October 10, 2023

Yamada, M. (1996b). Two regions' input-output table of Mie Prefecture: Estimation and its application. *The Journal of Law and Economics (hokei Ronso), 13*(2), 175–189. (in Japanese).

Yamada, M. (2015). Construction of a multi-regional input-output table for Nagoya metropolitan area, Japan. *Journal of Economic Structures, 4*, 1–18. https://link.springer.com/content/pdf/10.1186%2Fs40008-015-0022-7.pdf?pdf=core

Chapter 6
Summary and Future Tasks

6.1 Background, Aim and Structure of the Book

Since the early 1990s, the Japanese economy has been in a 30-year period of low growth. This is the result of a combination of factors, including a decline in demand since the collapse of the bubble economy, a drop in supply capacity due to sluggish productivity growth, a decline in the working-age population, and some redesign of the economic structure itself, including some response to the rise of international globalization. In the meantime, in Japan as in the rest of the world, economics and society at large have become more focused on taking action on global warming issues. This has further affected energy resources and uses of natural energy globally, as well as exerting pressure for social systems that do not depend on petrochemical resources. During this period, Japan also faced natural disasters such as the Great Hanshin-Awaji Earthquake and the Great East Japan Earthquake, which made it a priority for the country to build up resilient and disaster-resistant infrastructures, including its electric power supply. These natural disasters and economic pressures have had a major impact not only on Japan nationally, but also on its regional economies. For regional social capital, there is also a need to respond adequately to disasters while continuing to enhance regional economic vitality.

One of Japan's most pressing problems is population. This comes in the form of a rapid decline in numbers due to low birthrates and population ageing, while extreme depopulation is also on the rise locally. This problem of population decline is particularly severe at regional level, and one apt policy response would be promotion of tourism as a way of using local resources to increase inflows of people and demand. Tourism is also an expansive industry, in the sense that once promoted on this starting base of land resource exploitation, it can then spread its bounds by sending out ripple effects to other industries, contributing in the end to economic revitalization through the whole of the region concerned.

To address issues of productivity and population, resilience and revitalization, this book has offered an analysis of problems confronting Japanese regional economies

S. Asahi, *Econometric Analysis of Regional Economy*,
https://doi.org/10.1007/978-981-99-8707-8_6

in this period of rapid change. Most significantly, it has presented policy proposals capable of setting better perspectives for an economic future, and has aimed to ensure this by using economic data and econometric methods to identify mechanisms most actively at work in representative regional economies. After starting out from a general introductory chapter (Chap. 1), it has presented a collection of studies in four topic areas for which quantitative analysis can most profitably shed light on issues faced by Japan's regional economies: the decline in the total fertility rate (Chap. 2), which is connected via demographics to the fabric of social structure, tourism as an industry that interacts with population (Chap. 3), the sustaining resources of energy and environment (Chap. 4), and social capital (Chap. 5). If the issues in Chaps. 3 and 4 meet in a concern for a sustainable environment, the resources in Chaps. 4 and 5 also meet in their common role as public goods. For each of these issues and chapter topics, different analytical methods were also brought in, as outlined below.

6.2 Summary and Future Tasks in Each Chapter and Overall

6.2.1 Significance and Role of Regional Economic Analysis in Japan

Chapter 1 described the relationship between regional economics as a study field and regional economic analysis in Japan, and then provided explanations of statistical data and economic analysis methods. Beginning from previous studies of how regions can be characterized, a regional economy model and methodology were presented as contributing to the economic theorization of regional economics. Practical examples were then offered of policy analysis using this kind of model.

Starting from previous studies of how regions are characterized, I next presented the regional economy model and methodology as a contribution to the economic theorization of regional economics and offered some practical examples of policy analysis using this kind of model. Of particular importance here were the statistical techniques used in panel analysis and multivariate analysis, which have developed from input–output (I-O) analysis, econometric modeling, and multiple regression analysis. The examples were chosen from my own previous research. Next, the process of undertaking a typical econometric study of a regional economy was illustrated.

6.2.2 Study of Total Fertility Rate of Women in Employment, by Industrial Sector

Population decline, considered in Chap. 2, is a problem that cannot be ignored. The national and regional governments are working on policies to support child raising, but with no significant improvement to date. Population is a basic statistical indicator of social stability, and the current imbalance is having a significant impact on demographic trends. For this reason, regional population estimates, that is, estimated variations in total fertility rates (TFRs) and the economic variables that affect them in each region, were selected as an appropriate topic for this first topic chapter.

Another important objective was to demonstrate a method of data display for regional economic statistics that is capable of handling large quantities of data and a number of measurement methods. The case study chosen as an example was a revision of an earlier paper in which the period covered was extended by 5 years. As data for declining fertility, industry-specific TFR estimates were calculated for all 47 prefectures in the hope that this would encourage the various industry sectors to address the issue each from their own position. The study also examined relationships between these data and the respective regional characteristics.

An accurate scrutiny of the total fertility rate (TFR) is certainly one of the keys to Japan's population problems. A special feature of this study was that it examined TFR from an employer-side perspective. Accordingly, rates were calculated by industrial sectors. First, trends of childbirth and employment were summarized from Annual Population and Social Security surveys. Next, previous studies and sources were consulted for the Own-Children method and fertility rates. An outline was given of the data to which the method is applied in this paper, and procedures were explained in detail for estimating the characteristics of TFRs across industrial sectors for Japan and its 47 prefectures for the 16 years 2000–2015. Finally, a summary of results was displayed, including the relationships between TFRs in various industrial sectors and regions. Finally, the results were examined for their consistency with preceding research and surveys and in relation to agglomeration indicators.

The background reasoning behind estimating TFRs by industrial sector in this way is as follows. When a worker enters into employment in Japan, there is a bewildering diversity of contract conditions, and there are cases where even the work category is not clear or fixed. What is more, the type of work may change in the course of employment depending on the worker's aptitude, the economic health of the company itself, or evolution in the working environment. However, the sector of employment will not change unless the worker changes jobs. Within sectors, there are sometimes craft or industry unions that transcend the boundaries of individual enterprises. Labor unions in Japan are generally company unions, although many of them are also further organized into industry-wide alliances. For reasons like these, the issue of declining birthrate cannot well be discussed outside of the issues of employment choices and work environments within industrial sectors.

The TFR of employed women was 0.48 in 2000, 0.45 in 2005, 0.62 in 2010, and 0.80 in 2015. For non-employed women, the TFR was 2.89 in 2000, 2.79 in 2005, 3.06 in 2010, and 3.42 in 2015. Comparing these data, it can be seen that birth rates have held firm among non-employed women over this period. Regarding the "employed" figures, women of 25–44 accounted for 0.43 of the TFR in 2000 (25–29: 0.14, 30–34: 0.20, 35–39: 0.08, 40–44: 0.01), increasing to 0.56 in 2010 (25–29: 0.16, 30–34: 0.24, 35–39: 0.13, 40–44: 0.03), and 0.74 in 2015 (25–29: 0.19, 30–34:

0.32, 35–39: 0.19, 40–44: 0.04). This shows that late marriage and parenthood is increasing. Similar trends are also obtained for non-employed women.

Comparing TFRs by industrial sector in Japan as a whole, rates are highest in the primary industries, followed by the Government sector, Construction, Finance and insurance, Electricity, gas, heat supply and water, Combined services, and Medical, health care and welfare. Rates are particularly low in Accommodation, eating and drinking services, Wholesale and retail trade, and Transportation and postal activities. In 2015, Accommodation, eating and drinking services, Wholesale and retail trade, and Manufacturing showed low TFRs. These were sectors employing many women. Wholesale and retail ranked second for the number of female employees, Manufacturing third, and Accommodation, eating and drinking services, the sector with the lowest TFR, was fourth. In contrast, Medical, health care and welfare, the sector with the largest number of women employees, showed a relatively high TFR. An increase in the number of births in this sector can contribute greatly to Japan's national TFR.

Specific challenges confronting measures to reverse falling birthrates can be made more visible by comparing the wages, work rules, and working environment in industrial sectors with higher and lower TFRs. Sector-specific data are of vital importance when considering improvements in working conditions for the women in each industrial sector, in women's work choices more broadly, and for the overall problem of birthrate decline.

A further question investigated in this research were relations between TFRs and the agglomeration economy using TFR data drawn from different regions.

Sato (2007) and Morita and Yamamoto (2014) have shown that areas with stronger agglomeration economies have higher population densities. And as wage rates are higher in areas with agglomerated economies, it can be argued in theory that costs of obtaining child-rearing opportunities will be high and TFRs will be low. The results of this study confirmed a negative correlation between TFR and population density in most industrial sectors, with exceptions in 2015 for Electricity, gas, heat supply and water, Government, Transport, and Real estate. This is similar to what was found by Sato (2007) and by Morita and Yamamoto (2014). The dependence of the low fertility rate on the higher wage rate, and the reasons why TFRs, in an equilibrium state, are lower in areas of higher population density, are set out in Sato (2007). Sato also concludes that more populated areas favor fewer children per woman. From investigations of TFRs by industrial sectors in the period 2000–2015, this study confirmed that rates are higher in less populated, and lower in more populated areas so far as concerns the private sector. However, TFRs in the government sector are unlikely to be affected by agglomerated economies as there are no significant regional differences in wage rates and the ease of taking childcare leave is the same.

Sato (2007) shows that some people born in less populated areas will later move to more populated ones. In other words, there is a net movement of people from lower density to higher density population areas. Overall, areas of low population density will have a surplus of people moving out, and areas of high population density a surplus of those moving in. Year on year, sparsely populated areas have a net loss of population through migration, while densely populated areas have a net gain.

Finally, the study also investigated TFRs across various industrial sectors in connection with 8 different indicators of agglomeration economies. Indicators that were found to be consistent with predictions of agglomeration economy theory were the number and scale of employment locations (in Manufacturing), the number of employees per habitable area (in Manufacturing), and the agglomeration level, whether of the specialization or of the more general urbanization type. An agglomeration index will have its own characteristics depending on the data creation process. Analyzing relations between TFRs by industrial sector and agglomeration indexes shows that TFRs for the Government sector are different from those for other industries. This might indicate that regional differences in TFRs could be reduced by bringing the working environment in private companies closer to what is the norm in public employment.

It was important for the purposes of this study to estimate TFRs and demonstrate how the data obtained relate to other economic variables. From this, it may be possible to ascertain which industrial sectors need to improve their measures against low rates. In addition, the relationship with other economic variables may provide clues as to how best to overcome low fertility situations. For this reason, a future research task will be continuous estimates of TFRs across industrial sectors. There is also a need to estimate the actual extent to which the further dip in fertility due to the COVID-19 pandemic has affected TFR in the various sectors. Finally, a wider variety of analytical methods is needed to investigate TFR levels across sectors, including the relationship with the economy in each region.

6.2.3 Analysis of the Impact of Overtourism in Japan

Low regional birthrates lead to local depopulation, and decline in the regional economy. In response to this, the national government is promoting tourism as one of its policies to revitalize regional economies. International tourism, in particular, favors transfers of income from tourists' home countries to the destination areas they travel to. Chapter 3, accordingly, was in the form of a study of tourism guided by dynamic panel analysis.

The study estimated the tourism demand function of international visitors to Japan. The intention behind this was to analyze the impact of tourist congestion phenomena on international visitors and to discover which economic variables affect capacity numbers.

The average growth rate in the number of international visitors coming to Japan in the ten years 2010–2019 was 19%. In 2019, the number of international visitors staying overnight was 31.88 million, ranking 12th in the world and 3rd in Asia. By prefectures, the number of overnight stays by visitors to Japan is highest in Tokyo, followed by Osaka, Kyoto, Hokkaido, Okinawa, and Chiba. In 2019, these six prefectures accounted for 69% of all overnight stays, while the top nine accounted for 79%. As Japan has 47 prefectures in all, this gives an idea of how extreme the regional bias in inbound tourism is. What is noticeable from these figures is that the recent rapid growth in the numbers of tourists coming in has led to greater concentrations in the same limited group of tourist areas. This suggests that conditions of overtourism are occurring. It is true that in 2020 and 2021, numbers of tourists fell worldwide with the novel coronavirus (COVID-19) pandemic. Once this external factor is removed, however, there is every chance that the demand for tourism will gradually reappear. If demand levels return to what they were in 2019, many tourist areas will soon face the problem of overtourism again.

With this in mind, the aim of this study was to arrive at an estimate of the demand function of tourists visiting Japan on the basis of the TALC (Tourist Area Life Cycle) model using data from the top nine, and more especially the top six, prefectures in terms of the number of overnight stays by international tourists.

It was found that the cumulative effect of previous international visitors drawing new visitors is self-sustaining in prefectures where tourists from overseas are already numerous. The effect of this on the reputation of these tourist areas, and on problems of congestion, will work out negatively in the following year. As for the effect of elasticity of income in the country of origin, that is positive but its influence on numbers depends on the income level in each country. Further, visitor numbers were also affected by price changes.

Given that the reputation of a tourist area affects the visiting behavior of future tourists, national and local government, along with the tourism industry in each area, need to take measures to reduce congestion problems. This is not a policy that should focus only on numbers. Rather, what will increasingly count in future are efforts to enhance destination images. In the case of Japan, geographical distributions of tourist operations to date have been highly skewed. In order to overcome this problem, there is an urgent need to build up local attractiveness area by area, to disseminate information, and to follow the tourism strategies that fit best locally.

The need for the future is for careful analysis leading to new promotion policies. The downsides of congestion are apparent not only to residents but also to tourists visiting the area, but it is more difficult to know quantitatively what precise impact it is having. Without that precise knowledge, it is difficult to know where to look for solutions. Regional tourism research therefore needs to improve the accuracy of its statistics by continuing to strive for detailed surveys tailored to reality. In particular, many analysts could benefit from having closer access to the detailed and itemized tourism statistics published by the Japanese government at near-individual visitor level. Backed with data like these, it is possible to make an exact science out of tourism.

6.2.4 *Analysis of Environmental and Economic Effectiveness of Wind Power Generation in Japan*

A society with less environmental impact is a requirement not only for tourism, but for a range of economic activities. The power industry is also under social pressure not to seek energy from petrochemical resources due to global warming issues. At the same time, a stable energy supply is essential for Japan and its regions. Electric power is a private good, but can also be understood as a public utility and permanent necessity for all people. Chapter 4, then, was a study of wind power as a renewable energy source. This chapter argued that there is a positive cost–benefit balance in favor of the expansion of wind power generation capacity in Japan. This began from summarizing the economic and social background and the steps that this expansion has taken so far. In particular, the rise in the amount of power generated, the resulting CO_2 reduction effect, the cost of generating wind power, and the ripple effects on regional economies were analyzed.

The amount of energy generated from wind power in 2022 was 7.45 million MWh. It can be calculated that the equivalent output from a coal-fired thermal plant would have led to 7032 kt of CO_2 emissions. In other words, supplying this energy from wind power instead of coal has an effect of eliminating virtually all of this CO_2 load. Looking at individual regions, Tohoku stood out as saving the equivalent of 3020 kt-CO_2/year, accounting for 42% of the national total. The measured cost of wind power energy generation is found to lie between 13.4 and 29.7 yen/kWh, although this takes no account of the scale of the plant. Depending also on regional differences, there is no denying that wind energy can be more expensive than energy from other sources.

In Japan, as the environmental tax on CO_2 emissions is only 289 yen per ton, generating electricity from high-carbon energy resources has relatively little negative impact on the enterprise concerned, but once a more targeted carbon tax is introduced, as in many other countries, the cost benefits of wind power electricity are likely to rise.

The economic ripple effects of investments in wind power plant construction, estimated only within the same region, suggest that a direct investment of 141.718 billion yen results in a total output of 265.874 billion yen when indirect effects are counted in. The induced coefficient with these indirect effects included is 1.8. Increased production from this investment in plant construction also leads to the creation of 41,667 additional jobs.

From my analysis of the ripple effects in the case of very large investment projects involving contractors outside the home-region, the direct benefit to the whole Japanese economy from the building of wind power generating plants can be evaluated at 419.8 billion yen, while the total induced rise in production value, including indirect effects, comes to 758.4 billion yen. Increased production due to these investments in plant construction also results in the creation of 121,003 additional jobs. It is true that the construction of plants requires a certain cost of resource and energy consumption. But in view of the very small amounts of CO_2 involved, the carbon tax payable on this would come to no more than about 0.25% of the economic benefit from the increase in production. To conclude, then, wind energy results in very little release of CO_2, and the environmental loads of the plant construction and energy generation remain minimal.

Previous analyses of the economic effects of wind power abroad have revealed positive benefits in terms of production and employment, and the results of this study support that. In addition, if a targeted carbon tax is incorporated into the Japanese economic system, the advantages of new energy sources such as wind power could become highly competitive. At the same time, as it is not easy to tap new energy continuously as a base-load power source, Japan also needs to continue with its wider policy of finding the best mix of energies, which must certainly include the new energies.

This study was about what can be found in the way of quantitative data from an analysis of cost–benefit in wind power. Many researchers point out that there are also negative impacts in wind power construction that cannot be captured as quantitative data. This depends to a large extent on the suitability of the site where a wind power facility is installed, so it is important to conduct research in a way that includes the individual characteristics, not only the administrative location of the plant. A large-scale indication like prefecture is clearly not appropriate. A future research task will be to ensure that data are collected in ways that distinguish the physical conditions under which wind power facilities within a region are sited, and that studies are conducted to compare the cost–benefit impacts of variables in siting.

6.2.5 Economic Ripple Effects of Choice Factors and Disaster-Related Investments at Nagoya Port

Chapter 5, finally, was a study on the subject of social capital, including the role played by seaports as public assets, notably when a need arises to select an alternative port in disaster or disaster-avoiding situations. In this case, factor analysis was used to account for the choice of one alternative port over another. At a later stage, use was additionally made of regional input–output analysis to quantify the spillover ripple effects of administrative investments in ports, including investments for disaster prevention.

In the worst Japanese natural disaster of recent times, the Great East Japan Earthquake of March 2011, vessels in many affected ports were washed ashore by tsunami, causing extensive damage to the whole port area. At the same time, congestion in supply chains also reduced the production capacity of companies.

The impact of disasters on local economies varies in the extent and absolute severity of the actual damage sustained depending on the scale of the disaster, the level of production activities, and the local industrial structure. This chapter attempted to identify factors that affect companies' original decisions to use a port such as Nagoya and to review circumstances that might lead them to change such a choice, including options of ports in other areas. The study focused particularly on factors relating to natural disasters and countermeasures, first summarizing the investments required to ensure the port's safety and resilience against risks of major disasters and then analyzing the further impact they have on the Nagoya region.

The results of the initial survey showed that the factors most important in the original choice of the Port of Nagoya for exports were lower logistics costs, lower domestic transport costs to the port and lower port costs overall. For imports through Nagoya, the factors of importance were similarly lower domestic transport costs from the port and lower total port costs. A comparison was next drawn with "Hanshin Port," the port partnership of Kobe and Osaka. Regarding exports, while the first factor of choice for Hanshin Port related to "enhanced port service required for exports," the second factor was "reputation" relating to port functions for easy handling of exports. A third was "total logistics costs," taking in both port costs and inland freight costs. The order of these interests differs from the ones in Nagoya, above, where total costs and rapid handling come clearly first, with "port service for exports" second, and "reliability" (but here focused more on speed) third. On the imports side, for Hanshin Port, the order of the choice factors was first, again, "enhanced port service for imports," and then second, "promptness." In Nagoya, as was just said, the first-choice factor for imports was "total costs at port" (conjoined with speed at port). "Enhanced port services for imports" ranked second at Nagoya. Regarding the hypothesis of an earthquake or similar disruption, if the port of Nagoya were to become unusable, many companies were inclined to change to either Osaka or Kobe. Those with no plans for an alternative port accounted for 59% of all responses, however. For exports, the reasons for selecting Osaka as an alternative were "cargo handling capacity," "number of port calls," "frequency of port calls," "handling times," and other reasons, including the company's "existing business continuity plan." The results came out almost the same for choices of Kobe as an alternative. The fact that 59% of companies using the port of Nagoya are not even considering alternatives is likely an indication of the port's supreme importance for the surrounding region, and can be read as a timely warning of the existential need to develop Nagoya into a disaster-resistant port.

As for the regional economic ripple effects of the Port of Nagoya improvement projects budgeted for 2012, the effect in Aichi Prefecture was found to be 20.794 billion yen against a project cost of 12.948 billion yen, while the effect on Japan was 26.594 billion yen, with a production inducement coefficient of 1.6 for Aichi Prefecture and 2.1 for Japan. In terms of employment, there was an effect equivalent to 1616 jobs.

It will be recalled (see Chap. 5, above) that Measure 1 of the 2012 project aimed to ensure port safety and guard against damage to the local area in the event of a major disaster. Measure 2 aimed to raise the region's international and industrial competitiveness and create a port that can respond to changes in the port logistics environment. Measure 3 aimed to lead to a more environmentally friendly and people-friendly port in which visions, fulfillments and lively activities can coexist. In terms of their direct effects within Aichi Prefecture, Measure 1 was estimated to have a ripple effect of 3.9 billion yen, Measure 2 of 6.4 billion yen and Measure 3 of 2.5 billion yen. The total primary effect and secondary effects in Aichi came to 5.7 billion yen for Measure 1, 10.5 billion yen for Measure 2, and 4.4 billion yen for Measure 3. Finally, adding the amounts for smaller ripple effects outside Aichi Prefecture, the total for Japan as whole reached 7.4 billion yen for Measure 1, 13.2 billion yen for Measure 2 and 5.8 billion yen for Measure 3. The induced coefficient for Aichi Prefecture was 1.5 for Measure 1, 1.6 for Measure 2 and 1.7 for Measure 3.

Considering the financial situation of Japan in recent years, it is difficult to use all public investments in a region for social capital. However, renewal investment is necessary to replace those parts of the country's social capital that are of highest importance. But in order to accurately assess the importance of a stock of social capital, it is necessary to conduct a thorough study not only of the elements at work in the capital *per se*, but also of the many other possible impacts there may be on regions rather remote from the home location.

6.2.6 Future Tasks for This Study

Japan is caught up in numerous regional economic problems at present, in a climate of breathless change. The solution to such problems consists in taking exact stock of the current situation in the light of economic theory aided with other research results and information. The statistical data needed for the analysis can then be collected, and supplemented by estimates as necessary, to fill any gaps. The research results can then be obtained using these procedures and analytical methods.

This book has presented research into present-day regional economic problems in present-day Japan, drawing on different kinds of economic data and making various use of regional input–output analysis and factor analysis, together with other econometric methods. Through the studies included, ranging over topics of population, tourism, energy and environment, and social capital, I hope to have demonstrated the need and importance of having the right analytical methods and the newest regional data to respond smartly and aptly to varied regional issues like these.

It is true that this small number of studies brings its own topic span limitations, and I will need to extend my research to more regional problems in the future. There have also been limitations in my uses of data sources and analysis methods, and in my settings and divisions for the various kinds of "region" that provide the frames for my subjects of analysis. These issues are issues within me and will always remain over as a source for further reflection and exploration.

References

Morita, T., & Yamamoto, K. (2014). Economic geography, endogenous fertility, and agglomeration. RIETI Discussion Paper Series, 14-E-045 (July 2014). http://www.rieti.go.jp/en/. Accessed September 26, 2023.

Sato, Y. (2007). Economic geography, fertility and migration. *Journal of Urban Economics*, *61*(2), 372–387. https://doi.org/10.1016/j.jue.2006.08.002.

MIX
Papier aus verantwortungsvollen Quellen
Paper from responsible sources
FSC® C105338

If you have any concerns about our products,
you can contact us on
ProductSafety@springernature.com

In case Publisher is established outside the EU,
the EU authorized representative is:
Springer Nature Customer Service Center GmbH
Europaplatz 3, 69115 Heidelberg, Germany

Printed by Libri Plureos GmbH
in Hamburg, Germany